P9-AOR-101

The Arno Press Cinema Program

THE GANGSTER FILM:
EMERGENCE, VARIATION AND DECAY
OF A GENRE
1930-1940

By

Stephen Louis Karpf

ARNO PRESS
A NEW YORK TIMES COMPANY
New York • 1973

This volume was selected for the
Dissertations on Film Series
of the ARNO PRESS CINEMA PROGRAM
by Garth S. Jowett, Carleton University

First publication in book form, Arno Press, 1973

THE ARNO PRESS CINEMA PROGRAM
For complete listing of cinema titles see last pages

Manufactured in the United States of America

- -

Library of Congress Cataloging in Publication Data

Karpf, Stephen Louis.
    The gangster film.

    (The Arno Press cinema program. Dissertations on
film series)
    1. Moving-pictures--Plots, themes, etc.--Crime.
I. Title. II. Series: The Arno Press cinema
program. III. Series: Dissertations on film series.
PN1995.9.G3K35   791.43'0909353   72-555
ISBN 0-405-04098-9

NORTHWESTERN UNIVERSITY

THE GANGSTER FILM:

EMERGENCE, VARIATION AND DECAY OF A GENRE,

1930 - 1940

A DISSERTATION

SUBMITTED TO THE GRADUATE SCHOOL
IN PARTIAL FULFILLMENT OF THE REQUIREMENTS

for the degree

DOCTOR OF PHILOSOPHY

By

STEPHEN LOUIS KARPF

TABLE OF CONTENTS

TABLE OF CONTENTS

CHAPTER I

INTRODUCTION

A. Research Materials

The dissertation research included a survey of library materials, all available reviews, newspaper and magazine articles and books relating to the actors, production factors and general information on the films of the study. Additional research procedures: viewing the films under consideration; reading screenplays of the films; conducting personal interviews; 16mm rentals were utilized as well as television showings and 35mm prints provided by Warner Brothers Studio, Burbank, California. The 35mm screenings in studio theaters were of particular significance because they approximated most closely the original release viewing situation. With the aid of studio projectionists it was possible to closely examine certain sections of films through repeated projection. Several of these 35mm nitrate prints were in such an advanced state of decay that they had to be discarded after screening for this study.

Warner Brothers Studio provided original scripts as well as the use of studio files (memos, letters, press releases). Tape recorded personal interviews were conducted with members of the studio staff and with such contributors to the film art of the 1930's as Henry Blanke, Mervyn LeRoy, Edward G. Robinson and Bryan Foy.

Additional materials were obtained from the Academy of Motion Picture Arts and Sciences Library, Los Angeles, California.

B. Description of Study

This study delineates the emergence, variation and progressive decay of the gangster film genre. Initially it is concerned with the archetypical films, "Little Caesar" (1930), "The Publio Enemy" (1931), "Scarface" (1932), "The Petrified Forest" (1936). Through succeeding years of progressive decay, the gangster genre is traced -- mirrored in the changing roles of the four actors whose characterizations immortalized the archetypical films: Edward G. Robinson as Rico, James Cagney as Tom Powers, Paul Muni as Tony Carmonte and Humphrey Bogart as Duke Mantee.

The nature of the selected examples of the gangster genre is examined through the physical qualities of the films, the continuing character of the actors who created the archetypical characters, and the continuity of plot lines through the whole body of films. Many other interesting and significant approaches exist; for example, the study of the prominent directors, or the literature upon which the films were based. A subject with such wide-ranging possibilities as the gangster genre must be confined to a few topics for purposes of conciseness, however, thus the special focus on four actors and on ten years of films.

This study is historical-critical in concept. The two major
qualities of the archetypical films are explored -- their episodic,
socio-historical narratives, which serve as source material; and
the central characters, so powerfully established that satisfaction
could be drawn from later films by watching variations on the
familiar roles. These qualities are used to judge those films
coming later in the genre.

C. The Dissertation and Related Studies

It is the major purpose of this study to delineate the emergence,
variation and decay of the gangster film genre. The study also will
make observations about the entertainment media in terms of tendencies
to produce copies of successful original creations, the effort to base a
film genre on an era's "current events" and the common roots of the
gangster and socially conscious film genres. The major purpose of
the study, however, is to make known the origins and progression of
the genre, rather than supporting one or more theses concerning mass
communications in general or the film medium in particular.

The article "Mass Communications Research in Radio,
Television and Film"[1] by Martin Maloney suggested several facets
of approach for this study. Under the heading "Research Problems

---

[1]Clyde W. Dow (ed.), An Introduction To Graduate Study
in Speech and Theatre (East Lansing: Michigan State
University Press, 1961), pp. 312-320.

In Radio-Television-Film" it is noted that while there have been many historical studies dealing with broadcasting and film, many more are needed.

Maloney states "...the study of mass communications is by no means yet a science, or even particularly "scientific". Indeed, this may be said of the study of communication as a whole. Typically in the early stages of development of any field of study, the observer and collector -- the data-stuffers, as they are sometimes called -- are the first investigators, and their techniques are humanistic rather than scientific... Eventually, after enough data has been accumulated, we may expect the classifier, the Linnaeus of mass behavior; and ultimately the theorist and experimenter. "[1] Maloney holds that before the possibilities of observation and speculation had been exhausted, with classification almost untouched, communications researchers had moved on to theorize and experiment.

After two years as a writer in the film and television industry I can attest to the fact that there is a need for basic historical studies dealing with a wide range of topics. For example, it would be helpful to the writer if there were a comprehensive study of the American film hero.

This gangster film study should serve as a section of such comprehensive work. Other studies are needed to create links to the

---

[1]Ibid., 323.

era of Douglas Fairbanks and Richard Barthelmess and on into the

1940's (Bogart characters of "The Maltese Falcon" and "Casablanca"),

the 1950's (Marlon Brando and James Dean "rebels"), the 1960's

(Paul Newman, existential loner, etc.). In practical terms a par-

ticularly useful comparison of character motivations could be drawn by

an appraisal of Paul Muni's "I Am A Fugitive From A Chain Gang" (1932)

and Paul Newman's remake of the same theme "Cool Hand Luke" (1967).

Such a comprehensive study of the American film hero would allow

the practicing writer to gain perspective on his craft as well as

provide the mass media scholar with source material for theoretical

constructs.

Both Robert Warshow and Maloney note that communication criticism

and scholarship often by-pass the communicator to focus on the text

of the communication. This study also provides material on the "text"

of films under consideration; however, considerable effort is made

in this study to delineate the screen personality of Robinson, Cagney

and Bogart. Screen characters are thus used as units of analysis.

This unit of analysis would seem to be a useful addition to the textual

ones commonly employed by communication researchers.

The Maloney article cites "The Lone Ranger: A Dissertation

Involving Content Analysis",[1] which provided the "Lone Ranger's"

universe, i.e., settings, characters, outlook, etc. This study

---

[1]Ibid., 330.

provides the universe for the gangster films of an era. This universe
may be used as a framework of comparison for other films made in
the genre later and yet to come.

In his introduction to Gary A. Steiner's The People Look At
Television, Bernard Berelson stated the purpose for the Steiner study:
"It provides a factual platform from which the debate must subsequently
go forward. "[1] The debate to which Berelson referred involved questions
such as what public ends should television serve. The Steiner study
sought to report the attitudes of the audience toward television.

The information contained in the Steiner study was derived
from the results of two surveys each drawn from 1250 interviews. A
piece of data stems from a question such as "Generally speaking,
which of these do you think people are more satisfied with today?"
The distribution among the choices offered the interviewers were as
follows: Automobiles 57%, TV Programs 28%, Popular Music 5%,
Movies 2%, Womens Fashions 6%, None of them 0%, NA, DK 2%.[2]
This particular piece of information is contained in the chapter titled
"Satisfaction,The Degree and Nature of Public Acceptance". In the
chapter "What People Say", we find data such as thirty percent of those
with four years of high school say television should provide more

---

[1]Gary A. Steiner, The People Look At Television (New York:
Alfred Knopf, 1963), p. viii.

[2]Ibid., 28.

informational material while forty percent of those with four years of
college say they would like to see television providing more informational
material. The interviewees for this question were categorized by educational levels from those with none to six years of schooling to those with
education beyond college.[1] The study was organized to gather information about audience attitude in several broad areas. Additional chapters
in the study recorded audience attitudes in such areas as the conflict
between the leisure activity of watching television and perhaps during
something "more constructive", television commercials.

This study, like the Steiner study, is intended to provide a
kind of basic information. For example, this study could be used to
supply a historical perspective for a possible study of the 1960's Paul
Newman - Steve McQueen,   tough, existential film loner. Details
could be gleaned from the study for an inquiry into the political and
social tendencies of American films during the 1930's in the manner
of Robert Warshow's articles "The Anatomy of Falsehood" and "Father
and Son -- and the FBI"[2] drawn from the films "The Best Years of Our
Lives" and "My Son John".

Although the approach and type of data differ, this gangster
film study and the Steiner study have a similar goal -- to provide basic

---

[1]Ibid., 139.

[2]Robert Warshow, The Immediate Experience (Garden City:
Doubleday & Company, Inc., 1962), pp. 155-177.

information. This information can be of use simply for its own value or to support theses or propositions. Although supporting a hypothesis was not the primary goal any study tends to present a position or support a point of view if only through its methodology and selection of data reported. This study, for example, emphasizes the leading character and story in delineating the progression of the genre, while another might place emphasis on the directors.

In 1940 the Museum of Modern Art published a thirty-one page monograph by Alistair Cooke which detailed the creation and evolution of the screen personality of Douglas Fairbanks. In the 1960's a number of books have been published commercially to provide in depth information on film artists. To mention just two we have The Films of Bette Davis by Gene Ringgold and Humphrey Bogart: The Man and His Films by Paul Michael. There are also similar books on Jean Harlow, Laurel and Hardy and Greta Garbo.

These books have much in common. Each has an introductory essay outlining career highlights. The remainder of the books contain still pictures, credits and synopses from the films made by the personalities. With the exception of the Cooke monograph, which is written with some detachment, these books are written with obvious affection for their subjects, usually using the tone of newspaper or magazine articles. These books do not attempt to relate their subject

matter to trends in film making or art or society in general,
rather they try to make as much known about the films of their
subjects as possible.

A student of film can read a number of the "personality"
books then view the films enumerated in them. These chunks of
information -- the individual books -- will then begin to fit
together like pieces of a mosaic to form important observations about the film art. Falling into a similar category to
the personality picture books are the personality autobiographies or reminiscences. Going back to 1925 we find <u>When
The Movies Were Young</u> by Mrs. D. W. Griffith. This book and
others like it by individuals such as Jesse Lasky, Adolph
Zukor, Jack Warner and Colleen Moore tend to be rambling and
overly sentimental. These books, however, have value to the
mass media scholar through their presentation of first hand
accounts of those who helped shape the media. (Although quite
often these accounts come through ghost writers.) Mrs.
Griffith's book is particularly rich in detail concerning
production methods when David Griffith was first introduced to
film.

Moving from studies primarily intended to provide source
information to studies which use source material to support
theses note must be taken of Siegfried Kracauer's <u>From Caligari
To Hitler:</u> <u>A Psychological History of The German Film</u>.
Kracauer's work chronicles the history of the German film with
particular emphasis

on films made between the end of World War One until the coming
to power of Hitler in 1933.

In the preface Kracauer states, "This book is not concerned
with German films merely for their own sake; rather it aims at
increasing our knowledge of pre-Hitler Germany in a specific way.

"It is my contention that through an analysis of the German
film deep psychological dispositions predominant in Germany from
1918 to 1933 can be exposed - dispositions which influence the course
of events during that time and which will have to be reckoned with in
the post-Hitler era."[1]

Kracauer does not claim that the analysis of film motifs for
the period in question will reveal a national character which will remain unchanged for all time, rather the psychological dispositions for
that particular time. Kracauer is attempting something extraordinary
in scholarship with this study: "There is no lack of studies covering
political, social, economic and cultural history of the great nations.
I propose to add to these well-known types that of a psychological
history."[2]

Kracauer sees film as a unique medium to record a
people's psychological tendencies or dispositions, "Since any film

---

[1]Siegfried Kracauer, From Caligari To Hitler A Psychological
History of the German Film (Princeton: Princeton University
Press, 1947), p. 1.

[2]Ibid., 8.

production unit embodies a mixture of heterogenous interests and inclinations, teamwork in this field tends to exclude arbitrary handling of screen material, suppressing individual peculiarities in favor of traits common to many people. Second, films address themselves, and appeal to the anonymous multitude. Popular films or to be more precise, popular screen motif's,can therefore be supposed to satisfy existing mass desires."[1]

Kracauer holds that films reflect not so much explicit credos but psychological dispositions in the collective mentality lying beneath the level of consciousness. He sees these reflections in other media but he states that film exceeds these sources in inclusiveness.

Kracauer analyzes a number of German films made over the period between the end of World War One and Hitler's assumption of power. The following is an example of Kracauer's analysis. In "One ArabianNight" (1920) directed by Ernst Lubitsch he sees "...destroyed young lovers representative of all that counts in life. They characterized history as meaningless. History, they seemed to say, is an arena reserved for blind and ferocious instincts a product of devilish machinations forever frustrating our hopes for freedom and happiness."[2]

In two Lubitsch directed German films "Passion" (1919) and "All For A Woman" (1921) Kracauer finds, "Designed for mass consumption,

---

[1]Ibid., 5.

[2]Ibid., 52.

this nihilistic gospel must have satisfied widespread wants...
poured balm on the wounds of innumerable Germans who because of
the humiliating defeat of the fatherland, refused any longer to
acknowledge history as an instrument of justice or Providence...
Their basic nihilism made them indulge also into images of utter
destruction, which, like those of "The Student of Prague" or
"Homunculus" reflected forebodings of a final doom.[1]

In his history of film, The Liveliest Art, Arthur Knight
attributes the decline of the distinctive quality of German
films after 1924 to the number of Germany's leading motion
picture artists, including Lubitsch, who came to America to
work. Knight also sees the German film industry coming under
the domination of American companies.[2] In keeping with the
basic thesis of his study, Kracauer maintains these were not
the basic causes for decline rather it was another reflection
of the collective German mind which could not cope with the
attempt to establish democracy under the republic or the short-
lived period of stability introduced by the Allies through the
Dawes economic plan.

In the chapter "Frozen Ground" Kracauer states, "To
them the 'system' was a matter of indifference... This kind
of indifference is

---

[1]Ibid., 53.

[2]Arthur Knight, The Liveliest Art (New York: Macmillan
Co., 1957), p. 69.

their /the post 1924 films/ chief characteristic. They seem cut off
from all their inner most roots. The emotional grounds are frozen."[1]
Kracauer sees the German nation to be paralyzed by the trauma of defeat
and removal of authoritarian rule. Kracauer supports the assertions in
his text with still photographs from motion pictures. With a still from
"The Cabinet of Dr. Caligari" of the doctor and the somnambulist
Kracauer supplies the caption "Insane Authority", a still from "The
Street" of a man with his head slumped on a woman's breast carries
the caption, "This gesture -- recurrent in many German films -- is
symptomatic of a desire to return to the maternal womb." Whether one
agrees with Kracauer's thesis or not the book is an extraordinarily
useful source of material because of the wealth of detail on German
film production in that era.

Like Kracauer, Martha Wolfenstein and Nathan Leites hold in
their book Movies: A Psychological Study that it is possible to deter-
mine national psychological predispositions through analysis of film
motifs. Their study compares the psychological predispositions of
America, France and England. Wolfenstein and Leites consider films
as manufactured day dreams which relieve audiences of the burden of
day dreaming in these same themes themselves.

---

[1]Kracauer, loc. cit., p. 138.

For an example of their observations in the chapter
"Killers and Violence", Wolfenstein and Leites see the following national distinctions: "The split between hero and murderer is that between mere wishes and action. Human beings
have a tenacious susceptibility to feel guilt for mere wishes.
The American film melodrama expresses the effort to eliminate
such guilt..."[1] The American police bungle the situation to
the degree that the hero must step in and set the situation
right and clear himself. "British films... are more apt to
make the murderer known to us and to present him at least par-
tially sympathetic. He is the hero who is overwhelmed and
destroyed by his own violent impulses."[2] The Scotland Yard man
is efficient and father-like. "French films are less concerned
with the internal or external dangers of violent impulses.
Where crimes of violence occur, the central theme is more likely
to be that of the irony of human justice. There is none of
the confidence that we find in both American and British films
that everything will be cleared up and everyone gets his just
deserts in the end... French films sees murderer and victim,
the falsely accused and the police, each as mixtures of good
and bad impulses."[3]

---

[1]Martha Wolfenstein and Nathan Leites, _Movies: A
Psychological Study_ (Glencoe: The Free Press, 1950),
p. 176.

[2]_Ibid._, 178.

[3]_Ibid._, 179-180.

The Wolfenstein and Leites study has its greatest value for
the scholar in terms of basic approach and methodology rather than
standing as a source material supplying specific information on films.
Thus it is at the opposite pole from this gangster film study.

Both the Kracauer and Wolfenstein and Leites studies see film
as a kind of source material from which to draw support for observations
about societies. Neither are concerned with films for the value they
might have apart from this function.

Seymour Stern provides a most original study with Griffith:I,
The Birth of a Nation. In his study Stern provides extraordinarily detailed source material on one of motion pictures' great creators and
landmark works. Stern covers aspects of the film's production from how
illumination was provided for scenes to Griffith's part in the creation
of the musical accompaniment to the impact the film had on motion
picture criticism.

Mixed in with this high quality scholarship, but easily recognized
for what it is, we find Stern's diatribe against what he considers to be a
conspiracy by Stalinist Communists, film museum curators, university
theatre arts departments and capitalist film producers. Stern says they
are attempting to destroy Griffith's reputation and film art in general.

The Stern study does not resemble other books, dissertations

---

[1]Seymour Stern, Griffith:I The Birth of a Nation. New York:
Film Culture, 1965.

or monographs. It contains no table of contents thus the reader would
have to leave book marks to come back to a particular place. The
pages are printed in double columns frequently slashed with a black
print bar followed by bold headlines composed by Stern followed by
a quote that he feels is relevant.

Despite its eccentric form and frequent interjections of Stern's
political and social outlook, this study stands as an important reference
because of the vast amount and the excellent quality of the material
gathered into it. Like this gangster film study and the Steiner study it
draws its existence from the position that making an important subject
known as completely as possible rather than shaping material to prove
a thesis is a worthwhile and necessary goal in communications research.
Sharing this position is Case History of a Movie by Dore Schary.[1] Schary
set himself the task of chronicling the making of a feature film from its
origin as an idea for a script to its release as a finished film.

Schary's book stands as one of the best sources available on the
operation of giant film studios when feature films were still mass produced on an assembly line basis in Hollywood. Schary had first hand
knowledge of the subject because at the time of writing the book he was
in charge of production at Metro-Goldwyn-Mayer.

---

[1]Dore Schary, as told to Charles Palmer, Case History of a
Movie. New York: Random House, 1950.

Both the Kracauer and Wolfenstein and Leites studies are
based on the outlook that films reflect the psychological predispositions
of their audiences. The Payne Fund Studies under the general title
Motion Pictures and Youth in twelve volumes written in the early 1930's
are based on the view that "The motion picture, then, can give us data
about life. For example, if you carry out an experiment in chemistry
or physics or general science you find that when you ignite illuminating
gas and air mixed in certain proportion, you get a loud explosion. If
you always mix them in the same proportion, you always get this
explosion. In the same way the motion picture can give us the data
as to what happens when people make certain choices. The criminal
breaks the law; he is arrested. The motion picture should teach us
that in life certain effects follow from certain causes. "[1] In brief
the Payne Studies say films can play a part in shaping attitudes and
actions rather than just passively reflecting audience predispositions.

In a volume of the studies How To Appreciate Motion Pictures
Edgar Dale calls on his high school student readers to become selective
in their film diet, to choose films which will help them make better
decisions in life. Dale provides a short film history and calls

[1]Edgar Dale, How To Appreciate Motion Pictures
(New York: The Macmillan Company, 1935), p. 207.

attention to aspects of film craftsmanship so his readers may attend films with heightened appreciation. In this same volume Dale envisions an ideal motion picture studio where fewer and better films would be made, where a number of the films made would not be directed toward the largest possible audience. In Dale's ideal studio film artists would not just be in search of wealth and its trappings, as he says is the case in Hollywood of that era, rather they would work to satisfy a sense of artistic integrity.

In the volume of the Payne Studies Movies and Conduct, Herbert Blumer offers evidence that films influence conduct. Blumer draws his conclusions from the analysis of written movie autobiographies from high school and college students. These autobiographies had young people writing about how movies touch their lives. Boys reported that they used the plots of adventure films to structure their games of "cops and robbers" and "cowboys and indians". Young girls reported efforts to look like Mary Pickford by curling their hair or like society film heroines by draping themselves in curtains. Boys reported trying to look like John Gilbert.

A twenty-year-old female college student reported that after seeing "Romeo and Juliet" she acted out the plot with her sister in bed with the exchange of kisses. Blumer states that the imitation of adventure films by children can lead to physical injury by their attempting screen stunts. Blumer's investigations convince him that film influences

play but he states his uncertainty concerning the significance
of this influence. Interviewees reported forming racial stereo-
types and notions about what college life would be like from
films. There were reports of trying to emulate Clara Bow or
John Gilbert in relations with the opposite sex. We gain perspective concerning the outlook of the Payne Fund Studies
through Charles R. Wright's Mass Communication. Wright points
out that Herbert Blumer's model of the mass "from all walks of
life, anonymous to each other, with little interaction and
very loosely organized", does not take account of later evidence
that individuals are members of a network of primary and
secondary groups.[1] Wright makes the point that a model such as
Blumer's suggests that the individual has little to protect him
from the messages of mass communication media, as if the individual were being injected by a hypodermic needle. Wright
points to research by Elihu Katz, Paul Lazarsfeld and Robert
K. Merton among others pointing to the views that mass media
messages are filtered and edited through other people, groups
and the individual's own predispositions before affecting the
individual.

The Payne Fund Studies also devote a volume to physio-
logical responses to the stimuli of film scenes. The research
procedure was to show subjects film scenes while measuring
their psychogalvanic reflex. The results were inconclusive in
terms of proved dangers,

---

[1]Charles R. Wright, Mass Communication (New York:
Random House, 1959), p. 50.

"attendance at the motion picture theatre is a matter of individual mental lives and must be regulated or at least judged
according to the individual psychophysiological organism."[1]

In their conclusions the Payne Fund Studies say that
children get models for play, cues for conduct including delin-
quence (in the volume by Blumer and Hauser) and certain stereo-
types from films. These findings, however, were based on what
interviewees said rather than direct observation of action
other than psychogalvanic response triggered by watching a film
in a laboratory situation.

The Payne Studies summary stops short of saying that
movies are solely responsible for anti-social behavior rather,
"To say that movies are solely responsible for anti-social
conduct, delinquency or crime is not valid. To assert contrari-
wise that delinquents and criminals happen to frequent movies
and are not affected by them is clearly indefensible. Validity
probably rests with a combination of the two... The two factors
drive forward progressive aggravation of unhealthful conditions."[2]

The Payne Studies devoted one volume to analysis of the
content of motion pictures. The volume contains fifty-three
tables

---

[1] Windell S. Dysinger and Christian Ruckmick, The Emotional Responses of Children to the Motion Picture Situation: Motion Picture Standards of Morality (New York:
The Macmillan Co., 1933), p. 13.

[2] W. W. Charters Motion Pictures and Youth - A Summary
(New York: The Macmillan Co., 1933), p. 13.

which include "Comparison of the Types of Motion Pictures Produced in 1920, 1925 and 1930", "Types of Clothing Worn By Characters In 40 Pictures" and "Frequency of Lovemaking By Each Type of Character in the 40 Pictures". The first page of this volume says that it will be for the purpose of setting forth facts upon which enlightened discussion might be based.

The comparison of films made in 1920, 1925 and 1930, five hundred films from each year, was made from written plot outlines rather than viewing the films. After reporting the rise and fall over the decade of the several categories, crime, sex, love, mystery, war, children, history, exploration, travel, comedy, social propoganda, the analysis of the 1500 films concludes with, "The fact that two-fifths of the pictures are concerned with crime and sex indicate a belief that a purpose of the movies is to deal with life problems and their solution ... are there no social problems other than those of crime and sex which lend themselves to dramatic treatment?"[1]

A total of 115 films were actually screened over 1929, 1930 and 1931 for more detailed analysis than was attempted from the 1500 film analysis conducted from written plot outlines. The Payne Fund researchers' conclusions, supported by statistical evidence, were that films too often depicted the well to do, did not present rural

---

[1] Edgar Dale, The Content of Motion Pictures (New York: The Macmillan Co., 1935), p. 22.

settings often enough, youthful romance was frequently depicted while mature romance was not. Of course, the statistics on content are in themselves neutral, in order to interpret them as the Payne Studies do one would have to accept the studies' outlook.

Whether it is the textbook on appreciation by Dale or the Blumer volume or the statistical information on content, the studies do not reveal very much on the nature of film making. The studies were founded on the concept that film had the power to instruct its audience. To the degree film failed to do this along certain ethical lines it was criticized by the Payne Fund researchers. Today it is most likely that the Payne Studies are of value chiefly for their methodological, sociological and ethical points of view rather than for source material on the film medium itself. This gangster film study found the narrative method of reporting the progress of the genre more flexible to report variations in character and story than the categories of content analysis employed in Payne Fund Studies. Kracauer, in the study previously discussed, also employed the narrative method.

In terms of basic outlook this study owes much to a concept found in the volume of collected articles by Robert Warshow, The Immediate Experience. Warshow holds that the film critic or historian very often does not "see" films because of a tendency for critics and historians to feel they must look at films with a

thesis or point of view in mind. Warshow sees two major
strains of criticism: First, one which attempts to elevate
film to "equality" among the older arts, emphasizing the formal
qualities of the medium and the self-consciousness of the film
artist. This type of criticism usually sets up a clear definition of what is cinematic. This type of critic minimizes the
importance of the actor in favor of the director, who is considered the artist of the medium. Warshow places Arnheim and
Eisenstein in this category. Warshow's second category of
critics minimize or ignore the esthetic problem and treats
films as indices to mass psychology or sometimes the "folk
spirit." Warshow places Kracauer, for his history of German
films not for his work in esthetics, and Wolfenstein and
Leites in this second category.

Warshow sums up his feeling about both categories of
criticism by stating though they both are rich in many respects
they tend "to slight the fundamental _fact_ of the movies, a
fact at once aesthetic and sociological but also something
more: This is the actual, immediate experience of seeing and
responding to the movies as most of us see and respond to
them."[1]

---

[1]Warshow, _loc. cit._, p. 26.

This study of the gangster film attempts to meet its subject
directly or, as Warshow puts it, through immediate experience by
emphasizing the settings, the studio that made them and most importantly the evolution of the central characters and the stories which
gave the characters an arena.

Warshow used language with extraordinary facility and
economy. Warshow notes that modern egalitarian societies,
whether democratic or authoritarian in their political forms, always
base themselves on the claim that they are making life happier, that
America as a social and political organization is committed to a
cheerful view of life. He links this observation with a deep insight
into the gangster film; "In ways that we do not easily or willingly
define, the gangster speaks for us, expressing that part of the
American psyche which rejects Americanism itself."[1] We see the
accuracy of this observation in the outlook of the central gangster
characters of "Little Caesar", "The Public Enemy" and "Scarface,"
who hold that life is a matter of grabbing everything you can any
way you can, because if you don't the other man will.

Warshow's partaking in the immediate experience of the
gangster film allowed him to make a number of crisp observations

---

[1]Ibid., 130.

of which the following are representative (the accuracy of these
observations will be seen in the body of this study):"This gangster
is the man of the city, with the city's language and knowledge with
its queer and dishonest skills"[1] No convention of the gangster film
is more strongly established than this: it is dangerous to be alone.
(Rico in "Little Caesar", Tom in "The Public Enemy" and Tony in
"Scarface" were cut down when they were alone. "Scarface" begins
with a man foolishly allowing himself to be separated from the group.
He is being set up to be murdered.) Warshow sums up his article on
the gangster film with an observation which holds only for "Little
Caesar" and "Scarface". "At bottom, the gangster is doomed because
he is under the obligation to succeed, not because the means he employs
are wonderful...one is punished for success. This is our dilemma:
that failure is a kind of death and success is evil and dangerous, is -
ultimately - impossible."[2] Tom in "The Public Enemy" is not
ambitious, he is content to be a "rank and file" gangster, willing to
take orders from Paddy and Nails. His death comes when he is not
careful and to satisfy the tenets of the era's film censorship which

---

[1]Ibid., 131.

[2]Ibid., 133.

held since he was a murderer he must die. Duke Mantee in "The
Petrified Forest" is not in search of success or power.

Warshow's observations reflect best the archetypical gangster
films "Little Caesar" and "Scarface". However, the tone of his articles
(he continues his discussion of the gangster films in an article on the
Western) implies their applicability to all gangster films. Warshow's
observations do not cover the Cagney films too well. Cagney was so
vital and exciting in "The Public Enemy" that in his succeeding films
his characters did not have to pay for their criminal activities ("Lady
Killer" is an example). Robinson on the other hand died much as he
did in "Little Caesar" even when he played a policeman in "Bullets or
Ballots". The Bogart gangster film "The Petrified Forest" really was
not tragic in the terms Warshow applied to "Little Caesar". The
Bogart character risked his life to wait for his woman while the law
closed in. His men stayed with him not out of fear, rather out of
respect and friendship.

Warshow's concept of the tragic nature of the gangster hero
usually was not applicable to most gangster films. As this study will
show in the latter part of the 1930's in the Bogart program gangster
films ("You Can't Get Away With Murder" and "King of the Underworld")
the gangster was simply a rather low and distasteful creature without
the stature to challenge anything as mighty as America's commitment

27.

to happiness. Other attempts to resurrect the genre in the
1960's, "The Rise and Fall of Legs Diamond", "Portrait of a
Mobster", "Young Dillinger" similarly could not be thought of
as ever attempting a tragic quality. This study at once confirms a number of Warshow's observations and lends support to
them through specific examples. Because, however, this study
first compares and contrasts the archetypical films then goes
on to discuss the succeeding films it provides a more complete
view of the genre.

D. General Cultural Studies and Mass Communications
Research

The mass media are often not accorded the importance
they deserve in historical scholarship dealing with general
cultural development. This situation holds for several possible reasons: This kind of scholarship has yet to fully take
account of what is a relatively new human endeavor; the vast
phenomena connected with the mass media -- spanning artistic,
economic and social spheres -- are difficult to categorize and
define. There is a need for fundamental studies by those
engaged in mass communications scholarship which will make the
history, artistic achievement and workings of the media more
readily understood in other scholarly circles. Two respected
general cultural history studies, The Growth of the American
Republic

by Samuel Eliot Morison and Henry Steele Commager and The Rise of
the West by William H. McNeill, point up the need for this kind of
communications scholarship.

Morison and Commager's The Growth of the American
Republic has been a widely used college text for a number of years.
This study drew on the second volume of The Growth of the American
Republic for background on the 1930's. (Morison and Commager's
study spans from before the coming of Columbus to America through
1950.)

Morison and Commager simply lump the automobile, radio
and motion picture together, calling them a force which has promoted
urbanization of America in the years after World War One. The
authors spend about a page and a half discussing motion pictures. They
make several brief observations: David Griffith did much to advance
the dramatic power of film; film stars like Chaplin, Pickford and
Fairbanks became national favorites; sound films made classics like
David Copperfield available to vast numbers of people who would probably
never read the originals. Their summary view of the medium was rather
dim. Theystate that while motion pictures had demonstrated their
capability to handle themes of social criticism the medium placed overwhelming emphasis on fostering highly romantic and misleading notions
about life.

Morison and Commager saw film providing models for the audience in matters of dress, home furnishings, play, even marriage and family life. They saw human nature conforming to commercial art. Morison and Commager also saw this tendency in the big time sports of the 1920's and 1930's -- millions of small boys who had never heard of Charles W. Eliot or Justice Holmes held Babe Ruth and Joe DiMaggio national heroes. [1] It is, perhaps, unlikely that high quality fundamental studies of the mass communications media would change the opinions of those who see the media in a particular light. However, such studies might provide scholars of culture such as Morison and Commager with material, with which scholars could then point out the development and accomplishments in the media; how the media are an integral part of this era; how the media relate to other human endeavors such as statecraft and architecture.

William H. McNeill's vast study The Rise of the West, covers human civilization from its origins in the Fertile Crescent to the present. Like Morison and Commager's work it is a summary and integration of the scholarship of others, and could have benefited from fundamental communications studies. McNeill sees the modern era as

---

[1] Samuel Eliot Morison and Henry Steele Commager, The Growth of the American Republic (New York: Oxford University Press, 1950), II, 554.

characterized by two qualities: increasing human control over
inanimate forms of energy and increasing readiness to create
institutions and customs to attain social goals. [1]

Reliance on science, technology and vast physical resources
and the need for large numbers of people to make motion pictures and
bring them to the public would certainly qualify films (by McNeill's
construct) as an endeavor of the modern era. However, McNeill restricts his discussion of modern art to painting, music, architecture
and literature. The plates which accompany McNeill's text include
only examples of modern painting and sculpture. A strong case could
be made for the inclusion in this section of a still from a motion picture
of the stature of "The Birth of a Nation".

Perhaps studies such as this one, which are designed to de-
limit and elucidate occurrences and qualities of the mass media, such
as the gangster character, will aid future generalists in the tradition
of Morison and Commager and McNeill. Future general cultural
histories, by incorporating communications research could make
fuller observations about our age, an age in which so many of the
world's people spend so much time partaking of the mass communications
media.

---

[1]William H. McNeill, The Rise of the West (New York:
New American Library, 1965), p. 794.

E. Definition of the "Gangster Film"

Today, when a film is made and designated a "gangster
film", the label refers to a storyline concerned with criminals
employing physical violence, operating in a more or less
organized fashion during the period of the 1920's and early
1930's (for example, "The St. Valentine's Day Massacre",
"Bonnie and Clyde", etc.). Gangster films are based on this
period just as Westerns refer to the approximate period in
American history from 1870 to 1890. The archetypical gangster
films, "Little Caesar" and "The Public Enemy" were based on
the headlines, the news events of their era. These films laid
bare personalities symptomatic of an age: Duke Mantee ("The
Petrified Forest"), a rootless, bank robbing desperado of the
Depression; or Tom Powers ("The Public Enemy"), a rebellious,
first generation American youth, no longer to be bound by the
outlook of his parents in the burgeoning city after World
War I.

By 1939 Prohibition was past and the underworld had
become less open in its methods. The Dillinger-type killer
had been hunted down. "The Roaring Twenties" (1939) with James
Cagney and Humphrey Bogart, already carried a foreword which
called its story "a reminiscence." Edward G. Robinson's only
gangster film of 1940, "Brother Orchid," with Humphrey Bogart
as his one-dimensional adversary, will be found to be

categorized in this study under the heading "Comic Caesar" --
a shallow, humorous reminder of the character Robinson
created in "Little Caesar" ten years before.

By 1941 Cagney had moved out of the gangster genre as
had Robinson (both would return years later). Bogart was to
repeat his classic desperado in "High Sierra" (1941), but was
also to switch to a new career as the private eye in "The
Maltese Falcon" (1941).

Paul Muni's first successful film, "Scarface", was of the
gangster genre. He repeated a similar characterization in
"Bordertown" (1935). However, other than a minor film, "Dr.
Socrates" (1935), in which Muni played a physician involved with
gang leader Barton MacLane, Muni never again made a gangster
film. Muni, protean and versatile, made a wide range of characters
his trademark. While Robinson, Cagney and Bogart honed and redefined their singular gangster characterizations, Muni (donning
complex make-up and costumes) went through a series of roles
from Louis Pasteur to Juarez, from a Mexican to a Chinese.
Because of his early divergence from the gangster genre, Muni's
films will be treated in those specific cases which serve to point
up contrasts and contributions -- especially "Scarface" and
"Bordertown". Muni's diverse repertory is not germane to the
study. His work in the "socially conscious" and "historical-

documentary" films will, however, be discussed in Appendix I.

America's participation in World War Two developed a new concern among audiences. Films dealing with a domestic problem such as gangsters did not hold great interest for a country involved in world affairs. Patriotism was the order of the day, with a large helping of optimism. Our adversaries became foreigners, our violence had a noble purpose, our internal issues took second place. On screen, Robinson became a fatherly naval officer; Bogart a tank commander; Muni a Russian soldier; Cagney a flyer -- and the gangsters put away their guns for the duration.

F. The Gangster Film at Warner Brothers Studio

All four of the personalities most closely associated with the gangster film genre of the 1930's, Edward G. Robinson, James Cagney, Paul Muni and Humphrey Bogart, made the majority of their films for one studio, Warner Brothers. In the years when American feature film making was organized according to assembly line methods and each studio (whether consciously or not) left a stamp on its films, this genre came to be identified with Warner Brothers.

This is not to say that Warner Brothers was the only studio to make gangster films, but it was the studio which achieved the greatest success in the genre. Warner Brothers created more of the significant films and classic characters than its competitors and worked in the genre longest. Tracing the Warner Brothers films and their recurring stable of characters over the period 1930 through 1940, it is possible to delineate the thesis of variation and decay of the gangster film genre. To better understand the genre a discussion of the mode of operation of the Warner Brothers Studio is in order.

The Warners became the sensation of the entertainment industry with their presentation of "The Jazz Singer" in 1927. By 1930, Warner Brothers could be classed as the nation's leading motion picture production-distribution-exhibition organization.

Warner Brothers and Loews, Incorporated (Metro-Goldwyn-Mayer's parent company) alone among the theatre owning-producing firms were not forced into some form of bankruptcy, receivership or reorganization during the Depression. In the 1930's, Warner Brothers had larger gross assets ($177,500,000.00) than any other movie company.[1] This fact is all the more remarkable when it is remembered that film industry leaders in 1922 did not consider the Warner brothers important enough to be included as signatories to the agreement establishing the Hays Office.

_____

[1]"The Brothers Warner", Fortune, December, 1937, pp. 110-113.

The Warner Brothers Studio had grown to this position from rather unpromising beginnings. Benjamin Warner had brought his family to America from Poland in the 1880's. Not particularly successful at a variety of ventures, he pawned his watch to help his sons Sam and Albert buy a projection outfit, some posters, song slides and a print of "The Great Train Robbery".

In 1906 the Warners opened their first theatre, a converted store in New Castle, Pennsylvania. Business had to be suspended on the days the local undertaker commandeered his ninety-nine folding chairs. This was a family enterprise.[1] Jack, the youngest brother, sang illustrated songs and sister Rose accompanied him on the piano after she sold tickets to the show. Harry, the oldest brother, was booking agent for the firm. Warner Brothers was a family controlled enterprise from its inception through 1966.

In a St. Louis studio in 1912, the Warners produced their first film, a three reeler, "Peril of the Plains". By 1916 they had leased a small Hollywood studio with Sam and Jack in charge. Albert sold the pictures and Harry handled the firm's finances. Story lines were often taken from current happenings in the newspapers. The first major Warner success was drawn from the newspaper serialization of United States Ambassador James W. Gerard's

---

[1]Frederic M. Thrasher (ed.), Okay For Sound (New York: Duell, Sloan and Pearce, 1946), pp. 41-46.

"My Four Years In Germany" which appeared after Gerard
was recalled when America severed relations with Germany preceding the declaration of war.

Because they could not yet afford top stars or mount
spectacles, the Warners attempted to gain a public following
through timeliness. (Warners returned to timely topics with
success in later years with "Doorway to Hell", "The Public
Enemy", "Black Legion", etc.) "My Four Years In Germany" was
successful; their financial backer took more than fifty percent of the profits, the distributor, First National, made
$300,000.00, the Warners made $130,000.00.

During the 1920's Warner Brothers had under contract John
Barrymore, Wesley Barry, Lenore Ulric and Rin-Tin-Tin. Ernst
Lubitsch directed their films "Marriage Circle", "Three Women",
"So This Is Paris". Jack and Sam ran the studio on Sunset
Boulevard in Hollywood. By 1924 production funds were raised
through the sale of Warner Brothers films to regional franchise holders -- powerful independent distributors who advanced
them a portion of the money to make their pictures. Financier
Waddill Catchings later joined forces with the Warners to
raise money for the purchase of the Vitagraph Company with its
system of exchanges which freed Warners from the franchise
holders. During 1925 Warners concluded agreements

with Western Electric which initiated sound film experiments under Sam Warner's direction in New York. Back in California, Jack Warner, with assistants Darryl Zanuck and Bryan Foy, continued to produce silent pictures.

After the success of their sound films "Don Juan", then "The Jazz Singer" and "The Lights of New York" (the first all talking picture), Harry Warner set the family enterprise on a course which would make it an equal to the largest motion picture companies. Again in concert with Waddill Catchings, Warners acquired Stanley Company of America, which controlled some two hundred and fifty theatres and also owned a third interest in First National Pictures. With cash from banks and stock sales Harry Warner bought out additional First National stockholders; later they acquired the final interest in First National from William Fox for $10,000,000.00. During 1930 the Warner theatre chain was expanded to more than five hundred houses. Music publishing and record companies were added. Broadway plays were produced at this time. A raid on Paramount brought Kay Francis, William Powell and Ruth Chatterton to Warner Brothers. As previously noted Warner Brothers rode the Depression in relatively good condition although the period of acquisition and growth had passed with 1930. Darryl Zanuck, for several years head of production, left Warners in 1933 for Twentieth Century Pictures which later merged with Fox Film Corporation.

During the remainder of the 1930's, Jack L. Warner,
youngest of the brothers active in the firm, headed production
with Hal Wallis, next in command. Fortune Magazine noted the
following characteristics of Jack Warner's production organization:
"Sets were built using straight line production methods in a huge
central crafts building to release stages for more shooting time.
Art directors were sent on weekly tours of the scenery docks in
order that future productions might utilize sets on hand."[1]

Unlike Paramount which during the 1930's operated in
some respects like a loose federation of powerful producers,
Jack Warner's regime was founded on the notion that no producer
was bigger than the studio. Warner Brothers assigned the term
"supervisor" to the position other studios called producer. Later
in the decade the studio gave its supervisors the title "associate
producer" with Hal Wallis designated Associate Executive in Charge
of Production.

One of Warners' supervisors or associate producers was
Henry Blanke, Lubitsch's assistant during the 1920's. Blanke
handled such diverse assignments as "Convention City", "The
Petrified Forest", "Adventures of Robin Hood", "The Life of
Emile Zola", "The Story of Louis Pasteur", "Juarez" and "The

---

[1] "The Brothers Warner", loc. cit.

Maltese Falcon". Blanke, like the other Warner producers, moved

from assignment to assignment rather than carving out an "area"

as producers did at other studios.

Louis Edelman handled low budget service and newspaper

headline based stories. During the 1930's he produced "Devil Dogs

of the Air" (Cagney), "Here Comes the Navy" (Cagney), "Submarine

D-1". Edelman and his staff writers could often put a film together

for as little as $300,000.00, given the technical cooperation of one

of the armed services and a star. Edelman also maintained the

tradition of making films based on newspaper stories. "G-Men"

(Cagney) drew its impetus from the killing of John Dillinger. From

conception through end of production "G-Men" took eight weeks.

"Marked Woman" (Bette Davis and Humphrey Bogart) was based on

the Thomas E. Dewey vice investigations in New York City. Edelman

rarely purchased a story property.

Bryan Foy, son of stage star Eddie Foy, headed the Warner

"B" or program picture unit. (Foy directed the first all talking pic-

ture "The Lights of New York".) During the mid-1930's he was

assigned to make twenty-six features with a total budget of

$5,000,000.00. (The "A" picture, "The Life of Emile Zola",

cost approximately $1,000,000.00 in 1936). Foy's pictures

featured inserts (newspaper clips) which advanced the story

without using actors. He employed many closeups to keep

attention diverted from the sets. About half of Foy's pictures were remakes of past Warner Brothers films; for example, Bogart's "King of the Underworld" (1939) was a remake of Muni's "Dr. Socrates" (1935), "You Can't Get Away With Murder" (1939) was a remake of "San Quentin" (1937).

While Warner Brothers made the occasional big picture ("Anthony Adverse", "A Midsummer Night's Dream"), the company addressed itself to pictures which would produce a consistent, if relatively modest, profit in relation to what could be realized by making more expensive films. The gangster genre fitted the company's low risk outlook. The Warners realized financial stability enabled them to keep the Wall Street interests out of the operation of their business.

Only Mervyn LeRoy, director of "Little Caesar", "I Am A Fugitive From A Chain Gang", "Two Seconds", "Gold Diggers of 1933", "Anthony Adverse" and "They Won't Forget", held the position of independent producer at Warner Brothers Studio. He had players under personal contract and shared in his pictures' profits. He had, however, married into the Warner family. LeRoy left Warner Brothers in the later thirties for Metro-Goldwyn-Mayer. William Randolph Hearst's and Marion Davies' Cosmopolitan Productions also existed for a time as an independent unit at Warner Brothers.

Through 1966, Warner Brothers was headed by Jack L. Warner, last of the brothers active in the firm. Warner functioned both as head of the corporation and chief production executive. Today, with the present tax structure, the separation of production-distribution from exhibition, and the subsequent growth of independent production, no studio can leave as distinct a "company stamp" on all its pictures. However, certain characteristics consistently present in Warner pictures were still in evidence at the end of J. L. Warner's reign in 1966.

First, Warner Brothers films were relatively smaller in scope than those of other major studios. While Warner Brothers has produced "My Fair Lady" and "Camelot", the studio has left it to Twentieth Century-Fox, Metro-Goldwyn-Mayer and Columbia to create such "blockbusters" as "Cleopatra", "Ben Hur", "Dr. Zhivago", "Lord Jim", "Dr. Doolittle", "Bridge Over The River Kwai".

In recent years Warner Brothers has negotiated agreements whereby Paul Newman, Steve McQueen and Frank Sinatra made a portion of their pictures for the studio. The films of these individuals may be characterized as personality-story oriented as opposed to spectacles such as Metro-Goldwyn-Mayer's "Dr. Zhivago". The tradition of the personality-story oriented film reaches back to the Warner films of the 1930's with Robinson, Cagney and Bogart.

Warner Brothers has always had a tendency to take on
the controversial -- "I Am A Fugitive From A Chain Gang", "Black
Legion", "They Won't Forget", "Confessions of a Nazi Spy",
"Mildred Pierce", "A Streetcar Named Desire", "Baby Doll".
This too fits in with the notion of not risking all on super productions.
The controversial film has often proved to be most profitable for
the studio, permitting operation without large, high risk productions
which if unsuccessful might have compromised family control of the
studio.

In the year preceding Jack L. Warner's sale of his studio
holdings to Seven Arts his regime made two small films -- small
in relation to much industry practice of the 1960's -- which may
prove to be among the most important of recent times -- "Who's
Afraid of Virginia Woolf" and "Bonnie and Clyde".

CHAPTER II

THE ARCHETYPICAL FILMS

A. "Little Caesar" 1930

According to Warner Brothers, "Little Caesar" was not
a gangster picture, rather, through the telling of Little Caesar's
story, the producers sought to present to the American people an
expose of a national problem and a reassertion of traditional tenets
for human conduct:

> "For all those who live by the sword shall perish
> by it."
>
> Matthew 26:52

> "The first law of every being, is to preserve
> itself and live. You sow hemlock, and
> expect to see ears of corn ripen."
>
> Machiavelli

(Versions of the above were carried on "Little Caesar"
release prints over the years.)

Warner Brothers' "Little Caesar" (1930) and "The Public
Enemy" (1931) were extraordinary in that they were both singularly
successful in delineating episodic stories without lapses into non-
filmic exposition; the screenplays covered considerable expanses
of time. Both films explored the origins, motivations and social
conditions which led to the criminal careers of two men -- each

of whom was typical of an "antisocial" type of his era.

We find this kind of time span covered in other films, although not with the same action quotient: "I Am A Fugitive From A Chain Gang" (1932) directed by Mervyn LeRoy with Paul Muni, "Silver Dollar" (1933) directed by Alfred E. Green with Edward G. Robinson, "The World Changes" (1933) directed by Mervyn LeRoy with Paul Muni, "Angels With Dirty Faces" (1938) directed by Michael Curtiz with James Cagney, "The Roaring Twenties" (1939) directed by Raoul Walsh with James Cagney.

"Little Caesar" traces the career of Caesar Fredrico "Rico" Bandello from petty holdup artist in the hinterlands, quick with his gun, to chief of a big city gang (still relying on his gun), to his death at the hands of tommygun-armed city police.

After an opening sequence in which Rico (Edward G. Robinson) and his buddy, Joe (Douglas Fairbanks, Jr.) hold up a gas station and shoot the attendant, we find the pair in a diner. Rico notes a big city newspaper, "Underworld Pays Respects to Diamond Pete Montana". Montana does not have to waste his time on cheap gas station holdups; "He's in the Big Town, doin' things in a big way." Acutely aware of his own shabbiness, Rico is drawn by Montana's flashy jewelry and fine clothes.

In the space of two script pages the direction of the story

is established: Rico wants to be in on the action; he wants power.

Joe thinks only of big city good times; a career as a dancer. Even

before he has begun his climb in the underworld, Rico dreams.

Eating spaghetti in the roadside diner, Rico plots his course.

                    RICO
          I could do all the things that fellow
          (Diamond Pete Montana) does. More!
          When I get in a tight spot, I shoot my
          way out of it. Like tonight. . . sure,
          shoot first -- argue afterwards. If
          you don't the other feller gets you...
          This game ain't for guys that's soft!
                    (to Joe)
          Women. . . dancin'. . . where do
          they get you?
                    (shakes his head
                    violently)
          I don't want no dancin' -- I figure on
          makin' other people dance.

Once in the city this fierce aggressiveness propels Rico

to the top of the underworld in short order. But it is a drive that

is out of step with the times. An end to violence is desired by

both the city's "good people" and the underworld. Rico interprets

this as weakness. A creature like a dinosaur, unable to adapt to

or understand a changing environment, Rico condemns himself to

extinction. During the development of the story it is apparent

that Rico will die, but not because he is bad or, as the foreword

suggests, because he "lives by the sword" or "sows hemlock".

Rico's code for living is at odds with his environment and society will eliminate him. Rico emerges a tragic rather than an evil character; a man consumed by ambition who will not heed the warning of his gang boss that shooting is "old stuff".

Rico, always the gunman, shows his reliance on firearms early in the script. In the diner scene, the more passive Joe fears Rico's trigger-happy ways as they are questioned by police.

> JOE
> .....That was close. You got
> me kinda jumpy when I seen you
> reachin' for the...

> RICO
> Maybe I should o' done it, too.
> (pats his gun)
> That's all I got between me and
> them -- between me and the whole
> world....

James Cagney's Tom Powers in "The Public Enemy" is obviously Irish. In the early sequences laid in turn-of-the-century Chicago, emphasis is placed upon the still highly recognizable European ethnic groups living in the city. So, too, Edward G. Robinson's Rico is obviously Italian. (Although of Rumanian ancestry, Robinson often played Italians and a variety of "foreigners" -- a Portuguese in "Tiger Shark", a Frenchman in "Man With Two Faces", a Chinese in "The Hatchet Man", a Greek in "Smart Money", a Scandinavian in "Our Vines Have Tender Grapes".) After Rico has been admitted to Sam Vettori's gang headquarters at the Club

Palermo, Vettori introduces the gang members: Tony Passa,

Otero, Scabby and Killer Pepi. If not all Italian, no one in the

gang appears to be Anglo-Saxon.

"Little Caesar" chronicles the rise and fall of Rico

against the backdrop of the times. This same pattern -- a man's

story, a view of society -- is followed in other Warner films such

as "I Am A Fugitive From A Chain Gang", "The Frisco Kid", and

"The Roaring Twenties". In "Little Caesar", big city crime is

examined. A crime commission has recently been installed and

not even the Big Boy (as yet unseen and unknown head of crime in

the city) can fix things with the crusading commissioner. Diamond

Pete Montana tells Rico's boss, Vettori, and another gang leader:

> MONTANA
> The Big Boy wants me to tell you
> to put chains on your gorillas for
> the next few months 'cause if any
> of 'em go too far, it'll be just too
> bad...
> (to Vettori)
> It's guys like that torpedo of yours
> (Rico) that cause all the trouble...

When Montana leaves, Rico has a chance to have a close

look at Diamond Pete's jewelry. His rise in the underworld will be

paralleled by his own acquisition of jewelry. Diamond Pete, once

Rico's idol, now slips in the gunman's esteem. Rico scoffs at

Diamond Pete's desire to put aside violence. Not understanding
the forces at work, Rico labels discretion as a show of weakness.
Rico, the first-rate, steel-nerved gunman, has confronted the
organization-oriented, businessman crime boss.

The underworld of Little Caesar's city has thrived on a
coalition of crime and politics; an alliance conceived to prevent
city police from moving against organized crime. The mysterious
Big Boy enjoys connections in high places -- and low. The new
commissioner, apparently incorruptible, challenges Big Boy's
position from above. At the same time Rico, rising, unstoppable,
brutally ambitious, challenges from below. The result is fatal --
for the commissioner, for the crime organization and ultimately
for Rico. (The relationship between crime and politics is also
explored in "Bullets or Ballots", "The Frisco Kid", "Barbary
Coast", "Marked Woman" and "Angels With Dirty Faces" among
the films under consideration.)

Rico's longstanding dream to surpass even the legendary
Diamond Pete comes true. As he growled to Joe in the diner,
"When I get in a tight spot, I shoot my way out of it", Rico begins
his rise when he sets out to challenge the mob's "no violence"
policy. During the holdup of a nightclub owned by a rival gang
leader, Rico, with the Sam Vettori gang, personally shoots and

kills Crime Commissioner McClure, who is patronizing the

club. Sam Vettori, Rico's leader, crumples at the news.

Rico has killed the commissioner; Tony, the gang driver, has

fled in fear.

> VETTORI
> (to Rico)
> The head of the Crime Commission!
> The Big Boy can't do us no good --
> not this trip -- they'll get us dead
> sure now...what am I gonna do?

> RICO
> (to Vettori)
> Maybe you better go and give yourself
> up. You're slippin', Sam...

And later, after the police have paid a visit to Sam Vettori in

the Club Palermo office:

> RICO
> ....You've got so you can dish it out,
> but you can't take it no more. You're
> through!

Attention in setting detail and minor characters heighten

the historical quality of both "Little Caesar" and "The Public Enemy".

Before his murder on the steps of a church on his way to confession,

there is a scene between Tony Passa (the gang member who ran

after the commissioner's murder and who is now suspected of

turning informer) and his mother. The setting is described in the

script:

TONY'S FLAT EARLY MORNING MED. SHOT

This is a combination living and bedroom in one of
those wretched tenement houses that are typical Little
Italy. The apartment itself perhaps consists of a bedroom and kitchen in addition to this room, but we do
not see the other chambers at this time.... The door
opens quietly and Mrs. Passa -- an old Italian woman
with a parchment-like yellowed face, comes in.....
seeing her son is distraught and not being able to
find out what is going on--

> MRS. PASSA
> Listen, Antonio, I leave spaghetti
> on the stove. Yes? When you feel
> better, eat some, eh? Do you good...
> (she recalls)
> The church was beautiful...you little
> boy with long hair...the big candle...
> flowers...remember, Antonio?

After Rico has shot Tony on the church steps for his
defection from the gang, a decorous Italian style funeral scene is
played, complete with ornate floral blankets. There is similar
"color" in a number of sequences in "The Public Enemy" with
reproduction of the rows of bars, Tom's house and "Back of the
Yards" living conditions.

After his accession to the leadership of the gang, a dinner
is given in Rico's honor; a duplicate of the party honoring Diamond

Pete which inspired Rico long ago in the lonely diner. The
testimonial dinner with a newspaper photographer in attendance
serves as the ceremony Rico needs to confirm his new position as
leader -- a public strutting of his power. Rico is later wounded by
a rival gang leader's gunmen while taking a walk to buy a bunch of
newspapers featuring his banquet picture -- his ego overriding his
caution.

Rico is still true to his original code now that he is a
success in the big city. The banquet scene is as follows: Every
other seat is occupied by the ladies of the gang, cheap, semi-
prostitute, blondined, over-dressed types. There are, however,
no women around Rico.

> RICO
> All right, if you birds want me to
> make a speech, here you are. I
> want to thank you guys for this
> banquet. It sure is swell. The
> liquor is good so they tell me, I
> don't drink it myself, and the food
> don't leave nothing to be desired, I
> guess we all had a swell time and it
> sure is good to see all you guys gathered
> together. Well, I guess that's about all.
> Only I wish you guys wouldn't get drunk
> and raise cain, as that's the way a lot of
> birds get bumped off.

Rico has the opportunity for exercising cold power in the
city; the situation he wished for on the evening of the gas station

robbery. The gang even fulfills Rico's love of flashy jewelry; they steal a large platinum and diamond pocket watch to present to their boss at the banquet. Jewelry, clothes and lavish apartment give proof of Rico's rise in the world.

The policemen are a peculiar lot. They hound the underworld characters, dropping by their offices, crashing their parties, with no particular purpose other than routine harassment. The detective assigned to watch Rico's activities is named Flaherty. Slightly wounded by a rival gang's gunmen, his arms full of newspapers carrying his picture, Rico haughtily laughs off Flaherty's warnings of his impending fall. Flaherty turns to his fellow officers and says grimly: "I'll get that swell-headed mug if it's the last thing I ever do".

The police are a negative force in "Little Caesar". Next to Rico, his gang or the Diamond Pete Montana type of character, the police provide dull fare. In "The Public Enemy" Tom's policeman father; his streetcar conductor, night school student brother; his uncomprehending mother do not appear sympathetic but dully negative, as the police do in "Little Caesar".

The rival gang leader, Little Arnie Lorch, makes a great error in just wounding Rico. In a lightning move, Rico and his gang capture Lorch's headquarters without firing a shot. This stroke will propel Rico to leadership of the underworld, second only to

the Big Boy himself. Rico has the nerve he boastfully proclaimed

to Joe after the gas station holdup. This is evidenced in his take-

over of Little Arnie:

> (Little Arnie in a near
> state of collapse.)

RICO
You hired these mugs. They missed,
now you're through. If you ain't out
of town by tomorrow mornin', you won't
never leave it except in a pine box...

ARNIE
You're growin' Rico. This is what you
been after all the time, eh? I saw it in
your eyes the first time I met you...
You're a rat, Rico. But if you think you
can muscle in on me like you did on Sam
Vettori, you're off your nut. I guess you
forgot about Pete Montana?

RICO
And how's "Diamond" Pete gonna stop me?
He may be your boss but he ain't mine.

From the beginning of the film, Rico has stated that a

leader is no longer capable of holding his position when he no

longer has the capacity for physical action. Rico takes the

Palermo gang from Sam Vettori when Vettori tries to rule from

behind a desk. Rico gains the gang's respect by personally killing

Commissioner McClure. Rico now crushes Little Arnie because

Arnie has to hire killers and is not capable of personally facing a

showdown.

Diamond Pete has been seen only at a meeting where he acted the part of a boss solely through tough talk. To Rico's mind this means Diamond Pete too has lost his nerve. Rico still does not understand that big city vice operations seldom need shoot-outs. Vettori, Arnie and Montana, out of fear, give way to Rico; though they realize Rico's tactics mean ruin for the crime empire.

RICO
(to Arnie)
Better quit the racket, Arnie. You
got so you can dish it out, but you
can't take it no more.

The Big Boy sends Diamond Pete Montana to see Rico with an invitation to meet with the Big Boy himself for dinner. Despite Montana's bravado it's obvious that he is shaken by Rico's power. The Big Boy, taken by Rico's nerve, appoints him boss of the North Side over Montana.

It is apparent that the Big Boy is a person of position. He has used social connections along with the power of his gangs to build a crime empire. (Society people are painted as either dishonest or less than admirable in a number of the films under consideration: "The Public Enemy", "Blonde Crazy", "Little Giant", "Bullets or Ballots", "Angels With Dirty Faces".) Rico, though a bit ill at ease in the Big Boy's plush home, will not compromise himself; he will not drink.

Now that he is boss of the North Side, Rico moves out of
his dingy rooms in Little Italy into an elegant apartment. Here
Robinson shows one of the most celebrated qualities of his "Little
Caesar" characterization. As the scene opens in his new apartment,
he struts (according to script directions) "like a proud peacock".
The strutting, the rapid fire delivery and the thrusting motions at
an opponent's face with his index finger, are the symbols of the
Robinson screen character best remembered and most frequently
imitated.

As Rico prances up and down the room, he addresses his
chief henchman and most loyal admirer, Otero:

> RICO
> I knew it was coming. I knew he
> had his eyes on me. Let me tell
> you - it's not only Pete Montana
> that's through -- but the Big Boy
> himself....he ain't what he used
> to be neither. Pretty soon he won't
> be able to take it and then...watch
> me.

Both Rico and Tony Carmonte of "Scarface" have a peculiarly
possessive quality toward chosen people. This obsession is instrumental in the ultimate destruction of both characters. Now that Rico
is boss of the whole North Side and feels that it is only a matter of
time before he will control the entire city, he wants his friend Joe
Massara to quit dancing and rejoin him. In one of the most explicit

examples of the motivation of the possessive gangster character,

Rico confronts Joe:

>   RICO
> You didn't quit! Nobody ever quits me.
> Get that! You're still in my gang. I
> don't care how many fancy dames you
> got stickin' on to you. That skirt can go
> hang. It's her that made a softy outa you.

>   JOE
> You lay off Olga, Rico.

>   RICO
> I ain't layin' off her. I'm after her.
> She an' me can't both have you. One
> of us gotta lose -- an' it ain't gonna
> be me! There's ways of stoppin' that
> dame...!

>   JOE
>   (terror-stricken)
> You're crazy! Leave her out of this...

>   RICO
>   (his face distorted with
>   rage now, he is fairly
>   shrieking)
> It's curtains for her, see? She's
> through...she's out of the way...
> that's what she is!

>   JOE
>   (drawing back; almost
>   insanely)
> You're lyin'. You wouldn't....

>   RICO
> I wouldn't? I'll show you...that
> dirty, painted-up.....

>   JOE
> I love her! We're in love! Don't
> that mean nothin' to you?

RICO

Nothin'! Less than nothin'! Love --
soft stuff! When she's got you, you
ain't safe...you know too much. I
ain't takin' no chances. You're stayin'
here!

Robinson uses a tactic which helps him dominate all his films of the 1930's. Through his rapid, passionate delivery and hand gestures he overwhelms physically larger players. His delivery is the key. If Douglas Fairbanks, Jr. (Joe) were in the Rico role he could not have brought it off as effectively as Robinson. (Such a situation did arise in "Doorway to Hell" when Lew Ayres, with an appearance and low key delivery not too different from Fairbanks, played the gang leader with something less than convincing results.) Both Cagney and Robinson, through the power of their delivery, thrust themselves into a position of domination over larger and more "clean cut" male players.

Joe goes back to Olga's place in a state of near hysteria. Olga is determined to rid their lives of Rico. She calls Flaherty with an offer that Joe will turn state's evidence. As Olga and Joe nervously wait for the police, Rico and Otero burst into the apartment. Rico has come to silence Joe and Olga forever, but he cannot shoot. Otero accuses Rico himself of getting soft. As Rico and Otero struggle, Otero shoots Joe in the shoulder. The two gangsters escape as Flaherty arrives.

Rico and Otero are now fugitives. Olga and Joe will provide evidence that Rico killed McClure. As they stop for a minute, Rico says, "This is what I get for liking a guy too much".

Rico told Joe at the beginning that "This game ain't for guys that's soft!...That's (his gun) all I got between me and them -- between me and the whole world..." If he had eliminated Joe and Olga when he had the chance he would not be a fugitive; but at the crucial moment he lost his capacity to act.

With Joe Massara's testimony Rico's gang is dispersed and Sam Vettori executed. Rico escapes, however, and is hiding out in a flophouse. His ego has crumbled with his fall from power. Unwashed and unkempt, drunken and depressed he sits on his cot, another nameless man. He listens with contempt as a flophouse inmate reads about Vettori's execution; "Former gang chief faints on scaffold. After a futile battle in courts, Sam Vettori, former gang leader, today presented a pitiful figure as the hangman's noose was placed around his neck".

In the same newspaper story Detective Flaherty has planted the following item knowing it will reach Rico and bring him out of hiding:

                    VOICE OF MAN WITH PAPER
          "Little Caesar has never been found. He
          is hiding like a rat in his hole. The once
          swaggering braggart of the underworld wilted
                         (MORE)

> VOICE OF MAN WITH PAPER
> (continuing)
> in the face of real danger and showed the world
> his cowardice, thus contradicting his oftrepeated
> boast that he could dish it out and take it too.
> When the moment arose, Rico couldn't take it!
> Meteoric as his rise from the gutter has been,
> it was inevitable that he should return there..."

> VOICE OF ANOTHER MAN
> "Just the same, he was the real leader of that
> gang".

> VOICE OF THE MAN WITH
> PIPE
> "Don't you believe it! Sam was rotten but he
> was the real head. Rico didn't have the nerve
> and he didn't have the brains...He was yellow,
> like the paper says. That's what Rico was..."

As Rico hears these words, he springs into a sitting position

on the bed -- an ugly, threatening expression comes to his face. He

leaps up, about to start toward the group. His face clouds, he looks

at the whiskey bottle still in his hand, looks at it long and nods his

head as though saying to himself, "I'm not the same man any more!

This is the cause of it!..."

Rico telephones Flaherty and screams a challenge to him.

The policeman comes after Rico. His machine-guns cut Rico down

behind a billboard for a new gala musical starring Joe and Olga.

With Flaherty and the police gathered about, Rico gasps, "Mother

of Mercy -- is this the end of Rico...?"

Despite the foreword to "Little Caesar" to the effect that

"he who lives by the sword shall perish by the sword", even with

Rico's death it cannot in fact be said that the film taught a moral lesson. Rico was in many respects an admirable person. He bettered himself in the only way he understood. There was never indication that the more socially acceptable characters and their way of life were preferable to Rico and the road he had chosen. This point is made even more graphically in "The Public Enemy" when individuals on the right side of the law are shown to be either boring or hypocritical. Rico's death is in great measure gratuitous, a kind of sacrifice to an external code, enforced from outside the construct of the film.

"Little Caesar" never presents a force of good to strike down Rico, to effectively cancel Rico's code of living by the sword. Strangely enough, Rico's demise came about through a weakness in his personality, flaws which prevented Rico from carrying out the dictates of his code -- his desire to dominate Joe, compounded by his inability to kill his friend. This conclusion did not fundamentally discredit Rico's code, and so the film, despite the protestations of the producers, did not serve as a lesson to support conventional morality.

B. "The Public Enemy" 1931

Like "Little Caesar," the release prints of "The Public
Enemy" carried a careful rationalization in its foreword. The
audience was not about to see the glamorization of gangsters,
rather, a national problem would be explored through film.
The film did succeed in extraordinary measure in exploring the
factors which shaped the central character -- a gangster and
murderer. This exploration, despite the protestations of the
foreword, provided little in support of law, order and conventional morality.

"The Public Enemy" was classic in terms of its execution
of a broad narrative which through the progression of exqui-
sitely formed episodes, detailed every stage in the formation
of the hero's outlook. "Little Caesar" followed the same pattern. Perhaps Warners felt that the Cagney and Robinson
characters were so well established in these first films that
it was never again necessary to delineate the factors that
shaped their motivations. Certainly no succeeding Cagney or
Robinson film had the scope of "The Public Enemy" or "Little
Caesar". Succeeding films presented situations for the
already established Cagney and Robinson characters.

In approximately an hour and a half "The Public Enemy" traces the life of a young man who begins his career with petty theft, graduates to grand larceny, bootlegging, murder, and ends with his bullet-riddled body being dumped on his mother's front porch by a rival gang.

Tom Powers' brother, Mike, goes to night school while working as a streetcar conductor. Tom tells the older man who is teaching him the ropes of crime that his night school student brother is "learning to be poor". Tom scoffs at patriotism. Rather then enlisting in the service for the First World War he decides to make money in crime. The stern Irish father is seen only for a moment, but is clearly delineated. The loving mother understands nothing of the experiences of her young son growing up in a great, vibrant American city of the early 1900's. The diligent brother, Mike, chooses to set goals which consist in "joining up", at a modest level, with middle class culture.

There are no "good" people. Propriety is made to seem stuffy and absurd. A "solid citizen" who wishes to operate his brewery during prohibition finds it difficult to admit he is doing so for the money. Mike comes back from the war with nothing to show for his wounds but a medal. The brother faults Tom for bringing gangland beer into the family house, yet cannot answer to

Tom's rebuttal about his own "patriotic" forms of violence against the Germans.

The law itself is shown to be absurd. The national prohibition act is helping to promote the unparalleled level of crime. Although both "Little Caesar" (1930) and "The Public Enemy" (1931) were made during the period of Prohibition they both featured numerous drinking scenes as did countless films during the life of the Prohibition Act.

The various episodes of "The Public Enemy" are all part of a clear narrative line which traces Tom from his boyhood to his murder. The film consistently contributes to an understanding of his character and his times. In the opening, a half-dozen shots prefaced by the title "1909" establish the setting of the story - a Chicago working class neighborhood back of the yards.

We come upon young Tom Powers and his friend, Matt Doyle, both about 10 years old. In less than two script pages we discover some very important qualities in Tom's personality. The boys have been sent out to a nearby saloon by their families to get pails of beer for the evening meal. Tom looks around quickly then takes a swig of beer. Matt does not try to stop his friend.

A couple of girls, also on their way for beer, come up to the boys. Matt grins but Tom shies away as though he didn't want to talk to them. _coward_

                        FIRST GIRL
            Hello, Tommy.

                        TOMMY
                    (ill at ease, starting to
                    walk away)
            'Lo.

                        MATT
                    (more friendly, looks
                    into the girl's pail)
            Can greased?
                    (he quickly runs his
                    finger around inside
                    the pail, and nods)

                        SECOND GIRL
                    (looking at Tom who is
                    standing a few feet off,
                    hovering about uneasy)
            What's the matter with Tom, Matt?

                        MATT
                    (looking at Tom)
            He don't go for girls...that's all.

                        FIRST GIRL
            Nor for school either. He ain't been
            there for a week.

                        TOM
                    (scowling)
            C'mon, Matt. We got business.

    Matt playfully tweaks the hair of one of the girls, turns

and joins Tom. Tom gives him a scornful look. Later Tom steals

a pair of roller skates and gives them to Matt's sister just so he can

trip her. When Matt protests Tom answers scornfully, "What do you

care? It's only a girl."

Tom's brother self-righteously orders the girl to give back
the skates which he immediately suspects Tom of having stolen.
The incident ends with Tom going into his house to receive a beating
from his father. There is no protest, only cold insolence. It is
evident Tom has been beaten many times in the past.

Tom's house is a small free-standing affair, a duplicate of
others on the street. With its picket fence and wooden sidewalks,
it is a simple, dull place in contrast to the exciting city Tom and
Matt discover through their criminal activities.

In an episode prefaced by the title "1915" Tom and Matt
get involved in an abortive fur robbery which results in the death
of a young fellow from their neighborhood who was their accomplice.
They are brought into the robbery by Putty Nose, a ne're-do-well who
amuses young boys with dirty songs and serves as fence for the items
his youthful followers steal. Tom and Matt kill a policeman during the
robbery and when they turn for help to Putty Nose they learn he has
left town. Tom swears to kill Putty Nose when he finds him.

Conflict between Tom and his brother Mike, present even
in their childhood, grows with the years, underlining the divergent
attitudes toward life the brothers have adopted. When Mike enlists
for service in World War I, the following scene is played in the
boys' bedroom.

                    TOM
Gee, you're rushing it.

                    MIKE
                (seriously)
Well, Tom, when our country needs
us. . . she needs us.

                    TOM
I suppose so.
                (shifting uneasily from
                one foot to the other)
I suppose you think I ought to go, too.

                    MIKE
No.
                (goes over and lays his
                arm on Tom's shoulder
                in a big brother attitude)
Maybe it was selfish of me, Tom, but
one of us has got to stay and take care
of Ma. You earn more than I do...
and they'd have taken me first anyhow.

                    TOM
You always did get all the breaks.

                    MIKE
Don't look at it that way, Tom. You've
got to be the man of the family now.
                (turns back to his packing)

Tom watches him awkwardly for a moment.

                    MIKE
                (as he packs)
And while we're on the subject. . .
I wish you'd spend a little more time
at home.

                    TOM
                (quick to take offense)
I gotta work, ain't I?

                    MIKE
        I understand that, but . . . .
                    (he becomes serious, like
                    a teacher who has to correct
                    one of his pupils. He walks
                    over and shuts the door.)

Tom watches him with a slight scowl.

                    MIKE
                (coming back to Tom)
        Listen, Tom, I was in a place today
        . . . and
                (embarrassed)
        I heard someone saying something.

                    TOM
                (on guard)
        What of it?

                    MIKE
                (embarrassed)
        Well . . . . they were saying . . .
        well, it seemed like they were pointing
        a finger at you and Matt.

                    TOM
                (getting belligerent)
        Who was? What rat was saying any-
        thing about me? I'll show em.

                    MIKE
        Now, Tom . . .

                    TOM
                (in guilty anger)
        You're always hearing things.
        You'll get too much in your nose some
        day . . . and you'll wonder how you
        got it.

MIKE

Well, for cryin' out loud! I heard
a couple of guys talkin' about you....
as much as to say you were mixed
up in some crooked work. What am
I supposed to do . . . run?

TOM
(slowly)
Well. . . .you ain't asking me. You're
telling me . . . and I don't know nothin'
see?

MIKE

All I got to say, Tom, is that you got a
good job (Tom and Matt are drivers for
an express company) and you don't know
nothin' see?

TOM
(sneers)
I suppose you want me to go to night
school . . . and read poems.
(starts for the door)
I've heard some things myself . . .

MIKE
(jumps after him and
grabs his arm)
There's nothin' to hear about me!

TOM
(loftily)
No? That's all you know. You ain't
so smart. Books and that whoey don't
hide everything.

MIKE

You're a liar, Tom! You're covering up.

TOM
(wrenching his arm free)
Covering up? To you? Say . . . You're
only a sneak thief! A nickel snatcher!
Robbin' the street car company.

Mike lashes out in blind fury and catches Tom on the chin, knocking him down. As Mike stands glowering over him, Tom gets up slowly, for once his overbearing, brow-beating manner is conquered. Mike's glare plainly asks if he wants any more, but Tom shows no intention of returning the blow. Mike scornfully turns on his heel and walks out.

Tom glares after Mike malevolently, clenching his fist and gritting his teeth, furious at Mike but more furious at himself for having let Mike get away with it.

Mike talks about the country needing him, Tom regards any such call to duty with cynicism. Tom's values do not include "unselfish" love or patriotism. As far as he is concerned everyone is out to get something. Mike's blow, provoked or not, confirms Tom's beliefs.

It would seem that the ideals Mike held no longer rang true for many in 1931. The national disillusionment stemming from America's participation in the War and the despair brought on by the ever deepening Depression helped place "The Public Enemy" among the most popular films of the 1930's. Although never again reaching a comparable level of articulation, the Cagney character carried this cynical quality in all of his films between 1930-1940. This quality was evident in several recurring themes: A suspicion of women who "put on airs", of the motives of the well-to-do, a code of existence that says nothing comes in life save that which you beat the next fellow to.

The characteristic malevolent glare on Cagney's face as Mike leaves the room is repeated as a gesture in many of the Cagney films. Later in "The Public Enemy" and in successive films it portended the wreaking of merciless violence on an opponent. The forms varied from hitting a girl in the face with a grapefruit half, to firing round after round into a victim. Unlike the Western hero who, prodded into violence, used only enough force to counter that of his opponent, the Cagney character relished the use of more than enough.

        The title "The Eighteenth of January. . .The Eighteenth Hour. . .The Eighteenth Amendment", introduces the Prohibition era. With the Eighteenth Amendment Tom passes from occasional thievery to a full time membership in a bootlegging gang. Before beginning this episode the audience sees the following detail:

DOWNTOWN BUSINESS STREET. NIGHT:

LONG SHOT,

Sidewalks are crowded with pedestrians, the street crowded with traffic. Rich and poor carrying bundles, bottles, packages of all sizes.

SIDEWALK

The pedestrian crowd jostling along, through them

comes a young couple, the man wheeling a baby
carriage, piled high with bottled goods. The
woman carrying a six month old baby for whom
there is no room in the baby carriage.

LAP DISSOLVE TO:

STREET

Full Shot of a wild drinking party.

FADE OUT.

Reports have gotten back home of Mike's war heroism.
The express company they work for promotes Tom and Matt because
of local pride in Mike. The company has just gotten a contract to
carry alcohol from Government warehouses and distilleries to those
who have special permits to use alcohol -- manufacturers of hair
tonic and perfume and drug stores. Together with Paddy Ryan, a
local saloon keeper and gang boss, the boys start hijacking the
liquor they deliver. The boys become affluent and cocky with their
new found wealth.

The chance at easy bootlegging money interests not only
people of Tom, Matt and Paddy's social status, but also a well-to-
do brewery owner, Leeman, whose plant has been shut down by the
18th Amendment. At a meeting of the gang with Tom in attendance,

Leeman says:

> "You can understand, of course, that my
> desire is merely to furnish a better grade
> of beer than the working man can now obtain
> under the present...oh...unfortunate..."

Leeman is interrupted by the gangster "Nails" Nathan,

> "In your hat! I've heard that north wind
> before. If you're in this, you're in for
> the coin the same as the rest of us."

Tom and Matt come to have great respect for the dapper
but straight talking Nails Nathan.

Like Rico in "Little Caesar", Tom and Matt acquire
flashy possessions in keeping with their rise in the world. First,
custom-fitted clothes, then an expensive touring car. When the
boys grandly drive up to a night club Tom yells at the parking
attendant when he gnashes the car's gears.

> "Hey there, stupe! That's no Ford. . .
> It's got gears."

Once inside the Club the boys zero in on two girls who
attract them. They have the manager throw the girls' drunken
escorts out, then take their place at the table. Indicating his girl,
Matt says to Tom:

"Look what I got measured for, Tom".

The girls are in no way offended by the matter-of-fact

pickup. Although Matt and his girl will later plan marriage, the

whole affair is crude and direct.

Before cutting to a scene with Tom and Matt and their

girls in an apartment, there is a sequence which serves to sever

Tom once and for all from his home ties. Mike, nearly recovered

from his wounds, has returned from the hospital. At the welcome

home party, he is enraged to find Tom has become a full-time

gangster and has brought a keg of his beer into the house. Mike's

fury mounts as he sits at the dinner table, finally he jumps to his

feet:

>   MIKE
> You think I'd care if it was just beer
> in that keg? I know what's in it! I
> know what you've been doing all this
> time. . . where you got the clothes
> and those new cars--you've been
> telling Ma that you've gone into
> politics. . . that you're on the city
> payroll! I know everything!
>   (looking wildly from Tom
>   to Matt)
> YOU MURDERERS!! It's not beer in
> that keg! It's beer and blood. Blood
> of men!

Mike dashes to the side of the table, seizes the keg and

heaves it on to the floor with a crash. The women scream. Matt

looks stunned. Tom turns away with a sneer of contempt as Mike
collapses into a chair.

> TOM
> You ain't changed a bit. And say...
> you ain't so good yourself. You
> killed... and you liked it! You
> didn't get all those medals for holding
> hands with them Germans.

Tom does not trust his brother's motives. He sees no
difference between killing for "defense of country" and killing
to get rid of opposing bootlegging gangs. (Environment)
Immediately after this scene the famous grapefruit episode opens in an apartment occupied by Tom and Matt and their
girls. It is obvious that Matt and his girl have developed a
kind of domestic relationship. Tom is fed up with his girl's
fussing. He has rejected feelings of "home", and "patriotism"
before and he does not wish to have them with a pickup.
BREAKFAST NOOK
The usual two-seated affair off the kitchen. Kitty
is bustling about the table, on which she has laid
out breakfast. Tom enters. She is dressed in a
night gown and wrapper, he pajamas and robe.

> KITTY
> (brightly)
> Already, Tom.

                    TOM
               (surly)
          Nuts to that stuff. Ain't you got
          a drink in this house?

                    KITTY
          Not before breakfast, Tom.

                    TOM
          I didn't ask for any lip! I asked
          for a drink!

                    KITTY
          Yes, Tom but I wish.....
               (turns away to get
               the drink)

                    TOM
          There you go-puttin' on that wish
          stuff again. I wish you were a
          wishin' well, so I could tie a
          bucket onta' ya and sink ya!

Kitty comes back, has very serious expression on her
face.

                    KITTY
          Maybe you got someone you like
          better.

Tom stares at her ferociously for a second, then reaches
over on the table, picks up half a grapefruit, throws it
at Kitty's face and strides out. Kitty sinks down into
one of the seats at the table, stares after him broken-
hearted.

When the Cagney character smashes the grapefruit half

into the girl's face he again produces the menacing sneer first

seen when his brother knocked him down. There is nothing noble

about this character; he is capable of unlimited brutality and the restraints on this potential for violence are rapidly giving way.

Putty Nose, the saloon piano player, who introduced Tom

and Matt to crime, is spotted in the night club where Matt and his

girl are celebrating their engagement announcement. Nails Nathan

chides Tom, saying Putty Nose "has his number". Tom forces the

reluctant Matt to leave the party and they take after Putty Nose to

settle accounts.

PUTTY'S LIVING ROOM

MEDIUM SIZED ROOM with ordinary furniture. Against

one wall is an upright piano. Tom is standing facing Putty

who now is thoroughly alarmed.

PUTTY NOSE
What's wrong with you, Tom?

TOM
You know what's wrong. We ain't forgot
how you lammed out on us after that fur
heist. Left us to take the rap!
(Tom steps forward and hits
Putty a blow on the jaw.)

TOM
Sit down, you lyin' double crossin' rat!

Putty sinks into a chair feeling the bruise where Tom

hit him.

TOM
Don't make so much fuss over that
bump! You got a lot more comin'!

PUTTY NOSE
(terrified)
Gee, Tommy, Matt. . . .what you gonna
do? I don't wanna die!

TOM
(scornfully)
You don't wanna die? No?

PUTTY
(pleading)
Don't you remember, Tommy. . .and you
Matt. . .how you were just kids and we
were friends. . . .

TOM
Nix on that "soft stuff". You're going,
and you know it.

Matt is holding aloof and letting Tom handle the matter.

MATT
What are you going to do with him?

TOM
What does anyone do with a rat?

PUTTY NOSE
(in terror throws his arms
around Tom's legs, clutching
him wildly)
Don't let him, Matt! Don't let him!
I'll do anything for you from now on!
Ain't you got a heart, Matty boy? I
wouldn't hurt a fly! Remember how I
used to play for you. . . .tell me. . .
don't you? Didn't I always stick up for
you? I ain't got this comin'. . . .

Tom looks at him cooly without replying. . .his deadly

manner only terrifies Putty the more.

PUTTY NOSE
Please, Matt... tell him not to!
I ain't a bad fellow! Oh Tommy,
Tommy, don't. Ain't you gotta heart?
    (wildly to Matt)
You won't let him, Matt? You remember
the old days! Remember that song I
taught you...

He jumps over, runs to the piano, sits himself with his
back to Tom and Matt, starts playing "Frankie and
Johnny."

PUTTY'S LIVING ROOM

MEDIUM SHOT OF MATT. He turns away as though the sight
was a little too much for him. He is not going to take
any more hand in it himself, but at the same time he's
not going to interfere with Tom. We hear the piano
off scene. Putty, playing, trying to sing the song in
a cracked voice, quivering with terror. Matt watches
him out of the corner of his eye. As he reaches the
filthy lines where he was interrupted when he was playing in the Club room, there is a sound of a pistol shot,
then a crash of the keys as though someone had fallen
forward with both arms on the keyboard. There is
another shot. Matt turns away and walks toward the
door, his face expressionless.

Putty asked Tom, "Ain't you got a heart?" By this episode Tom has no "heart".

The small boy who tripped a girl on skates now brutally
abuses his mistress. The clumsy, fearful boy who stole for
Putty Nose has now become a collector-killer for a bootlegging gang.

It may be said that Tom's "heartlessness" is the result
of never knowing anything better. Matt, too, follows a life of
crime, perhaps for the same reason. Matt simply does not have
the drive that propels Tom. The story never has the boys confronting "good". The hypocritical brewer Leeman is the "higher type"
person they encounter.

While cruising about in their new touring car, Tom and
Matt see Gwen (Jean Harlow). She evidently comes from a family
of means and lives in a fashionable hotel. Matt makes a try for
Gwen but is no match for Tom. (In a sense Matt's attachment for
his girl does not show a finer side to his character, rather an outlook which tells him to settle for things the way they are. In the
killing of Putty Nose, while he shows distaste for the business, he makes
no attempt to stop it.) After Tom has made a date with Gwen, and
they have dropped her off:

> MATT
> Gee! What a jane. I could go for
> her myself.

> TOM
> What do you mean you could go for her
> yourself? You'd go for an eighty year
> old chink with rheumatism.

> MATT
> Find out if she's got a friend.

                    TOM
        What do you want of a friend? You
        got Mamie, ain't you?
                    (mimicking)
        Ain't you gonna kiss yer honey?

                    MATT
        Hell, you got Kitty, ain't you?

                    TOM
        I ain't going to have her much
        longer. I'm gettin' fed up. And
        you can tell her so from me. Step
        on the gas.

The car drives off.

A remarkable scene is played between Cagney and Harlow

in which the high class Gwen tells what she sees in the crude,

uneducated, tough Tom Powers.

GWEN'S APARTMENT AFTERNOON

The sitting room of a high class hotel suite. Gwen in

a stunning negligee is stretched out on a couch. Tom,

ill at ease, is sitting in a chair. Between them is a little

taboret of drinks laid out from which they are sipping as

they talk.

Tom is dressed more fashionably than we have ever seen

him before. Something is preying on his mind. His

trouble is that Gwen is several notches higher in the

social scale than any other girl he has known and he

doesn't know how to handle her. Gwen realizes something

of this and is playing with him in a cat and mouse fashion.

GWEN
I may leave town next week, Tom.
(pause)
You don't care, do you?

TOM
(uncomfortable)
Gee, ... if you go, you go ... that's
all.

GWEN
(laughs and gets up)
You're a funny boy.
(comes over to him, cups
his face in her hands, and
kisses him full on the lips)
You're a funny boy, I like you immensely.

TOM
What's funny about me?

GWEN
I don't mean funny in that sense. I
mean you're different.
(she goes back and sits
on the couch)

Tom is uncomfortable, silent for a moment, then starts

to talk jerkily.

TOM
No. . .but. . .gee! How long can a guy
hold out?
(jumps to his feet)
I'd go screwy!
(he picks up his hat and
starts for the door.)

GWEN
Where are you going?

                    TOM
    I'm gonna blow.

Tom stands shifting his weight from one foot to the other.

Gwen goes over and takes his hat from his hand and throws

it across the room.

                    GWEN
    You're a spoiled boy, Tommy. You
    want things!.....and aren't content
    until you get them. Well, maybe I'm
    spoiled too. . .but you're not running
    out on me like this, come over here.

With mock indignation she leads him over to the couch,

pushes him down onto it and sits herself on his knees.

                    GWEN
    Now you stay put, if you know what
    that means.
            (puts her arms around
            him and draws his head
            down to her breast)
    Oh, my bashful boy.

They are silent for a moment.

                    GWEN
    You are different Tommy. . .very
    different. And I discovered that it's
    not only a difference in manner and out-
    ward appearances. It's a difference in
    basic character. Men that I know, and
    I've known dozens of them. . .they're so
    nice, so polished, so considerate. Most
    women like that type. I guess they're
    afraid of any other kind. I thought I was,
    too, but you're so STRONG. You don't
    give. . .you take! Oh Tommy! I could
    love you to death.

Throughout the scene the background music has been "I Surrender, Dear". As they embrace, news comes via Matt that Nails Nathan, always the dandy, has been killed while out horse back riding. Tom leaves Gwen instantly and sets off to avenge —*business first* his leader by shooting the horse. After he leaves, Gwen smashes a vase against the door.

The well bred girl is out for excitement. Again the motive which occurs throughout the film, "everybody is out for something, take what you can get", is reinforced. There is no suggestion that Gwen wanted Tom to be her husband and build with her a "home-family" life. Rather, her only interest in this savage young man is his physical prowess.

With Nails Nathan dead, his gang has scattered, the rival "Schemer" Burns gang has encroached on Tom's gang's territory. Paddy Ryan's place has been bombed, the brewery set on fire. Rather than attempt a raid on the rival gang, Paddy wants his boys to stay in hiding until he can regroup forces. The rival gang finds the hideout and stations machine gunners across the street.

Tom storms out of the hideout with Matt tagging along when he finds the woman who owns the hideout has made love to him when he was helplessly drunk the night before. Tom strikes the woman much as he smashed the grapefruit into the face of his *no home for him*

girl, both scenes take place when the women have set out breakfast
and try to surround Tom with a home-like atmosphere.

Matt is gunned down in front of the hideout. Tom escapes
and going to Gwen, finds a note saying that she has returned home.
After holding up a pawn shop for two revolvers, Tom sets out single-
handedly to wipe out the Burns gang.

It is at night, a steady rain falls. Tom, hands thrust into
his jacket pocket, advances. The look of menace mixed with a
maniacal smile are frozen on his face as he approaches the hideout.
He goes in. There are repeated shots and screams. He comes out,
attempts to shoot back at the wounded gangster shooting from the doorway but finds that his guns are empty. He flings them through the
store hideout's plate glass windows; all the while he is uttering
guttural moans; he stiffens, says, "Aw, I ain't so tough", and falls
in the wet gutter.

Later in a hospital bed he tells his family that he is sorry.
Mike will have nothing of apologies; rather, in a tender way he
answers him that his only concern is for Tom's recovery. Both this
scene and the line, "Aw, I ain't so tough", force the film to break
stride. It is as if some outside source said this killer must recognize
and pay for his crimes. Tom's demise is the result of the most
exciting quality of his personality, rash courage, rather than the

triumph of a power for good in the society.

Later, Tom is taken from the hospital by the remnants of the rival gang. Paddy sends out all his men to find Tom and even offers to quit bootlegging in exchange for Tom's safe return. Tom is murdered. His corpse, wrapped and bandaged, is propped against the Powers' front door. When Mike answers the doorbell, Tom falls in face first like a beef carcass.

Cagney, at least in terms of number of films, was Warner's most popular star of the four actors being considered during this period. The essential character was delineated in "The Public Enemy". The Cagney character is always cynical. He must work for a living -- legal or otherwise, and entertains no false hopes for human charity -- everybody is "out for himself".

His love interests are never described as anything more than physical attraction. In "Lady Killer" he pulls Mae Clarke (his girl who got hit with the grapefruit in "The Public Enemy") around by the hair and kicks her into a hallway.

Traditional, happy endings, were not in the Cagney mold. "Blonde Crazy" ended in a lengthy term in prison; "The Roaring Twenties" saw death at the hands of Humphrey Bogart's gang on the steps of a church; "Angels With Dirty Faces" offered death in the electric chair for killing Bogart; in "The Fighting 69th" death by a German hand grenade. In "City for Conquest" his fate was blindness.

The Cagney character was most effective through vocal delivery in "The Public Enemy". His breathy, staccato voice created something of a sensation with the likes of:

> "There you go -- puttin' on that
> wish stuff again. I wish you were
> a wishin' well, so I could tie a
> bucket onto ya' and sink ya!"

In almost every Cagney film of this era his character was identified by name or other means as being Irish. This ethnic identification and blue collar economic status were aspects of the character begun in "The Public Enemy."

Ingenious settings and supporting and bit players lent a distinct quality to "The Public Enemy" as they did to "Little Caesar". The Warner set department's lower class homes and apartments and hotel rooms were created with such a dismal reality they lent a particular aura to these films throughout the 1930's. The Warner stock company with Allan Jenkins, Frank McHugh, et al. lent immeasurable support in the form of accomplished sidekicks and colorful bit parts. Twentieth Century-Fox Television rented the Warner Brothers back lot "New York Streets" so frequently seen in the films of 1930-1940 for the Batman television show's Gotham City.

C. "Scarface" 1932

The highly derivative quality of "Scarface", particularly in relation to "Little Caesar", is set forth in the following description. It is very likely, however, that the Howard Hughes production "Scarface" (1932) is the best of the gangster films. If "Scarface" cannot be commended for its originality, its successful reiteration of the familiar on a grand scale with an overall excellence of execution marks Hughes' effort as one of the most outstanding and enduring of the genre.

Like "Little Caesar" and "The Public Enemy", "Scarface" carries a prologue which was meant to serve as a palliative to the censor boards across the country. "Scarface's" prologue, signed by Edward P. Mulrooney, Police Commissioner of the City of New York, stated that it was the film's purpose to impress upon the audience the need for rigorous firearm regulation laws.

Another important similarity to the other two gangster film classics is the episodic form of "Scarface". Rico Bandello and Tony Carmonte rise to greatness and fall to their deaths against the fabric of the beer wars which stretched from World War I into the hard Depression days.

Perhaps because the elements of this story were familiar, director Howard Hawkes channeled his creativity toward a greater

emphasis on sheer brilliance of image; his variation on a theme.
This insistence on visual interest is initiated when the film opens
on an empty dance hall. The camera, a careful observer, tracks
past a janitor cleaning up the debris of a riotous party. At the end
of the shot at the edge of the frame a waiter's hand picks up a
brassiere from the rubbish on the floor.

Three men have lingered, early-morning tired, satiated from
their revel. One rises from the table, leaving his cronies to take a
phone call. The call is a ruse; a killer in the shadows shoots the
man dead. A waiter wisely walks away after the murder; experience
with gangland ways has taught him the value of non-involvement.

Newspaper headlines predict the killing will touch off a gang
war. Young, cocky gangsters Tony Carmonte and Rinaldo treat the
police with utter contempt when they are questioned. When Tony is
arrested his boss, Johnny Lovo, has him out instantly through a writ
of habeus corpus. The law is powerless in Tony's eyes.

Lovo, impressed by the gunman's nerve, asks Tony up to
his expensive apartment. Tony takes the whole place in, including
Johnny's blonde mistress, Poppy. Tony, boldly, crudely seductive,
mimics the elegant Poppy's eyebrow plucking. It is obvious Tony
plans to acquire these "status symbols" just as Rico of "Little Caesar"
coveted the jewelry, clothes and apartments of his betters on the way

up. Just as Rico remarked about Sam Vettori, and Little Arnie,
Tony says, "Say, Lovo's soft...I'm going to run the whole works...
There's only one law -- do it first, do it yourself and keep doing
it". This parallels Rico's "You're getting so you can't take it no
more...you can dish it out but you can't take it".

The stories of "Little Caesar" and "Scarface" are rooted
in an Italian-American background. As Tony becomes more pros-
perous he continues to live in the semi-slum of Little Italy, the
favored haunts of Rico. Both men are fiercely possessive of family
and friends. When Tony comes home to find his pretty younger
sister Cesca kissing a young man in the hall, he flies into a rage
and jealously throws the intruder out. Tony is as possessive of those
around him as was Rico of Joe Massara in "Little Caesar" or Nick
Donati (Edward G. Robinson) of his convent-raised sister in "Kid
Galahad". Tony gives Cesca a roll of bills to soothe her feelings.
Their mother warns her, however, that it is bad money, that Tony's
obsession is to possess. Rinaldo, Tony's partner, sees the
flirtatious Cesca and they fall in love. (George Raft, playing
Rinaldo, practices his famous coin flipping in "Scarface".)

Johnny Lovo, crime boss of the South Side territory with
its thousands of saloons and half million customers, sends out
Tony and Rinaldo to drum up business. In a violent saloon smashing

sequence the gang forces owners to buy more beer. "The Public
Enemy" has a similar scene but "Scarface" has it on a much larger
scale.

Tony begins his rise in the world of crime. He shows
Poppy his recent acquisitions - silk shirts, a new bed bought at
an auction, jewelry, a hideout with steel shutters. From his window
can be seen the sign "The World Is Yours, Cook's Tours".

Johnny Lovo is flabbergasted when he learns that Tony is
starting to carve out additional territory on the forbidden North
Side. Tony snarls that Lovo is afraid; and the boss does quake,
as Sam Vettori did in the face of Rico's ambition. Gaffney (Boris
Karloff) and his gang from the North Side hunt down Tony and
Rinaldo in a restaurant. An enormous battle ensues. The restaurant is raked with submachine gun fire, windows shatter, tables
splinter, the air is filled with chatter of the guns. (Gaffney had
previously demonstrated the power of the new machine guns for
his gang by cutting pool balls in half.) Tony must have one of the
weapons. Rinaldo, fearless, the willing lieutenant, works his way
out front to pick off a member of the opposing gang with his pistol.
One of the armada of attacking black sedans races past; Rinaldo
fires and drops his man. He proudly takes the prize, the machine
gun, to Tony.

Lovo loses his nerve completely as Tony wreaks terror across the city with his new submachine guns. There is a re-enactment of the St. Valentine's Day murder. Girders in the garage where the murder takes place form a shadow X like the scar on Tony's cheek, a recurring symbol. Gaffney, the North Side boss, is left alone, beaten, cringing in a dingy room. Gaffney is eventually found by Tony's gang at a bowling alley. His murder is synchronized with the falling of a final pin.

At a nightclub, Poppy lets the failing Lovo know that he is out and that she is now Tony's woman. Cesca, oblivious of her brother, dances suggestively in front of Rinaldo, but he will not respond, knowing Tony's attitude. Cesca taunts Rinaldo and dances off with another man. Tony watches Cesca dancing; enraged, he drags her home. Once there, Tony almost tears Cesca's dress off. She screams at him that he is jealous. Their mother calms the sobbing Cesca. "Tony hurts everyone" is the old woman's rationalization.

A machine gun is fired through the Carmonte's door. Tony, unhurt, jumps in his car and gives chase to his attackers. Bullets from a sedan rake Tony's car; the vehicle crashes. Tony walks to a phone and calls Rinaldo who is at a woman's house. Rinaldo, ever loyal, comes for his boss obediently. Tony then calls Lovo and tells him he missed. Lovo, completely broken now, falls to Rinaldo's bullets at Tony's order. Tony, in triumph, thrusts his hand through the glass in the door of Lovo's office, thus getting rid of Lovo's name. A new glass replaces it. "Antonio Carmonte" has his name on a door.

Tony, surrounded by bodyguards, goes to Florida for a month. Cesca uses her temporary freedom to accelerate her pursuit of Rinaldo. The handsome gunman likens her determination to Tony's; and Rinaldo is a follower, ready to carry out the dictates of either brother or sister. Tony returns and listens hurriedly to his mother's information. Cesca is living with a man. Waiting for no details, the incensed Tony races to the couple's apartment. The door opens to reveal Rinaldo in pajamas and robe. With a cross of light at his back, the X of his scar, Tony shoots Rinaldo before he can give a word of explanation. Cesca calls Tony a butcher; she and Rinaldo had been married. The killing of Rinaldo makes Tony a fugitive. A similar situation occurs in the wounding of Joe Massara in "Little Caesar". In both instances overwhelming possessiveness leads to the gangster's downfall.

Cesca joins her brother in Tony's fortress hideout. As they shoot it out with the police, brother and sister alike revel in the situation. They are joined as one at last in their fatal battle;

their strange bond culminated. They embrace. She is laughing, exhilarated.

The police shoot Cesca. She asks Tony to hold her as she dies. Tony realizes he is alone. He comes out after a tear gas attack and begs for his life. (One version had Tony hanged.) Knowing he will be killed, suicidal now, Tony makes a break. The police machine-gun him to death. There is a tilt up to the sign "The World Is Yours...Cook's Tours". The tour's sign and Rico's newspaper stories of action in the big city serve the same function -- they foster dreams. The film fades out on an X -- the ever present symbol of Tony's scarred face; the mark of the underworld on his countenance.

Paul Muni had only one other part remotely like that of Tony in "Scarface", that of the ambitious, bitter Johnny Ramirez in "Bordertown". Initial success in a gangster portrayal had considerable influence on the careers of Robinson, Cagney and Bogart for years to come. Muni was the protean actor. He never created a "personality". Tony Carmonte was an entity in Muni's repertory. While he brought to the character the recognizable Muni force and involvement, the gangster did not become his trademark. As was his style, he slipped in and out of the character, going on to an ever changing gallery of roles.

D. "The Petrified Forest" 1936

"Little Caesar" (1930) and "The Public Enemy" (1931) and
"The Petrified Forest" (1936) each introduced a gangster character
with such impact that it was to be continued in varying forms, by
the creating actor in a succeeding series of films.

"The Petrified Forest"'s gangster "Duke Mantee", played
by Humphrey Bogart, was a supporting character as opposed to a
leading character as in the earlier archetypical films. The
succeeding Bogart gangster films also placed the character in a
subsidiary position, or, if in a leading one, in quickly made, low
cost program pictures with nothing to suggest the quality of the
archetypical films.

It is possible, however, to see certain elements in Bogart's
portrayal of Duke Mantee which were to be a part of his continuing
screen personality even after he was no longer working in the
gangster genre.

First, his appearance -- three or four day beard, black
hair combed straight back, moody, haggard eyes, unsmiling mouth,
rough work shirt open at the neck. This created the believable look
of a man who had spent his life in violent conflict with the law.
Creating a particular appearance was absolutely necessary for
working in the gangster genre. The importance of appearance

for gangster roles is shown by viewing Lew Ayres' clean cut
and unbelievable racketeer in "Doorway to Hell" (1930).

Second, "The Petrified Forest" had Bogart's peculiar flat
delivery of dialogue which was to prove so effective years later
in major films such as "The Maltese Falcon" (1941) and
"Casablanca" (1943). With quiet authority Mantee gives orders
to the Alan Squier character in "The Petrified Forest".

> MANTEE
> Sit down, pal.

When he is considering life past and prospects for the
future he says:

> MANTEE
> I've spent most of my time since I grew
> up in jail...and it looks like I'll spend
> the rest of my life dead.

Bogart's capacity for powerful, moody near-soliloquy was
later used with extraordinary effect in "Casablanca", when Rick
sits in his night club after closing time thinking of his lost love.

Unlike James Cagney, Bogart was never a "physical" actor.
The action always came to him. This quality is first found in "The
Petrified Forest". The studio script gives the following directions
to explain the situation of Mantee holding a gun on the other characters
in the restaurant:

> For the remainder of the picture, we create the
> feeling that Duke, on the dais, controlling the
> destinies of those on the lower level, is in nature

an evil god who must be feared and looked up to...
Just as in reverse he looks down upon those he
controls.

An "evil god" quality was not apparent in the Mantee
character, however, there was a feeling of disinterest. He
observed the intrigue of the other characters then brought
this intrigue to resolution. This disinterest and power of
resolution was also to be found later in "The Maltese Falcon",
in which the thieves fight for possession of the precious
statue only to have Sam Spade turn their plots back against
them.

In "Little Caesar" the police are shown to be dull
creatures, opposing the central character because of his
aspirations. The head of the city's crime organization is a
man of wealth and position. "The Public Enemy" shows the
middle class in an unfavorable light. Each of these films
shows the gangster character to be more admirable than the
society he opposes. The situation holds true in "The
Petrified Forest."

The leading character, Alan Squier, is a writer who
never fulfilled his early promise and who now wanders the
face of America in search of a reason to live.

On his trek through America's Southwestern desert,
Squier encounters Gabby Maple, who, with her father, runs a
restaurant

and gas station on a highway. She wishes to escape from what she
believes to be an oppressive atmosphere and go to France to study
art. She is prepared to run off with Squier after knowing him just
a few minutes. Her father also feels that he never had a chance.
His passion is jingoistic patriotism and membership in a local
vigilante group which gives him the opportunity to dress up in a
ridiculous pseudo-military uniform. Gabby's uniformed father
cowers before Mantee and later exults when he hears by radio that
the gang has been taken by a posse. Grandpa Maple completes
the family. Though he has a considerable amount of money he
refuses to help Gabby realize her ambition to study abroad. He
prattles about supposed encounters with the desperado Billy the
Kid.

To complete the cast of characters there is a thick-headed
former college football player who works for the Maples pumping
gas and a wealthy couple whose life is an endless round of petty
bickering. Unlike the more filmic episodic narratives of "Little
Caesar", "The Public Enemy", and "Scarface", "The Petrified
Forest" is a dramatic situation in which characters are thrown
together for a limited time and in a limited space to interact.

Duke and the men with him could have made good their
escape across the border into Mexico were it not for Duke's

insistence that they wait for other members of the gang, including his girl, to join them. Duke's men agree to wait, although they know the police are drawing closer, because of their respect for Duke. To the consternation of her husband, the wealthy woman expresses her admiration for Duke's romantic gesture.

There is an interesting exchange between the colored member of Duke's gang and the wealthy couple's colored chauffeur. Duke's confederate is in every sense an equal to the other members of the gang, while the chauffeur is obsequious before his employers. The gang member asks derisively if the chauffeur has heard of "...the big liberation".

Alan Squier, who in his world weariness would not accept the offer of the attractive Gabby, decides to give her the opportunity to study abroad. He makes her the beneficiary of his life insurance policy. He needs Duke to bring his noble act to fruition. He forces the reluctant gangster to shoot him by blocking the restaurant door when Mantee is making his getaway.

In the context of such characters, Duke Mantee could not help but appear in a favorable light. He alone has the capacity and desire to take action in the world. He is both the giver and receiver of unswerving loyalty. He brings resolution to each of the other characters' stories.

Bogart's portrayal of Duke Mantee was very well received.
After the release of "The Petrified Forest" his career was to be
totally in motion pictures. He had made a number of indifferent
films earlier in the 1930's only to return to the Broadway stage.

With the release of "The Petrified Forest" Humphrey Bogart
became a member of the "Warner stock company". For the next
six years, however, most of his parts were poor in conception but
executed by Bogart in a manner which showed professional
dedication.

Capitalizing on the fame which came to Bogart for his gangster
portrayal in "The Petrified Forest", Warner Brothers cast him as a
gangster in a number of films from 1936 through 1941. As Nick "Bugs"
Fenner in "Bullets or Ballots" (1936), Turkey Morgan in "Kid Galahad"
(1937), Rocks Valentine in "The Amazing Dr. Clitterhouse" (1938),
and Jack Buck in "Brother Orchid" (1940), Bogart played "second
banana" gangster to the main character played by Edward G. Robinson.
In each of these roles the Bogart character was without any redeeming
traits. The purpose of this character was to provide the Robinson
character with opposition which could be eliminated without the
audience feeling any remorse.

Bogart characters fulfilled the same function for James

Cagney's leading parts in "Angels With Dirty Faces" (1938),
"The Oklahoma Kid" (1939), and "The Roaring Twenties" (1939).
What had begun as a balanced, moving portrayal in "The Petrified
Forest", had been transformed in succeeding films into a one-
dimensional foil whose sole reason for being was to provide the
star with a convenient target.

Bogart was to play a sympathetic criminal in Samuel
Goldwyn's "Dead End" (1937), Warner's "High Sierra" (1941),
and "The Big Shot" (1942). None of these three involved Robinson
or Cagney, however, nor were any of them Warner program
pictures.

Most of Bogart's starring gangster parts during this
period were also one-dimensional. The character was totally
black and the plot revolved simply around efforts to erase the
character from the world. Films in this group include "Racket
Busters" (1938), "King of the Underworld" (1939), "You Can't
Get Away With Murder" (1939).

As Grandpa Maple put it, Duke Mantee was a "desperado",
like Billy the Kid, a real American desperado. Grandpa Maple
considered "gangsters" to be foreigners. Whereas Robinson
generally played foreign types -- Italians, Portuguese -- and
Cagney most often portrayed characters of Irish background,

Bogart consistantly was cast as non-ethnic, or "American"
gangsters.

Bogart played the Duke Mantee character of "The Petrified
Forest" in three productions: first in the New York stage version
which preceded the Warner Brothers film of 1936 and in 1955 on
television with Henry Fonda as "Alan" and Lauren Bacall as
"Gabby".

CHAPTER III

VARIATION AND DECAY OF THE GANGSTER FILM: HOW IT CAME ABOUT

Using the four archetypical films as critical bases, judge-
ments and inferences may be made concerning the development of
the gangster film during the 1930-1940 decade. The progressive
changes, the variations on the archetypical characterizations, are
noted in selected films of Edward G. Robinson, James Cagney and
Humphrey Bogart. Paul Muni branched into a variety of non-gangster
films after "Scarface". His films will therefore only be used in
certain cases for the purpose of specific comparisons.

Although the decline of the genre is associated with factors
other than characterizations - repetitive scripts, overworked
situations, cliche'-ridden dialogue - it is through the "constant",
the recognizable archetypical character, that the comparison
between the first product in the series and the last may be made
and the degrees of change between noted.

The corruption of the "Little Caesar" character can be
charted through two categories of films -- each successive stage
marking a dissolution and weakening of the original character into
a convenient stereotype. One group of Robinson vehicles may be
classed "Little Caesar Syndrome" films -- characterizations most

closely related to the original and most in keeping with the essential
message of "Little Caesar".

The second category "Comic Caesar", marks the generalization of the "Little Caesar" character into a "useful" stereotype --
the comic gangster. In these films "Little Caesar" is rendered
innocuous, only the symbols and signs of the role remain stripped
of social comment, devoid of violence.

The films of James Cagney follow a similar course. Watered
down by successive stages of comic emphasis, the "Public Enemy"
character created by Cagney travels through three classifications:
Derivitive "Public Enemy" characterizations, drawing heavily on
the original; secondly a step toward a less villanous, more comedic
"Public Enemy" in the group of "Con Man" films and finally into the
demise of the original character in the broad, humorous, light
pieces grouped under "Service-Action-Vocation" films.

The Humphrey Bogart films, being much more uniform in
their characterizations, progress from the original "Petrified
Forest" desperado to a series of generally dismal "B" pictures
in which Bogart appears as a second-banana gunsel or as the
sneering "all-black" heavy.

A. Edward G. Robinson: The "Little Caesar" Syndrome

"Smart Money" 1931,"Dark Hazard" 1934, "Bullets or
Ballots" 1936, "Kid Galahad" 1937.

The "Little Caesar" character reappeared yearly throughout
the decade and indeed has become a film classic. Robinson's swaggering, cigar smoking, snappily dressed little tough with the
stabbing forefinger was used again and again. The "Caesar Syndrome"
is in evidence in a number of notable films. Robinson's portrayals
are closely allied, in story line and more importantly in characterization, to his performance as Rico Bandello. "Little Caesar's"
spectre stalks the screen again in "Smart Money" (1931), "Dark
Hazard" (1934), "Bullets or Ballots" (1936), and "Kid Galahad" (1937).
The "Little Caesar" traits and acting techniques (as well as restatement of the philosophy of Rico) are apparent in these films. Within
the genre the "Little Caesar" character transgresses against society
and must in all cases pay the price of his misdirected ambition,
often with his life.

"Smart Money" (1931) came soon after "Little Caesar" and
"The Public Enemy". Robinson, fresh from his success as Rico,
was cast in a similar role, thus capitalizing on the popularity of
his classic characterization. Publicity for "Smart Money" calls
attention to "Little Caesar" and "The Public Enemy" and at the

same time echoes the force of pressures against glorification of

gangster films. In "Smart Money" the "Little Caesar" character

is not a killer or gang leader but rather a tough gambler:

> "Two Great Stars Together!...A small town barber
> who cleaned up big city gamblers...but who was
> cleaned himself by a bevy of blondes!...twice as
> good as he was in "Little Caesar"...with James
> Cagney, sensational star of "The Public Enemy"
> ...they give up gunning and take up gambling.
> Tough as ever but twice as likeable!"

The last sentence in this enthusiastic publicity blurb is a

key to the development and change of the "Little Caesar" character

in "Smart Money". Nick the barber is clever, tough, and ready

for a fight (or a blonde) but he is not sinister. He is compassionate

(taking in a drowning girl) and loyal (repaying his original small town

backers many times over). He kills only by error and deeply regrets

it (the accidental death of his lieutenant, Cagney).

Nick the Barber retains Rico's strutting "little tough man"

braggadocio: "Yeah, my brother works in the mint" (flashing a

roll of bills.) "These are made for me by a fellow in Havana"

(passing out his favorite brand of huge cigars). Like Rico, Nick

favors outlandishly fancy clothes as a sign of his success, but

unlike the cynical woman-hating Rico, Nick has his weaknesses,

his "human streak". Superstitious, he carries a rabbit's foot

and rubs Negroes' heads for "good luck". Nick has a propensity

for blondes (symbolized by his pet, a yellow canary). He is
cheated of his first $10,000.00 stake by a beautiful blonde hotel
counter girl who traps him in a confidence game. He finally
meets his downfall because of circumstances surrounding the
suicidal young blonde he pulls from the river. Even the police
recognize the chink in Nick's armor and send a blonde agent to
try and trap him.

"Dark Hazard" (1934) is a lesser Robinson vehicle but
typical of the dissolution of the "Little Caesar" character. The
film calls forth certain themes which proved successful in "Little
Caesar", but there is no cohesive story line or forceful
characterization to back them up.

As in "Smart Money", Robinson is a compulsive gambler,
a braggart. Genevieve Tobin as his troublesome wife affects
"gentility". The theme of the "lower class" man (gambler, con-
man, gangster) who wants to marry the "higher class" woman
(rich or good, or socially prominent) is evident, with the resultant
problems of acceptance in this "higher" or more respectable level.
This is a recurring story line. The rich, the small town bigots,
et al., are the corrupt forces, worse than the "shady" characters
they scoff. In keeping with this theme, Robinson finds happiness
with a woman on his own level; a "heart of gold" if amoral woman,

an old mistress.

"Bullets or Ballots" (1936) is a notable "Caesar Syndrome" film in that the tough "Caesar" character is made even more palatable by being transposed to the side of the law. The title of "Bullets or Ballots" refers to the union in American life between organized crime and politics. In a typical opening technique, "Bullets or Ballots" begins with a sequence which will set the ensuing story in its period's social-economic context.

A newsreel draws gang chief Al Kruger (Barton MacLane) and henchman "Bugs" Fenner (Humphrey Bogart) into a theatre. The newsreel narrator delivers a rapid fire exposition on the extent of the hold of organized crime on the American economy: Crime is stealing billions of dollars from the American people every year by placing a levy on the transportation of fresh produce; by seducing the young into gambling with slot machines placed near schools; by controlling restaurant supplies, etc. A crusading news-paperman ends the program, swearing that his paper will continue to expose racketeering despite threats leveled against him. As a result of the newsreel, Fenner kills the publisher.

The major portion of the story pits the Bogart character (Fenner) against the Edward G. Robinson character (Police Detective Johnny Blake). Blake and Fenner are old-fashioned men alike in their use of force, different only in their goals. Both

are wholly committed to their professions and will hear nothing

of "peaceful coexistence" with the other side. Blake's script

description paints him boldly:

> "A powerful face... stocky in build...the toughest,
> hardest-hitting detective in the New York Police
> Department. He knows New York like a book...
> is familiar with all its haunts. He has been kicked
> down the ladder and has ended up a plain detective
> in the Bronx district. Beneath his cold-shell
> exterior are two driving emotions...hatred of the
> underworld, its racketeers and its rates...and a
> tremendous loyalty to his old friend Police Captain
> Dan McLaren, a square-shooting veteran of the
> Department. Blake will strike a "mug" or "rat"
> when he will not tip his hat to a police officer."

Johnny Blake thus bears a close resemblance to Rico

of "Little Caesar". Blake, however, is ostensibly on the side

of the law. This "legalizing" of violence is also especially

apparent in Cagney's portrayal of a rather violent law officer

in "G-Men" (1935). The brand of violence of earlier gangster

films is maintained intact, but dealt out at the hands of a "law

officer" it becomes "good over evil". The objections of various

censoring groups are met.

Blake has a warm friendship with a lovely female cafe owner,

Lee Morgan (Joan Blondell), however, a romantic attachment is

not possible for the detective:

> "I'm not dumb, Lee. You like me pretty
> well...and that goes both ways. If women
> and home life had been in my line, I'd have
> fallen for you a long time ago."

The Johnny Blake of "Bullets or Ballots", never having won

the girl, dies after he smashes the city's rackets. This is in

keeping with the non-romantic character set by "Little Caesar".

Robinson was never a romantic figure. Robinson is either used

and deserted by a woman ("Tiger Shark" and "Smart Money") or

maintains a relationship based on mutual need with a semi-

prostitute (Bette Davis in "Kid Galahad").

The film loses believability when, in order to gain the

upper hand in the rackets and to meet the bosses known only to

Kruger, Blake organizes the most profitable and widespread racket

of all, numbers. For a substantial portion of the film, crime

fighter Blake is the city's greatest criminal (thus playing the

gangster role while not "glorifying gangsterism").

Even though the Robinson character was on the side of the

law, he died at the end of the film as he did in "Little Caesar". In

each instance the character is too inflexible to survive - a man who

fitted into no system.

This film, like many others in the study, is totally devoid of glamour. Dingy offices, public buildings, cafes, hotel lobbies form the background. The players are found at their work. The script consistently describes characters as having grim looks on their faces because their tasks require complete concentration.

An example of this insistence on commonplace backgrounds is Joan Blondell. An attractive and appealing woman, her appearance in these films was always of a person in action or on the job. Contrast the loyal secretary or gold-digging chorus girl to Garbo and Dietrich whose languid presence invited extended contemplation. Later in the 1930's and into the 1940's, Warners continued this type of tough "woman on the go" with Ann Sheridan and Ida Lupino.

"Kid Galahad" (1937) combines Robinson and Bogart in a popular theme of the period - a fight picture. Bogart plays a role to which he had become well accustomed - the second banana gangster, the one-dimensional, all-bad-villian. Bogart is required to snarl and bridle under the more clever Robinson, fight dirty against his competition and die for his sins in the end in a gun duel.

Robinson's role is the much better one in the film, although also tried and true after so many airings. Again Robinson is "Little Caesar" without the menacing overtones. He is expansive and jovial and at the same time vicious and unrelenting - unflinching in the face of his opponents but with a soft spot for his girl.

The treatment of the female characters in "Kid Galahad" is typical of "Caesar Syndrome" films. There is the "bad" girl with the "heart of gold" (Bette Davis), and the "good" girl (Jane Bryan). Robinson's over-protectiveness of his younger sister whose innocence he wishes to preserve is similar to Muni's obses- sion with his sister in "Scarface" - both familial relationships having southern European overtones complete with an understanding Italian mother standing over the stove in the background. In each case the brother was either a criminal or had shady dealings but could not tolerate the least indiscretion on the part of his sister - she, perhaps, symbolized the preservation of all the "good" ideals he had foregone.

Robinson once again followed the established "romantic" pattern of his films. Although he has Fluff (Bette Davis), the relationship is not a love match - rather a convenience, a business relationship, Fluff being bought and paid for (as is demonstrated by her hopeless attraction to the young fighter). Robinson, perhaps not being a character who fits well into a romantic situation, once again ended without the girl (in this case through his death after she had left him). This "tragic" ending with the girl who has forsaken

him feeling some remorse at her actions now that her kind benefactor
is dying is quite similar to the ending of "Tiger Shark", in which
Robinson's wife (who married him in return for his kindness) falls
in love with a young man thus inadvertantly causing her vengeful
husband's death.

"Kid Galahad" is a cliche ridden film, one of the most
interesting being Miss Davis' departure into the fog in the final
reel - an ending exactly like that in "Marked Woman", another
"shady lady" role released the same year.

B. Edward G. Robinson: Development of the "Comic Caesar"

"Little Giant" 1933, "A Slight Case of Murder" 1938
"Brother Orchid" 1940

A deterioration of the "Little Caesar Syndrome" can be
noted in "Little Giant" (1933), "A Slight Case of Murder" (1938)
and "Brother Orchid" (1940).

These films still reflect the "Little Caesar" characteristics -
cockiness, swaggering, desire for power gained by illegal means,
control of a mob or gang. The physical traits are also the same -
the strutting walk, the jabbing forefinger, the cigar, the wicked,
expansive smile, the flashy clothes. The films, however, represent
a change in the "Little Caesar" character - a softening achieved by
placing Robinson in a comic situation and using the "Little Caesar"

type as the brunt of the jokes and satirical social comment. This was due in part to the discouragement of violent films glorifying the criminal element by certain censoring groups, official and unofficial.

The gang leader's desire for acceptance in "society" and his attempt at securing "class" were particular areas at which the comedic thrusts were aimed.

"Little Giant" (1933) was a natural development of the successful gangster film cycle. It is a variation on a theme Little Caesar doing comedy instead of melodrama. Although some mourned "Little Giant" as a "farewell" to lively and enter-taining genre (satire on the gangster film being its death knell) it was proved that these fears were unfounded since many years of gangster films stretched ahead (albeit a great many of them mediocre).

The film demonstrated that Robinson was not only an excellent serious stage actor and the dean of movie gangsters, but also an accomplished comedian.

The preposterous situation of a gang lord trying to break into posh society has built-in comic elements and Robinson's "Little Caesar", perhaps because it was close to a caricature to begin with, lends itself easily to physical gags, jokes on verbal characteristics, etc.

"Little Giant" is certainly not "high" comedy - in fact the
"Little Caesar" type is played for "cheap" and obvious laughs.
Perhaps the most effective comedic section is the rowdy polo game
featuring Bugs Ahern and his mob. The humor takes on a sadistic
note in a scene featuring the lit cigar torturing of an old man. The
weakest aspect of this first "Little Caesar" comedy is that the
character himself bears the brunt of the humor. In later films,
such as the successful "A Slight Case of Murder" the character
moves within a comedic plot which is not centered on his own
ineptitudes and traits but on a situation to which he is a party.

"Little Giant" has two important themes which are evident
in films throughout the decade. The first is the desire on the part
of a gangster, a con man, a fighter -- any "rough" or "crude"
character -- to achieve a higher social situation or "class". As
in "Little Giant", the affections of a society girl are often involved.
The plots normally explore the blundering attempts of the "commoner"
to emulate his betters.

Bugs Ahern, the Little Giant, blatantly sets out to emulate
the social set, and the second continuing theme is employed - the
idealized upper crust is in reality more disreputable and corrupt
than the aspiring roughneck. Wealthy businessmen are really the

the "Mr. Bigs" of crime in "Bullets or Ballots" and "Little Caesar"
Bugs Ahearn finds that the socialites he is trying to impress have
him marked as the victim of their swindle. In a time of depression
it was perhaps comforting to the audiences to think that the common
man, the low man on the totem pole was in reality the ideal type
and that wealth and culture were cover ups for hypocrisy and
dishonesty.

"A Slight Case of Murder" (1938) is, perhaps, the best
gangster-comedy of the period. Again the theme of a crude
gangster taking on the airs of the rich or respectable provides
the comic situations as in the other "Comic Caesar" films.
"A Slight Case of Murder" was taken from the mildly successful
Broadway play of the year before. It was the most popular of the
Robinson gangster-comedies and received the most critical acclaim.
The piece was transferred to the screen without the staginess which
plagued other stage play adaptations. The fact that the story was a
tightly written comedy situation rather than a play on the personal
foibles of the "Caesar" character could count in part for its
superiority over "Little Giant" and "Brother Orchid" as screen
comedy.

Beyond the comedy played off the Robinson character, "A
Slight Case of Murder" has two important comic themes -- the

successful handling of four corpses as continuing "sight gags"
throughout and the part of the youthful delinquent, Douglas
Fairbanks Rosenblum, played by Bobby Jordon, who constantly
acts to deflate Robinson's beneficent pretentions.

"Brother Orchid" (1940) is in the same family of gangster-
comedies as "Little Giant" and "A Slight Case of Murder". Earl
Baldwin wrote the scripts for "Brother Orchid" and "A Slight Case
of Murder" and the same treatment of humorous situations can be
seen throughout. The essence of this type of hard-boiled, impudent comedy is the use of amusing contrasts and incongruous
situations.

When Edward G. Robinson and Warner Brothers decided
that the actor would play Dr. Ehrlich ("Dr. Ehrlich's Magic Bullet",
1940), it was announced that as part of the agreement Robinson
would play one more gangster role for the studio. "Brother Orchid"
was that gangster film.

All of Robinson's comic gangsters seem to be cultural
snobs, superior to the mob, and thus a perfect set up when he
storms the bastions of society. Robinson, as the gang leader,
is his usual on-screen self -- aggressive, domineering, "telling
off" the boys, a cigar in his mouth, thumbs in his lapels, eyebrows
raised as his forefinger stabs the air in his characteristic

intimidating gesture. This was the Robinson so familiar to the audience - the tough gangster in control of the situation with pretensions to the grand life, the "class".

"Brother Orchid" differs from other gangster-comedies because of its serious overtones. The touchy subject of religion is introduced. The outcome of the mixing of gang comedy and monastery life could conceivably have ended in an irreverent and very unfunny treatment; however, "Brother Orchid" balances the two well. The humor comes from the contrasts of the uncompre-hending amoral gangster living among monks - and following their rules by his own dishonest methods (watering the milk to get a greater yield, having a boy tend his zinnia beds).

Robinson had the difficult task of introducing a tenderness into the stereotyped character of the blustering gangster about halfway through the film - to make the final conversion believable. Robinson does this gradually and thus effectively -- as a novice he still has the old swagger as witnessed by his affectation of a jaunty feather in his monk's hat. In the last scene the converted and happy Brother Orchid milks a cow and states his philosophy, "This is real class". The ending is acceptable because we see Robinson not as a pious, praying, solemn monk but as a man who is still essentially gangster Little John Sarto - fitted into another stream of life.

Again in "Brother Orchid" the character Robinson plays
does not "get the girl". The Robinson character most often ends
up "paying" in one way or another for his crimes or social
transgressions -- usually by dying ("Little Caesar", "Barbary
Coast", "Tiger Shark", etc.). In "Brother Orchid", Robinson
pays again, this time by giving up his life and retiring to the
monastery.

It is interesting to note the role of Ralph Bellamy as
Clarence Fletcher in the film. This is the emergence of the type
which might be termed the "All-American Boob". This fellow is
healthy and wholesome, robust and passably good-looking, pure
of heart and simple of mind. He loves completely, hates no one
and blunders to a happy ending. He is the opposite of the gangster
hero and provides a rather bland protagonist after a fare of
Robinson and Cagney. In the early forties one sees him rise to
prominence over his more jaded brothers as Wayne Morris and
Eddie Bracken cavort harmlessly over the screens ripped by
bullets a decade earlier.

C. James Cagney: "The Public Enemy" Revisited

"Sinner's Holiday" 1930, "Doorway to Hell" 1930,
"G-Men" 1935, "Angels With Dirty Faces" 1938
"The Roaring Twenties" 1939

The form Cagney set in "The Public Enemy", is the basis
of classification for "archetypical Cagney" films. These films
show Cagney as the hard-bitten criminal, tough and unrepentant,
his actions punctuated by a maniacal laugh and quick, brutal movement. Unlike later films these show few comic elements nor do
they allow Cagney's light touch. The themes are generally more
serious than the other two categories, "con man" or "action"
films, and they are often of wider scope and more social significance than works falling under the latter two classifications.

"Sinner's Holiday" (1930) was Cagney's first film,
preceding "Doorway to Hell" and "The Public Enemy". Cagney
and Joan Blondell appeared in the original stage version "Penny
Arcade". Warner Brothers bought the play for the screen and
brought Cagney and Miss Blondell to recreate their stage roles.

The Cagney of "Sinner's Holiday" is a very youthful one.
The characteristics, mannerisms and vitality which came to
fruition in the classic "Public Enemy" and developed into the
unmistakable Cagney style can be seen in "Sinner's Holiday"
in their beginning stages.

Cagney's portrayal shows traces of restraint in this film. His cockiness, swagger, darting hands are slightly unsure - perhaps because he is not in the starring role. The sneer, the bravado of the "tough little guy" are there, however, and shine out far about the patterned and self-conscious ogling of the leading man, Grant Withers. Withers adopts the exaggerated hand, head and eye gestures (and also falsetto, mocking voice) seen so often in the period. Dick Powell was a leading proponent, Paul Muni used these techniques to some extent in "Bordertown", "Hi, Nellie!", and with great effectiveness in "Scarface".

Cagney's "Harry Delano" in "Sinner's Holiday" is identical in many respects to the string of roles he filled over the decade. He uses his ill-gotten bootlegging gains to buy a new suit (a typical move in numerous Cagney, Robinson, Muni and Dead End Kids films). In "Sinner's Holiday" the Cagney character is forced to kill his gang boss after being caught stealing from the mob's till. Harry Delano's mother helps her favorite child, her black sheep, though his acts fill her with anguish. (Similar mother-son relationships appear in "The Public Enemy", "Scarface", "Kid Galahad".) Harry, weeping at his mother's knee, was one of Cagney's rare weaklings. He again played a coward in "The Fighting 69th", but Harry Delano delivering a tearful confession and plea for help at his mother's knee with the police approaching in "Sinner's Holiday" was a broken man Cagney never included again in his repertory.

"Doorway to Hell" (1930) was Cagney's second film and one of his few in a non-starring role (he received sixth billing). As in his first film (and his succeeding ones) Cagney playes a hoodlum - a charming, boyish roughneck with a selfish streak.

In a period when it seemed everyone took a turn at playing gangsters (Spencer Tracy, Clark Gable, et al.), Lew Ayres is badly miscast as the Italian gang leader in "Doorway to Hell". Ayers too much resembled a "color ad" type and the tough, gangster dialogue was delivered slowly and awkwardly. ("Any mug who don't think so, will be treated to the swellest funeral that ever stopped traffic.") This ineptitude is especially apparent in contrast to Cagney's portrayal of Ayres' lieutenant. Cagney's rapid fire delivery and New York accent fit perfectly into the gangster's image ("Why you doity greaseball!"). In addition, Cagney's "business" is quick and aggressive - brazenly pulling a cigar out of an adversary's pocket, sniffing it and replacing it with an arch smile; snapping a man's suspenders and skipping off.

As in following gangster films, certain common themes

may be found to "Doorway to Hell" - Ayres quits the rackets and looks for "respectability" (as in "Little Giant", "Picture Snatcher", "Lady Killer", "Brother Orchid" and others). The gang leader wishes to protect his "good" younger brother (similarly Robinson's sister in "Kid Galahad", Bette Davis' sister in "Marked Woman", Cagney's brother in "The Crowd Roars", Muni's sister in "Scarface"). As in "Little Caesar" the gang leader has a "Napoleon complex", played on visually in "Doorway to Hell" by Ayres' fascination with the painting of Napoleon in exile and his statement about his brother's posh military school: "Gee, war is a great racket".

The film ends with the epilogue, "The Doorway to Hell is a one way door and they soon forget about him". As previously noted, similar warnings or declarations that the films explored "national problems" were run with the credits of "Little Caesar", "The Public Enemy", and "Scarface", supposedly marking these films as socially conscious exposes.

"G-Men" (1935) is an attempt by Warner Brothers to maintain the old successful ingredients of their gangster films - fast action, chases, shoot-outs, tough characters - while avoiding any glamorization of the criminal type. Public opinion had been raised against "films not suitable for impressionable youth" and "G-Men" was a round about way of meeting this problem.

Essentially, "G-Men" is a violent gangster film but it
looks at the action from the top (the law men) rather than from
the bottom (the criminals). There are mass killings but all in
the name of law and order - which supposedly made them all
right. This switch to violent law men rather than violent criminals
saw the police force enlarged by detective Robinson in "Bullets or
Ballots" and carried on eventually into the private eye and police
films of the forties.

After the acquisition of arms for their branch of service,
government agents became involved in a vast campaign against
crime. The action in "G-Men" is largely based on authentic cases -
the pursuit of John Dillinger and Baby Face Nelson, the Kansas City
Union Station massacre, the Dillinger shoot out in Wisconsin, and
various well known kidnap cases.

Despite the realistic quality of the material and the
supposedly commendable purpose of the film's exposition, critics
still found "G-Men" only a loosely disguised sequel to its gangland
predecessors[1] and still unfit for young audiences.[2] The city of
Chicago barred "G-Men" from its theatres when H. M. Costello

---

[1]"G-Men", The Literary Digest, May 11, 1935, p. 30.

[2]The New York Times, April 25, 1935, p. 17:1.

of the Crime Prevention Division of the police department declared that the machine-gun killings were in violation of Chicago film standards and over-stimulating for children. None the less, it played twenty hours a day at the New York Strand.

Warner Brothers was the first studio to make a government man film. The detective branch of the Department of Justice had begun in 1908 and expanded with the Mann Act in 1912. "G-Men" came to prominence during World War I handling alien cases but the branch developed to major proportions during the "public enemy" era of early Prohibition. At the time of the film the service numbered eight hundred men and had only recently come to widespread public attention.

Although "G-Men" provided Cagney with a more meaningful role than his lightweight work in the Cagney-Pat O'Brien series of army and navy films then in production, it was still bogged down by trite dialogue and situations highly reminiscent of Cagney-O'Brien sparring. (1) Cagney joins the government service with a chip on his shoulder. He is dedicated to a goal and undertakes quick revenge of his friend's death. (2) G-Man Cagney, too eager and contemptuous of authority in his desire to take on the killers, comes into conflict with a hard-bitten superior and (3) immediately falls for the superior's aloof and haughty sister. Thus Cagney

typically must not only fight the criminals but must also prove
himself to his fellow G-Men and at the same time win over the
girl and her brother.

"G-Men" may be counted as the last truly "archetypical"
Cagney film. In it, Cagney hit his prime. Quick and brutal in
his movements, the Cagney gestures give the story its pace.
The bouncing gait, the flippant tough talk (Robert Armstrong)
to Cagney derisively, "Oh, Phi Beta Kappa, eh?" Cagney: "Yeh,
flatfooted coppa!") are Cagney at his best. After "G-Men" Cagney
made other films in which he handled a gun or played the "tough
little nut", but the Cagney fire was not the same. An example of
this maturing of the Cagney character is evident in "City for
Conquest" (1940), in which he imbues his struggling boxer with
little zest; in "Torrid Zone" (1940) where Cagney-O'Brien fire-
works lose their boyish charm and become arguments between two
grown men.

"Angels With Dirty Faces" (1938) is a study of a great
city's slums and specifically of how these environs affect the lives
of boys growing up in such an unattractive and vice-ridden atmosphere. The opening sequences, scanning the "Streets of New York"
set, very effectively create a crowded, seething, melting-pot
neighborhood. The boys involved, Rocky (James Cagney) and Jerry

(Pat O'Brien) as children and later the Dead End Kids, provide believable inhabitants - tattered, tough, wise beyond their years, scrambling for life. Their filthy basement hideout, the sopping, rusty tenement gymnasium communal bathroom where they wash up after basketball, set an undertone of decay and environmental ugliness which supports and explains their attitude toward life. This is further developed through the street scenes - vignettes of the boys committing minor acts of violence as they make their way through the milling crowds; Rocky and his girlfriend Laury (Ann Sheridan) pushing their way through waves of people on the sidewalks without giving the obstructions a thought - the anonymous horde being so much a part of their everyday lives. The milieu comes into particularly sharp relief when the world of Rocky, now grown up and a gangster, is contrasted with the quiet interior of the church where Jerry, now a priest, has his office. Father Jerry has created an island of order, morality and purpose in a sea of squalor. These settings thus parallel the conflicts of the film - the dedicated priest fighting the debilitating forces of the surrounding slum, personified by Rocky.

James Cagney recreates much of his familiar "Public Enemy" self in this film. As Frank Nugent stated, "No one resents type-casting more than Mr. Cagney and no one justifies

it more completely."[1] He had tried to break away from the tough-
guy image in several succeeding pictures - such as his less than
satisfying portrayal as a comical screenwriter in "Boy Meets Girl"
(1938). Cagney slipped easily back into the familiar mold in
"Angels With Dirty Faces" - squared shoulders, arms poised to
show the world aside, the pugnacious jaw, Irish nose and bared
teeth, either charging about a scene in his stiff-legged gait or
balancing menacingly on the balls of his feet. In "Angels With
Dirty Faces" a vintage Cagney outwits police by using his
juvenile gang as lookouts and couriers; dupes his fellow gangsters
by spotting the men Frazier has following him and tricks one of
the tails into the telephone booth to be shot in his place; by
double-double crossing his cowardly partner Frazier, stealing
his "incriminating documents" and locking the tuxedoed lawyer
in a basement under a boiler where he is forced to spend the
night with the rats. Rocky is the type of character who grace-
fully eludes all traps and with great humor inflicts appropriate
retribution in all quarters. He is a smilingly unscrupulous
racketeer and murderer yet so engaging that he wins the
immediate love of the good Laury, the devotion of the boys, and

---

[1]The New York Times, Nov. 27, 1938, p. 5:IX.

even the lifelong friendship of the crusading anti-crime priest,
Father Jerry.

Cagney has a tremendous capacity for participating in
violence. He moves through the gunfight scenes like a ballet
dancer. While others may appear scared or vicious or obsessed
while killing, Cagney does this, his primary occupation, with
zest and staccato efficiency - his mode of moving through a mass
killing or gunfight is identical to his mode of acting in verbal
situations - sure, poised movements; aggressive, thrusting gestures;
his "machine-gun" pronunciation and speech rate a counterpart
to the reports of his guns; a basic animal pleasure in every life
act whether talking quietly or killing. In his scenes with the Dead
End Kids, he follows them to his old hideout and intimidates them
into returning his money, then wins their friendship; and later,
when he takes them to the basketball court, he referees in a style
they can understand -- he strikes them when they do something
wrong.

Cagney's treatment of the death scene is a frightening
episode. Done in shadows and silhouette, his agonizing screams
for mercy, the sound of a man crying, shows a depth to Cagney's
gangster characterization that he was rarely permitted to show -
an unsure man eaten with fear. (It was said in a publicity release

at the time that during a rehearsal of this scene an irreverent press
agent on the sidelines made a remark about "fried ham" when the
power was turned on and Rocky died. The good-natured Mr. Cagney
merely corrected him with the single word, "Baked".)

Humphrey Bogart played a supporting role in "Angels With
Dirty Faces". His attorney, Frazier, was unscrupulous yet
cowardly about finaglings as opposed to the aggressive Cagney.
Frazier was "dishonestly dishonest" as opposed to being "honestly
dishonest"; he betrayed his peers (the city politicians, et al., he
had material on) and his gangster associates as well. Bogart played
him as a weak-willed and fearful wrongdoer - intimidated by Cagney.
Frazier did not meet aggression with force, rather he withdrew.
A characteristic technique of Bogart's is to be seen in Frazier, the
rapid smoking under pressure, the lowered chin, hunched shoulders,
refuge behind a large desk, eyes jerking from side to side, unable
to gaze directly into the eyes of someone confronting him, nervous
lips jerking in greed or fear. (This type can be seen as the
thwarted ring promoter in "Kid Galahad" or as the black-clad
saloon owner in "The Oklahoma Kid", both rather one-dimensional
supporting roles.)

Pat O'Brien is Cagney's friend-nemesis. This relationship
can be found in many films ("Devil Dogs of the Air", "The Fighting

69th", "Here Comes the Navy", etc.). They did make perfect foils
the quick gleeful, shorter Cagney; the taller, stodgier leader O'Brien
whose authority Cagney was constantly challenging. Although both
were Irish types in these films, both always with a good deal of
nerve and charm, Cagney's cockiness was countered by O'Brien's
steady confidence and knowledge of what was correct. Cagney was
boyish; O'Brien manly. Cagney was an exciting companion; O'Brien
a comforting one. Cagney fascinated the girl and after offending
her, won her. O'Brien was her brother, her priest or the losing
suitor.

Pat O'Brien as Father Jerry displays his usual characterization - strong, correct, yet a vigorous fighter when aroused by an
obvious wrong. (Cagney would usually fight when personally offended
or challenged.) O'Brien and "right" ostensibly triumph but it is the
prodigal racketeer Cagney who wins your attention and interest.

Newspaper advertising for "Angels With Dirty Faces"
carried a famous blurb, "Last one over the fence lands in the
chair". This captured the essence of the story that while Rocky
and Jerry as boys both lived in the slums and engaged in petty
thievery, it was Rocky's initial capture that led one boy to become
a criminal and the other a priest.

One of the strengths of "Angels With Dirty Faces" is a relatively realistic point of view. The priest, while still somewhat larger than life, admits to the gangster Rocky that crime does appear to pay. He further concedes that recklessness and a distorted kind of heroism tend to glorify the gangster, to make him a juvenile idol. When the priest enters the tear gas filled warehouse to bring Rocky out, the hunted man does not concede to the call of morality but rather uses the well-intentioned priest as a shield to try a last-ditch escape.

In the end Father Jerry has to appeal to Rocky's courage - not really his sense of good or bad - to turn "yellow" in the chair and thus smash his image as idol of the slum boys. One has the feeling that Rocky dies completely unrepentant and unchanged. He has put on this final act more as a tribute and a gift to an old friend than for any noble reasons. (Under the same motivation, loyalty to Father Jerry, he had only recently murdered his two partners, Frazier and Keefer, to prevent them from killing the priest.)

The finale of Rocky dying in the electric chair offered an interesting dilemma to the Hays Office. While ostensibly this is an acceptable ending - the murderer is punished, the slum boys are saved - in reality the ending offered a moral defeat for a crusading priest and a conclusion which, while convincing a handful of make-believe juvenile delinquents that Rocky Sullivan was a coward, would convince the audience of real small boys of precisely the opposite.

"The Roaring Twenties" (1939) was considered at the time of its release a "well documented period piece" recreating with exceptional reality the mood and appearance of the era it explored. By present standards, the late twenties and the thirties may seem to be a continuous period, particularly viewed after the "cut off" period of the Second World War. At the time, however, the twenties were considered to be a distinct and historical period, far enough removed to deserve a "period" treatment.

With "The Roaring Twenties" Warner Brothers reverts to a popular picture type - the first "serious" 1920's bootlegging and gangster film in which the criminals are the main characters since the 1931-1932 series ("The Public Enemy", "Little Caesar" and others). Since that period, owing in part to censorship, code rulings and pressure groups, the "pure" gangster film had been shunted off into gangster-comedy, con man films and films dealing with gangsters as villains supporting an essentially "good" hero ("G-Men", "San Quentin").

"The Roaring Twenties" was given "prestige" publicity in

keeping with its "historical" qualities and the documentary aspects

of its format. At least once critic, Frank Nugent, found this

glorification of an old form to be "pretentious".

> As though it were not already the most thoroughly
> cinematized decade of our history, the Warners
> are presenting the "Roaring Twenties" with the
> self-conscious air of an antiquarian preparing to
> translate a cuneiform record of a lost civilization
> ...The dirty decade has served too many quickie
> quatrains to rate an epic handling now. Stripped
> of its false whiskers...the picture merely marks
> the Warners return to the profitable and visually
> exciting field where once sprouted such horrendous
> nosegays as "Public Enemy" and "Little Caesar".[1]

"The Roaring Twenties" somehow lacks what might be

called the "innocence" or originality of "The Public Enemy" and

"Little Caesar". The later film is, if not a copy, at least a

tribute to its gangster predecessors. It is an attempt to raise

the genre from the "B" picture and program picture status to which

it had been consigned as the 1930-1940 period wore on to its place

once more as major film material. To achieve this the gangster

story is placed in a setting which points up the social issues which

caused this era. Authenticity is added by a "March of Time" format,

newsreel clips and a narrator. Background music and nightclub

acts featured songs popular in the twenties   "Melancholy Baby"

and "I'm Just Wild About Harry" were used under the credits.

---

[1]The New York Times, Nov. 11, 1939, p. 12:1.

Emphasis is given to the effects on the gangsters-to-be of the
First World War (not unlike the "Forgotten Man" number in
"Golddiggers of 1933"). The reasons behind their choice of
occupation are explored, the social pressures and injustices
(no jobs after the war, etc.) are revealed. (This "sociological
significance" approach was applied to many gangster films to
help alleviate the risk of criticism aimed at the possible
"glorification" of gangsters. "Little Caesar", "The Public Enemy",
"The Roaring Twenties" and others carried forewords to this
effect. In the beginning of the latter film Mark Hellinger stated,
"The film is a memory and I am grateful for it...Now as we face
a world shaking before power made men...")

The effect of the war on shaping these men is constantly
emphasized. When Cagney, out of a job upon returning and trying
to deliver illegal liquor to make ends meet, is thrown in jail his
cell mate is a veteran also. This man is wanted for armed robbery,
a route he chose out of desperation, and he states that if he had a gun
he'd kill himself. When Bogart commits murder, during the warehouse
robbery, it is of his hated former sergeant, "Leather Lungs", now
a government guard.

As the three soldiers who are followed from their army
days to the beginning of the Depression, Cagney, Bogart and Jeffrey

Lynn represent three ways of meeting the crisis of the new times.
Bogart is marked early as a "totally bad" character. In the first
scene in the trenches he rises and shoots a German soldier. Lynn
refused to shoot the soldier saying that the boy wasn't a day over
fifteen. Bogart replies, "Well, now he'll never make sixteen". Lynn
is cast as the "good" character of the trio. He announces in the
trench that he wants to go back to law school. Later, although he
works as his bootlegging friend's lawyer for a time he finds the
business distasteful and leaves. He marries the "good" girl of the
film, Priscilla Lane, who spurns Cagney because of his motives.
Cagney plays a "gray" character, as opposed to Bogart's "black"
and Lynn's "white". Cagney wants to make a living, preferably at
his old garage job. Whereas Bogart went into his bootlegging profession by design, Cagney gets drawn in little by little as the bleak-
ness of his future becomes more and more apparent. Bogart remains
the "professional gangster" throughout - killing without qualms,
betraying friends, working coldly and without emotion. Cagney, on
the other hand, still holds his old friends dear - Frank McHugh
and Jeffrey Lynn, for whom he sacrifices his life in the final scene
with Bogart. Cagney aspires after "respectability" as witnessed
in his pursuit of the "good" girl, whose virtue he respects, rather
than settling for an easy relationship with the loyal but "common"

Panama. Cagney, the man undone by the war is again undone by the stock market crash when he loses the "good" girl to his lawyer. His emotional involvement is deep, despite his toughness in his profession. He turns to drink, becomes a bleary-eyed bum.

"The Roaring Twenties" offers Bogart in a traditional gangster role - the hardened criminal with no redeeming qualities. Cagney's gangster is sympathetic - a product of his environment and of his times, the gangster with a streak of humanity, with an inner urge toward respectability and "hearth and home", a man who turns to crime to survive in a society that seems to have turned against him. The irony of his fruitless striving is seen in two sequences - when the faded Panama says to the drunken, broken Cagney in a cheap bar, "I always knew we had the same taste..." and when Cagney lies in his rags, dying of a bullet wound on the snowy steps of a darkened church, a passer-by offers his epitaph, "Gee! He used to be a big shot!"

D. James Cagney: The Con Man Films

> "Blonde Crazy" 1931, "Hard To Handle" 1933,
> "Lady Killer" 1933, "Picture Snatcher" 1933,
> "Jimmy The Gent" 1934

The Cagney "con man" films can be traced as a direct development from the character set in the "archetypical Cagney" films. Cagney is still outside the law, the treatment is much lighter with more comic elements (compared with the development of Robinson's "Little Caesar" into "Comic Little Caesar"). Cagney's actions are much more exaggerated -- his bouncing step, his quick movements. He is still easily angered, ready to fight, but the consequences are rarely grave. Romantic interests are always present, as well as wisecracking dialogue and a preoccupation with puncturing pomposity.

The con man believes the world owes him a living. As Cagney says in "Blonde Crazy", "It is the age of chicanery". The con man is charming and roguish and slightly shady -- but he rarely pays for his crimes, nor do we want him to. He is "The Public Enemy" -- but this time he is only kidding. Critics of film violence were mollified and the audience was fed a lighter dose of the pugnacious Cagney gangster.

Con men crooks and humorous approaches to crime allowed the screen to deal with the usual pyrotechnics and violence while softening the much-criticized crime themes with lighthearted banter and comedy, tongue-in-cheek murders and Robin Hood thievery. Perhaps influenced by the various pressure groups and Code supporters, the Cagney public enemy -- tough, flippant, cocky -- found his way into the part of the bumptious con man and finally

into the innocuous "tough little guy versus the system" roles in the
Cagney-O'Brien service-action films.

In "Sinner's Holiday", "Smart Money" and "Doorway To
Hell", Cagney still had co-starring or supporting roles -- a ne'er
do-well brother, a second banana gangster. He could not fully
dominate the screen as he did in succeeding roles. His style was
therefore restricted, overshadowed, subject to story and star.
In "Blonde Crazy" Cagney is given free reign, and he turns from
"blue-collar" crooks (killers, thieves) to "white-collar" crooks (con
men, tricksters).

"Blonde Crazy" (1931) is a prime example of the beginnings
of the Cagney con man characterization. The formative stages of
his unique "con man" portrayal can be seen in this film. Although
the essential Cagney gestures are here -- the quick, graceful movements, the cocky stride, the maniacal laugh, the salacious yet
boyish smile -- some aspects still lack definition; some movements
still lack the complete assurance of the finished con man as seen in
"Lady Killer" or "Jimmy the Gent".

Although released the same year as "The Public Enemy",
"Blonde Crazy" is a lesser film in every aspect and cannot be
compared fairly with its classic predecessor. Whereas, "The
Public Enemy" offered Cagney the choicest of roles, perfectly suited

to his talents -- rough action, suspense, tightly constructed drama --
"Blonde Crazy" is on the lighter side, with inklings of humor.
Crooks cheat crooks; badger games are played on deserving
"suckers". The latter film, however, bogs down considerably in
the final third. Clever chicanery is replaced with thievery and the
melodramatic climax features retribution and just deserts. Cagney's
charming, if disreputable, Bert Harris grinds to a halt when he
remorsefully gives up his "trade" after losing his partner in crime,
Ann, to an "honorable" bridegroom. Topping this in nobility,
Bert self-sacrificingly tries to cover Ann's husband's embezzlement
by taking the rap himself. To see the swindler, Cagney, at last in
prison, paying for his crimes, with the tearful Ann promising to
"wait for him" may prove crime doesn't pay, but it provides a much
less satisfactory ending than does the success of the unremorseful
con man of "Lady Killer" who escapes all punitive measures.

Cagney's portrayal in "Blonde Crazy" is closer to his work
in "Sinner's Holiday" and "Smart Money" than to his later films.
Cagney's characteristics are forced into a recognizable "method"
in "Blonde Crazy" -- a type of contemporary flippant bravado that
he redefined and adapted to his own needs with great success in
later films. In "Blonde Crazy" these gestures and intonations are
still somewhat foreign to Cagney, not completely osmosed. This

"method" can be seen in the work of Grant Withers in "Sinner's Holiday" and in Dick Powell in "Gold Diggers of 1933" among many others. It involves extreme facial reactions to every situation, particularly humorous or titilating ones. The typical reaction is rolling eyes, raised eyebrows, an appreciative whistle or an exaggerated grin, the chin pulled in and the head cocked to one side. Often in combination with this ogling reaction, the hat is tipped over one eye. Grant Withers also hooked his thumbs under his suspenders and talked out of the side of his mouth. As was typical of this group of gestures, Cagney also used a falsetto voice to imitate "grand" or "phony" people or to make fun of various aspects of "culture" such as reading Browning's poems in this tone. Cagney's most obvious borrowing from this syndrome was his constant and forced use of the word "Ho-o-on-ee" when addressing women in "Blonde Crazy". (This type of intonation was evidently popular at the time, being a trademark of actress Alice White.)

"Blonde Crazy" is a comment on the times. Bert Harris is a down and out bellhop, supplementing his salary by selling bootleg whiskey and shaking down hotel customers. His partner, Ann, is an out-of-work girl looking for a job in the hotel linen room. Disillusioned by the times ("It's the age of chicanery, not of chivalry, honey."). Bert is goaded by the rich and foolish

hotel guests. A quick-thinking and ambitious young man, held down
by his position, Bert turns to crime as his only way to rise in the
world (as did his counterpart in "The Public Enemy", "The Roaring
Twenties"). Cagney once again plays the product of his times and
the victim of it.

In "Hard to Handle" (1933) Cagney cons the suckers again.
Cagney plays a charming, fast-talking, quick-thinking, unscrupulous
publicity agent -- but whether he is bellhop, usher-turned-movie
star, or a locator of missing heirs; the shrewd, crude, engaging
rascal characterization is the same.

Mordaunt Hall called Cagney "alert and fiery"; the story
of "Hard to Handle" "a violent, down-to-the-pavement, slangy
affair".[1] These descriptions could well apply to any of the con man
films -- and to the majority of Cagney films of this period. The
story of "Hard to Handle" has a basic theme of toughness, of
survival. Although "Hard to Handle" is essentially comedy, the
wryly cynical knowledge of motives and human reactions is impressive -- especially as seen in Cagney's relationship with his girl's
lovable gold-digging mother. The two are the same breed and they
know it. They peddle what they have for all it's worth. Cagney

---

[1]The New York Times, Feb. 21, 1933, p. 21:5.

can sell "suckers a bill of goods" whether it is useless "reducing cream" or a grapefruit diet, the mother has a beautiful and ingenuous daughter whom she peddles.

The use of a grapefruit campaign for the climax of the film smacks of an "in" joke. The grapefruit scene with Mae Clark in "The Public Enemy" was Cagney's most famous piece of work. Grapefruit halves keep turning up in his later films as appetizers for on-screen meals, and in "Hard to Handle" the Grapefruit Acres hoax becomes a pivotal point of the story.

As in numerous other Cagney, Robinson and Muni films of the period, "Hard to Handle" shows the fallibility and corruption of the idealized "upper classes". The aspiring lowly con man proves to be the better of two evils, the most "honest" of two dishonest parties. Cagney always treats the common man -- the poor average man of the depression -- with fairness, as witnessed by the dance marathon in the first scene. The final contestants are a penniless girl and a delivery man and a hillbilly couple. Cagney runs the contest with every intention of giving the deserving couple the prize; it is his partner who runs out with the money. Later, however, Cagney feels guiltless when bilking the rich. He schemes invariably victimize only the greedy The plan to publicize the amusement park by hiding money on the ground and opening the gates to the money-hungry hordes, his sale of useless reducing cream and his promotion of three-week grapefruit diets are formulated to ensnare the corpulent, the gluttons -- those who spend money to gorge in a time of breadlines. Cagney's rival is a rich society photographer (as it is the well-bred stockholder in "Blonde Crazy", the phoney-elegant geneologist in "Jimmy the Gent"), but as usual, the common, hard-headed, broke today-rich tomorrow Cagney wins the heart of the girl who wavers between loving a scoundrel and obtaining security and social position. The average man is thus made to seem more desirable than his rich and important counterpart.

The theme of the rich with "feet of clay" is treated with particular effectiveness in the scene in which Cagney talks a socially prominent matron into endorsing his fake reducing cream. The matron sniffs at the thought of being photographed for publicity but is induced to do so after being assured her social rival has done a similar ad. As Cagney advances with his photographers ("Quick! I got the old bag in the bag!"), the matron drops her haughty exterior to haggle with Cagney over her honorarium in street corner terms. After a satisfactory price has been reached, the matron composes herself once again and poses regally for Cagney's camera.

"Lady Killer" (1933) is an implausible story, an usher becomes a jewel thief and is then "discovered" by Hollywood and made into a star. Despite this handicapped plot, Cagney's well-defined and enthusiastic portrayal of Dan Quigley makes it a prime example of the full force of his characteristic style in all its aspects. The film is possibly the best of the con man Cagney series.

Cagney's flippant character is marked by the rapid fire quips of the dialogue, shopworn as they may be. An usher in a Warner Brothers theatre, Dan Quigley is asked by a pompous patron why there is no "Mickey Mouse" that night. Quigley replies with a devilish grin, "He's makin' a poisonal appearance in Joisey City". When a blonde gives him a drink and inquires, "Chaser?" Quigley archly replies, "Always have been". When a movie star (Margaret Lindsay) requests his name (the former usher is now in the costume of an Indian for his job as a movie extra), Quigley replies with the Yiddish term for "sore derriere" referring to his pains after riding a fake horse all day.

"Lady Killer", in the tradition of "The Public Enemy", has some notable displays of the Cagney violence. In one sequence Mae Clark (the girl in the famous grapefruit scene of "The Public Enemy") is dragged by the hair out of Dan Quigley's bed and booted into the hall. Another piece of action has Quigley confronting a movie critic -- perhaps reflecting industry feelings on the matter. Cornering the critic in a men's room Quigley advises him to "write about motion pictures and leave the personal lives of people alone...,

"or I'll cut your ears off and mail them to your folks". As a climax

to the scene Quigley, with a maniacal grin, pushes the critic into

one of the nearby stalls, his laughter drowned out by the sound of

flushing.

Like Cagney's "Boy Meets Girl" (1938), "Lady Killer" is

a self-inflicted satire on the movie industry. Cagney starts as a

Warner Brothers usher (the theatre has a marquee for Robinson

in "Little Giant"). The star system bears the brunt of the joke:

Cagney is picked up on the street for a part; becomes an extra;

writes himself hundreds of fan letters and finally shoots to stardom

overnight. Margaret Lindsay, the established star, is lavishly

housed. The parody continues with Cagney's boyishly extravagant

and prankish presents to her -- yodelers, a cage of monkeys, an

elephant, a "Hollywood" party.

Quigley is tricked at his own game by a confidence gang

"moll"; an attractive blonde as were her counterparts in "Smart

Money" and "Blonde Crazy". As in numerous other films of the

period ("Bordertown", "Winner Take All", "Little Giant", etc.)

Cagney, an usher who tries his hand as jewel thief on his way to

becoming an actor, fights to improve his lot (socially, monetarily)

and at the same time desires the attentions of a woman of a "higher

class".

Despite Cagney's last minute help to the police in rounding up the jewel gang (formerly his partners), it is unusual that the character of Dan Quigley receives no punishment (either from the law or by any other methods such as dying nobly or losing the girl or forsaking his fame and fortune). Although the brains of a jewel stealing and confidence gang, who is responsible for a murder (albeit not under his orders), Cagney is "cleared of all charges" because of his aid in the final gunfight and allowed to continue his lucrative film career. This reflects the desire for "happy endings"; a hesitancy to kill off the leading man in the final reel, a further "softening" of the genre. In "Blonde Crazy", Cagney (in a con man role similar to that in "Lady Killer") had "paid" for his past by going to prison and this did cast a pall over the previously lively proceedings.

"Picture Snatcher" (1933) is a film built around one "headline" event. The actual event which spurred the story was the printing in The New York Daily News of a picture taken secretly at the execution of Ruth Snyder. Around this piece of news an action-love story is strung, composed of all the heretofore popular elements in other Cagney films.

Although it would seem an unnecessary hook-up with popular criminal motifs, the film opens with Cagney's release from a three

year prison term. The fact that he immediately gives up his
lucrative business as gang leader to become a low paid, but
"respectable" photographer, seems too near a convenient reformation. It was a popular theme to "kick off" a picture by showing the
comic-dramatic elements of a gangster who desires to change his
social position -- Robinson in "Little Giant", and "Brother Orchid".
This play introduces Cagney in his expected gangster role while
still allowing him to be a non objectionable character.

The appealing elements of the Cagney con-man films are
also evident: Cagney's clever trick to get the picture of the
murderer and his wife from the deranged man; his tricking pursuers
in the newspaper office by hiding in the ladies room; his scheme for
getting into the death house and secretly snapping the execution picture.

Cagney's rough treatment of Alice White is reminiscent of
the violent Mae Clark scenes in "The Public Enemy" and "Lady
Killer". In all three cases Cagney manhandles a "loose" woman
whose attentions at last disgust him. Critics at the time suggested
that a "manhandling" scene was almost obligatory and expected by
Cagney fans.

The two themes of the "lower class" tough trying for
respectability and the same type desiring a "good" or rich girl of
a "higher" class, are seen again in "Picture Snatcher". Also

repeated is the familiar theme (to be found also in Cagney-Pat O'Brien films) in which the pugnacious Cagney, in his head-long pursuit of his desires (a woman, power, revenge against a superior, defiance of authority) causes death or disgrace to come to some innocent friend. The outcome is predictable -- righting this wrong "reforms" the upstart and restores him to society. The innocent friend of "Picture Snatcher" is his girl's policeman father. The Captain is demoted after Cagney sneaks past him into the death house to snap a forbidden photo. The remorseful Cagney writes a newspaper article which neatly clears all this up; wins the father's approval and the girl.

"Picture Snatcher" is a composite of typical Cagney themes. It is also an "occupation" picture. Cagney is always involved in the problems of a particular occupation and "making good" in his job. Boxer, racing driver or newspaperman; occupations are always "proletarian" in nature, and often effected by the depression, as opposed to stories centering around professional men or "society" groups.

"Jimmy the Gent" (1934) is Cagney at his fullest "con man" development. By this time Cagney had completely solidified his characterization seen in its beginnings in "Blonde Crazy". The awkward and derivative gestures and intonations are now gone. Cagney has great control of his portrayal and dominates the film.

Comparing "Jimmy the Gent" and "Blonde Crazy" one notes that this is an older, more mature and much more secure Cagney. In three years Cagney has obviously become the master of his own technique.

Even if overdrawn, Jimmy "The Gent" Corrigan is the ultimate in crudity, energy and shrewdness. Never was Cagney's New York accent so heavy, his tone more sneering, his manner more pugnacious. In fact, looking back, it would seem he spent the entire film with his lower lip out-thrust and his shoulders hunched, ready for action.

It was reported at the time that Cagney carefully prepared for this role and it is evident that he had has character clearly in mind. He arrived at the studio for the first day's shooting with a haircut he felt suited the part. This involved having his head shaved high up the sides and the back. Supposedly the director objected to working with a leading man whose head "looked like a pig's knuckle", particularly where romantic scenes were involved. Cagney obviously won his point, however, for the film opens on the back of his head with a full view of his "tough" haircut.

As Bert Harris bested master con man Dapper Dan (Louis Calhern) in "Blonde Crazy" so Jimmy Corrigan bests the elegant James J. Wallingham (Alan Dinehart) in a similar way. Crook

cheating crook seems to make the bilking palatable. There is the
pleasure of seeing the little man with a few rough edges put one
over on his suave and self-important contemporary.

As in "Lady Killer", Cagney is deeply and cheerfully
embroiled in less than moral doings -- and pays no price for his
shady occupation. The lesson learned from Cagney's soggy ending
in "Blonde Crazy" saves Bert Harris from paying for his transgressions. The clever and charming rascal made to face reality and
punitive measures is not in keeping with the light and flippant tone
of these films.

An old theme is basic to "Jimmy the Gent", one which had
strong appeal to audiences of the time: The desire for respectability
of "class" seen before in "Scarface", "Little Caesar", "Little
Giant", "Brother Orchid" and "A Slight Case of Murder". Cagney
as the gang boss left the mob for a "respectable" job on a newspaper in "Picture Snatcher". The desire to rise above one's lowly
stratum was basic to the bilking of the rich in "Blonde Crazy" and
"Lady Killer".

In combination with the "rise to respectability" theme is
the desire for society women, rich girls, good girls as opposed to
the gun molls or heart-of-gold chippies who usually accompanied
Cagney or Robinson in their less comic ventures.

Following this much-used line, Cagney strives for "culture"

in "Jimmy the Gent" as is indicated by the title. The important point

is, of course, that the "classy idol" -- competitor James J.

Wallingham -- is in reality a worse crook than Jimmy Corrigan.

This sub-theme, that the holders of the much sought after respec-

tibility are actually "lower" than the aspirants is repeated again.

The rich girls are invariably heartless and untrue; the syndicate

is really run by wealthy pillars of society ("Bullets or Ballots",

"Little Caesar"); the society lawyer is cowardly and untrustworthy

("Angels With Dirty Faces"). In "Blonde Crazy" Cagney's girl

married a "worthy" suitor instead of the less than respectable con

man and found that her husband was a weakling and an embezzler.

Thus the shady con man, striving for respectibility, finds

that his own brand of chicanery is more "honest" than the hypocritical

respectibility of his betters.

E. James Cagney: Service-Action-Vocation Films

"The Crowd Roars" 1932, "Winner Take All" 1932,
"Here Comes The Navy" 1934, "The St. Louis Kid" 1934,
"Ceiling Zero" 1936, "Frisco Kid" 1935, "The Irish In
Us" 1935, "The Oklahoma Kid" 1939, "City For Conquest"
1940, "The Fighting 69th" 1940, "Torrid Zone" 1940

The furthest departure from the "archetypical Cagney" is

found in a group of films a step beyond the "con man" in the dissolution of the original "The Public Enemy" characterization. The "service-action-vocation" films feature the familiar Cagney -- beligerent, rebellious, quick -- but the tone is largely comedic. Cagney has acquired a humorous side-kick in the majority of these films (often Frank McHugh) as well as a likable opponent (Pat O'Brien) with whom he battles good-naturedly (rebellious upstart against staid professional).

In all of these films Cagney is a "common man" with a job -- sailor, prize fighter, truck driver, et al. He is a man completely involved with his work and all conflicts center around his occupation.

Action is the underlying theme, and spectacular chases and stunts are commonplace, along with the accompanying heroics and romance. Little or no social comment is apparent and the plots are of a non-serious and melodramatic nature.

Service-action-vocation films treat the language and implements and equipment of the work involved -- whether it be "flight lingo" or navy talk, control room radios or communication in battle-ship gun rooms. The characters cannot be separated from their work and have no life apart from it. Cagney did not play a man in search of himself or a man involved in internal meditation of problems -- he was a taxi driver with taxi problems or a sailor with navy problems.

It is difficult to judge the first of this series, "The Crowd
Roars" (1932), in that only an edited television version is in existence. It is evident, however, that it may be classed as one of
Cagney's lesser portrayals. At the time of its release a critic
called it "Mr. Cagney's least important production, not through
his fault, but because the story, in which the director, Howard
Hawks, had a hand, is so childishly transparent."[1]

"The Crowd Roars" is typical in that it capitalizes on the
car racing sequences which are in part interesting but extremely
repetitious. Cagney goes through the old routine of being the bad
brother (drinking, women), mistreating his faithful mistress and
allowing his self-indulgence and conceit to cause the death of his
best friend. (Frank McHugh dies in this film for Cagney's faults,
the same fate relegated to this unfortunate "best friend" in
"Ceiling Zero"). Turned on by his friends and fellow drivers for
this (as he was by companions in "The Fighting 69th"), Cagney
must pay for his sins through self-banishment. All too conveniently
he wrests himself from his hobo's alcoholic stupor in time to drive
for his noble younger brother in an important race and thus redeem
himself. This pat and predictable melodramatic plot unfolds quickly

---

[1] The New York Times, April 3, 1932, p. 4.

and without time for motivation, character development or even
explanation. The winning of the race is capped with a slapstick
comedic ending in which the injured Cagney races his ambulance
against another carrying other racetrack victims in a mad chase
to the hospital. This ending seems tacked on and is out of context
when viewed as the ending of a largely medodramatic, even tragic
film.

Cagney's role in "The Crowd Roars" is a cheap imitation
of several of his other portrayals constructed on some of the
basic elements of the "Public Enemy" character. The plot being
as sketchy and hastily drawn as it is, these elements are touched
upon quickly as if that were enough to draw a meaningful characterization: Cagney brutally discards his girl friend; Cagney's maniacal
laugh echoes during the harrowing race; Cagney's flippant attitude
prevails in the face of advice from his girl friend and family.

In "Winner Take All" (1932) identification of Cagney's
"working man" character is particularly easy. Jimmy Kane, the
fighter proudly sports a scrambled ear and mashed nose.

Out of his element, Kane is ill at ease. His life has been
divided between fighting and making the rounds of New York nightclubs.
He is completely at a loss in the sleepy health resort where he has
been sent after a collapse in the ring. The fresh air and scenery of

New Mexico make no impression on Kane. He asks in disgust,
"What do you do from gettin' daffy around here?" Kane meets the
predictable "good girl" at the resort -- a deserving young widow
with an asthmatic little boy.

Fresh from his rest cure, Kane returns to New York and a
stunning victory in his first bout. After the fight, the exuberant
Kane is told in his dressing room that some people want to meet
him. Naturally this appeals to his ego. A stylishly dressed young
woman steps forward to be introduced to Kane. He reaches out for
her hand, "Lay it in dere, baby". The "high society blonde" is
fascinated by Kane's sweaty body and cannot resist the temptation
to touch him with her fingertips. The little widow in New Mexico
is forgotten.

Paul Muni's Mexican-American Johnny Ramirez in
"Bordertown" first came to the attention of his society girl when
he started a brawl in a court of law which led to his disbarment.
Neither Ramirez nor Kane realize that their upper class women
are fascinated by the "animal" they have found in a world
populated by the Warner Brothers issue of the foppish upper class
male. These "society" girls are not looking for lasting relationships with Ramirez or Kane, rather excitement.

We find Kane totally out of his element with the girl and

her social set in a nightclub scene. All the girls are flitting
around the fighter; they ask if they may feel his muscles, etc.
One girl inquires seriously as to what was his most difficult
fight. He replies with a leer, "With a bouncin' blonde in a taxi
over in Jersey". Everyone considers him a boor. He is kept
on in the group as long as he remains a novelty.

Cagney played the role of Jimmy Kane with realistic make-
up which gave him a smashed nose, bent lip and cauliflower ear.
Kane, ever the egotist, believes he can make himself acceptable
to the society girl if he has these marks of his profession removed.
After absenting himself for a time he returns and presents himself
at the society girl's apartment and asks, "How do yah like dah
landscape?"

She is less than enthusiastic about his reconstruction and
confides in a friend:

> "Oh, the fool took me seriously -- went
> and had his face done over -- he's lost the
> things that made him colorful and different...
> He looks ordinary now -- like any other man --
> and one thing I can't stand is bad grammar
> spoken through a perfect Grecian nose."

Eager to protect his new face, Kane changes from his wide
open slugging tactics to a "bicycling" technique in the ring. The
crowds boo the change and the society girl loses interest in him
even more rapidly. The newspapers accuse him of having become

a society lap dog.

Cagney always relied on movement for his effectiveness.
Of all the films made by Cagney between 1930 and 1940, "Winner
Take All" provides the widest range for his extraordinary
physical dexterity. First, of course, there are numerous fight
scenes where Cagney used a "slugging" style, then the defensive
bicycling. Between rounds in the final climactic fight he
bounces up and down like a burly child, waiting for the bell
which will free him again for combat. The bicycle tactic was
not unlike a dance.

Not only did "Winner Take All" provide the opportunity
for Cagney to display his spectacular physical dexterity but
also his breathy staccato delivery. Before meeting an opponent,
Kane tells the fighter's manager, "Have a pick and shovel handy
tuh pick dat mug's skull outta dah rosin". His proposal to
his true love is equally straightforward as he boards the train
bound to New York, leaving New Mexico. He leaves the girl
with the parting remark:

> "Listen -- you know I'm goin' to
> send for you in a couple of months.
> We'll have dough for a swell
> honeymoon. We'll give that Niagara
> Falls a good kickin' around."

The film ends with Kane and the widow reunited. Kane
has just won the lightweight championship. His nose smashed
anew he kisses his girl gingerly, "Look out for the schnozzle,
it's full of firecrackers."

If "Winner Take All" had not been one of many similar
Cagney films of the early 1930's it would have seemed a more
important entry in film history. It was preceded, however, by
"The Public Enemy", "Smart Money", "Taxi" and "The Crowd
Roars", and so seemed to be just another vehicle for a well known
personality. By the release of "Winner Take All" reviewers had
already begun to classify Cagney's films by the central character's
occupation. Here he was a fighter; in the past, a gangster, gambler,
taxicab driver, et al. Future films would similarly be providing
"employment" for the essential Cagney character.

"Here Comes The Navy" (1934) is a film tailored for
Cagney with an eye on the Legion of Decency and the Production
Code. Cagney had gained great popularity not only for his acting
style but also for the rough and tumble films he had appeared in.
As The Literary Digest put it, "He has a generally subversive way
of mocking the sentimental weaknesses of mankind with uninhibited
honesty."[1]

"Here Comes The Navy", was the first in a chain of Cagney-
O'Brien films with similar themes. All of them were service or

---

[1]"Here Comes The Navy", The Literary Digest, August 4,
1934, p. 26.

occupation oriented and featured conflicts between the bumptious
newcomer Cagney and the dedicated "old pro" O'Brien.

The film is a product of a rather bland era of movie making --
a result in part of the stepped up pressures of various "purity"
leagues. The fighting Cagney is transposed out of a criminal or
con man context to the innocuous personal conflicts of a comic
situation with a dash of patriotism thrown in for good measure.
Rather than hurting society, Cagney's belligerence brings harm
only to himself (scorn of his fellows, losing the girl, etc.).

Cagney is allowed rage, some chicanery and many fist
fights -- but nothing more deadly. Furthermore, this series in-
vests him with a comical sidekick (often Frank McHugh) and involves him in large scope heroics (saving burning ammunition
magazines, rescuing O'Brien from dirigible ropes, and, in other
films of this genre, sacrificing himself to test the defrosting device
in "Ceiling Zero", taking the fighter's place in the ring in "The Irish
In Us", bringing in the burning plane in "Devil Dogs of the Air",
leading the final charge in "The Fighting 69th").

"Here Comes The Navy" won Warner Brothers some ridicule
from certain critics for its "glorification of preparedness". This
cry was echoed in many criticisms of Warner films of the period
such as "Devil Dogs of the Air" (1935) and particularly "Confessions
of a Nazi Spy" (1939). These films were often dedicated to the service

they honored. Glowing pictures of dedication to the armed forces were drawn. Service maneuvers and war games were shown to be great adventures. (In "Here Comes The Navy", stock footage of large scale war games was used for the first time in films.)

"Here Comes The Navy" and the others of its ilk that followed suffered from several common weaknesses. Cagney and O'Brien's old boys school plot, rewritten for battleships or airplanes, grew all too recognizable. Cagney inevitably falls in love with his superior's haughty or unobtainable sister. The services were shown as overly benevolent and noble (they try to reform and "save" Cagney rather than punish him). The humor employed is exceedingly broad and often crude -- a prime example of this is the ending of "Here Comes The Navy" in which Frank McHugh's screen mother sings "Oh, Promise Me" at the wedding of Cagney and O'Brien's sister. While valiantly holding in her new dentures (a running joke in the film), she sings her son's favorite song from the words tattooed on his bare chest and back.

Although these films were formulated to present Cagney in a totally acceptable situation the actor himself added something to the script that was not intrinsically there. Even when required to reform at the end by the Navy and the girl, Cagney plays the role with a sardonic, amused sort of mocking which suggests that the reformation is at best reasonably ironic. While on the surface the film reflects the reform wave, Cagney still maintains the maniacal laugh, the sneer that keeps intact the essential Cagney image -- untouched by censorship.

"The St. Louis Kid" (1934) a typical example of a minor action film with fleeting pretentions of social comment. First, the story is set in the context of its times. In this instance it is the battle being waged by farmers to stay alive during the depression. The issues of the contest between the farmers and dairy firms are described in some detail. The social context does not receive the emphasis found in Warner Brothers "Black Fury" (1935) or "Black Legion" (1937), however "The St. Louis Kid" was essentially a light film designed to provide action for the Cagney character.

The name "St. Louis Kid" had no particular significance other than suggesting a "locale". Warners used their backlot for St. Louis as in other films it was used for other cities. During these years Warners would "plug" a city or state -- "The Frisco Kid", "The Oklahoma Kid" -- or a branch of the armed forces -- "Here Comes The Navy", "Flirtation Walk" -- to create added interest in their films.

The film is wholly caught up with physical action. Something was happening every moment. There is no time or place for opulent sets or costumes.

"The St. Louis Kid" offered many opportunities for Cagney
to present the bouncy, youthful, blue collar effervescence he had
been developing since "The Public Enemy". There is not a serious
moment for the Cagney character in the entire film. No matter the
predicament he is bouncing about like a boxer looking for an opening.
When he is threatened with the loss of his job, he gives in but exits
with the line "Some day, when the weather is nice and clear I'm
going to knock your nose right around to your ear".

During the great battle with the truck drivers led by Kennedy
(Cagney) against the goon squad in the employ of the companies we
see Cagney dancing around with his fists raised. He finds an opening and knocks one man after another cold with his head rather than
a fist. "Comical sidekick" Buck Willetts (Alan Jenkins) tries the
same attack only to knock himself out.

Kennedy and Willetts are blue collar in every detail. They
do physical labor, their dress is always workshirts and trousers.
Their idea of a good time is to go dancing, fight and drink.

"The St. Louis Kid", despite the background of the story is
in no sense a "socially conscious" Warner film such as "Black Fury"
or "The Life of Emile Zola". True enough, there is criticism of
the dairy companies for their treatment of farmers and considerable
exposition of the farmers' plight, but the overall thrust of the film
is blunted by a slapstick comedy laced into a clinche'-ridden plot.

"Ceiling Zero" (1936) was adapted from a play of the same name, by Commander Frank Wead, which enjoyed considerable success on the Broadway stage in 1935. As a film, "Ceiling Zero" was named one of the ten best pictures of 1936 in various publications. Appraising the film in modern terms, the enthusiastic reviews and favorable criticism the film received in 1936 come as something of a surprise. To an audience of today, "Ceiling Zero" presents a shopworm plot in a restricted setting. At the time, however, the film was hailed for its utilization of only one main set and two sub-sidiary sets. This limited setting supposedly proved that the script was so strong and exciting that it could survive complete intact transplantation from the stage to the screen.

The film's popularity can probably be attributed to the fact that a story of air heroism, even one confined to a field control room, was completely new and fresh to the 1935-1936 audiences. The "flight lingo" was strange to their ears. The equipment and airplanes had not been seen before. The tribulations of running mail flights out of Newark, New Jersey was something for young boys to dream about.

With the exception of some process shots of pilots at the stick and several miniaturized crashes, the major action takes place in and around the main office -- control room or in a nearby

Italian restaurant. The effect is very stagey and confining, especially in an action picture. By making an entrance, telephoning or radioing in, everyone in the cast is obliged to bring all of life's problems into this room. When Texas (Stu Erwin) is about to crash, most of the action is seen through the stage technique of watching the reactions of the gathered cast in the control room as they listen to the radio. When the pilot hits, a miniature crash scene is inserted. Back in the control room all gather at the windows to look off into the cyclorama and register horror as lights are flashed in their faces. They do not run to the field or ride out in the crash truck or go to the hospital with Texas. Even the wife conveniently comes to the control room at the right moment and is comforted there.

Publicity compared "Ceiling Zero" to other aviation films: "More exciting than "Wings"." "More colorful than "The Last Flight"," etc. Actually, this Howard Hawks air film comes closer to being categorized with other Cagney-O'Brien service-adventure films such as "Devil Dogs of the Air" or "Here Comes The Navy". The plot may be somewhat more sophisticated, but Cagney and O'Brien are playing familiar characterizations.

Pat O'Brien is soft-hearted and hard-shelled as usual. Hard-working, conscientious and no-nonsense, he provides the foil for devil-may-care James Cagney; impudent, rebellious, disdainful of authority. As Dizzy Davis, Cagney is attractive to all women (even nice girls, who are at first offended -- as in "The Irish In Us", "Devil Dogs of the Air", "Taxi", etc.). He is a reckless,crack flyer, arriving at the field upside down (in "Devil Dogs of the Air" he arrived at the field doing tricks). As in all other service-adventure pictures, Cagney immediately proves himself to be a cad, turning his friends and co-workers against him. In the end he performs the required act of heroism, vindicating himself and winning the affection of all. In "Here Comes The Navy" he saves Pat O'Brien, hanging from the rope of a flying dirigible. In "The Fighting 69th" he performs courageously in battle. In "Ceiling Zero" Cagney alienates his friends by feigning illness and causing the lovable Texas to take his run and ultimately lose his life. He casually wins over Tommy, the "good" girl, from her deserving fiance. Turned on by everyone, he absolves himself by heroically taking the mail run in bad weather and sacrifices his life to test the new de-icers under storm conditions while he is up. Cagney's physical characterization is similar to his former ones -- cocky, ready to fight, light on his feet, flirtatious, ribald where women are concerned. In this film Cagney also affects a small moustache as he did later in "Torrid Zone".

"Devil Dogs of the Air" (1935) carries on several familiar Warner Brothers themes and is noteworthy because of its repetitious quality. It is a patriotic film, glorifying a branch of the armed services (as did "Here Comes The Navy" and "Flirtation Walk").

As in "Here Comes The Navy" and "Ceiling Zero", Cagney plays a cocky, ready-for-a-fight extrovert, attractive to women and highly disrespectful of the service to which the clean living and serious O'Brien has dedicated his life.

The stories of all these "service" films are formula pieces with slight variations and Cagney and O'Brien, invariably Irishmen (Tommy O'Toole and Lieutenant Brannigan in "Devil Dogs of the Air"), recreate their specialized characterizations again and again -- Cagney, bouncing gleefully through the fast action of the scenes -- punching someone at a moment's notice; laughing in the face of authority and tradition represented by O'Brien; stopping at no trick or deception to win the girl whom he has fallen in love with at first sight. These films are not notable for their dialogue. This is Cagney amidst frantic action (disasters, fights, troop maneuvers, etc.) and thus many of the Cagney characteristics are lost or glossed over in the confusion and mass action. There is not so much time for his side long look, his maniacal laugh, his dancing movements on the balls of his feet, his taunting sense of only lightly restrained violence in scenes of conflict.

Perhaps more notable than the stories or sterotyped portrayals in these action films were the reaction of certain critics to
the basic purpose Warner Brothers had in making this genre. One
comment called "Devil Dogs of the Air" a film "loaded with pictorial
dynamite even if it is only an advertisement for the preparation of
boys".[1] Another article states, "It seems that the sternly militarist
Warner Brothers became so enamored of the two-fisted details of
life among the boys in khaki that they scorn to introduce anything so
effete as a story among all the glamorous recruiting paraphenalia
which Washington so thoughtfully places at their disposal".[2]

Warner Brothers was noted for its predilection for patriotic
themes and these service-action-vocation films run hand in hand
with less obvious pieces such as "The Life of Emile Zola" and
"Juarez" and later, the undisguised warnings of "Confessions of a
Nazi Spy".

"Frisco Kid" (1935) placed Cagney in San Francisco in the
1850's. In spite of this historical setting the Cagney character (the
pugnacious upstart, cocky, violent, attractive to women, given to
quick "short arm" punches) and the usual action-love story are

[1] The New York Times, Feb. 7, 1935, p. 23:2.
[2] The New York Times, Feb. 24, 1935, p. 5:1.

predicatable. A critic calls Cagney the "Al Capone of San Francisco's vice district"[1] and this is quite correct, for the gangster characters and gangland plot (taking over a gang leader's territory, organizing gambling and vice, etc.) are easily recognizable and publicized as such. Newspaper advertising in connection with the release of the film called attention to Cagney's gangster image: "...with a blast of dynamite he rocks the bloody cradle of modern gangdom...in this sensational screening of Vigilante Vengeance...(a picture of Cagney pointing in an "Uncle Sam wants you" pose). It's time to get these killers!...as prophetic as 'The Public Enemy'!"

"Frisco Kid" was not only an entry in the gangster genre but also followed two other contemporary trends: According to code suggestions the "hero" is reformed and comes to the side of law and order; and, secondly, it is set in the Barbary Coast in the 1850's.

Barbary Coast stories enjoyed some vogue in these years. Howard Hawks made "Barbary Coast" with Edward G. Robinson (1935) and the year before a Barbary Coast play, "Golden Eagle Guy", had a successful Broadway run.

"Barbary Coast" and "Frisco Kid" show a great similarity. Both of them begin at the water's edge -- the harbor is full of fog,

---

[1]The New York Times, Nov. 25, 1935, p. 22:1.

rowboats slip noiseless y on nefarious errands. Both of them have a great deal of action -- fights, shootings, gaming tables, loaded dice, "palaces of sin". Both show a crusading newspaperman murdered after daring an expose. Both of them show the newspaper plant being wrecked. Both bring in the vigilantes (large bearded men) to hang the leading villain and restore order.

Thornton Delehanty in the New York Post, suggested that the only difference in the two films was their treatment of theme: "Barbary Coast" was sentimental melodrama. Delehanty qualified this by stating, "In case the distinction isn't clear, let me say that "The Barbary Coast" was the superior by virtue of a definite and conscious romanticism which enabled the authors to leave their melodrama with humor".[1] The general agreement among critics was that Howard Hawks had done the better job with his "Barbary Coast". One critic went on to say that Cagney's curled and bleached hair for "Frisco Kid" became him "scarcely more than did the jackass mask" in "Midsummer Night's Dream".

Certain familiar themes are repeated in "Frisco Kid" which link it with other films under consideration: the Frisco Kid, like Little Caesar, Duke Mantee and Scarface, is a gangster type

---

[1] "The Barbary Coast", The Literary Digest, Dec. 7, 1935, p. 29.

who is on the verge of being outmoded in his society -- in this case
in the burgeoning city about to be civilized. As in "Bullets or
Ballots" and "Little Caesar" there is a linkage of politics and
business corruption. Cagney does anything to "get ahead" and climb
in power and position ("The only thing I'm guilty of is trying to get
ahead..."), especially to win the favor of a "higher class" woman
(a motivating force in "Bordertown", "Lady Killer", "Winner Take
All" and others).

"Frisco Kid" is greatly hampered in its development with
reversion to overly melodramatic and maudlin scenes. Cagney's
character becomes unbelievable when he begins to reform. This
is particularly true in such sequences as Cagney standing before
the angry mob about to burn the newspaper office and in best
declamatory style and oratorical gesture giving a speech on "There's
been enough killing..." the contrived ending in which Miss Lindsay
saves Cagney from being hanged with the other Coast criminals by
pleading for his life is weak. (Robinson being led off to be hung by
vigilantes in "Barbary Coast" seems a much more believable climax
to such a career.)

"The Irish In Us" (1935) is perhaps the weakest entry in the
Cagney-O'Brien action films. The familiar plot is once again
employed -- Cagney, the charming but ne're-do-well brother

competes with O'Brien, the solid citizen, for the favors of the girl.
Cagney wins the girl despite his faults and finally proves himself
to his family and friends in a dramatic and self-sacrificing interlude.

This theme was used with diminishing success in this series
of films. Critics and audiences were becoming tired of the
repetitious quality of the formula. These films always relied on the
excitement of the climatic scene in which Cagney proves himself to
his fellows. In "The Irish In Us" this high point takes place in the
boxing arena. Admittedly, this is the best sequence of the film but
far from believable. (Cagney, a trainer and manager, steps into
the ring in place of his indisposed boxer to face the champion, never
having boxed before.)

The fight scene was carefully planned and imaginatively shot.
Publicity centered on this scene: How Cagney did his own boxing,
construction of the set, how many days the scene took. It was
obviously hoped that the sequence would bolster and carry the entire
film. The rest of the script leans heavily on maudlin sentiment,
however, so that the ring scene is merely a reminder of a better
Cagney film, "Winner Take All". (Cagney was also a fighter in
"City For Conquest".)

As the title suggests the film deals with an Irish family
and as such comes off as a satire on Cagney-O'Brien films. Without

fail, Cagney and O'Brien sport Irish names in the service-action pieces. It would seem that "The Irish In Us" carries this aspect to the extreme and succeeds in making a joke of itself.

The Irish mother is a replica of the wise, self-sacrificing old world mother of other films such as "Scarface", "Kid Galahad" and "Bordertown". Except in this case, rather than being in the background, a symbol of the "old values", she is a major character or more precisely, caricature. Her brogue is extremely thick, her hovering maternalism and sage advice are obtrusive.

Cagney as the rebellious, yet-to-make good fight promoter, O'Brien as the steadfast Irish policeman, Frank McHugh as the dim-witted fireman brother are all in their predictable roles. The play on "Irishness" and the "humor" of casting the trio as brothers seem to have taken precedence over the plot which is a trite version of Cagney meets "nice" girl and, though a crude roughneck, wins her from respectable older brother O'Brien.

"The Oklahoma Kid" (1939) is one of the most unusual pairings of Cagney and Bogart. It is noteworthy mainly because of the choice of these two actors to portray Western gunmen. Certainly one of the most amusing lines of all time occurs when Bogart appears dressed completely in black from Stetson to jangling spurs and sneers in a lower Manhattan accent, "I'm Whip McCord from the Panhandle".

One has the feeling throughout the film that Cagney and Bogart have been transplanted from some New York alley into the Old West. Their dialogue is the same, their accents the same. They are 1930's gangsters thrust into the Oklahoma land rush to take advantage of a new setting (and perhaps a more palatable one to certain pressure groups) in which to have murders, gun fights and robberies. Publicity showed Cagney with guns drawn and the caption, "Outlaw...Killer".

"The Oklahoma Kid" was another Warner's bid at the burgeoning Western cycle -- "Stagecoach", "Union Pacific", "Dodge City", "The Return of the Cisco Kid" (even the Marx Brothers came up with "Go West".). Cagney plays the character with a light, tongue-in-cheek touch, as if not fully believing himself that he has forsaken shoulder holsters for six guns at the hip. The rest of the cast plays the piece with almost as straight a face, but lacks Cagney's jauntiness at a good joke. As it is the film rests precariously on the edge of satire.

"City For Conquest" (1940) is another Warner Brothers tale of New York. As Bosley Crowther wrote, "Sometimes we wonder whether it wasn't really the Warners who got New York from the Indians, so diligent and devoted have they been in feeling the great city's pulse, picturing its myriad facets and recording with deep compassion the passing life of its seething population".[1]

Warners used a newly popular device of the time to string this story together -- the "Our Town" type of narrator. Frank Craven was again recruited for this commentator's role, this time as a ragged bum popping up in alleys and on street corners and passing sage remarks about the developing plot. This seems to add a pronounced artificiality and staginess to what is essentially of plebian, "slice-of-life" nature -- a story of the slums told in tabloid terms. Another continuing device uses the "Symphony of a Great City" composed by Eddie Kenny, a struggling young musician of the slums. "A symphony of its seven millions with all the color of a hundred different races, and the harmony of a thousand discords like the dizzy mad whirl of an ambulance siren screaming across Forsythe and Delancy". His brother's composition spurs trucker Danny (James Cagney) to make more money for Eddie's training. Seeing no other route, Danny reluctantly becomes a fighter.

On the surface, it would seem that "City For Conquest" could be called a picture in the usual Cagney vein -- a spunky slum kid grows up to become a fighter to win his girl and help boost his talented kid brother out of their degrading environment.

---

[1]The New York Times, Sept. 28, 1940, p. 9:2.

Somewhere along the line, however, the essential Cagney was
softened and slowed in the part of Danny Kenny. He plays a young
man pushed into a conquest of New York not through ambition or
desire for personal advancement but because of the ambitions of
two people he loves -- his drive to get ahead is thus "second hand"
or reflected rather than originating in the Danny character. Those
making decisive moves are his girl friend, Peggy, who runs off with
a sharpie for a glittering life in show business, and his brother, who,
afire with creative zeal, composes a great "song of the city" in the
Kenny's humble flat on a broken down upright piano. Happy as a
modestly paid truck driver, Danny sees that a simple, steady life
will not win back Peggy, nor will it pay for the training and opportunities
a promising young composer deserves. Thus, a pushed and passive
Cagney reluctantly "conquers the city" by giving in and becoming
a fighter. This is in contrast with, say, the prize-fighter Cagney
portrayed in "Winner Take All". In the latter film, Jimmy Kane
also pursued the fight game to gain the woman he loved but he was
the decision maker, the prime motivator of his own actions; he
loved to fight and did it with zest and skill.

In "City For Conquest" the bounce and nerviness so
remarkably Cagney are muted by the overriding tones of maudlin
melodrama -- the sad and quiet scenes with his "fallen" girl whom

he still believes will come back to him when she has had her fill
of dancing; the scenes in which he admires but does not understand
his brother's musical genius; the overtones of sacrifice and disillusionment. These points combined with an overlong and ponderous
story deaden the Cagney characterization. As a wronged but trusting
boy friend; as a sacrificing, father-like older brother; as a reluctant and peaceable fighter; as a pitiful blind news vendor making
the best of things, Cagney does not live up to his potentialities as
a dynamic, pivotal character. This Cagney is older, slower,
resigned, acted upon. The vicious action achieved in his well-
photographed and highly authentic fight scene is not enough to
balance the rest of the film which trails off from this high point
into a tedious compendium of tears, recriminations, disillusionment and failure through which stumbles a scarred and blinded
Cagney, tapping his cane, smiling wanly and twitching his ruined
eyes in the offending light while Donald Crisp stands tsk-tsking in
the wings to see his fine young fighter get such a raw deal.

As Googi, Elia Kazan put in an inspired performance.
Bosley Crowther called him "enough to scare Eddie Robinson".[1]
In passing one wonders if this new Warners bad man had happened
earlier in the prime of the gangster film he might well have

---

[1]The New York Times, Sept. 28, 1940, p. 9:2.

developed in this vein along with Cagney and Robinson.

"The Fighting 69th" (1940) follows in Warners' tradition
of taking its action films from real events. In this case the film
cannot be put in the same category with such historical biographies
as "The Story of Louis Pasteur", "The Life of Emile Zola", "Juarez",
"Dr. Ehrlich's Magic Bullet", or "A Dispatch From Reuter's".

The film treats a famous New York regiment, the 69th
(The Fighting Irish), during the time they were incorporated into
the Rainbow Division, summoned for training at Camp Mills,
Long Island and sent to France in November, 1917. Camp Mills
was reconstructed at West Providence ranch across from the
Burbank Studio. Three hundred actors were involved and four
technical advisors: Captain John T. Prout, a commander of the
69th; George Boothby, New York newspaperman who covered the
69th in France; Mark White, a soldier from the ranks of the 69th
to add the "doughboy's slant"; and Father John Devlin to advise
O'Brien in the Father Dully role. This constituted more technical
advisors than had ever been used on a Warner Brothers production
to date.

This true life story, combined with the regiment's wide
renown and well-known officers, would seem to mark it as an
excellent choice for a semi-documentary action film. Though

Joyce Kilmer and others are included prominently in the screenplay, the story revolves around the personal problems of a fictious
soldier, Jerry Plunkett. The New York Times suggested that the
film should be called "Personal History of Private Plunkett and
How He Became A Hero", and found the emphasis on the Cagney
character "embarrassingly unconvincing".[1]

"The Fighting 69th" is a factually based film upon which
has been grafted the traditional Cagney-O'Brien service-action film
characterizations. In "The Fighting 69th" their relationship is more
restrained, much less humorous -- especially because of O'Brien's
role as Father Duffy, a part which required dignity and fidelity
to the actions of a well-known and well-liked chaplain. Cagney,
however, as Plunkett is a carbon copy of Chesty of "Here Comes
The Navy", and his upstart successors who balked at authority in
"Devil Dogs of the Air", "Ceiling Zero", etc.

The Cagney-O'Brien banter is still there -- with O'Brien
less volatile, more understanding. Plunkett says, "Hi, they
call me Smilin' Jerry. Who are you?" Father Duffy answers
(not wearing his insignia) "Oh, they call me Fiery Frank".

As in the former service-action films his lack of

---

[1]The New York Times, Jan. 27, 1940, p. 9:2.

discipline brings injury or death to Cagney's friends. "The
Fighting 69th" treats this more seriously than the other films,
however. Cagney turns into a coward, not merely a rebel, and
causes the death of the famous and beloved Joyce Kilmer as well
as that of his sergeant's brother.

As in the other films, O'Brien's dedication and honor bring
Cagney back into the fold. The scene of Father Duffy kneeling in
the Lord's Prayer and joined by Plunkett is far more effective and
meaningful than any of Cagney's other "redemptions". In "The
Fighting 69th" Cagney also "pays" for his cowardice and at the
same time finds his reward -- in this case the satisfaction of
valiant behavior rather than the girl -- by sacrificing his life
in a charge on the enemy.

A great deal of publicity was attendant upon the film.
(Some called it patriotic, others militaristic; it was banned in
Australia in March of 1940 because of the war conditions.)
Councilman Sharkey of New York suggested January 24th as 69th
Day but was opposed by Councilman Baldwin, who noted that this
was the day the Warner Brothers film was set to open and
labeled the measure a "publicity trap", especially in view of the
previous anti-uniform bill before the council that elicited publicity
during the opening of "Confessions of a Nazi Spy".

"The Fighting 69th" is also a preparedness film and mirrors Warners' policy of growing concern with the world situation ("Confessions of a Nazi Spy" was issued the same year). The first film does not have the impact nor the "shock value" of the second -- first of all because it was historical, the other contemporary; and secondly because of the predictable Cagney characterization (even that of O'Brien closely resembles the priest of "Angels With Dirty Faces" more than all new and factual representation of Father Duffy's personality). "The Fighting 69th" loses its sense of real happenings, its documentary quality and becomes easily categorized as the entry in the Cagney-O'Brien service-action series (albeit the most "prestigious" and ambitious one).

"Torrid Zone" (1940) paired Cagney and O'Brien for the last time. Their traditional banter and rivalry is in evidence following the theme of their films over the preceding six years. Once again O'Brien is in a position of authority (top boss of a U.S. fruit company) and Cagney is his upstart subordinate. Compared with the earlier teamings, however, Cagney seems much more mature, less endearing and boyish and more O'Brien's contemporary -- although O'Brien says, "I've treated you like a son..." (Cagney's lessened exuberance and youthfulness is also notable in "City for Conquest" made the same year).

By this time not only had Cagney outgrown his pugnacious "tough kid" but the Cagney-O'Brien conflict, replete with yelling and wisecracks, had grown stale. The whole picture tries for a more mature treatment of the usual theme, perhaps to accomodate Cagney's development -- Ann Sheridan, a sultry girl with a "past", is the love interest rather than the traditional "good" girl of such films as "Here Comes The Navy", "The Irish In Us", or "Devil Dogs of the Air". The repartee is also much stronger in its sexual implications as Sheridan says, "I'm used to sleeping outdoors...I used to be a Girl Scout", causing Bosley Crowther to note that the Hays Office must have stopped its eyes and ears.

The Cagney-O'Brien conflict is further dampened by the introduction of comic soldiers and bandits, which make "Torrid Zone" a candidate for the old Ziegfield school of banana country musical comedies of which "Rio Rita" was the prize example.

>   F. Humphrey Bogart: The One-Dimensional Bad Man
>   And The Second Banana Gunsel
>
>   "Dead End" 1937, "San Quentin" 1937, Racket Busters,
>   1938, "You Can't Get Away With Murder", 1939

The films of Humphrey Bogart during the 1930-1940 decade can be divided roughly into two categories. The first is what is generally considered his most "typical" role -- the unrepentant, hard-bitten criminal. The powerful and well-defined Duke Mantee of "The Petrified Forest" degenerates to a one dimensional "bad man" in such films as "King of The Underworld" (1939) and "Racket Busters" (1938).

Bogart also often played a "second banana" criminal to major criminals Cagney and Robinson in such films as: "Bullets or Ballots" (1936), "Kid Galahad" (1937), "The Amazing Dr. Clitterhouse" (1938), "Angels With Dirty Faces" (1938) "The Roaring Twenties" (1939), and "Brother Orchid" (1940). The Bogart gangster, however, refined in these productions, was distilled to a few gestures and cliche situations and used time and again in a plethora of Warner program pictures. These characterizations are noteworthy becuase of their remarkable consistency and repetition.

"Dead End", Goldwyn Studios (1937), was a film version of the Broadway play and as such suffered somewhat from the effects of extensive consoring to suit the material for the screen. This affected the role of "Baby Face" Martin which Bogart played.

Essentially, the tough gangster part was kept intact, however, and is a classic Bogart portrayal -- he lounges about the waterfront tenement district of his youth, the bad boy grown up into the gunman. Bogart's gangster is thoroughly bad -- a killer, a

despoiler of youth. He sneers and smokes. He dresses in sharp,
flashy clothes. He brazenly shows his disregard for the law by
coming back to his old neighborhood when he is wanted throughout
the country. The human touch in this cold-blooded killer is the fact
that he has risked this journey in order to visit his aged mother and
his boyhood sweetheart. His mother looks upon him with disgust and,
although this is softened from her reaction in the play, he shows his
desperate character by remarking to her, "I've killed men for
looking at me like that".

The impact of his meeting with his old girl loses much of
its strength in the film version. In the play his girl, now a prostitute,
is ravaged by syphilis. In the film this is only lightly and decorously
touched upon and the horror of Martin's wrecked dreams are not fully
exploited. "Why didn't you starve?" he says to her. "Why didn't
you?" is her reply.

The film version is further idealized by making the hero
(an idealistic architect turned house painter) a strong, whole young
man who kills Baby Face in the end rather than the cripple of the play
who calls in the G-men to do the job.

"Dead End" is important in the development of the "gangster"
genre. It is similar in many instances to other vehicles which initiated
"gangster" trends and also contains numerous elements which were to
effect succeeding "gangster" films.

Like Bogart's original and classic portrayal of Duke Mantee
in "The Petrified Forest", the role of Baby Face Martin comes
from a stage play -- in literary works of this period the American
desperado was the symbol of corruption in the system. As in "The
Petrified Forest", Bogart finds himself opposing an idealistic hero,
a thinker, a dreamer, as well as a strong-willed young woman
(Gabrielle in "The Petrified Forest", Drina in "Dead End") who is
willing to go to great lengths to change her presently unacceptable
mode of life.

Bogart's Baby Face Martin is so typical and standard in
his actions that comparison with other film gangsters is unnecessary --
the common elements are present in scores of films. "Dead End",
however, presaged the development of a new "tough group" --
the "Dead End Kids". These boys, from the original stage play,
were brought to Hollywood for the film version and went on to make
numerous other pictures. (It is interesting to note that only Huntz
Hall actually came from lower Manhattan where his father was a
tinsmith.) The Dead End Kids' delivery and the frightening reality
of their street talk and violent natures was new to audiences and
quite provocative.

The development of the Dead End Kids parallels the
development and degeneration of the gangster film groups in many

ways. Playing essentially the same roles, the Dead End Kids made
several other "crime" pictures for Warner Brothers (e.g. "Crime
School" 1938). Their talents were never developed further, however, and their portrayals were often hurried copies of their original
outstanding roles. Eventually, the bitterness and social comment was
lost and only the gutter humor (also deprived of its sting) was left.
With new "leaders" graduating upward from within their ranks
(Billy Halop, Bobby Jordon, Leo Gorcey), the Dead End Kids became
the stars of B pictures and cheap comedies as the Bowery Boys on into
the early fifties. (It is interesting to note that at the time of their
original success several copy groups emerged in their mold such as
the Gas House Gang.)

A theme of "Dead End" -- the brave sister struggling to
keep her younger brother out of trouble while providing for the
family -- is found in many similar films of the period. In "You
Can't Get Away With Murder" (1939), Billy Halop is again the wayward brother as his sister fights to keep him out of the clutches of
gunman Bogart and set him on a good life. In "Crime School" (1938),
gang leader Halop once again grieves his worthy sister by going
wrong in the face of her efforts to support him.

Like many Warner Brothers films (e.g. "City For Conquest",
1940), "Dead End" is a story of New York, and a social comment on

conditions there. It is noteworthy that Goldwyn took two of the Warner Brothers players to fill the roles in "Dead End" -- tried and true gunman Bogart and Allen Jenkins in his traditional role as the gangster's sidekick.

"San Quentin" (1937) is a usual entry in the long line of Warner prison pictures -- the prison corridors being a permanent set on the lot. This tried and true formula turned out many success-ful, if minor, films.

The prison film casts Bogart and O'Brien in stereotyped roles with which audiences had long before learned to identify them -- Bogart as the criminal beyond redemption, given on one hand to viciousness and on the other to fear, reflected in his drawn face, twitching mouth and darting eyes; O'Brien as the "All-American cop", dedicated, loyal and true, wise and understanding, yet quick with a yelled command to correct a situation. Although Captain O'Brien meets opposition in prisoner Bogart, whom he is trying to rehabilitate, there is none of the personal exchange that marked similar Cagney-O'Brien relationships. Bogart is unapproachable, cold, unsympathetic.

"San Quentin" (with a few ideas from Warners' "Mayor of Hell", 1933) was remade as "Crime School" (1938) with Bogart oddly recast in the second piece as the warden. Neither film rose to the promised publicity of "showing the problems of the men (or boys) in our prisons". In each case the possible social commentary was muffled by a trite love story between the warden and the inmate's sister and a melodramatic ending: Bogart beating the corrupt assistant warden in "Crime School"; Bogart crawling back to die at the prison gates in "San Quentin" in a last gesture of humanity to save the warden's reputation.

Certain scenes for "San Quentin" were shot at the actual prison. Governor Frank Merriam threatened an investigation of these practices after being informed that a near riot took place when the cameras were trained on the inmates. Warners replied that their camera crew, headed by Lloyd Bacon, took only long shots which revealed no faces and had entered with the permission of the prison board which, in turn, censored the footage.

"Racket Busters" (1938) is a treatment of the Thomas E. Dewey investigations into racketeering in New York. At the time these proceedings were headline news and figured prominently as story material for several films. Released simultaneously with Warners' "Racket Busters" was a similar film, "Smashing the Rackets" (RKO-Radio). The latter piece featured Chester Morris as the crusading young district attorney and was based on a series of Saturday Evening Post articles by Forrest Davis. RKO's Dewey tackled the white slave trade by rounding up a gang of streetwalkers and using their testimony to jail a racketeer. The film disintegrated into a confusing melodramatic ending and District Attorney Dewey threatened to sue the producers if his name was connected with the enterprise.

"Marked Woman" made by Warners in 1937 dealt with much of the same story -- from the girl's point of view -- with Bogart in the dull and unrewarding role of the district attorney, playing second fiddle to Bette Davis as the beleagured "hostess".

"Racket Busters" takes a less spicy avenue and fights the rackets in the fields of food and trucking. Warners claimed authenticity by drawing its script from actual court records and testimony. Critic Bosley Crowther noted this documentation and marked the film as "instructive and compelling".[1] Certain critics also conceded that Warners was one up in the "Dewey Sweepstakes" in that Walter Abel looked more like the real Dewey than anybody else's.

It is interesting to note that Warners' Dewey had to settle for fourth billing behind Bogart, the star of the film and the racket boss whom the district attorney was battling. In fact, the film centers around Bogart's gangster character and the crime fighter is largely

---

[1]The New York Times, August 11, 1938, p. 13:1.

ineffectual -- his only weapon is to ask honest truckmen not to join the dishonest union; those who oblige him are intimidated, thrashed and pushed in front of subway trains. In sheer desperation, two foolhardy young truckers take the matter into their own hands and sort out the mess for personal reasons. This is still glorifying the criminal in the name of law and order and indulging gunfights and killings with the justification that the criminal somehow meets retribution in the end. Bogart plays his well-defined and typical gangster, unrepentant, hard-bitten, lacking all compassion or concern for human life. (It was reported that District Attorney Dewey, busy preparing his case against Tammany District Leader Jimmy Hines attended neither production.)

"You Can't Get Away With Murder" (1939) might be termed a retread of "Dead End". Although based on the play "Chalked Out", the similarities are undeniable -- even to the use of the same actors in nearly identical roles. Billy Halop plays the wayward slum youth in both films, Humphrey Bogart the hardened, all-bad public enemy who instructs the eager youth in the ways of crime.

In both films the boy has a self-sacrificing older sister who has raised her brother and is valiantly trying to find a way out of the slums so the youth may have a decent life. In scenes very similar to those between Sylvia Sidney and Billy Halop, Gale Page remonstrates

with Halop for being out all night, running with bad people, etc.,
and in turn holds and comforts him when he becomes involved in a
crime.

"You Can't Get Away With Murder" is a "B" picture.
Bogart turns in his usual role of a thoroughly bad character --
beyond redemption without morals or remorse. He is steely-eyed
and hissing, with fear darting intermittently across his drawn face.
He uses an innocent boy as his accomplice and the impressionable
lad is soon willing to pin the wrap on his unsuspecting and upright
brother-in-law. Bogart's character has no spark of humanity, no
feeling of responsibility for his action (this spark of humanity was
what made the hardened criminal Duke Mantee a believable and
compelling character whereas Frank Wilson is stereotyped and
shallow).

Bosley Crowther noted that this film, yet another entry in
Warners' prison pictures, proved at least that the producers could
"get away with murder" and that Bogart must be signed to a five-
year "sentence" rather than a five-year contract.[1] "You Can't
Get Away With Murder" is another in line with get-the-Governor-
on-the-wire prison films with the notable change being that prospective
public enemy number one, Billy Halop had now graduated to a man's

---

[1]The New York Times, March 25, 1939, p. 19.

estate, being sent to the penitentiary instead of reform school. Crowther pointed out that Halop had been reclaimed for society so often he was beginning to consider him a sociological pushover.

CHAPTER IV

VARIATION AND DECAY OF THE GANGSTER FILM:

WHY IT CAME ABOUT

A. Contributing Factors: The Copies,

The Formula and The Code

The gangster genre owes its decay in part to the amazing
durability and excellence of the two archetypical films, "Little Caesar"
and "The Public Enemy". A motion picture will usually attract the greatest
portion of its audience to the theaters during the first six months of
its release. A short life in the theaters was particularly true prior
to the introduction of television when the American feature film industry
produced approximately five hundred features per year in a system
designed to give theaters a weekly change of program. (In recent
years the industry has devoted a considerable portion of its resources
to the production of spectacular films designed to play at a limited
number of theaters in a given area for extended periods.)

"Little Caesar" and "The Public Enemy" proved to be not only
the archetypes in terms of the development of the gangster film genre
but also to be enormously popular with audiences in theaters for over
twenty years. Warner Brothers rereleased the two gangster classics
repeatedly. Eventually, they were teamed. Each film carried a
foreword which made reference to the other, pointing out how the two
films explored a national problem rather than glorifying the gangster.

Today the surviving 35 mm prints at the Warner Brothers Studio are from the 1949 reissue.

(The Warner Brothers pre-1948 films were sold to an organization headed by Eliot Hyman in 1956. Hyman in turn licensed these films to television. Hyman's Seven Arts Productions bought all Warner assets in 1966. The production-distribution company is now known as Warner Brothers-Seven Arts. The films under study passed from Hyman's control to United Artists Television. No new 35 mm prints have been made for many years. 16 mm prints for television were made in the 1950's.)

No other films of the genre received comparable audience support. Both in critical terms and in relation to public acceptance, "Little Caesar and "The Public Enemy" stand as archetypes for the gangster film genre. Because of the continuing presence of the archetypical gangster films over two decades, succeeding films could not help but stand as anecdotes in relation to them. Perhaps the continuing presence in the theaters of these films inhibited film makers of the 1930's and 1940's. Little more than copies of the archetypical forms or the archetypical characters were attempted.

"Scarface", an admitted copy, was the best. In terms of character and attempt to execute an episodic plot, the film mirrored the form of "Little Caesar". Its brilliance lies in the production, i.e. the tommy-gunning of cue balls, a murder synchronized with the falling of a final bowling pin. "The Roaring Twenties" (1939) emulated the broadguaged episodic form of the archetypical films, even borrowing a March of Time-type narrator, but failed to revitalize the genre. Usually, however, later films in the genre were not ambitious in concept; they were shorthand copies, relying on the characters established in the archetypical films.

For example, "Little Giant" (1933) proceded on the assumption that the audience knew the Edward G. Robinson-Little Caesar character. "Little Giant" was simply a comedic situation for the already established character. There was no attempt to show origins or motivation. "Kid Galahad" (1937) was another Edward G. Robinson-Little Caesar anecdotal film. The Cagney films succeeding "The Public Enemy" were also anecdotal in quality, trading on the character established in the archetypical film. These films made little attempt to show motivational development of the central character or the tenor of the times. It was assumed everyone knew the "tough little nut" Cagney created in "The Public Enemy" and it was now merely necessary to provide this character with a pretext for action.

Linked to the importance of anecdotal copies in the decline of the genre is the accompanying insistence on what might be called "formula gangster plots". These plots and the familiar characters who came as part of the package, were imposed upon the genre in film after film. There were several reasons for relegating gangster films to the mediocre morass of backlot, two week wonders. First of all, the films fit easily into program picture requirements -- no location work or outdoor scenes were necessary that could not be covered by standing backlot city streets and perhaps a few country roads in the San Fernando Valley. No costuming or special effects were called for. Furthermore, the action of the plot (gun fights, brawls, bombings) carried an anemic story line without reliance on dramatic invention or meaningful dialogue.

The formula had a built-in antagonist-protagonist situation. It was the crooks against society, or good against evil or just cops and robbers. The de rigueur confrontations of traditional motion picture stories were easily obtained: Gang chief versus newspaperman; gang chief versus crusading priest, et al. The common point comes, when, in the last reel, the major evildoer inevitably meets death.

The fact that Robinson, Cagney or Bogart must pay for his transgressions is one of the formula restrictions which hindered the dramatic growth of the genre. This factor in the decay of gangster films is directly related to the fact that the major criminal character in the majority of the films is the most interesting character; he is the "hero" despite all the mouthed protests of compensatory forewords. This central character's vitality is based on his blatant anti-social behavior. The narrative flow of the film follows his commission of

unlawful acts. Although violent death would seem to be the ultimate
fate of most men in the hazardous profession of crime, to have a neat
and proper retribution at the end of every film saddles the plot
development. No individual's story can be told if he must be fitted
into this pattern.

The number one cause of death in the gangster film is a hail
of bullets: Robinson in "Little Caesar", "Bullets or Ballots", "Kid
Galahad"; Cagney in "The Public Enemy", "He Was Her Man", "The
Roaring Twenties"; Bogart (who suffered the most consistent fatalities)
"The Petrified Forest", "Dead End", "San Quentin", "King of the
Underworld", "You Can't Get Away With Murder", "Bullets or Ballots",
"Kid Galahad", "The Roaring Twenties", and "Brother Orchid". As a
nonviolent alternative, criminals are sometimes allowed to pay by
being dragged off snarling to await their punishments at the hands of
the law: Robinson in "Smart Money", Cagney in "Sinner's Holiday" and
"Blonde Crazy", Bogart in "Racket Busters". This less gory ending,
however, was not widely used.

Although it is a common misconception that many of the
gangster films ended with a "walk down the last mile", few state
executions were performed. Robinson is electrocuted in "Two Seconds",
a melodrama of 1932. Cagney screams all the way to the "chair" in
"Angels With Dirty Faces". It would seem that justice is fulfilled most

often by the self-appointed executioners of the back alleys. Variations in gunshot deaths do occur, but these are infrequent and most often are found in films outside the gangster genre but loosely related to it through the Robinson, Cagney or Bogart characterization: Robinson is killed by sharks in "Tiger Shark" and hanged by vigilantes in "Barbary Coast"; in "I Loved A Woman" he is relegated to the living death of a madman tormented by his misdeeds. Cagney, as a repentant wrongdoer, sometimes saved society the trouble and takes upon himself the task of chastisement by crashing his plane in "Ceiling Zero" or falling on a German hand grenade in "The Fighting 69th". Gang leader Robinson atoned for his sins by smilingly choosing the monastic life in "Brother Orchid". Bogart seldom escaped the more common forms of violent death, however, he went peacefully in "The Amazing Dr. Clitterhouse" after unwittingly accepting a vial of poison from Robinson.

The gangster formula was not applied merely to the obligatory death scene. Aside from the obvious repetition of the archetypical Robinson, Cagney and Bogart characters is the repetition of story elements and in some cases entire scripts.

"San Quentin" (with elements of "Mayor of Hell") survived intact to become "Crime School". (The Warner newspaper film "Five Star Final (1931) with Robinson was remade with Bogart in 1936 under the title "Two Against the World"). Bogart, the recalcitrant convict of "San Quentin", graduated to Commissioner of Correction in "Crime

School". The Dead End Kids were incarcerated in "Crime School" to

replace the inmates of the earlier "San Quentin". "Dr. Socrates"

became "King of the Underworld", the only change of the plot being

the substitution of Kay Francis in Paul Muni's role of unwilling physician

to the mob.

It is interesting to note that Bogart as gang chief in "King of the

Underworld" was shot to death on the same stair case set where his

predecessor Barton MacLane had tumbled to his death in "Dr. Socrates".

Warner Brothers standing backlot New York street set appears, with a

few additions, in virtually every gangster film of the period.

Certain character traits and important motivations essential

to the development of the archetypical gangster characters became

familiar formula elements. After Little Caesar and Scarface celebrated

their ascension to power by the acquisition of flashy clothes, this

symbolic act became a traditional rite. Even the Dead End Kids under

the leadership of Bogart or Cagney could be expected to turn up in

fedoras and three piece suits the day after they "knocked off" their first

pawn shop ("Crime School", "You Can't Get Away With Murder").

In the tradition of Scarface's beloved Cesca and Little Caesar's big

brother love of Joe Massara, gangsters throughout the era doted on

their chosen "good" counterparts -- Robinson's convent raised little

sister in "Kid Galahad"; Cagney's love of sweet and unattainable Priscilla

Lane in the "Roaring Twenties", et al. Coupled with the gangster's secret love of purity, an aging and devoted mother often waited in her kitchen, doling out advice and love to her erring son. The cause of good was also carried on among the younger lawbreakers in the form of stereotyped older sister (delineated most effectively in the character of Drina in "Dead End"). This sister, although attractive, passed up marriage and happiness to work in a backbreaking job in order to someday move her delinquent teenage brother out of the unhealthy environment of the slums ("Crime School", "You Can't Get Away With Murder").

The most important aspect of the sister-mother-best friend involvement was that it came to provide a convenient avenue toward the death of the gangster. Normally clever, unafraid, and consistenly able to outwit rival gangsters and police, his love of the unattainable and/or his possessiveness prove to be his "fatal flaw". Without believable motivation and often with a noble intent foreign to his character, the "fatal flaw" causes the steel-nerved gangster to commit an unreasonably foolish act in the next to the last reel of the film. This act is his death knell. He lies bleeding in the gutter. Society is preserved. For ninety percent of the film, crime may have paid, but the last thing the audience sees is the death grimace on the face of Robinson, Cagney or Bogart.

Tightening censorship contributed to lowering the quality of the products of the gangster genre. Since the late 1940's a succession of court decisions have struck down the power of city and state censor boards. More important, perhaps, are our society's changing mores. Together, these two factors have given motion pictures increasing freedom to portray sex and violence in the 1960's. There has also been, of course, a tendency for films to deal more openly with social problems in recent years. The opposite situation prevailed in the early 1930's. The American motion picture industry found itself subject to increasing pressure to curb sex and violence. The power of this censorship is epitomized by the film industry's production code of 1934 and the establishment in that same year of the Legion of Decency.

The gangster genre was a particular target of 1930's film censorship. As noted, gangster films such as "Little Caesar", "The Public Enemy" and "Scarface" carried forewords to the effect that the films were performing some kind of public service by exploring social problems. "The Roaring Twenties" (1939) had a foreword which maintained that the film, including by necessity its violence, was an effort to portray the history of an era. These disclaimers were obvious attempts on the part of the producers to molify the censorship pressure groups operating in America in the 1930's.

B. General Trend of the Entertainment Media
   to Make Copies of a Popular Genre

The yearly repetition of the gangster film -- stretching from
the late ninetten twenties to the present -- as well as its depiction in
forms varying from the classic to the mediocre -- is a history which
is no surprise to any student of the entertainment media. We have
come to expect a flood of copies following in the wake of nearly any
commercially or artistically successful film, television show, play,
novel or even advertising campaign. The rule would seem to be, "If
it worked once, it will work again" -- and again and again, ad nauseum.
The financial advisability of following up on a "sure thing", the
sentimental security of trodding on a favorite and familiar ground on
the part of the audience have combined to insure the birth of film
dynasties, particularly the indestructable Western and the gangster
film in the field of drama. These two forms have much in common in
the history of American films and a comparison of their respective
developments shows interesting parallels.

Gangster and Western films may both be labeled pure Americana.
The realities upon which both are based could be best termed American
folklore and the social conditions leading to both eras -- the 1870's-'1880's

and the 1920-1930's -- are well-known eras of "hardship and individualism", both beloved American qualities. The Western cowboy and the prohibition gunman may have been men of violence, but each epitomized the kind of action and adventure, based on historical fact, that appealed (and continues to appeal) to audiences.

Whereas Western films occupied the creative talents of film makers from the beginning ("The Great Train Robbery"), gangster films had to wait for their creation in history. Gangster films appeared in the 1920's (Robinson's "The Bright Scarf") but the events were still too contemporary, still too much in a state of evaluation to be put on film with the objective definition achieved in "The Public Enemy". Cagney appeared in "Doorway to Hell" and "Penny Arcade" shortly before "The Public Enemy" and it is important to note that the gangster character which became an oft-repeated classic is still in an embryonic stage. Lew Ayres, while playing a ruthless Napoleonic Italian hoodlum in "Doorway to Hell" manages to remain wholesome and clean cut. Grant Withers as the ex-con in "Penny Arcade" is a posturing, eye-rolling con man cum vaudeville comic.

After the advent of the archetypical and highly successful "Public Enemy" and "Little Caesar" everyone concerned had learned the route. The predictable imitations probably reached their highest achievement in the derivative yet dramatically excellent "Scarface". At the time, Paul

Muni voiced doubts about playing the role of Tony Carmonte in the wake of Robinson's and Cagney's triumphs. While "Scarface" is more concerned with spectacle (the machine gun fights were central to the film, more elaborate than the violence of the former films) the character development and involvement with social comment is on a par with its predecessors.

Perhaps one could take "Smart Money" (1932) as a harbinger of copies to come. The publicity attendant upon the use of Robinson and Cagney smacked of "cashing in" on their recent successes. Robinson's role as Nick the barber is a hurried sketch of Little Caesar all the trimmings but none of the depth. Cagney's role as Nick's lieutenant is that of a minor, second-banana gunsel; one which takes small advantage of Cagney's talents and is certainly no continuation of the "Public Enemy" characterization as overly enthusiastic publicity blurbs promised.

In no genre can such a wealth of repetition be found as in the Western. The film form that produced "Stagecoach" (1939) also provided the fodder for the innumerable and forgotten cowboy heroes who rode across the screens of America for decades. There was John Wayne and Gary Cooper stalking tall through the best of the entries and and at the other end of the scale, Monogram and Republic sent out the likes of Don "Red" Berry, Charles Starett and Lash LaRue to fight the never-ending wars between cattlemen and sheepmen while bringing justice to bear on the ubiquitous black-mustachioed villain waiting in his office at the back of the saloon.

The restatement of classic Western themes reached its zenith via the modern television Western cowboy. Although every season produces a fresh crop of Western hopefuls, all of them cut basically from the same cloth, the most blatant copies can be observed in the wake of "Bonanza". This "classic" television Western is mirrored weekly in its companion pieces, "The Big Valley", "High Chaparral" and "Lancer".

The private eye genre (a cousin to the gangster genre) has followed a smilar course. Such films as "The Maltese Falcon" 1941 (which had been made unsuccessfuly twice before) and "The Big Sleep" (1946) were outstanding entires in a plethora of private eye films which at their most mediocre offered such fare as the Hugh Beaumont-Producers Releasing Corporation "Mike Shane" series. Innumerable private eye series have filled the film industry's program film ranks as well as radio and television: To name a few, Philo Vance, Charlie Chan, Mr. Moto, Sam Spade; television has swelled the ranks of private eyes with Rocky King, Martin Kane, Mike Hammer (there were also several Mike Hammer features) and the Warner Brothers' "77 Sunset Strip" which the studio then copied with "Hawaiian Eye" and "Surfside Six".

The entertainment media follows its tendencies to produce copies of successful originals not only in the areas of a genre or a story line but also indulges in the copying of popular personalities. CBS saw a second Lucille Ball in Cara Williams. Jayne Mansfield, Sheree North and numerous other hopefuls already forgotten were groomed in the shadow of Marily Monroe. During the middle 1950's the success of Tab Hunter sparked the creation of Troy Donahue. Today the familiar face and gestures of James Dean can be seen in the performance of Christopher Jones.

Despite constant copying on what is often a painfully mediocre level the gangster genre and the Western genre have proved to be amazingly durable. This would seem to be due in part to a revival phenomenon. Every few years, out of the morass of cowboy retreads a "Shane" or "The Professionals" will appear. The private eye gained new life through "Harper (1965) (the success of which is directly responsible for Universal's new television series "The Outsider"). The last ten years saw no better gangster films than such naive and minor entires as "Young Dillinger" and "The Bonnie Parker Story". What would seem to be a tired and over-worked genre was given new life through the amazing popularity of "Bonnie and Clyde". Despite a strong anti-violence movement, the gangster film refreshed, is being viewed with new interest and respect. The copies of the "new look"

in gangster films are beginning already: A film treatment of Ma
Parker has been announced and "They Only Kill Each Other", the
story of "Bugsy" Siegel with Tony Curtis, is being planned at
Paramount.

Although the gangster genre may at the moment be
experiencing the effects of the revival phenomenon, its decline in
the past can be attributed to a kind of erosion caused by hundreds
of quickly made, ill-conceived pictures produced in an effort to
play on the consistent popularity of the genre. Films tended to
become a copy of a copy of a copy, etc., until only the "shorthand"
remained -- enough familiar elements to provide the film with some
action, some suspense, a villain and a hero, but little else.

     C. Difficulties Encountered in Basing a Genre
         on "Stories From the Headlines"

The gangster films of the 1930's were very topical in nature.
Warners prided itself on the semi-documentary quality of its product.
"Stories taken from the headlines" was a catch phrase Warners
boastfully repeated. "The Public Enemy" and "Little Caesar"
were realistic treatments of the American gangster figure, at
least in terms of the image fostered by the other media. For
United Artists, Howard Hawks patterned "Scarface" after Al Capone.

"Bullets or Ballots" was based on the real life New York City police detective, John Broderick. "G-Men" was inspired by the pursuit of John Dillinger.

"Picture Snatcher" was inspired by the secret photograph taken at the Ruth Snyder execution. "Racket Busters" and "Marked Woman" drew their bases from the Thomas Dewey vice campaign. "Black Legion" was drawn from contemporary KKK activities. These are specific examples. Nearly all the pictures of the genre were timely; although fictional they were obviously drawn from the social issues of the period. This was particularly true in the case of the James Cagney films which have been labled service-action-vocation. Employment was important to the Depression-oriented audiences and this may have influenced Cagney's change into "working man" action films.

The reliance on "stories from the headlines" which gave the gangster genre its life blood in the 1930's became the cause of its decline as the decade wore on. The situations which had given rise to the notoriety of the gangster had passed. America was entering a new era. This change is mirrored in the changing themes of Warners "headline" pictures. As the country advanced toward involvement in World War Two the preparedness picture began to appear -- votes of confidence for the armed forces such as "Here

Comes the Navy", "Devil Dogs of the Air" and "The Fighting 69th".
By 1939 Warners was receiving criticism for a film which was
slightly ahead of its time. "Confessions of a Nazi Spy" was a
thoroughly anti-Nazi picture that was meant to sound a warning.
It was the forerunner of the patriotic films produced by all the
studios during the early 1940's.

As this new genre gained prominence, the demise of the
gangster film could be seen in full evidence -- "The Roaring
Twenties" produced the same year as "Confessions of a Nazi Spy"
labeled itself "a reminiscence". The stories in the headlines were
no longer gangster stories and social problems at home were giving
way to a new involvement in world affairs.

CHAPTER V

THE SOCIALLY CONSCIOUS QUALITIES

OF THE GANGSTER GENRE AND THE

HISTORICAL DOCUMENTARY DRAMAS:

OUT OF DECAY, NEW GROWTH

The archetypical gangster films "Little Caesar" and "The Public Enemy" were considerably more than action pieces featuring well staged shootouts. Rather, both films delineated the motivations of their central characters as they developed in the context of a particular era in American life. There was the implicit statement in both films that organized crime was the product of growing materialism in America combined with the ill-conceived Prohibition Act.

Both film's drew their strength from plots rooted in a particular time. Rico, a petty holdup artist operating in a small town, is influenced by newspaper coverage of the blatant power and prestige of big city crime leaders. Rico resolves to leave the hinterlands for the big city where he intends to rise to the top in crime. American society's esteem for gangsters such as Al Capone during the Prohibition era was a fact and by the films making note of this, it was possible to lend movement to the plot and incorporate an overall documentary feeling in the film.

The Tom Powers character in "The Public Enemy" sees no difference between his brother earning a medal in the army by killing Germans in the First World War and his own gangland killing of rival bootleggers during the Prohibition wars. A general cynicism concerning America's reasons for involvement in the war "to end all wars" grew throughout the 1920's and 1930's. (Tom Powers' outlook makes "The Public Enemy" peculiarly contemporary in the 1960's.)

Both Rico and Tom were members of relatively under-privileged groups of their era, the Italians and Irish. Rico and his friend Joe turn to crime and show business, respectively. The other gang leaders are also of Italian extraction. Tom and his associates find advancement in crime and crime-linked politics. Neither film shows members of these ethnic groups working in banks and insurance companies. "Little Caesar" has Rico living in dismal quarters in his city's Little Italy. When he rises to gang chief he moves to a fashionable apartment. Before he gains money through his criminal activities, Tom lives in his family home, a small, drab, free-standing affair on a street with a number of identical houses. The sidewalk is of wood. Tom's neighborhood is back of the yards in Chicago.

Neither "Little Caesar" nor "The Public Enemy" presents

another road of advancement for the ambitious Italian-American Rico

or Irish-American Tom. Rico's friend Joe who becomes a dancer is

shown to be a weakling, allowing his girl to make his decisions.

Tom's brother Mike finds a place as a streetcar conductor but it is

made clear that this job will not get him out of the back of the yards

neighborhood. Though both gangster films claimed to be exposing

the evils of gangsterdom, in fact they both pointed out that Rico and

Tom probably chose the only roads for advancement open to them in

our society.

Later gangster films departed from this approach of

rooting the central character's motivation in a social context.

These gangster films were often comedic in nature. In

Robinson's "Little Giant" and "A Slight Case of Murder" the

sociological causes of criminal behavior were of no consequence.

In other cases trite formula plots painted the gangster as simply

and thoroughly "no good". The second category included the in-

expensively and quickly produced Bogart "B" films. In "You Can't

Get Away With Murder" and "King of the Underworld" the Bogart

character's criminal behavior was never explained -- he was

simply evil. The plots consistently build to the inevitable

elimination of Bogart's character at the film's conclusion.

Just as Warners led the American film industry in the

creation of the outstanding gangster films and characters of the 1930's, the studio also successfully turned to making the most significant of the "socially conscious" films. When the gangster genre turned to comedy, formula and con man formats, it was the socially conscious film which carried on the exploration of the roots of social problems as did the archetypical gangster films.

The best of the socially conscious films had a quality in their conception which formed a common bond with the archetypical gangster films. These films placed their stories in the context of an era. The characters drew their motivations from the demands of their times. As they lost this quality, the gangster genre declined as the 1930's wore on. The socially conscious group gathered strength by retaining it. A shorthand way of looking at this phenomenon might be to note that the era began with "Little Caesar" and ended with "The Grapes of Wrath".

Both the gangster film and socially conscious film of the 1930's American motion picture industry were instruments of social criticism. They were based on problems in society. The reasons for the censorship of the gangster film probably extended beyond their violence and graphic sex. The gangster film questioned the very foundations of American society.

It was and is popularly held that an individual can become a success in America by studying and working hard, being thrifty and having respect for family and institutions. Of course, the individual

must have the ambition to bring about change where events show

them necessary in his surroundings. Mixed in with this general out-

look is an adherence to the Ten Commandments or some similar set

of moral values. The gangster film in its fullest development rep-

resents anarchy in the above scheme. The genre states that you

take whatever you can by any means available. Any rules of the

game are strictly for the weak. As Tony Carmonte in "Scarface"

said, "There's only one law -- Do it first, do it yourself and keep

doing it".

Tom Powers of "The Public Enemy" did not believe in

playing by the rules as did his staid brother. He looked at the

world and came to the conclusion that being able to take something

was all the justification necessary for having it. Rico of "Little

Caesar" unabashedly dreamed of coming to the big city and "making

people dance". Might decided everything. Despite the somber pic-

ture "I Am A Fugitive From A Chain Gang" paints, it does not

suggest the total disruption and turn-about of society put forth by

the archetypical gangster films. Later gangster films such as

"King of the Underworld" had none of this challenge to society. If

anything, they proved "crime doesn't pay" by the unsympathetic

treatment of the criminal and his required demise in the last reel.

The socially conscious films can be roughly divided into two categories: The contemporary films "I Am A Fugitive From A Chain Gang", "Black Legion", "Black Fury" and "Confessions Of A Nazi Spy" -- which dealt with social problems of the 1930's (penal cruelty, bigotry, labor strikes, fascism). The historical films: "The Story of Louis Pasteur", "The Life of Emile Zola", "Juarez" -- which treated both long-standing social ills and contemporary ones alike in the semi-documentary treatment of the lives of great men.

First of the socially conscious films was "I Am A Fugitive From A Chain Gang" (1932) directed by Mervyn LeRoy, who also directed "Little Caesar". As in his classic gangster film, LeRoy told a story which sprang from the revolutionary changes taking place in post-World War One American society. The film was based on a book by Robert Burns entitled "I Am A Fugitive From A Georgia Chain Gang". While the film was in production author Burns was in fact a fugitive from the law and often slept in LeRoy's office.

"I Am A Fugitive From A Chain Gang" opens with newsreel footage of American troops returning after World War One. The film then depicts the life of one veteran, James Allen, played by Paul Muni. Allen returns to his home town to pick up his life once again. He begins working at his old job in a factory. Despite the urging of his mother, minister brother and boss, Allen quits his dull but secure job to make something of himself. He is not willing to accept the regimentation of the factory after his army experience.

America is in the depths of a postwar depression. Allen, like hundreds of thousands of other veterans, cannot find a job. He wanders across the country penniless and hungry like countless others. Eating a rare meal in a shabby diner, Allen is witness to a robbery which he tries to stop. Although innocent, he is arrested because of his ragged appearance and summarily sentenced to a chain gang.

Allen is caught in the brutal world of life on the road gang. He and his fellow inmates are treated inhumanly. There is considerable attention to the detail of how the chain gang works and lives. The food is inedible, the barracks dismal, the bosses vicious; but worst of all, the chain gang breaks the spirit of the men. Allen desperately decides even death is preferable to existence on the chain gang. Risking a smashed foot, Allen persuades a Negro inmate to sever his chains with a sledge hammer. Free at last, Allen miraculously escapes through the bushes as the gang works the road.

The fugitive Allen, once again a nameless, wandering man, joins a construction crew, work he had liked in the army. Over a decade, through study and hard work, he becomes an executive.

Well fixed and respected, Allen's past is suddenly revealed by his wife in a fit of jealousy. He is returned to the chain gang with a hurried promise of a swift pardon in view of the exemplary life he has led. Vengeful penal authorities have no intention of pardoning him. Once again he escapes. In a brilliant closing scene, Allen furtively returns to his faithful love (the woman who had inspired his wife's ire). The girl asks how will he live. Allen retreats into the night--bearded, shabby, his eyes wild -- "I'll steal" he says, and disappears.

The plot of "I Am A Fugitive From A Chain Gang" was meant to move its audience. The involvement of the plot with social problems makes it among the finest films of its time. The motivation is clear -- a man is restless with his meager lot after seeing the world. Given the chance, he pursues material success and prestige. Allen's life is changed by events beyond his control, so too he is crushed by these events. "I Am A Fugitive From A Chain Gang" contains much of Franklin D. Roosevelt's early depression political philosophy. Post-World War One social pressures created a generation of forgotten men. Although the film ends on a somber note, it carries a message -- if we were to salvage our humanity we would have to regain control of the forces the age had unleashed.

"Black Legion" (1937) is another of a series of films that sought to expose threats to American democracy -- this time through a ficticious story of a Midwestern organization modeled on the Ku Klux Klan.

Frank Taylor (Humphrey Bogart) is an average man. He works in a factory, is well-liked by his fellow workers, and lives in a modest home with his wife and son. Taylor has seniority in his machine shop and expects to be named foreman. So sure is he of the promotion that he prepares to buy a new car on the install- ment plan. A sincere, hardworking man, he is crushed when the job goes instead to an ambitious foreign born newcomer. At the urging of a fellow worker, Taylor attends a meeting of the Black Legion. The speaker, urging Americans to unite against the foreigners, seems to make sense to the disgruntled Taylor. He rashly joins the Legion and is initiated in an outdoor night cere- mony with a pistol held to his head.

Taylor finds he must pay out hard earned money for dues, a pistol and costume. The Legion comes to the aid of Taylor by staging a raid on the farm of the new foreign foreman, driving him off and securing his job for Taylor. Taylor finds he must pay for his position with increased participation in Legion activities. Taylor's wife leaves because of the change that has come over her

husband. A friend of Taylor's learns of the activities of the Legion
and is marked for death. Taylor is instructed to kill him. Completely indoctrinated, he carries out his orders and is arrested for
the murder.

Taylor is warned by a Legion lawyer not to say anything about
the Legion at his trial. But upon seeing his loyal wife in the court he
makes a full confession.

There are several brilliant touches in "Black Legion" which
ally it to the archetypical gangster films. Frank Taylor is shown
as "typical". He likes to listen to adventure shows on the radio
with his son. He yearns for a new car. The immigrant worker who
gets the foreman's job spends his every spare moment studying books,
an occupation scoffed at by Taylor. Taylor is part of a "friendly
group". He feels he deserves the promotion because he was there
first and because he "gets along". His only form of retribution,
however, is to lead the group in mildly ridiculing the immigrant
for studying so much. It takes the Klan-like Legion to force Taylor
into the mold of a brutal bigot.

The "message" of the film seems to be that we easy-going
Americans must be vigilant, or else fall prey to the merchants of
hate. Although the dramatic touches which fill in Frank Taylor's
outlook raise "Black Legion" above the level of a formula film, it

lacks the conception and scope of execution of "I Am A Fugitive
From A Chain Gang". Taylor's motivations are one-dimensional;
his capitulation to the philosphy of hatred is melodramatic.

The New York Times called "Black Legion" the editorial
cinema at its best -- "ruthless, direct, uncompromising".[1]
As Mr. Sinclair Hill, the noted British motion picture producer
observed, "Hollywood's flair for showmanship has been admirably
exemplified in its habitual practice of going to the newspaper headlines for its story material".[2] This comment was aimed specifically
at the time at Warner Brothers and applied very well to "Black Legion".

The film was a treatment of hooded society terrorism and
stemmed directly from the Ku Klux Klan activities in Michigan the
preceding years. Robert Lord specifically drew his dramatization
from the killing of Charles Poole and the testimony of Dayton Dean,
a legion executioner, who was State's evidence at the trial.

It is interesting to note in passing that the American film
industry showed considerable courage in the treatment of American
social problems but was more cautious where more international
issues were concerned. Hollywood halted production of "It Can't
Happen Here" because Italy and Germany would have taken offense

---

[1]The New York Times, Jan. 18, 1937, p. 21:1.

[2]James P. Cunningham, "The Black Legion", The
Commonweal, Jan. 27, 1937, p. 37.

at the anti-Fascist message; the negative of "The Devil is a Woman"
was destroyed because of a Spanish protest about its disrespectful
treatment of Spain's Civil Guard; all mention of the War of 1812 was
omitted from "Lloyd's of London" rather than risk offending Britain;
the original film production of "Paths of Glory" was abandoned when
it was learned that France would prefer to forget the World War I
incident. "The Forty Days of Musa Dagh" was shelved in Turkey's
interest.

Like "Black Fury" and "I Am A Fugitive From A Chain Gang",
"Black Legion" makes no effort to soften its message -- it is meant
to be a startling experience, to evoke the proper sort of public indignation against hooded secret societies and false Americanism.
Because of the very nature of this prodigious undertaking, "Black
Legion" has some basic production problems. The film approaches
its theme from three angles -- the effect on Frank Taylor; the
legion purpose of making money for a crew of cold-blooded organizers;
and the mob activities of the legion (night raids, night beatings,
murder). The problems would seem to arise in the characterization
of the legion as an "evil" force and in working the plot into a fictional
story with fictional characters.

The legion is portrayed as a completely anti-social organization composed of hate-filled rabble rousers, bigots and money-grabbing

organizers. Although Frank is persuaded to join after losing the
foreman's job to a "foreigner", the prospect of even the most
bitterly disappointed workman joining such a frightful and menacing
group may seem a little far-fetched, especially when Frank Taylor
is portrayed basically as such a decent sort. The film creates a
completely "black" villain in the person of the legion and then goes
about heaping abuse and accusations on this undeniably loathsome
target. This, of course, has elements of truth, but the message
would be stronger if the villainous group were portrayed at first in
a more deceptive light -- an organization with which one could identify, with ideals and purposes cloaked in a greater degree of
respectability. Then, as the group developed into its true form --
after the unsuspecting and trustful Frank had been taken in -- it
would have been more believable and all the more frightening.

Perhaps the greatest problem, however, is the forming of
the theme into a fictional story of ninety minutes duration. It was
necessary to put the story of the legion in terms of specific human
experience -- Frank and his family and friends. Thus the characters
had to be developed and time taken to weave the story about them.
This burdened the actual telling of the tale and compressed it into a
very short space. Of course, to fully understand the implications
and causes of the Black Legion, one would have to be presented a sort

of socio-economic history of such movements complete with Molly Maguires and Know-Nothings -- obviously this is neither feasible nor desired. The answer to this in the film is to build the story of the legion activities through a series of short vignettes and montages. This results in a jerky presentation -- flashes of life in the shop; domestic life at home; back to the shop; back to the house; to the drugstore; the legion meeting; the first raid; the shop, etc. Each one is good but the end result is too much crowded on the screen to build a tightly-woven dramatic experience.

The characters have a certain stereotyped quality -- the noble, sweet, long-suffering wife, the good-guy best friend who gets killed, the sneering, vicious legion members, the tough blonde of easy virtue, etc. This plus the all-too-convenient ending (confession in the courtroom) weaken a strong and important theme. The judge's closing speech on the virtue of democracy and the evils of "false patriots who prey on national and racial prejudices" is well-intentioned and underlines the message of the film but again is too pat a tie-up, too expected and obvious an instruction to do justice to the theme.

Publicity for "Black Legion" centered around its uncompromising attack on an American problem, all the more frightening because it was "close to home". One newspaper called the film

"vastly important" and suggested that it be seen by everyone. Much
was made in the attendant newspaper and magazine coverage to laud
the film's intentions and the screen's "power for indignation" and,
at the same time, roundly slam all hooded societies.

Director Archie Mayo was reported to research the history of
American secret societies. Mayo studied the Know-Nothings, the
Molly Maguires, the A.P.A., the Ku Klux Klan, and the Silver Shirts.
He stated that he found in the Molly Maguires the closest parallel to
the Black Legion -- workers recruited in a definite field, starting as
a protective group, soon dominated by lawless elements fighting for
their own personal benefit, eventually infiltrated and broken by a
Pinkerton man, James McParian.[1]

Mayo felt that the day of such groups was past but that the
incentive remained and the cause would die out only when the mass
saw that such organizations, however benevolent their apparent
purpose, were "dedicated to class and racial hatred and the
furtherance of bigotry and oppression". Mayo felt he had in "Black
Legion" put on record "for all time" a vigorous warning against and
an exposure of such secret orders by showing how the members
became dupes of racketeers who are involved in crime and terroristic

[1]The New York Times, Jan. 17, 1937, p. 4:4.

campaigns. As did "I Am A Fugitive From A Chain Gang" which did,
in fact, take place in the South, this film chose to portray an all-
white story. There is no hint here of this kind of organization's
activities against Negroes.

In the ads for "Black Legion" Humphrey Bogart was billed as
"The Killer of Petrified Forest" while a malevolent hooded figure
with up-raised fist was shown. The two roles -- of Duke Mantee
and Frank Taylor -- are obviously quite different, however. Whereas Mantee is waging a battle against the forces of society, he still
has a certain surety in his actions -- he is a professional desperado
who handles his own affairs with dispatch and strength. Taylor is
also beset by societal problems, but of his own making. Where
Mantee is driven by something akin to greed to strike out at society,
Taylor is driven by fear and jealousy and this same basic weakness
prevents him from either reconciling his emotions or taking independent action. Thus Taylor readily allows the legion to fight his battles
for him and desires the anonymity of the cloak. Soon, however, the
weak Taylor cannot control his situation -- blindly he follows legion
orders, although beginning to have second thoughts, and gets further
and further into beatings and vandalism. Where Mantee kills those
who stand in his path of escape, Taylor kills for no such clear-cut
reason. He kills under a sudden shouted command and is then

overtaken by fear and remorse at killing his best friend.

Bogart portrays Frank Taylor as a sympathetic character despite his weaknesses. He achieves this by projecting a very for- givable and human quality into a well-meaning but easily misled "follower" type. Bogart's scenes with the boy in the Taylor's small home give a deep feeling of domesticity, the quiet, simple, yet happy life he had built -- the wife preparing dinner when he comes home, listening to a serial on the radio. He "goes for" the radio-adventure just as does his son. Frank Taylor is just an average little man who becomes a symbol in "Black Legion".

One finds that the leading characters of "social conscious" films are often symbols, many times eclipsing the usual on-screen personality of the actor. Thus Bogart as Frank Taylor is a subor- dinated Bogart, secondary to the message. The same can be seen by comparing the gangster Muni of "Scarface" and Muni as the beleaguered hero of "I Am A Fugitive From A Chain Gang". The Bogart or Muni characterization, while still forceful and recognizable, find themselves fitted into a message or "social conscience" theme which is central to the film.

Paul Muni appeared again in a contemporary socially conscious film, "Black Fury" in 1935, a story of the management -- labor problems of foreign-born coal miners. After years of struggle

a coal miners' union has wrested a contract from the mine owners.
The agreement provides some recognition of the miners' needs, but
the situation still leaves much to be desired. A gang of racketeers
plans to force the union to break its contract with the owners. A
strike call will provide an opportunity for the gang to move into the
situation, restore order with their "police force" of armed thugs,
and collect a large fee from the mine owners.

Joe Rodek, is a very popular miner in the company town
which is populated largely by immigrants from Eastern Europe.
Rodek has no interest in union affairs. He has been saving his
money to buy a pig farm with Anna Novak, the girl he plans to
marry. Anna, however, cannot wait. Unable to bear life in the
drab mining town, she runs away with a company policeman who is
being transferred to Pittsburgh.

Rodek is blind with grief. He starts drinking. A racketeer
spots the popular Rodek and nominates him to head a group of union
dissidents and start a strike. Rodek, a simple workman who has
never interested himself in such matters, has no understanding of
what he has set into motion.

Work comes to a standstill. A judge rules the union has
violated its contract thus the owners are no longer bound by it.
The owners import scab labor to work the mines. The racketeer

police force keeps order. Families are evicted from their company owned houses. The people are on the brink of starvation.

Rodek's best friend, a staunch union man who had always tried to make Rodek take part in union affairs to no avail, is killed by a thug policeman. His friend's death clears Rodek's mind. He sets out to undo the trouble he has caused. Rodek sadly learns that the men can return to work only under a contract which will take away all the benefits they have won over the past twenty years.

With the help of Anna, who has returned from the city disillusioned, Rodek makes his way into the mine with a load of dynamite. He sends the girl out with the message that unless the men can return to work under decent conditions he will blow up the mine, ending all operations. Newspaper headlines announce "MINE OWNERS HELPLESS IN ONE MAN STRIKE" and "WASHINGTON STEPS IN TO SETTLE STRIKE". After a settlement is reached guaranteeing the rights of the miners, Rodek comes out of the mine and announces to the world that he and Anna will "settle down and raise pigs and kids".

A government investigator points out the futility of the situation. There was never any reason for the strike.

Realism and a documentary quality were hallmarks of the socially conscious film; Muni's characterization of a common

working-man sought to point this up. The first time we see Joe
Rodek he is getting up in the morning to begin the day's work. He
puts his work clothes on over the underwear which served as his
pajamas. He sleeps with a large dog. Later at a party Rodek
wears the immigrant's "uniform" -- a too tight suit and derby.

At a dance Rodek drinks beer, crudely wipes his mouth with
his hand and dries his hand on his pocket. As he dances with Anna
she closes her eyes in dread. He always talks of taking his savings
and buying a farm and raising kids and pigs with his Anna. After the
girl runs off with a company policeman, Rodek reacts by bellowing
like an animal, "Why she do this to me? We raise pigs and kids...
all women are pigs..." He has no understanding of leadership, a
perfect tool for racketeers. When he decides to take action, he
just charges dumbly ahead.

The audience is given the background of the conflict and the
forces at work; the social milieu is carefully drawn. The opening
shots show the miserable, dreary company town. The worker's
houses are little more than shacks. We are given details concerning
the coal miners' job. They are paid only for the coal received. The
miners must remove the material around the coal on their own time,
this is called "deadwork". We learn from a discussion among the
miners in the shaft that while conditions are bad, they have been

improving over the years. The mine owners have come to recognize the miners' right to be represented by a union and a fairly comfortable situation exists.

One group of miners supports the union, another says the union serves only to keep the status quo. It is interesting to note that the miners themselves do not rise in a strike. The racketeers (undefined, generalized, evil-doers) are used to exploit the miners. Thus the real social issues were skirted and a safe, traditional "villain" took their place.

The mine owners are of old American stock while the miners are obviously recent immigrants. At the big dance, company police refer to the miners as "Hunyaks". The agitator sent in by the racketeers refers to Rodek as a "dumb Hunyak". The gangster chief tells the mine owners that he will use mounted police to control the miners and their families because "they respect that from the old country".

The mine owners are shown to be harsh but it is made clear that conditions will improve slowly if the men will bargain with the owners through their union. Attempts at radical change in working conditions are shown to play into the hands of those who would exploit the miners. Thus the film takes a middle-of-the-road approach.

As in "Racket Busters" (1938) management and labor are brought together by the heroics of a single man. The film does not expound the ideological solution to the problem, but would seem to be on the side of a status quo gradualism.

"Confessions of a Nazi Spy" (1939) was taken from the front pages of the nation's newspapers. The year before, trials in Manhattan had disclosed a Nazi organization which was working to gain secret information from American sources. From this trial came G-man Leon G. Turrou's book, Nazi Spies in America. Warner Brothers purchased Turrou's book for $25,000 and, hiring the G-man as technical advisor, set about to make a film pointing out the dangers of the German-American Bund.

Although, according to court rulings, persons involved in trials cannot be represented on the screen without their consent, the characters of "Confessions of a Nazi Spy" are readily identifiable: Edward G. Robinson as Ed Renard is Turrou; Otto Kruger, Francis Lederer, Dorothy Tree, Lya Lys and George Sanders play characters suggested by the convicted spies Dr. Ignatz T. Briebl, Gunther Gustav Rumrich, Johanna Hoffman, Mrs. Kate Moog Busch and Darl Schluter. Warner's even considered eliminating the usual disclaimer legend at the beginning of the film.

With faith in the public's reaction Warner's specified a

$1,500,000 budget with a fifty-five day shooting schedule. Most of the budget went for physical mountings -- some ninety sets including offices, public buildings and stages in German bund meeting halls and camps in the United States. The costume supply houses having no such apparel, it was necessary for the wardrobe department to manufacture 600 uniforms for the Storm Troopers and Silver Shirts at a cost of $15,000.

Article C of the Production Code regulates the representation of other nationals on the screen and Warner's anticipated that certain difficulties would arise over their uncomplimentary representation of Germans in the film. Reactions did come from the German consul in Los Angeles who stated, "the German Government will not be responsible for the results if the picture is filmed". In Washington, Hans Thomsen, acting chief of the German Embassy, suggested to the State Department that the film might cause resentment between his country and the United States. Secretary Hull referred Thomsen's letter to Will H. Hays, President of the Motion Picture Producers and Distributors of America. Mr. Hays referred the complaint to Warner Brothers. As spokesman for the studio, Harry Warner said the film would continue to be shown and that approval of the picture by strict British censors would have banned the film had it been made in the days when Germany and Italy made up 10% of the market.

"Confessions of a Nazi Spy" was banned in Denmark and Norway and in Havana following a protest by the German Minister there. In Poland, Stefan Kalamajski, president of the Poznan Chamber of Commerce was deported to Germany and sentenced to twenty years at forced labor for showing the film in a theatre he owned.

Warner Brothers was well aware of the publicity potential of their controversial film and the papers were full of articles pointing up the dangers inherent in the filming and showing of the piece. It was reported that for the sake of security only the pages of the script to be shot that day were given out to the cast. The stages were locked and guarded. Much was made of the fact that no actor (19 had refused) could be found who was willing to imper-sonate Hitler. This was compounded by the statement of the Hollywood Makeup Men's Association that none of their number would be allowed to make up an actor as the Fuhrer. One extra playing a storm trooper marched angrily off the set refusing to speak the words "Heil, Hitler" aloud, a mike boom broke and for a while sabotage was mentioned and it was suggested that actress Lya Lys had had trouble with the Nazis while in Europe for refusing to appear in Nazi propaganda films.

In New York the City Council viewed the film as an

inducement to pass a bill against the wearing of foreign uniforms in the city. In Hobbs, New Mexico, a man intent on destroying the anti-Nazi film, broke into the projection booth at the theatre where it was playing but destroyed a Warner Brothers Western short by mistake.

Although no incidents occurred, police protection was granted to the opening of the film. Police lines formed in a two block radius around Warners' Beverly Hills theatre and 104 officers in uniforms and plain clothes watched the crowd. The film was shown at the Strand in New York under a police guard and grossed $45,000 in its first week. No local censorship plagued the film as was feared except for a few communities where the swastikas in Warners' outdoor advertising were prohibited.

With the initial success of the film (450 advance bookings) other studios went immediately into production on similar themes: At MGM Sinclair Lewis' "It Can't Happen Here", Charlie Chaplin in "The Great Dictator"; independent producer Al Rosen began work on a Hitler biography, "The Mad Dog of Europe"; and Paramount announced "Heil America".

Despite heavy publicity ("It was our American duty to make this picture! It's your American privilege to see it!") and initially heavy response the Warners admitted a year after the film's release that it was not "very successful" from a commercial viewpoint. This was blamed on the fact that the film was "ahead of the times". As one spokesman explained, "people still were inclined to scoff at the film's expose of the methods of the Nazi spy ring then, but now (late 1940) they'll realize the truth of its predictions".

"Confessions of a Nazi Spy" was greeted with mixed feelings. It was readily admitted that it was an outstanding endeavor. It's techniques and acting were lauded, particularly the effectiveness of the quasi-documentary approach which lent authority and believability to what was essentially a propaganda approach. The film opened without credits and advanced into a "March of Time" presentation using a narrator, real film clips, maps, etc. This was excellently interwoven not with acted vignettes but with a whole story in which the characters were allowed to grow and develop.

On the other hand was the argument that Warners had "held an excellent hand and overplayed it". This was in reference to the overdrawn "blacker than black" villains, the sneering, rat-faced or brute browed portrayal of all Nazis. Other critics remarked on the lack of motivation or social reasons on the part of the Americans who were taken in by the Nazi propaganda and became the spies of the film. Stronger criticism centered around the basic concept of the film and its effect on the viewing audience. One magazine stated, "A little too terrific, perhaps. The film is a hate-breeder if there ever was one, and when even our playboy intellectuals are charging around proclaiming the duty to go into battle of somebody else, any

aid to national hatred is dynamite."[1] Another publication wondered,

"Are we now to have a series similar to those "Beast of Berlin" films

that fanned our hatred in 1917?"[2]

As Ed Renard, Edward G. Robinson presents his definitive

portrayal as the "super sleuth". This type of Robinson screen

characterization is in direct opposition with his "Little Caesar"

image and was a later development in his repertory. The super

sleuth is a learned man, smooth, controlled, understated, yet

strong and unbeatable through his use of logic, reason or intelligence.

This is the mentally-dominant Robinson rather than the physically-

dominant Robinson. Rather than out-yelling or out-fighting the

opposition, this Robinson out-thinks them.

The mature and polished super-sleuth is seen again in such

Robinson films as "Dr. Ehrlich's Magic Bullet" and later in "The

Stranger" with Orson Welles (a Robinson role with a great many

similarities to his portrayal of Ed Renard).

The super-sleuth is fiercely dedicated yet patient and level-

headed, he is contempletive and brooding yet decisive and fast-moving

when the solution has been reached. On the surface he holds himself

[1] "Confessions of a Nazi Spy", New Republic, May 10, 1939, p. 20.

[2] "Confessions of a Nazi Spy", The Commonweal, May 19, 1939, p. 106.

emotionally aloof from his job" yet is deeply involved because of the principles concerned (Ed Renard's only show of emotion is the snapping of his pipe stem--the pipe being his trademark). The Robinson of "Little Caesar" and "Smart Money" delighted in snappy clothes. The super-sleuth is neat and conservative to a point of being nondescript. He is not interested in his physical appurtenances, only in the problem at hand that must be solved.

It is Robinson's controlled performance in "Confessions of a Nazi Spy" that helps save the film from being a straight propaganda piece. The other characters come dangerously close to all being "types". In a film where black is black and white is white the depth of the Robinson character helps to out-balance the burgeoning melo-drama. In the face of ranting, steely-eyed arch villains, Robinson's calm and calculating G-man adds a note of restraint and reality that a compaigning "hero" or love interest character could never have achieved.

The socially conscious genre took a turn toward exploring contemporary problems by examining similar problems faced by men in the past. The 1930's saw the filmed lives of Pasteur, Zola, Juarez, Edison, Florence Nightingale, Samuel Mudd, Ehrlich and Reuter.

The most ambitious in terms of concept of the historical

socially conscious films are "The Story of Louis Pasteur" (1936),

"The Life of Emile Zola" (1937), "Juarez" (1939) and "Dr. Ehrlich's

Magic Bullet" (1940). All these films were made by Warner Brothers,

produced by Henry Blanke and directed by William Dieterle. The

first three starred Paul Muni, the last Edward G. Robinson. Muni

won the Academy Award for his portrayal of Pasteur.

These films are optimistic in tone as compared to "I Am A

Fugitive From A Chain Gang". They have a quality which points to

a problem in American society and suggests solutions based on

traditional values already inherent in the country. In short these

films say that if we live by the ideals which are a part of our heritage,

a heritage which has produced much good, we can correct the

inadequacies and inequities of our system.

"Pasteur" was released in 1936 -- a time when the Depression

seemingly had become a way of life in America and there existed a

growing realization of the possibility of a second world war.

Pasteur was a very affirmative film.

Pasteur's filmic struggles had a definite Rooseveltian quality

about them -- the established and honored medical profession opposed

Pasteur and his revolutionary concepts which, though addressed to a

great and urgent need in this time, shook the very roots of the medical

profession as well. Roosevelt's legislation challenged vested interests

who put up bitter opposition to his program. According to Warners,
Pasteur (and Roosevelt) were opposed by factions which were in ways
"misguided" but still looking for the good, encumbered only by their
own traditions. The Pasteur of the film and Roosevelt shared a wish
to win their detractors over rather than destroy them. This feeling
toward the opposition was a distinct contrast to that held in the
communist and fascist countries.

"Pasteur" carries the message of man's concern for the
well-being of his fellow man and advocates the position that this
love of humanity and struggle for the improvement of the human
condition must continue in the face of all opposition, against enormous
odds, even when confronted by power, stupidity or loss of status. This
could be inspiring stuff for an audience faced with national economic
troubles, widespread human deprivation and world-wide political unrest, just as "The Plow That Broke The Plains" and "The River" were
so powerful in the face of the great dustbowl and the floods on the
Mississippi and Tennessee Rivers. These films showed that something could be done.

"Pasteur", like other message films, ended with a plea
which verbalized the underlying moral of the story and which was
aimed more at the audience than at the characters to whom it was
addressed on the screen. As the crippled Pasteur is led to the podium

in the ampitheatre of the Sorbonne the great men of medicine rise

and give him the ovation which is the culmination of his lifetime

struggles in behalf of his theories.

CLOSE SHOT OF PASTEUR. He starts to speak.

> PASTEUR
> I--I have no words to express--

His voice falters. He stops. The ovation dies down
rapidly. There is complete silence. Pasteur gains
possession of himself, looks up at the gallery.

FULL SHOT GALLERY, which is crowded with the
young medical students of France. They have
resumed their seats; their eager faces are peering
down at him intently.

CLOSE SHOT PASTEUR. He slowly looks over the
auditorium, his eyes filled with tears of emotion.
He lifts his head toward the gallery.

> PASTEUR
> (addressing his remarks to
> the students, his voice
> ringing with conviction)
> You young men -- doctors and scientists
> of the future -- do not let yourselves be
> tainted by a barren skepticism, nor dis-
> couraged by the sadness of certain hours
> that creep over nations. Do not become
> angry at your opponents, for no scientific
> theory has ever been accepted without
> opposition. Live in the serene peace of
> libraries and laboratories. Say to your-
> selves first: "What have I done for my
> instruction?" and as you gradually advance:
> "What am I accomplishing?", until the time
> comes when you may have the immense
> happiness of thinking that you have contributed
> in some way to the welfare and progress of
> mankind.

He falters again, his voice fails; he steps back, unable
to go on. Lister on one side and Thiers on the other,
anxiously support him. The applause that greets his
words is deafening. Pasteur is overwhelmed by the
triumphant acclaim. His family is joyous.

FADE-OUT.

"The Life of Emile Zola" (1937) is not merely the story of the

author but rather of the universal issues he met and challenged in

his lifetime. Anti-Semitism; the danger of an entrenched, unchecked,

corrupt military to the democratic process; the rights of the individual

man; the importance of justice were all pertinent issues to the

audiences of the 1930's. It was a powerful reminder that a country

must never forget that democracy requires constant vigilance.

Director William Dieterle said of Zola, "The message of

Zola is that there are millions of people in the world today like the

persecuted Dreyfus and there is not always a Zola. Yet there is no

reason to despair. For at any time, through any chance, there

might come along a Zola".[1]

"Zola" brings a message concerning the rights of the

individual against the organization; the responsibility of everyone

to defend the rights of each of his fellow men; the courage to do so

in the face of all opposition (Zola lost his case and had to flee to

England, until two years later, the corrupt military was broken from

within and the truth revealed); and the fact that although injustice and

---

[1]The New York Times, September 26, 1937, p. 4.

persecution do exist there is always the power of truth and those who would risk their futures to uphold it.

Zola's famous "J'Accuse" address to the jury, like Pasteur's speech at the Sorbonne, Juarez's talk with Diaz and Ehrlich's death scene, restates the basic theme of the picture -- the importance of truth and the worth of the individual. Zola, in the film, is speaking to the jury but he is actually addressing the American people -- "Is the suffering of one worth the disturbance of a country?...I'm not defending myself...save the army and France by letting truth conquer...a great nation is in danger of forfeiting its honor...Show how important an individual can be...I swear by all my works, may my name perish if Dreyfus is not innocent".

This speech is six minutes long and made in one continuous shot -- the longest such film speech to that time and probably till today. The original script called for the camera to move away from Zola -- to show reactions from the jury and from various members of the courtroom audience, but in final form it became a Muni tour de force. Muni had memorized the speech perfectly by working with a tape recorder at home. (Henry Blanke claims Muni was the first actor to use this rehearsal technique.) The scene was shot twelve times and Muni was said to have never faltered once. Zola is shown mostly in close-up, addressing the camera. The jury is never studied, nor are reaction shots used, thus heightening the effect that Zola is speaking to the theatre audience. (It is unlikely that such a lengthy "message" speech in a cinematically static presentation could have been tolerated by the audience had it not been rendered so strikingly by Muni's elaborate characterization.)

At the bier of Zola, Anatole France delivers a second "message" oration. Again, it is addressed in actuality to the audience. He "enlightens the younger generation" (just as Pasteur spoke to the medical students). He speaks to "those who are now enjoying freedom" and admonishes them not to forget those who fought for them against fanatical intolerance. He asks them to be human -- for Zola fervently loved humanity (as did Pasteur). He cited Zola turning his back on security and fame to fight injustice, "There is no serenity save in justice". "Zola" was a call to America to "wake up" and not sit idly by, happy with what it had while the world was beseiged with problems and America herself ultimately threatened. In a famous closing line Anatole France calls Zola "a moment of the conscience of man".

In "Juarez" (1939) Warner Brothers reached the zenith of their development of documentary biographies. This film involved the longest preparation and shooting period (two years) and the largest expense (over two million dollars), the services of six

Academy Award winners and a cast of 1,188 including an imposing

list of stars. "Juarez" also had the largest publicity campaign in

the periodicals and newspapers. It was also a box office failure.

(A break came between Muni and Warners sometime later, based

partly on the lack of success of this and other "prestige" pictures of

this persuasion).

     Again, physical accuracy was stressed to underline the

documentary quality and sense of reality it was hoped the film

would express. More than a year of intense research was put in

by Warner Brothers in preparation for the film. The Mexican

government contributed access to the correspondence of Juarez,

to that of the Foreign Affairs Department during Maximilian's

reign and Juarez' presidency; also facsimile copies of Mexican

newspapers of the period as well as innumerable pictures, transcripts

of letters and other documents.

     Hal Wallis the executive producer, Henry Blanke the associate

producer, William Dieterle and Paul Muni spent six weeks in Mexico

visiting localities associated with Juarez -- Oaxaca where he was

born, Guanajuanto and Guadaljara, temporary seats of government

and headquarters of the army, and Mexico City. They visited the

National Museum, inspected relics, portraits, letters and personal

possessions. They spoke with two of Juarez's soldiers, Colonel

Gabriel Moreno and General Ignacio Valasquez and obtained first

hand accounts of battles and their impression of Juarez.

All of this research not only added greatly to the authenticity

of the film but the pre-publicity for the film constantly stressed this

approach, building the idea that this picture would be the ultimate

of filmic reality and historical validity. Warner Brothers billed

"Juarez" as "how great the screen can be". (A critic predicted that

by Thanksgiving, "Juarez" would be the "biggest turkey around" and

he hit closer to the truth.[1]) This was a unique wedding of the best

exploitation Hollywood could offer and the greatest attempt yet to pro-

duce a documentary feature. While the gangster genre sank to backlot

mediocrity, the historical film carried on the banner of social comment

to epic proportions.

Muni's makeup was superb -- he _was_ Juarez and was un-

recognizable as himself. Brian Aherne as Maximilian was also a

masterpiece of costuming and make-up -- his princely adornment

was correct to the last curled hair on his beard. The court sets

were detailed, lavish and accurate. Carpenters and plasterers

recreated a hundred-year-old Mexican village and it was peopled

with one thousand authentically garbed soldiers, peons and market

women who swarmed on cue.

---

[1]"They're Up, They're Down", The New Republic,
May 10, 1939, p. 20.

The question may be raised as to where the emphasis on facts and visual accuracy should leave off and the emphasis on acting skill and effective film techniques should begin. The time needed for making a complicated political situation understandable and usable automatically hampered the execution of the equally im-portant task of bringing the characters to life. The major characters, Juarez and Maximilian, who had to carry the theme of the picture wavered on the verge of becoming symbols instead of living persons. Minor characters, in particular Diaz (John Garfield) were less bur-dened and could develop as humans.

Perhaps this '"unbalance" of historical accuracy and filmic technique is natural in the development of this genre. It was far from the earlier overblown fake historical pageants but not yet the perfect ideal -- as The Nation called it, "The great vision of his-torical truth in the tense perspective of pure art".

The commitment to a large body of historical fact and the task of presenting it, interweaving it and explaining it to the audience shackled the film with a certain stiffness at various points -- all the more noticiable when compared to the several moving and well-photographed sequences. Reviewers found the film more intellectual than physical. There is an extended reliance on close-ups, two-shots and medium shots of persons

talking at great length, explaining themselves and their causes. This
is a stage technique, rather than a cinematic one and this type of
exposition tends to make the picture static -- as Napolean III lectures
to his ministers on dictatorship, Maximilian addresses his advisors
advocating monarchy and Juarez constantly instructs his aids on the
good of democracy. Dieterle seems to have mounted them on soap-
boxes for the purposes of declamation.

Dieterle has achieved some good filmic moments. Juarez
in his wagon-office going about the countryside; Juarez when he boldly
walks through the courtyard filled with hostile townspeople to confront
the traitor Uradi and thus regain the support of the Mexican people;
Napolean III on a fake horse posing for a heroic painting and strutting
about in obvious imitation of Adolf Hitler; the mad scene of Carlota,
as the disconsolate Empress of Mexico fluttering off into consuming
darkness.

Maximilian and Juarez never met -- their common ground
was the question of which would head the Mexican government and
whose ideology would triumph. Juarez had his separate problems
of maintaining his diverse and widespread following and dealing
with dissension within his ranks. Maximilian and Carlota were
involved in their relationship with Napolean III, their personal love,
their dawning disenchantment with their roles as unwanted rulers

and puppets of Napolean III. It seems, despite the emphasis of his

character demanded by Muni, to have been something of a struggle

to keep the stolid character of Juarez from being drowned in a story

awash with the too-sweet sadness of the honor-bright sincerity of

the mis-used Maximilian, the pitifulness of his mad, beloved Carlota,

their adoption of a Mexican boy in the place of a child of their own,

the repetition of their song "La Paloma", and Maximilian, noble

aristocrat to the end, gently giving himself over to certain death.

The problems of Mexico in the 1860's had many similarities

to the world problems of the 1930's and "Juarez" makes an obvious

statement concerning social and political issues. The 1930's found

people being confronted by competing and powerful political

ideologies -- fascism, communism, American style democracy and

their shadings. The choice between them was at the time not as

clear cut as it may seem today. In America itself there was con-

siderable unrest in the midst of the Depression and Nazi bunds were

organized and found sympathizers. "Juarez" is essentially an

argument for democracy as a better form than dictatorship or

monarchy. It also deals with the persecution and equality of minority

groups (as did "Zola") in the person of Juarez himself. Juarez was

a Zapotec Indian who rose from poverty as a sheep-herder to make

his way through law school and into local, and finally national,

government as President of Mexico. A member of his staff, Uradi

(a fictional creation of the film) seeks the presidency himself and gives as a reason the idea that the leader of the Mexican people should be "of pure Spanish blood" like himself. Juarez's success is a reaffirmation of the tenet that all men are created equal and should be given the right to rule themselves and the opportunity to rise to any position which they are capable of attaining.

The basic theme of the film, the superiority of democracy as a political system, is best stated in the "message" speech of the picture, in this case a conversation between General Diaz (John Garfield) and Juarez.

                    DIAZ
Señor Juarez.

                    JUAREZ
Porfirio.

                    DIAZ
It has been a long ride to reach you
here on the border.

                    JUAREZ
So you escaped, Porfirio?

                    DIAZ
No, Senor Juarez, I was given my freedom,
Maximiliano ordered it. Maximilian himself.

                    JUAREZ
You saw him?

                    DIAZ
He came to the prison, to my cell, alone.
He talked. At first I supposed trickery,
but that --

                    JUAREZ
What did he talk about?

DIAZ

About his ideas of government. I
doubted my own ears, for what I heard
was you speaking, your words out of
his mouth. Like you, Señor Juarez,
he wants to help our people.

JUAREZ

How?

DIAZ

By protecting them from those who
would oppress them.

JUAREZ

Virtue is a formidable weapon in the
hands of the enemy.

DIAZ

But he is not your enemy. Your aims
are his aims. He says only a word,
democracy, lies between him and you.

JUAREZ

Only a word?

DIAZ

He is honest, Señor Juarez. You will
know how honest when I tell you his
message.

JUAREZ

So there is a message.

DIAZ

He wants you to be Prime Minister of
Mexico -- in a monarchy founded upon
the principles of your own constitution.

JUAREZ

But it is the constitution of a republic,
Porfirio.

DIAZ
Well, he swears he will defend its
principles against the politicos and
selfish interests. He says that such
principles must always be defined by
someone like himself, someone who
is above all factions and parties.

JUAREZ
Maximiliano says only a word stands
between him and me -- only the word
democracy -- Porfirio, what does it
mean this -- this word?

DIAZ
Democracy...
           (laughing)
Why it means liberty: liberty for a
man to say what he thinks. To worship
as he believes. It means equal opportunity.

JUAREZ
No. No that cannot be its meaning, Porfirio.
Maximiliano offers us these things without
democracy. What is it then that he would
withhold from us?

DIAZ
Er -- only the right to rule ourselves.

JUAREZ
Then that must be the meaning of the word,
Porfirio, the right to rule ourselves. The
right of every man to rule himself. The
right of every man to rule himself and the
nation in which he lives and since no man
rules himself into bondage, therefore liberty
flows from it as water from the hills.

DIAZ
I understand, Señor Juarez.

JUAREZ

I say to entrust one's fate to a superior
individual is to betray the very spirit of
liberty. The spirit by which each man
may raise himself to that level of human
dignity where no man is superior of any
other. Where even the lowliest is up-
lifted to the worth of his manhood and is
able to rule with wisdom, justice and
tolerance toward all men. Should I not
know it, Porfirio? Am I not of the lowest?

DIAZ

Señor Juarez, I was a fool.

JUAREZ

Only a word, democracy, stands between
Maximiliano von Hapsburg and myself,
but it is an unbridgable gulf. We represent irreconcilable principles. One or
the other of which must perish. You see,
Porfirio, when a monarch misrules he
changes the people; when a president misrules the people change him.

Warners sought to invest these films with the same kind of

"background" and setting possessed by "The Public Enemy" and "I

Am A Fugitive From A Chain Gang". For example, we learn that

the medical profession is against Pasteur because he is a chemist

and is working in areas they hold to be the domain of doctors. The

historical socially conscious films were produced with great attention

to authenticity in order to create mood. "Pasteur", "Zola" and

"Juarez" were among the most expensive films produced by Warners

during the 1930's.

Thus, as has been noted, the best of the socially conscious films shared a conceptual bond with the archetypical gangster films. As the 1930's came to an end the all important elements -- stories placed in the context of an era, characters who drew their motivations from the demands of their times, social comment, documentary quality -- were passed on to genre which did not include the gangster film. Out of touch with new ideas, new fears, new headlines, the gangster genre sank to the obscurity of backlot program picture fodder while new forms took precedence. Greater villains, greater social ills loomed on the horizon. The gangster -- temporarily, at least -- was shelved until such a time when his bravado, his challenge of society, would again catch the interest of film makers and audiences alike after World War II.

The era that began with "Little Caesar" as one of its most significant films ended with films such as "Grapes of Wrath". Despite the decline of the gangster film, however, the era had given birth to an enduring, a classic genre which takes its place among the most influential and enduring forms in the history of American film.

APPENDIX I

SYNOPSES OF PERTINENT SUBSIDIARY FILMS OUTSIDE THE GENRE

"BARBARY COAST" 1936

SYNOPSIS:

Swan, a beautiful young woman, disembarks from a sailing vessel in the raucous young city of San Francisco. She has come to marry a rich man but finds that he has been killed shortly before her arrival. Undaunted by this and seeing that her beautiful clothes and blonde hair make her an unusual attraction in this city of frontier men and sailors, she accepts the offer of the local underworld boss and saloon owner, Chamalis, to work in his establishment.

Chamalis is occupied in taking over the city. He is being opposed by the reform minded newspaper editor and by the locally formed vigilantes. Chamalis and his henchman, Knuckles, stop at nothing in their fight for power, including the murder of the newspaperman.

Chamalis constantly meets defeat, however, in his attempts to win Swan. She works for him, attracting men to his gambling tables, but she refuses all of Chamalis' advances.

Jim, a young poet from New York who has come west for

the gold strike, brings his earnings into the casino and loses them
in an unfair game. Swan feels sorry for the young man and is
attracted to him. Jim gets a job in the saloon as a kitchen helper.

Out riding one day, Swan is caught in the rain and takes
shelter in a house where Jim happens to also be staying. Jim explains his hopes and plans to her and she is touched by his intelligence
and sincerity. It becomes apparent to both that they are falling in love.
Chamalis later learns of the meeting and is extremely jealous.

Swan and Jim plan to flee San Francisco together. Chamalis,
himself pursued by vigilantes who have already hung Knuckles,
follows the pair as they row toward the sailing ship through the dense
fog. Jim is wounded by Chamalis' men.

Chamalis apprehends them as they board. Swan, in a self-
less act to save Jim, offers to stay with Chamalis and even to give
her love to him if he will let Jim go on alone. At the last moment
Chamalis relents and lets the pair go, seeing that Swan's forced love
for him would be a hollow victory.

As the lovers leave, Chamalis is caught by the vigilante
party. He accepts his fate and still his arrogant self, goes smiling
to the gallows.

"BORDERTOWN" 1935

SYNOPSIS:

In Los Angeles a young Mexican man, Johnny Ramirez,
has worked his way up from a beginning as a juvenile delinquent to
his present position as a graduate of a local non-prestigous law
school. Mama Ramirez pawns her wedding ring to buy the sign,
"J. Farada Ramirez Attorney At Law" and Johnny quits his job in
the gas station to open a modest office in his home. During the
first month of practice, however, he earns only two dollars in
fees from his impoverished clientele. The Padre counsels Johnny
to have patience.

Rich Dale Elwell and her boyfriend, attorney Brook Manville,
are out on a slumming tour. Leaving the Cafe La Paloma, the exhuber-
ant Dale slams her roadster into a Mexican fruit peddler's truck.
The peddler goes to Johnny and begs him to take his case.

In court Johnny presents the case, and although justice would
seem to be on his side his inadequate knowledge of the law and of
court procedures allows Manville to make a fool of him and win the
case in Dale's favor. Johnny is enraged and losing control strikes
Manville in the courtroom, an action which causes the young Mexican
to be disbarred. Dale, unimpressed by the hearing, has spent the

the time sketching Johnny and over the picture of his face writes
"Savage".

Determined to make the "big time" yet, Johnny goes to
the border town of Mexacali. He eventually finds himself in the
cabaret owned by Charlie Roark. After stopping four syndicate
men from taking over the establishment, Johnny is given the job of
bouncer. A year later he is Roark's trusted manager. Finally he
persuades Roark to make him a partner.

Meanwhile Roark's young wife, Marie, has become flirtatious with her husband's young and attractive partner, but Johnny
will have nothing to do with her. Bored and feeling rejected, Marie
takes the drunken Roark home one night and leaves him asleep in the
car with the motor running and the garage door closed. After Roark's
"accidental" death Johnny builds a new night club, a much larger and
more elegant one, the "Rueda".

The new club becomes a favorite spot of socialites and one
night Dale Elwell and Brook Manville arrive. They are surprised to
find Johnny is the owner. Johnny and Dale are attracted to one
another and after that night begin going out.

Marie confronts Johnny and he still rebuffs her. In revenge,
Marie goes to the police, confesses the murder of her husband and

implicates Johnny in the crime. The two are brought to trial but
Marie goes mad on the stand and the case is dismissed.

Free at last, Johnny picks up Dale at her home and drives
her to a party. On the way Johnny professes his love but Dale informs him that he has been merely a passing fancy and that they
are from "different tribes". Johnny is hurt and angry. Dale flees
from the car and is killed in the street by a passing automobile.

Johnny goes back to his home and announces his intention
to stay "with his own people" and that he will sell his night club and
donate the money to endow a law school.

"TIGER SHARK" 1932

SYNOPSIS:

Mike Mascarena, a Portuguese owner of a tuna boat, is,
as he styles himself, the best fisherman of the Pacific. He is a
liar when he thinks the occasion demands it, and a fiend when
aroused. But, most of the time, he is a good fellow. He loses a
hand to a shark during a shipwreck and, thereafter, goes about
with a hook attached to his left arm. Mike is told that he will not
be permitted to enter the Celestial Regions because St. Peter
frowns upon those who are not bodily whole.

He goes to see Quita, the daughter of Manuel, who is a victim of sharks. He finds she is unusually attractive. He gives her money, saying that it is her father's life insurance. He brings her food, and in the course of time, Mike, who had never found a woman who would pay attention to him, has won a certain favor with Manuel's daughter, who is recovering from an unfortunate love affair.

Mike's good-looking fellow-fisherman, Pipes Boley, learns from "the best fisherman of the Pacific" that he is going to marry Quita. His girl must have a fine wedding gown, and he must be made to look beautiful. He is barbered; perfume is poured over his hair. His shoes are shined until he can see his reflection in them. Even the hook he uses for a hand is polished up, and his clothes would put any racetrack tout to shame. The marriage takes place. Mike, drunk, passes out on his wedding night.

Mike goes out on one of his fishing trips, and each man with two rods hauls in big tuna. The fish are put ashore and Mike hastens to his bride, who is awaiting him on the little pier. His life is complete. But Quita, at first grateful, has become sad in Mike's arms.

It is another fishing trip. The catch is big. Suddenly a hook catches in Pipes' neck. Pipes is taken ashore and a doctor attends him. Quita nurses him back to health.

Little does Mike know that Quita and Pipes are in love and

that they have admitted it to each other. One day, on the boat, they

embrace, and at the door first the girl and then Pipes see Mike's

face. Mike reaches out with his hook and strikes Pipes. He tries

to throw Pipes to the sharks, but Pipes is spared, through the fact

that Mike himself is caught in a rope and flung overboard.

Before he passes away, Mike avers that

St. Peter will take him aboard for he was the "best damn fisherman

of the Pacific".

APPENDIX II

CAST LISTS OF PERTINENT FILMS

THE AMAZING DR. CLITTERHOUSE

1938

First National

Director, Anatole Litvak; screenplay by John Wexley and John
Huston; from the play by Barre Lyndon.

Edward G. Robinson. . . . . Dr. Clitterhouse
Claire Trevor. . . . . Jo Keller
Humphrey Bogart. . . . ."Rocks" Valentine
Allen Jenkins. . . . . Okay
Donald Crisp. . . . . Inspector Lane
Gale Page. . . . . Nurse Randolf

ANGELS WITH DIRTY FACES

1938

Warner Brothers

Director, Michael Curtiz; screenplay by John Wexley and Warren
Duff; from the story by Rowland Brown.

James Cagney. . . . . Rocky Sullivan
Pat O'Brien. . . . . Jerry Connolly
Humphrey Bogart. . . . . .James Frazier
Ann Sheridan. . . . . Laury Ferguson
George Bancroft. . . . . Mac Keefer
Bobby Jordan. . . . . .Swing
Leo Gorcey. . . . . .Bim
Billy Halop. . . . . Soapy

BARBARY COAST

1936

A Samuel Goldwyn Production

Director, Howard Hawks; story and adaptation, Charles MacArthur and Ben Hecht.

Edward G. Robinson......................................Chamalis
Miriam Hopkins..Swan
Joel McCrea...Jim
Walter Brennan...Atrocity
Frank Craven...Cobb
Brian Donlevy..Knuckles

BLACK FURY

1935

Warner Brothers - A First National Picture

Director, Michael Curtiz; screenplay by Abem Finkel and Carl Erickson; from an original story "Jan Volkanik" by Judge M. A. Musmanno; the play "Bohunk" by Harry R. Irving.

Paul Muni...Joe Rodek
Karen Mosley...Anna Novak
William Gargan...Slim
Barton MacLane...McGee

BLACK LEGION

1937

Warner Brothers

Director, Archie L. Mayo; screenplay by Abem Finkel and
William Wister Haines; original story by Robert Lord.

Humphrey Bogart. . . . . Frank Taylor
Dick Foran. . . . . Ed Jackson
Erin O'Brien-Moore. . . . . Ruth Taylor
Ann Sheridan. . . . . Betty Grogan

BLONDE CRAZY
(formerly: LARCENY LANE)

1931

Warner Brothers & Vitaphone Corporation

Director, Roy Del Ruth; story by Kubec Glasmon and John Bright.

James Cagney. . . . . Bart Harris
Joan Blondell. . . . . Anne
Louis Calhern. . . . . Dapper Dan
Ray Milland. . . . . Anne's Husband

BORDERTOWN

1935

Warner Brothers & Vitaphone Corporation

Director, Archie L. Mayo; suggested by Carroll Graham's novel;
story by Robert Lord; screenplay by Laird Doyle and Wallace Smith.

Paul Muni. . . . . Johnny Ramirez
Bette Davis. . . . . Marie Roark
Margaret Lindsay. . . . . Dale Elwell
Eugene Pallette. . . . . Charlie Roark

BOY MEETS GIRL

1938

Warner Brothers

Director, Lloyd Bacon; screenplay and stage play by Bella and Samuel Spewack.

James Cagney	Robert Law
Pat O'Brien	J. C. Benson
Marie Wilson	Susie
Ralph Bellamy	C. Elliott Friday
Frank McHugh	Rossetti
Dick Foran	Larry Toms

BROTHER ORCHID

1940

Warner Brothers - First National Picture

Director, Lloyd Bacon; screenplay by Earl Baldwin, based on the Collier's Magazine story by Richard Connell.

Edward G. Robinson	Little John Sarto
Ann Southern	Flo Addams
Humphrey Bogart	Jack Buck
Donald Crisp	Brother Superior
Ralph Bellamy	Clarence Fletcher
Allen Jenkins	Willie the Knife

BULLETS OR BALLOTS

1936

A First National Picture

Director, William Keighley; screenplay by Seton I. Miller, from a story by Martin Mooney and Seton I. Miller.

Edward G. Robinson.............................Johnny Blake
Joan Blondell................................. Lee Morgan
Barton MacLane............................... Al Kruger
Humphrey Bogart............................. Bugs Fenner
Frank McHugh.................................Herman

CEILING ZERO

1935

Warner Brothers - A Cosmopolitan Production

Director and producer, Howard Hawks; stage and screenplay, Frank Wead.

James Cagney.................................Dizzy Davis
Pat O'Brien....................................Jake Lee
June Travis..................................Tommy Thomas
Stuart Erwin................................ Texas Clark
Barton MacLane...............................Al Stone

CITY FOR CONQUEST

1940

Warner Brothers - First National Picture

Director, Anatole Litvak; screenplay by John Wexley; from the novel by Aben Kandel.

James Cagney............................. Danny Kenny
Ann Sheridan..................................Peggy Nash
Frank Craven................................Old Timer
Donald Crisp............................. Scotty MacPherson

CONFESSIONS OF A NAZI SPY

1939

Warner Brothers - First National Picture

Director, Anatole Litvak; screenplay, Milton Krims and John
Wexley; based on the Articles of Leon G. Turrou.

Edward G. Robinson...................... Edward Renard
Francis Lederer............................... Schneider
George Sanders................................ Schlager
Paul Lukas.................................. Dr. Kassel

CRIME SCHOOL

1938

Warner Brothers

Director, Lewis Seiler; screenplay, Crane Wilbur and Vincent Sherman;
from a story by Crane Wilbur.

Humphrey Bogart........................... Mark Braden
Gale Page.................................. Sue Warren
Billy Halop................................ Frankie Warren
Bobby Jordan............................... Squirt
Huntz Hall................................. Goofy
Leo Gorcey................................. Spike

THE CROWD ROARS

1932

Warner Brothers

Written and directed by Howard Hawks.

James Cagney............................... Joe Greer
Joan Blondell.............................. Anne

Ann Dvorak . . . . Lee
Guy Kibbee . . . . Dad Greer
Frank McHugh . . . . Spud

A DISPATCH FROM REUTER'S

1940

Warner Brothers

Director, William Dieterle; screenplay, Milton Krims; from a story
by Valentine Williams and Wolfgang Wilhelm.

Edward G. Robinson . . . . Julius Reuter
Edna Best . . . . Ida Magnus
Eddie Albert . . . . Max Wagner
Albert Basserman . . . . Franz Geller

DARK HAZARD

1934

A First National Picture

Director, Alfred W. Green; screenplay by Ralph Block and Brown Holmes;
based on a novel by W. R. Burnett.

Edward G. Robinson . . . . Jim (Buck) Turner
Genevieve Tobin . . . . Marge Mayhew
Glenda Farrell . . . . Valerie Wilson
Robert Barrat . . . . Tex Willis

DEAD END

1937

United Artists - A Samuel Goldwyn Production

Director, William Wyler; screenplay, Lillian Hellman; based on the
play by Sidney Kingsley.

Sylvia Sidney.................................... Drina
Joel McCrea............................... Dave Connell
Humphrey Bogart....................... Baby Face Martin
Wendy Barrie.............................. Kay Burton
Claire Trevor................................. Francey
Allen Jenkins.................................. Hunk
The Dead End Kids

DEVIL DOGS OF THE AIR

1935

Warner Brothers - A Cosmopolitan Production

Director, Lloyd Bacon; screenplay, Malcolm Stuart Boylan and Earl Baldwin; based on a story by John Monk Saunders.

James Cagney........................... Tommy O'Toole
Pat O'Brien.................... Lieutenant William Brannigan
Margaret Lindsay........................... Betty Roberts
Frank McHugh............................ Crash Kelly

DR. EHRLICH'S MAGIC BULLET

1940

Warner Brothers - First National Picture

Director, William Dieterle; original screenplay, John Huston, Heinz Herald and Norman Burnside; from an idea by Norman Burnside.

Edward G. Robinson...................... Dr. Paul Ehrlich
Ruth Gordon............................. Mrs. Ehrlich
Otto Kruger........................ Dr. Emil Von Behring
Donald Crisp........................... Minister Althoff
Albert Basserman........................ Dr. Robert Koch

DR. SOCRATES

1935

Warner Brothers

Director, William Dieterle; screenplay, Robert Lord; adaptation, Mary C. McCall Jr.; story W. R. Burnett

Paul Muni	Lee Cardwell
Ann Dvorak	Josephine Gray
Barton MacLane	Red Bastian

DOORWAY TO HELL

1930

Warner Brothers

Director, Archie Mayo; screenplay by Rowland Brown.

James Cagney	Mileaway
Lewis Ayres	Louie Ricarno
Dorothy Mathews	Louie's girl

THE FIGHTING 69TH

1940

Warner Brothers - First National Picture

Director, William Keighley; original screenplay, Norman Reilly Raine, Fred Niblo, Jr. and Dean Franklin.

James Cagney	Jerry Plunkett
Pat O'Brien	Father Duffy
George Brent	"'Wild Bill' Donovan"
Jeffrey Lynn	Joyce Kilmer
Alan Hale	Sgt. 'Big Mike' Wynn
Frank McHugh	Crepe Hanger' Burke
Dennis Morgan	Lieutenant Ames
Dick Foran	Lt. 'Long John' Wynn
William Lundigan	Timmy Wynn

FRISCO KID

1935

Warner Brothers

Director, Lloyd Bacon; story and screenplay, Warren Duff and Seton I. Miller.

James Cagney. . . . . Bat Morgan
Margaret Lindsay. . . . . Jean Barrat
Ricardo Cortez. . . . . Paul Morra

G-MEN

1935

Warner Brothers

Director, William Keighley; story and screenplay, Seton I. Miller.

James Cagney. . . . . Brick Davis
Margaret Lindsay. . . . . .Kay McCord
Ann Dvorak. . . . . Jean Morgan
Robert Armstrong. . . . . .Jeff McCord
Barton MacLane. . . . , ... Collins
Lloyd Nolan. . . . . Hugh Farrell

HARD TO HANDLE

1933

Warner Brothers

Director, Mervyn LeRoy; screenplay, Wilson Mizner and Robert Lord; based on an original story by Huston Branch.

James Cagney. . . . . .Lefty Merrill
Mary Brian. . . . . .Ruth Waters
Allen Jenkins. . . . . Radio Announcer
Ruth Donnelly. . . . . Lil Waters

HERE COMES THE NAVY
(formerly: Hey Sailor)

1934

Warner Brothers

Director, Lloyd Bacon; screenplay, Earl Baldwin and Ben Markson;
original story by Ben Markson.

James Cagney. . . . . Chesty
Pat O'Brien. . . . . Biff
Gloria Stuart. . . . . Dorothy
Frank McHugh. . . . . Droopy

HI NELLIE

1934

Warner Brothers

Director, Mervyn LeRoy; screenplay, Abem Finkel and Sidney
Sutherland; story by Roy Chanslor.

Paul Muni. . . . . Brad
Glenda Farrell. . . . . Gerry
Ned Spark. . . . . Shammy
Robert Barrat. . . . . Brownell

I AM A FUGITIVE FROM A CHAIN GANG

1932

Warner Brothers

Director, Mervyn LeRoy; screenplay, Brown Holmes and Howard J.
Green.

Paul Muni. . . . . James Allen
Glenda Farrell. . . . . Marie
Helen Vinson. . . . . Helen
Preston S. Foster. . . . . Pete

I LOVED A WOMAN

1933

A First National Picture

Director, Alfred E. Green; screenplay by Charles Kenyon and Sidney Sutherland from a story by David Karsner.

Edward G. Robinson. . . . . John Hayden
Kay Francis. . . . . Laura McDonald
Genevieve Tobin. . . . . Martha Lane
J. Farrell MacDonald. . . . . Shuster

THE IRISH IN US

1935

A First National Picture

Director, Lloyd Bacon; screenplay, Earl Baldwin; based on an idea by Frank Orsatti.

James Cagney. . . . . Danny O'Hara
Pat O'Brien. . . . . Pat O'Hara
Olivia de Havilland. .Lucille Jackson
Frank McHugh. . . . . Mike O'Hara
Allen Jenkins. . . . . Carbarn

JIMMY THE GENT

1934

Warner Brothers

Director, Michael Curtiz; screenplay by Bertram Mihouser based on a story by Laird Doyle and Ray Nazarro.

James Cagney. . . . . Jimmy Corrigan
Bette Davis. . . . . Jean Martin
Alice White. . . . . Mabel
Allen Jenkins. . . . . Louie
Alan Dinehart. . . . . .James J. Wallingham

JUAREZ

1939

Warner Brothers

Director, William Dieterle; screenplay, John Huston, Wolfgang Reinhardt and Aeneas MacKenzie.

Paul Muni. . . . . Juarez
Bette Davis. . . . . Carlota
Brian Aherne. . . . . Maximilian
Claude Rains. . . . . Napolean III
John Garfield. . . . . Porfirio Diaz

KID GALAHAD

1937

Warner Brothers

Director, Michael Curtiz; screenplay, Seton I. Miller; from the Saturday Evening Post story by Francis Wallace.

Edward G. Robinson. . . . . Nick Donati
Bette Davis. . . . . Fluff
Humphrey Bogart. . . . . Turkey Morgan
Wayne Morris. . . . . Ward Quisenberry aka Kid Galahad
Jane Bryan. . . . . Marie Donati
Harry Carry. . . . . Silver Jackson

KING OF THE UNDERWORLD

1939

Warner Brothers

Director, Lewis Seiler; screenplay, George Bricker and Vincent Sherman; based on the Liberty Magazine serial, "Dr. Socrates" by W. R. Burnett.

Humphrey Bogart. . . . . Joe Gurney
Kay Francis. . . . . Carol Nelson
James Stephenson. . . . . Bill Forrest
John Eldredge. . . . . Niles Nelson

LADY KILLER

1933

Warner Brothers

Director, Roy Del Ruth; screenplay, Ben Markson and Lillie Hayward; from the original story by Rosalind Keating Shaffer.

James Cagney. . . . . Dan
Mae Clark. . . . . Myra
Margaret Lindsay. . . . . Lois
Leslie Fenton. . . . . Duke
Douglas Dumbrille. . . . . Spade

THE LIFE OF EMILE ZOLA

1937

Warner Brothers

Director, William Dieterle; screenplay, Norman Reilly Raine, Heinz Herald and Geza Herczeg.

Paul Muni. . . . . Emile Zola
Joseph Schildkraut. . . . . Capt. Alfred Dreyfus
Donald Crisp. . . . . Maitre Labori
John Litel. . . . . Charpentier
Morris Carnovsky. . . . . Anatole France

LITTLE CAESAR

1930

A First National Picture

Director, Mervyn LeRoy; screenplay, Francis Edwards Faragoh; from a novel by W. R. Burnett; adaptation by Robert W. Lee.

Edward G. Robinson........................... Little Caesar
Douglas Fairbanks, Jr........................... Joe Massara
Glenda Farrell................................. Olga Strassof
Sidney Blackmer................................ The Big Boy
Thomas Jackson.................... Police Sergeant Flaherty
Ralph Ince................................... Pete Montana

THE LITTLE GIANT

1933

A First National Picture

Director, Roy Del Ruth; screenplay, Robert Lord and Wilson Mizner; based on the original story by Robert Lord.

Edward G. Robinson........................... Bugs Ahearn
Mary Astor................................. Ruth Waybourn
Helen Vinson.................................. Polly Cass

MARKED WOMAN

1937

A First National Picture

Director, Lloyd Bacon; original screenplay by Laird Doyle and Abem Finkel.

Bette Davis...................................... Mary
Lola Lane.. Gabby
Eduardo Ciannelli.......................... Johnny Vanning
Humphrey Bogart............................ David Graham

THE OKLAHOMA KID

1939

Warner Brothers

Director, Lloyd Bacon; screenplay, Warren Duff, Robert Buckner
and Edward E. Paramore; from an original story by Edward E.
Paramore and Willy Klein.

James Cagney.................................. Jim Kincaid
Humphrey Bogart............................. Whip McCord
Rosemary Lane.............................. Jane Hardwick
Donald Crisp.............................. Judge Hardwick

THE PETRIFIED FOREST

1936

Warner Brothers

Director, Archie L. Mayo; screenplay, Charles Kenyon and Delmer
Daves; play by Robert Emmet Sherwood.

Leslie Howard............................... Alan Squire
Bette Davis............................... Gabrielle Maple
Genevieve Tobin.......................... Mrs. Chisholm
Dick Foran.............................. Boze Hertzlinger
Humphrey Bogart........................... Duke Mantee

PICTURE SNATCHER

1933

Warner Brothers

Director, Lloyd Bacon; screenplay, Allen Rivkin and P. J. Wolfson;
original story by Danny Ahearn.

James Cagney................................... Danny
Patricia Ellis................................. Patricia
Alice White.................................... Alison
Ralph Bellamy................................ McLean

THE ROARING TWENTIES

1939

Warner Brothers

Director, Raoul Walsh; screenplay, Jerry Wald, Richard Macaulay and Robert Rossen; from an original story by Mark Hellinger.

James Cagney. . . . . Eddie Bartlett
Priscilla Lane. . . . . Jean Sherman
Humphrey Bogart. . . . . George Hally
Gladys George. . . . . Panama Smith
Jeffrey Lynn. . . . . Lloyd Hart

THE ST. LOUIS KID

1934

Warner Brothers

Director, Ray Enright; adapted by Warren Duff and Seton I. Miller; from a story by Frederick Haxlitt Brennan.

James Cagney. . . . . Eddie Kennedy
Patricia Ellis. . . . . Ann Reid
Allen Jenkins. . . . . Buck Willetts
Robert Barrat. . . . . Farmer Benson

SAN QUENTIN

1937

Warner Brothers - First National Picture

Director, Lloyd Bacon; Screenplay, Robert Rossen and Abem Finkel.

Pat O'Brien. . . . . Capt. Stephen Jameson
Humphrey Bogart. . . . . Joe "Red" Kennedy
Ann Sheridan. . . . . May
Barton MacLane. . . . . Lt. Druggin

THE PUBLIC ENEMY

1931

Warner Brothers

Director, William Wellman; story, Kubec Glasman and John Bright; adaptation, Harry Thew.

James Cagney	Tom Powers
Edward Woods	Matt Doyle
Donald Cook	Mike Powers
Joan Blondell	Mamie
Jean Harlow	Gwen Allen
Mae Clark	Kitty

RACKET BUSTERS

1938

Warner Brothers - A Cosmopolitan Production

Director, Lloyd Bacon; screenplay, Robert Rossen and Leonardo Bercovici.

Humphrey Bogart	Martin
George Brent	Denny Jordan
Gloria Dickson	Nora Jordan
Allen Jenkins	Horse Wilson
Walter Abel	Allison

RETURN OF DOCTOR X

1939

Warner Brothers - First National Picture

Director, Vincent Sherman; screenplay, Lee Katz; from a story by William J. Makin.

Wayne Morris. . . . . .Walter Barnett
Rosemary Lane. . . . . Joan Vance
Humphrey Bogart. . . . . Marhsall Quesne
Dennis Morgan. . . . . .Michael Rhodes
John Lytel. . . . . .Dr. Francis Flegg

SCARFACE

THE SHAME OF A NATION

1932

United Artists - A Howard Hughes Production

Director, Howard Hawks; screenplay, Seton I. Miller, John Lee
Mahin, W. R. Burnett and Ben Hecht; based on a novel by Armitage
Trail (pen name of Maurice Coon).

Paul Muni. . . . . Tony Carmonte
Ann Dvorak. . . . . Cesca Carmonte
Karen Morely. . . . . Poppy
Osbood Perkins. . . . . .Johnny Lovo
Boris Karloff. . . . . Gaffney
George Raft. . . . . Rinaldo

SINNER'S HOLIDAY

1930

Warner Brothers

Director, John Adolfi; screenplay, Harvey Thew; from the play
"Penny Arcade" by Marie Baumer.

Grant Withers. . . . . Angel Harrigan
Evelyn Knapp. . . . . Jennie
James Cagney. . . . . .Harry
Joan Blondell. . . . . Myrtle

A SLIGHT CASE OF MURDER

1938

Warner Brothers

Director, Lloyd Bacon; screenplay, Earl Baldwin and Joseph Schrank;
based on the play by Damon Runyon and Howard Lindsay.

Edward G. Robinson . . . . Remy Marco
Jane Bryan . . . . Mary Marco
Allen Jenkins . . . . Mike
Bobby Jordan . . . . Douglas Fairbanks Rosenbloom

THE STORY OF LOUIS PASTEUR

1935

Warner Brothers - A Cosmopolitan Production

Director, William Dieterle; story and screenplay, Sheridan Gibney
and Pierre Collings.

Paul Muni . . . . Louis Pasteur
Josephine Hutchinson . . . . Marie Pasteur
Anita Louise . . . . Annette Pasteur
Donald Woods . . . . Dr. Jean Martel
Fritz Leiber . . . . Dr. Charbonnet
Henry O'Neill . . . . Dr. Emil Roux

SMART MONEY

1931

A First National Picture

Director, Alfred Green; screen story and dialogue by Kubec Glasmon,
John Bright and Joseph Jackson.

Edward G. Robinson . . . . Nick
Evelyn Knapp . . . . Irene
James Cagney . . . . Jack
Noel Francis . . . . Marie

TIGER SHARK

1932

A First National Picture

Director, Howard Hawks; dialogue and adaptation by Wells Root based on "Tuna" a story by Huston Branch.

```
Edward G. Robinson..................... Mike Mascarena
Zita Johann................................. Quita
Richard Arlen............................. Pipes Boley
J. Carroll Naish.......................... The Man
```

TAXI

1932

Warner Brothers

Director, Roy Del Ruth; adaptation and dialogue by Kubec Glasmon and John Bright.

```
James Cagney.............................. Matt Nolan
Loretta Young............................. Sue Reilly
George E. Stone........................... Skeets Nolan
Dorothy Burgess.......................... Marie
Guy Kibbee................................ Pop Reilly
```

TORRID ZONE

1940

Warner Brothers - First National Picture

Director, William Keighley; screenplay, Richard Macaulay and Jerry Wald.

```
James Cagney.............................. Nick Butler
Ann Sheridan............................. Lee Donley
Pat O'Brien............................... Steve Case
Andy Devine.............................. Wally Davis
```

WINNER TAKE ALL

1932

Warner Brothers

Director, Roy Del Ruth; adaptation and dialogue by Wilson Mizner
and Robert Lord based on a story by Gerald Beaumont.

```
James Cagney.................................. Jim Kane
Marian Nixon................................. Peggy Smith
Guy Kibbee........................................ Pop
Clarence Muse................................. Rosebud
```

YOU CAN'T GET AWAY WITH MURDER

1938

Warner Brothers - First National Picture

Director, Lewis Seiler; screenplay, Robert Bruckner, Don Ryan and
Kenneth Gamet; based on the play by Lewis E. Lawes and Jonathan Finn.

```
Humphrey Bogart......................... Frank Wilson
Gale Page................................ Madge Stone
Billy Halop.............................. Johnnie Stone
John Litel............................... Attorney Carey
```

BIBLIOGRAPHY

I. Newspaper Articles and Motion Picture Reviews

Archer, Eugene, "Other Heroes Are Dust But Bogart Snarls On," Kansas City Star, Jan. 24, 1965, p. 12.

New York Times. "The Amazing Dr. Clitterhouse," Apr. 10, 3:8, 1938.

_____. "The Amazing Dr. Clitterhouse," July 21, 14:2, 1938.

_____. "The Amazing Dr. Clitterhouse," July 24, 4:1, 1938.

_____. "Angels With Dirty Faces," Aug. 14, 3:7, 1938.

_____. "Angels With Dirty Faces," Nov. 26, 18:1, 1938.

_____. "Angels With Dirty Faces," Nov. 27, 5:1, 1938.

_____. "Big City Blues," Sept. 10, 18:5, 1932.

_____. "Big City Blues," Sept. 18, IX 33, 1932.

_____. "Black Fury," April 6, 21:2, 1935.

_____. "Black Fury," April 7, 3:1, 1935.

_____. "Black Fury," April 11, 27:2, 1935.

_____. "Black Fury," April 21, 3:6, 1935.

_____. "Black Fury," April 28, 3:4, 1935.

_____. "Black Fury," June 23, 2:3, 1935.

_____. "Black Legion," Jan. 17, 4:4, 1937.

_____. "Black Legion," Jan. 18, 21:1, 1937.

_____. "Black Legion," Jan. 24, 5:1, 1937.

_____. "Blonde Crazy," Dec. 4, 28:2, 1931.

_____. "Blonde Crazy," Dec. 20, 3:4, 1931.

_____. "Humphrey Bogart," Feb. 19, 4:2, 1939.

_____. "Humphrey Bogart," April 15, 1:1, 1940.

_____. "Humphrey Bogart," Aug. 21, 21:2, 1940.

_____. "Humphrey Bogart," Jan. 15, 1:43, 1957.

_____. "Bordertown," June 24, 22:5, 1935.

_____. "Bordertown," Feb. 3, 5:2, 1935.

_____. "Boy Meets Girl," March 27, 5:7, 1938.

_____. "Boy Meets Girl," May 22, 3:7, 1938.

_____. "Brother Orchid," June 8, 18:2, 1940.

Literary Digest. "James Cagney," April 17, 117:43, 1934.

New York Times. "James Cagney," June 28, VIII 5:4, 1931.

_____. "James Cagney," March 20, VIII 6:2, 1932.

_____. "James Cagney," April 27, 13:5, 1932.

_____. "James Cagney," April 28, 17:2, 1932.

_____. "James Cagney," April 30, 19:4, 1932.

_____. "James Cagney," Sept. 29, 19:6, 1932.

_____. "James Cagney," July 29, IX 3:1, 1934.

_____. "James Cagney," Aug. 19, 6:2, 1934.

_____. "James Cagney," Nov. 24, IX 4:5, 1935.

_____. "James Cagney," July 14, 22:1, 1936.

_____. "James Cagney," July 19, IX 3:3, 1936.

_____. "James Cagney," July 26, IX 3:2, 1936,

_____. "James Cagney," Jan. 9, X 5:8, 1938.

_____. "James Cagney," Jan. 3, 18:5, 1939.

_____. "James Cagney," Jan. 8, IX 5:1, 1939.

_____. "James Cagney," Jan. 9, 10:2, 1939.

_____. "James Cagney," Feb. 24, 9:3, 1939.

_____. "James Cagney," Jan. 23, 16:2, 1940.

_____. "James Cagney," Feb. 29, 2:2, 1940.

_____. "James Cagney," Aug. 15, 1:1, 1940.

_____. "James Cagney," Aug. 20, 14:8, 1940.

_____. "James Cagney," Aug. 21, 21:2, 1940.

_____. "Confessions Of A Nazi Spy," Feb. 5, IX 5:2, 1939.

_____. "Confessions Of A Nazi Spy," Feb. 19, IX 4:1, 1939.

_____. "Confessions Of A Nazi Spy," April 2, X 5:3, 1939.

_____. "Confessions Of A Nazi Spy," April 23, X 6:21, 1939.

_____. "Confessions Of A Nazi Spy," April 26, 25:8, 1939.

_____. "Confessions Of A Nazi Spy," April 29, 13:2, 1939.

_____. "Confessions Of A Nazi Spy," May 7, X 5:1, 1939.

_____. "Confessions Of A Nazi Spy," May 7, X 5:7, 1939.

_____. "Confessions Of A Nazi Spy," May 16, 26:4, 1939.

_____. "Confessions Of A Nazi Spy," June 7, 26:4, 1939.

_____. "Confessions Of A Nazi Spy," June 21, 27:3, 1939.

_____. "Confessions Of A Nazi Spy," June 22, IX 3:5, 1939.

_____. "Confessions Of A Nazi Spy," July 14, 10:8, 1939.

_____. "Confessions Of A Nazi Spy," Aug. 17, 4:4, 1939.

285.

_____. "Confessions Of A Nazi Spy," Nov. 28, 10:3, 1939.

_____. "Confessions Of A Nazi Spy," Dec. 25, 28:4, 1939.

_____. "Crime School," May 11, 17:2, 1938.

_____. "Crime School," May 15, X 3:1, 1938.

_____. "The Crowd Roars," March 23, 25:4, 1932.

_____. "The Crown Roars," April 3, VIII 4:4, 1932.

_____. "Dark Hazard," Feb. 7, 23:2, 1934.

_____. "Dark Hazard," March 11, X 5:2, 1934.

_____. "Dark Victory," April 21, 27:2, 1939.

_____. "Devil Dogs Of The Air," Feb. 7, 23:2, 1935.

_____. "Devil Dogs Of The Air," Feb. 10, VIII 4:5, 1935.

_____. "Devil Dogs Of The Air," Feb. 24, VIII 5:1, 1935.

_____. "Dieterle, Wm.," Sept. 26, 4:2, 1935.

_____. "Dr. Ehrlich's Magic Bullet," Jan. 14, 4:2, 1940.

_____. "Dr. Ehrlich's Magic Bullet," Feb. 24, 9:3, 1940.

_____. "Dr. Ehrlich's Magic Bullet," Mar. 12, 5:2, 1940.

_____. "Doorway To Hell," Nov. 1, 23:3, 1930.

_____. "Doorway To Hell," Nov. 23, 4:2, 1930.

_____. "City For Conquest," May 19, IX 4:3, 1940.

_____. "City For Conquest," Sept. 28, 9:2, 1940.

_____. "Confessions Of A Nazi Spy," Jan. 6, 3:6, 1939.

_____. "Confessions Of A Nazi Spy," Jan. 15, IX 4:2, 1939.

_____. "The Fighting 69th," Jan. 17, 25:4, 1940.

_____. "The Fighting 69th," Jan 23, 16:2, 1940.

_____. "The Fighting 69th," Jan. 25, 23:5, 1940.

_____. "The Fighting 69th," Jan. 27, 9:2, 1940.

_____. "The Fighting 69th," Feb. 4, IX 5:1, 1940.

_____. "The Fighting 69th," March 6, 13:5, 1940.

_____. "French Pasteur," Jan. 30, 14:4, 1936.

_____. "G Men," April 25, 19:3, 1935.

_____. "G Men," April 28, X 4:2, 1935.

_____. "G Men," May 2, 17:1, 1935.

_____. "Hard To Handle," Feb. 2, 21:5, 1933.

_____. "Hard To Handle," Feb. 12, III 5:1, 1933.

_____. "Here Comes The Navy," July 21, 14:2, 1934.

_____. "Here Comes The Navy," July 29, IX 3:1, 1934.

_____. "I Am A Fugitive From A Chain Gang," Nov. 11, 17:2, 1932.

IX IX 5:1, _____. "I Am A Fugitive From A Chain Gang," Nov. 20, 1932.

_____. "I Am A Fugitive From A Chain Gang," Dec. 23, 22:4, 1932.

_____. "The Irish In Us," July 28, X 4:1, 1935.

_____. "The Irish In Us," Aug. 1, 15:1, 1935.

_____. "Jimmy The Gent," March 26, 22:3, 1934.

_____. "Jimmy The Gent," April, IX 3:2, 1934.

_____. "Juarez," Feb. 5, 5, 1939.

_____. "Juarez," May 28, p. 4, 1939.

_____. "Juarez," July 2, p. 1, 1939.

_____. "Juarez," Nov. 7, p. 4, 1939.

_____. "Kid Galahad," May 27, 21:3, 1937

_____. "Kid Galahad," May 30, X3:2, 1937

_____. "King of the Underworld," Jan. 7, 6:2, 1939

_____. "The Life of Emile Zola," April 26, p. 27,
1937

_____. "The Life of Emile Zola," May 16, p. 4:3,
1937

_____. "The Life of Emile Zola," July 11, p. 3:2,
1937

_____. "The Life of Emile Zola," Aug. 12, p. 2:2,
1937

_____. "Little Giant," May 27, 11:5, 1933

_____. "Marked Woman," April 12, 15:2, 1937

_____. "Mayor of Hell," July 9, X 3:1, 1933

_____. "Reporter Sees Ghosts," Aug. 15, p. 2, 1937

_____. "Paul Muni," March 5, p. 17:3, 1937

_____. "Paul Muni," Nov. 18, p. 22:4, 1939

New York Times Magazine. "Paul Muni," May 22, p. 17, 1955

New York Times. "Oklahoma Kid," March 11, 21:1, 1939

_____. "Racket Busters," Aug. 11, 13:1, 1938

_____. "Racket Busters," Aug. 14, IX 3:2, 1938

_____. "Roaring Twenties," Nov. 11, 12:1, 1939

_____. "Edward G. Robinson," Nov. 9, IX 1, 1930

_____. "Edward G. Robinson," Sept. 20, VIII 3:1,
1931

_____. "Edward G. Robinson," Dec. 12, 23:4, 1931

_____. "Edward G. Robinson," May 29, VIII 4:1,
1932

_____. "Edward G. Robinson," Feb. 3, 21:3, 1933

_____. "Edward G. Robinson," May 28, IX 3:2, 1933

_____· "Edward G. Robinson," Jan. 13, IX 5:6,
1935

_____· "Edward G. Robinson," Feb. 9, II 1:1,
1936

_____· "Edward G. Robinson," June 14, X 3:8,
1936

_____· "Edward G. Robinson," Nov. 22, II 4:1,
1936

_____· "Edward G. Robinson," Jan. 22, IX 5:1,
1939

_____· "Edward G. Robinson," Sept. 1, 8:2, 1939

_____· "St. Louis Kid," Nov. 1, 25:2, 1934

_____· "St. Louis Kid," Nov. 11, X 5:1, 1934

_____· "San Quentin," Aug. 4, 15:2, 1937

_____· "Scarface," March 13, VIII 4:6, 1932

_____· "Scarface," May 12, 23:1, 1932

_____· "Scarface," May 20, 22:3, 1932

_____· "Scarface," May 29, VIII 3:3, 1932

_____· "Scarface," June 14, 26:4, 1932

_____· "Sinners' Holiday," Oct. 11, 21:4, 1930

_____· "A Slight Case of Murder," Jan. 27, 17:2,
1938

_____· "A Slight Case of Murder," Mar. 6, XI 5:3,
1938

_____· "Smart Money," June 19, 21:4, 1931

_____· "Smart Money," June 28, VIII 3:1, 1931

_____· "Taxi," Jan. 8, 27:3, 1932

_____· "Torrid Zone," April 7, IX 4:3, 1940

_____· "Torrid Zone," May 18, 11:3, 1940

_____· "Torrid Zone," May 26, IX 3:1, 1940

_____· "Warner Brothers," May 9, 40:2, 1930

_____· "Warner Brothers," May 26, 25:4, 1930

_____. "Warner Brothers," May 27, 27:2, 1930

_____. "Warner Brothers," May 30, 22:1, 1930

_____. "Warner Brothers," June 8, IX 4:1, 1930

_____. "Warner Brothers," Aug. 21, 1:1, 1930

_____. "Warner Brothers," Jan. 7, 32:4, 1931

_____. "Warner Brothers," Jan. 25, II 9:2, 1931

_____. "Warner Brothers," Feb. 19, 21:1, 1931

_____. "Warner Brothers," Feb. 26, 31:2, 1931

_____. "Warner Brothers," April 21, 35:5, 1931

_____. "Warner Brothers," May 8, 36:2, 1931

_____. "Warner Brothers," May 14, 37:2, 1931

_____. "Warner Brothers," May 22, 39:1, 1931

_____. "Warner Brothers," May 26, 33:3, 1931

_____. "Warner Brothers," June 21, VIII 5:1, 1931

_____. "Warner Brothers," June 29, 20:5, 1931

_____. "Warner Brothers," July 3, 22:2, 1931

_____. "Warner Brothers," July 22, 37:1, 1931

_____. "Warner Brothers," July 23, 22:4, 1931

_____. "Warner Brothers," Aug. 19, 29:5, 1931

_____. "Warner Brothers," Sept. 12, 15:3, 1931

_____. "Warner Brothers," Oct. 23, 26:4, 1931

_____. "Warner Brothers," Oct. 26, 22:3, 1931

_____. "Warner Brothers," Nov. 13, 35:1, 1931

_____. "Warner Brothers," Dec. 1, 23:5, 1931

_____. "Warner Brothers," Dec. 10, 28:1, 1931

_____. "Warner Brothers," Dec. 15, 39:4, 1931

_____. "Warner Brothers," April 12, 28:1, 1932

_____. "Warner Brothers," June 9, 36:1, 1932

_____. "Warner Brothers," Aug. 10, 25:1, 1932

_____. "Warner Brothers," Nov. 3, IV 3:2, 1932

_____. "Warner Brothers," Jan. 6, 23:4, 1933

_____. "Warner Brothers," Feb. 16, 2:4, 1933

_____. "Warner Brothers," March 16, 18:5, 1933

_____. "Warner Brothers," Aug. 2, 18:5, 1933

_____. "Warner Brothers," Sept. 8, 22:1, 1933

_____. "Warner Brothers," Nov. 8, 32:2, 1933

_____. "Warner Brothers," July 22, 19:4, 1933

_____. "Warner Brothers," Nov. 13, 27:2, 1933

_____. "Warner Brothers," May 25, 24:7, 1934

_____. "Warner Brothers," June 1, 22:4, 1934

_____. "Warner Brothers," June 26, 18:6, 1934

_____. "Warner Brothers," July 4, 18:1, 1934

_____. "Warner Brothers," July 17, 21:1, 1934

_____. "Warner Brothers," Sept. 23, II 21:4, 1934

_____. "Warner Brothers," Nov. 1, 25:4, 1934

_____. "Warner Brothers," Nov. 25, IX 5:2, 1934

_____. "Warner Brothers," Dec. 1, 20L, 1934

_____. "Warner Brothers," July 10, 24:4, 1935

_____. "Warner Brothers," Jan. 11, 9:2, 1936

_____. "Warner Brothers," Jan. 14, 24:4, 1936

_____. "Warner Brothers," Feb. 8, 18:6, 1936

_____. "Warner Brothers," Feb. 8, 19:1, 1936

_____. "Warner Brothers," March 17, 24:4, 1936

_____. "Warner Brothers," May 3, X 4:3, 1936

_____. "Warner Brothers," June 4, 27:1, 1936

_____. "Warner Brothers," July 12, IX 3:1, 1936

_____. "Warner Brothers," Aug. 16, X 3:1, 1936

_____. "Warner Brothers," Oct. 16, 22:4, 1936

_____. "Warner Brothers," Oct. 24, 23:6, 1936

_____. "Warner Brothers," Jan. 5, 43:3, 1937

_____. "Warner Brothers," March 3, 12:2, 1937

_____. "Warner Brothers," April 29, 17:2, 1937

_____. "Warner Brothers," May 4, 29:2, 1937

_____. "Warner Brothers," July 30, 17:6, 1937

_____. "Warner Brothers," May 2, 26:1, 1937

_____. "Warner Brothers," May 14, 42:4, 1937

_____. "Warner Brothers," June 20, X 4:6, 1937

_____. "Warner Brothers," Oct. 17, II 10:1, 1937

_____. "Warner Brothers," March 13, XI 5:5, 1938

_____. "Warner Brothers," May 13, 17:1, 1938

_____. "Warner Brothers," Jan. 15, IX 5:2, 1939

_____. "Warner Brothers," Jan. 15, IV 8:4, 1939

_____. "Warner Brothers," Feb. 5 IX 5:3, 1939

_____. "Warner Brothers," March 13, 12:5, 1939

_____. "Warner Brothers," Jan. 23, 16:2, 1940

_____. "Warner Brothers," Aug. 11, IX 3:7, 1940

_____. "Winner Take All," June 18, 9:2, 1932

_____. "Winner Take All," June 26, IX 3:3, 1932

_____. "You Can't Get Away With Murder," March 25, 19:2, 1939

II. Periodicals

Commonweal. "The Amazing Dr. Clitterhouse," Aug. 5, 1938

New Republic. "The Amazing Dr. Clitterhouse," Aug. 10, 1938

Newsweek. "The Amazing Dr. Clitterhouse," July 4, 1938

Time. "The Amazing Dr. Clitterhouse," July 18, 1938

Commonweal. "Angels With Dirty Faces," Nov. 25, 1938

Time. "Angels With Dirty Faces," Dec. 5, 1938

Atwood, William. "Bogart on Hollywood," *Look*, Aug. 21, 1956

Canadian Magazine. "Barbary Coast," Dec., 1935

Newsweek. "Barbary Coast," Oct. 19, 1935

Scholastic. "Barbary Coast," Nov. 2, 1935

Time. "Barbary Coast," Oct. 21, 1935

Baskette, Kirtley. "Hollywood's Trigger Man," *American Magazine*, June, 1943

Beatty, Jerome. "The Man Who Is Always Somebody Else," *American Magazine*, Feb., 1938

Canadian Magazine. "Black Fury," June, 1935

Literary Digest. "Black Fury," April 27, 1935

The Nation. "Black Fury," April 24, 1935

New Republic. "Black Fury," April 24, 1935

Newsweek. "Black Fury," April 13, 1935

Theater Arts Monthly. "Black Fury," June, 1935

Commonweal. "Black Legion," Jan. 22, 1937

Literary Digest. "Black Legion," Jan. 26, 1937

The Nation. "Black Legion," Jan. 30, 1937

New Republic. "Black Legion," Feb. 17, 1937

Scholastic. "Black Legion," Feb. 6, 1937

Time. "Black Legion," Jan 25, 1937

Saturday Evening Post. "I Stuck My Neck Out" - Humphrey
      Bogart, Feb. 10, 1945

Life. "Eulogy For A Tough Guy" - Humphrey Bogart, Jan. 28,
      1957

Time. "The Survivor" - Humphrey Bogart, June 7, 1954

Boynoff, Sara. "The Life of Dr. Ehrlich," Hygeia, Feb.,
      1940

Commonweal. "Brother Orchid," June 14, 1940

Time. "Brother Orchid," June 17, 1940

Collier's. "James Cagney," Oct. 28, 1955

Parents Magazine. "Portrait," James Cagney, Sept., 1937

Saturday Evening Post. "How I Got This Way" - James
      Cagney, Jan. 7, 1956

Saturday Evening Post. "How I Got This Way" - James
      Cagney, Jan. 14, 1956

Saturday Evening Post. "How I Got This Way" - James
      Cagney, Jan. 21, 1956

New Republic. "Ceiling Zero," Feb.5, 1936

Newsweek. "Ceiling Zero," Jan. 18, 1936

Time. "Ceiling Zero," Jan. 27, 1936

Canadian Magazine. "Ceiling Zero," Oct., 1936

Literary Digest. "China Clipper," Aug. 22, 1936

Scholastic. "China Clipper," Oct. 3, 1936

Time. "China Clipper," Aug. 24, 1936

Commonweal. "City For Conquest," Oct. 4, 1940

Newsweek. "City For Conquest," Sept. 30, 1940

Time. "City For Conquest," Oct. 7, 1940

Clausen, Bernard. "A Moment In The Conscience of Man,"
      The Christian Century, Dec. 1, 1937

Cooke, Alistair. "Epitaph For A Tough Guy," The Atlantic
      Monthly, Jan., 1957

Cole, Toby and Chinoy. "Actors on Acting," Crown Publications, 1949

Commonweal. "Confessions of a Nazi Spy," May 19, 1939

Nation. "Confessions of a Nazi Spy," May 20, 1939

New Republic. "Confessions of a Nazi Spy," May 10, 1939

Newsweek. "Confessions of a Nazi Spy," May 8, 1939

Scholastic. "Confessions of a Nazi Spy," May 27, 1939

Time. "Confessions of a Nazi Spy," May 15, 1939

Commonweal. "Crime School," May 27, 1938

New Republic. "Crime School," May 25, 1938

Commonweal. "The Crowd Roars," May 27, 1938

Nation. "The Crowd Roars," April 13, 1932

Time. "The Crowd Roars," Jan. 27, 1936

Commonweal. "Dark Victory," May 5, 1939

Commonweal. "Dark Victory," July, 1939

New Republic. "Dark Victory," July 5, 1939

Newsweek. "Dark Victory," April 24, 1939

Time. "Dark Victory," May 1, 1939

Commonweal. "Dead End" Aug. 20, 1937

Literary Digest. "Dead End," Sept. 4, 1937

New Republic. "Dead End," Sept. 1, 1937

Newsweek. "Dead End," Aug. 28, 1937

Scholastic. "Dead End," Sept. 25, 1937

Time. "Dead End," Sept. 6, 1937

Commonweal. "Dr. Ehrlich's Magic Bullet," March 1, 1949

Life. "Dr. Ehrlich's Magic Bullet," March 4, 1940

Nation. "Dr. Ehrlich's Magic Bullet," March 9, 1940

Newsweek. "Dr. Ehrlich's Magic Bullet," Feb. 26, 1940

New Yorker. "Dr. Ehrlich's Magic Bullet," Feb. 24, 1940

Time. "Dr. Ehrlich's Magic Bullet," Feb. 19, 1940

Durant, John. "Tough On and Off," Collier's, Aug. 31, 1940

Eustis, Morton. "Paul Muni, A Profile And Self-Portrait,"
    Theater Arts, March, 1940

Commonweal. "The Fighting 69th," Feb. 9, 1940

Life. "The Fighting 69th," Jan 29, 1940

Time. "The Fighting 69th," Feb. 12, 1940

Frazier, George. "Humphrey Bogart, He Has A Hard Unhappy
    Face And A Hard But Happy Life," Life, April 17, 1944

Literary Digest. "The Frisco Kid," Dec. 7, 1935

Nation. "The Frisco Kid," Dec. 18, 1935

Newsweek. "The Frisco Kid," Nov. 30, 1935

Literary Digest. "G Men," May 11, 1935

New Republic. "G Men," May 15, 1935

Theater Arts Monthly. "G Men," June 1, 1935

Literary Digest. "Here Comes The Navy," April 4, 1934

New Republic. "Here Comes The Navy," Aug. 15, 1934

Literary Digest. "The Irish In Us," Aug. 10, 1935

Time. "The Irish In Us," Aug. 12, 1935

Jacobs, Edward. "Cagney And The American Hero," Hound And
    Horn, April, 1932

Johnston, A. "They Toughened Him Up," Woman's Home Companion,
    Nov., 1934

Commonweal. "Juarez," May 12, 1939

Nation. "Juarez," May 6, 1939

New Republic. "Juarez," May 10, 1939

Newsweek. "Juarez," May 8, 1939

St. Nicholas. "Juarez," June, 1939

Time. "Juarez," May 8, 1939

Kennedy, J.B. "Tough As Velvet," Collier's, Jan 2, 1932

Literary Digest. "Kid Galahad," May 15, 1937

New Republic. "Kid Galahad," May 19, 1937

Newsweek. "Kid Galahad," May 29, 1937

Time. "Kid Galahad," May 31, 1937

Literary Digest. "Lady Killer," Jan 20, 1934

Commonweal. "The Life of Emile Zola," July 30, 1937

Literary Digest. "The Life Of Emile Zola," Aug. 14, 1937

New Republic. "The Life Of Emile Zola," Aug. 18, 1937

Time. "The Life Of Emile Zola," Aug. 16, 1937

Commonweal. "Little Giant, " June 16, 1933

Nation. "Little Giant," June 14, 1933

Nation. "Marked Woman," May 8, 1937

Time. "Marked Woman," April 19, 1937

Newsweek. "Mayor of Hell," July 8, 1933

American Annual. "Paul Muni," 1957.

Newsweek. "Paul Müni," Aug. 14, 1937.

Commonweal. "Oklahoma Kid," March 17, 1939.

Newsweek. "Oklahoma Kid," March 6, 1939.

Time. "Oklahoma Kid," March 20, 1939.

Commonweal. "Racket Busters," Aug. 5, 1938.

Time. "Racket Busters," Aug. 22, 1938.

Commonweal. "Roaring Twenties," Nov. 10, 1939.

New Republic. "Roaring Twenties," Dec. 6, 1939.

Literary Digest. "Edward G. Robinson," Jan. 9 , 1937.

Life. "Edward G. Robinson," Feb. 27, 1956, p. 40.

Life. "Edward G. Robinson," April 15, 1957.

Theater Arts Monthly. "Edward G. Robinson," April 29, 1931, p. 242.

Time. "Edward G. Robinson," Feb. 5, 1951, p. 48.

Time. "San Quentin," Aug. 16, 1937.

Literary Digest. "Scarface," July 30, 1932, p. 14.

Shipp, Cameron, "The Adventures of Humphrey Bogart," Saturday
    Evening Post, Aug. 2, 1952, p. 32.

Skinner, R. D., "Little Giant and Mr. Robinson," Commonweal,
    June 16, 1933, p. 190.

Commonweal. "The Story of Louis Pasteur," Jan. 24, 1936.

Literary Digest. "The Story of Louis Pasteur," Feb. 1, 1936.

Nation. "The Story of Louis Pasteur," Feb. 17, 1936.

Newsweek. "The Story of Louis Pasteur," Feb. 15, 1936, p. 46.

Time. "The Story of Louis Pasteur," Feb. 17, 1936, p. 46.

Van Doren, Mark, "The Novelist as Hero," The Nation, Sept. 4,
    1937, p. 246.

Fortune. "Warner Brothers," Dec., 1937, p. 110.

Newsweek. "Warner Brothers," Dec. 26, 1936, p. 23.

III. Books

Barnouw, Erik. Mass Communication. New York: Rinehart and
     Company, Inc., 1956.

Blumer, Herbert. Movies and Conduct. New York: The Macmillan
     Company, 1933.

Blumer, Herbert and Hauser, Philip M. Movies, Delinquency and
     Crime. New York: The Macmillan Company, 1933.

Cameron, Ian and Elisabeth. The Heavies. London: Movie Paperback,
     1967.

Charters, W.W. Motion Pictures and Youth. New York: The
     Macmillan Company, 1933.

Conway, McGregor and Ricci. The Films of Greta Garbo. New York:
     Citadel, 1968.

Cooke, Alistair. Douglas Fairbanks, The Making of A Screen
     Character. New York: The Museum of Modern Art, 1940.

Dale, Edgar. The Content of Motion Pictures. New York:
     The Macmillan Company, 1935.

Dale, Edgar. How To Appreciate Motion Pictures. New York:
     The Macmillan Company, 1933.

Dow, Clyde W. An Introduction to Graduate Study in Speech and
     Theatre. East Lansing: Michigan State University Press, 1961.

Dysinger, Wendell S. and Ruckmick, Christian A. The Emotional
     Responses of Children to the Motion Picture Situation.
     New York: The Macmillan Company, 1935.

Griffith, Mrs. D. W. When Movies Were Young. New York: E. P.
     Dutton, 1925.

Griffith, Richard and Mayer, Arthur. The Movies. New York:
     Simon and Schuster, 1957.

Jacobs, Lewis. The Rise of the American Film. New York:
     Harcourt, Brace and Company, 1939.

Knight, Arthur. The Liveliest Art. New York: The Macmillan
     Company, 1957.

Koenigil, Mark. Movies in Society. New York: Robert Speller and
     Sons, Publishers, Inc., 1962.

Kracauer, Siegfried. From Caligari to Hitler A Psychological
    History of the German Film. Princeton: Princeton University
    Press, 1947.

McNeill, William H. The Rise of the West. Chicago: The
    University of Chicago Press, 1963.

Morison, Samuel Eliot and Commager, Henry Steele. The Growth
    of the American Republic Volume II. New York: Oxford
    University Press, 1950.

Payne Studies. Motion Pictures and the Social Attitudes of
    Children. New York: The Macmillan Company, 1933.

Rosten, Leo C. Hollywood the Movie Colony and the Movie Makers.
    New York: Harcourt, Brace and Company, 1941.

Schary, Dore (as told to Charles Palmer). Case History of a
    Movie. New York: Random House, 1950.

Schickel, Richard. The Stars. New York: Dial Press, 1962.

Schramm, Wilbur (ed.). The Process and Effects of Mass Communications.
    Urbana: University of Illinois Press, 1955.

Steiner, Gary A. The People Look at Television. New York: Alfred
    A. Knopf, 1963.

Thrasher, Frederic (ed.). Okay For Sound. New York: Duell, Sloan
    and Pearce, 1946.

Warner, Jack L. My First Hundred Years in Hollywood. New York:
    Random House, 1964.

Warshow, Robert. The Immediate Experience. Garden City, N. Y.:
    Doubleday and Co., Inc., 1962.

Wolfenstein, Martha and Leites, Nathan. Movies A Psychological
    Study. Glencoe, Illinois: The Free Press, 1950.

Wright, Charles R. Mass Communication, A Sociological Perspective.
    New York: Random House, 1959.

The Arno Press Cinema Program

THE LITERATURE OF CINEMA

Series I & II

Agate, James. **Around Cinemas.** 1946.

Agate, James. **Around Cinemas.** (Second Series). 1948.

American Academy of Political and Social Science. **The Motion Picture in Its Economic and Social Aspects,** edited by Clyde L. King. **The Motion Picture Industry,** edited by Gordon S. Watkins. *The Annals,* November, 1926/1927.

L'Art Cinematographique, Nos. 1-8. 1926-1931.

Balcon, Michael, Ernest Lindgren, Forsyth Hardy and Roger Manvell. **Twenty Years of British Film, 1925-1945.** 1947.

Bardèche, Maurice and Robert Brasillach. **The History of Motion Pictures,** edited by Iris Barry. 1938.

Benoit-Levy, Jean. **The Art of the Motion Picture.** 1946.

Blumer, Herbert. **Movies and Conduct.** 1933.

Blumer, Herbert and Philip M. Hauser. **Movies, Delinquency, and Crime.** 1933.

Buckle, Gerard Fort. **The Mind and the Film.** 1926.

Carter, Huntly. **The New Spirit in the Cinema.** 1930.

Carter, Huntly. **The New Spirit in the Russian Theatre, 1917-1928.** 1929.

Carter, Huntly. **The New Theatre and Cinema of Soviet Russia.** 1924.

Charters, W. W. **Motion Pictures and Youth.** 1933.

Cinema Commission of Inquiry. **The Cinema: Its Present Position and Future Possibilities.** 1917.

Dale, Edgar. **Children's Attendance at Motion Pictures.** Dysinger, Wendell S. and Christian A. Ruckmick. **The Emotional Responses of Children to the Motion Picture Situation.** 1935.

Dale, Edgar. **The Content of Motion Pictures.** 1935.

Dale, Edgar. **How to Appreciate Motion Pictures.** 1937.

Dale, Edgar, Fannie W. Dunn, Charles F. Hoban, Jr., and Etta Schneider. **Motion Pictures in Education: A Summary of the Literature.** 1938.

Davy, Charles. **Footnotes to the Film.** 1938.

Dickinson, Thorold and Catherine De la Roche. **Soviet Cinema.** 1948.

Dickson, W. K. L., and Antonia Dickson. **History of the Kinetograph, Kinetoscope and Kinetophonograph.** 1895.

Forman, Henry James. **Our Movie Made Children.** 1935.

Freeburg, Victor Oscar. **The Art of Photoplay Making.** 1918.

Freeburg, Victor Oscar. **Pictorial Beauty on the Screen.** 1923.

Hall, Hal, editor. **Cinematographic Annual,** 2 vols. 1930/1931.

Hampton, Benjamin B. **A History of the Movies.** 1931.

Hardy, Forsyth. **Scandinavian Film.** 1952.

Hepworth, Cecil M. **Animated Photography: The A B C of the Cinematograph.** 1900.

Hoban, Charles F., Jr., and Edward B. Van Ormer. **Instructional Film Research 1918-1950.** 1950.

Holaday, Perry W. and George D. Stoddard. **Getting Ideas from the Movies.** 1933.

Hopwood, Henry V. **Living Pictures.** 1899.

Hulfish, David S. **Motion-Picture Work.** 1915.

Hunter, William. **Scrutiny of Cinema.** 1932.

Huntley, John. **British Film Music.** 1948.

Irwin, Will. **The House That Shadows Built.** 1928.

Jarratt, Vernon. **The Italian Cinema.** 1951.

Jenkins, C. Francis. **Animated Pictures.** 1898.

Lang, Edith and George West. **Musical Accompaniment of Moving Pictures.** 1920.

London, Kurt. **Film Music.** 1936.

Lutz, E ⌈dwin⌉ G ⌈eorge⌉. **The Motion-Picture Cameraman.** 1927.

Manvell, Roger. **Experiment in the Film.** 1949.

Marey, Etienne Jules. **Movement.** 1895.

Martin, Olga J. **Hollywood's Movie Commandments.** 1937.

Mayer, J. P. **Sociology of Film: Studies and Documents.** 1946. New Introduction by J. P. Mayer.

Münsterberg, Hugo. **The Photoplay: A Psychological Study.** 1916.
Nicoll, Allardyce. **Film and Theatre.** 1936.

Noble, Peter. **The Negro in Films.** 1949.

Peters, Charles C. **Motion Pictures and Standards of Morality.** 1933.

Peterson, Ruth C. and L. L. Thurstone. **Motion Pictures and the Social Attitudes of Children.** Shuttleworth, Frank K. and Mark A. May. **The Social Conduct and Attitudes of Movie Fans.** 1933.

Phillips, Henry Albert. **The Photodrama.** 1914.

Photoplay Research Society. **Opportunities in the Motion Picture Industry.** 1922.

Rapée, Erno. **Encyclopaedia of Music for Pictures.** 1925.

Rapée, Erno. **Motion Picture Moods for Pianists and Organists.** 1924.

Renshaw, Samuel, Vernon L. Miller and Dorothy P. Marquis. **Children's Sleep.** 1933.

Rosten, Leo C. Hollywood: The Movie Colony, The Movie Makers. 1941.

Sadoul, Georges. French Film. 1953.

Screen Monographs I, 1923-1937. 1970.

Screen Monographs II, 1915-1930. 1970.

Sinclair, Upton. Upton Sinclair Presents William Fox. 1933.

Talbot, Frederick A. Moving Pictures. 1912.

Thorp, Margaret Farrand. America at the Movies. 1939.

Wollenberg, H. H. Fifty Years of German Film. 1948.

RELATED BOOKS AND PERIODICALS

Allister, Ray. Friese-Greene: Close-Up of an Inventor. 1948.

Art in Cinema: A Symposium of the Avant-Garde Film, edited by Frank Stauffacher. 1947.

The Art of Cinema: Selected Essays. New Foreword by George Amberg. 1971.

Balázs, Béla. Theory of the Film. 1952.

Barry, Iris. Let's Go to the Movies. 1926.

de Beauvoir, Simone. Brigitte Bardot and the Lolita Syndrome. 1960.

Carrick, Edward. Art and Design in the British Film. 1948.

Close Up. Vols. 1-10, 1927-1933 (all published).

Cogley, John. Report on Blacklisting. Part I: The Movies. 1956.

Eisenstein, S. M. Que Viva Mexico! 1951.

Experimental Cinema. 1930-1934 (all published).

Feldman, Joseph and Harry. Dynamics of the Film. 1952.

Film Daily Yearbook of Motion Pictures. Microfilm, 18 reels, 35 mm. 1918-1969.

Film Daily Yearbook of Motion Pictures. 1970.

Film Daily Yearbook of Motion Pictures. (Wid's Year Book). 3 vols., 1918-1922.

The Film Index: A Bibliography. Vol. I: The Film as Art. 1941.

Film Society Programmes. 1925-1939 (all published).

Films: A Quarterly of Discussion and Analysis. Nos. 1-4, 1939-1940 (all published).

Flaherty, Frances Hubbard. The Odyssey of a Film-Maker: Robert Flaherty's Story. 1960.

General Bibliography of Motion Pictures, edited by Carl Vincent, Riccardo Redi, and Franco Venturini. 1953.

Hendricks, Gordon. Origins of the American Film. 1961-1966. New Introduction by Gordon Hendricks.

Hound and Horn: Essays on Cinema, 1928-1934. 1971.

Huff, Theodore. Charlie Chaplin. 1951.

Kahn, Gordon. Hollywood on Trial. 1948.

New York Times Film Reviews, 1913-1968. 1970.

Noble, Peter. Hollywood Scapegoat: The Biography of Erich von Stroheim. 1950.

Robson, E. W. and M. M. The Film Answers Back. 1939.

Seldes, Gilbert. An Hour with the Movies and the Talkies. 1929.

Weinberg, Herman G., editor. Greed. 1971.

Wollenberg, H. H. Anatomy of the Film. 1947.

Wright, Basil. The Use of the Film. 1948.

DISSERTATIONS ON FILM

Karpf, Stephen L. The Gangster Film: Emergence, Variation and Decay of a Genre, 1930-1940. First publication, 1973.

Lounsbury, Myron O. The Origins of American Film Criticism, 1909-1939. First publication, 1973.

Sands, Pierre N. A Historical Study of the Academy of the Motion Picture Arts and Sciences (1927-1947). First publication, 1973.

North, Joseph H. The Early Development of the Motion Picture, 1887-1909. First publication, 1973.

Rimberg, John. The Motion Picture in the Soviet Union, 1918-1952. First publication, 1973.

Wolfe, Glenn J. Vachel Lindsay: The Poet as Film Theorist. First publication, 1973.

They Call Her Pastor

SUNY Series in Religion, Culture, and Society
WADE CLARK ROOF, Editor

THEY CALL HER PASTOR

A New Role for Catholic Women

RUTH A. WALLACE

STATE UNIVERSITY OF NEW YORK PRESS

Published by
State University of New York Press, Albany

© 1992   State University of New York

For information, address State University of New York
Press, State University Plaza, Albany, N.Y. 12246

Production by Bernadine Dawes
Marketing by Fran Keneston

Library of Congress Cataloging-in-Publication Data

Wallace, Ruth A.
    They call her pastor : a new role for Catholic women / Ruth A.
Wallace.
        p.   cm. — (SUNY series in religion, culture, and society)
    Includes bibliographical references and index.
    ISBN 0–7914–0925–2 (alk. paper) : $44.50. — ISBN 0–7914–0926–0
(pbk. : alk. paper) : $14.95
        1. Women in church work—Catholic Church. 2. Women clergy—United
States.   I. Title. II. Series.
BX2347.8.W6W34   1992
262' . 142' 082—dc20
                                                                91–15121
                                                                CIP

10 9 8 7 6 5 4 3 2 1

To the Women Pastors Who Made This Possible

CONTENTS

Chapter 5. PARISH RESTRUCTURING / 87

Chapter 6. SUPPORT SYSTEMS AND RESOURCES / 105

Chapter 7. CONSTRAINTS, CONFLICTS, AND TENSIONS / 125

Chapter 8. GENDER AND THE PASTORAL ROLE / 151

Chapter 9. FINAL OBSERVATIONS / 167

PREFACE

This book is the result of my study of twenty Catholic parishes administered by women, as seen by the women themselves, their parishioners, and the priests who travel to the parishes to preside at Mass and the other sacraments. Such parishes are often referred to as "priestless parishes" because they are without a resident priest.

I am deeply indebted to these women who allowed me to intrude on their very busy lives. Without their cooperation, and that of their parishioners and priests, this book would not have been possible. Although their names will not appear, they are deeply etched in my memory.

By the time this book goes to press I will have spent the better part of two years working on the research project that is the foundation for these chapters. In addition to the professional gratification resulting from the opportunity to get in on the initial stages of a "cutting-edge" phenomenon, I want to mention briefly some of the personal compensations for the time and energy that I expended on this project.

Chronologically the first reward was the astounding cooperation I received from the women pastors. When I contacted them as potential subjects, they did not know me, and yet all of them agreed to participate in the study. Moreover, most of them invited me to stay with them in their homes when I visited their parishes for the weekend. Even more important, they were so generous with their time for interviewing, touring the parish, and letting me accompany them on their various duties over the weekend, that I came away with data that was not only extremely rich in quality, but also more than enough for a book.

Secondly I had a number of unforgettable encounters in my travels to these parishes. A chance meeting in an airport with the bishop who headed the diocese where one of my parishes was located was one of these. Because he had the power to prohibit me from gathering data in his parishes, this unexpected encounter could have sabotaged the project, had it not been for the quick thinking of a woman pastor, which I describe later in the book.

Some of my most profoundly moving experiences occurred when I accompanied women pastors to visit sick and dying parishioners. I will never forget the loving atmosphere in those rooms that in my view transformed their seemingly bleak living conditions. Likewise, I was enriched culturally time and time again as I took part in community gatherings on such occasions as weddings and wedding receptions, baptisms and baptismal parties, and numerous parish dinners all over the United States. Needless to say, a key ingredient at most of these gatherings was the food, the wonderfully fresh produce from the parishioners' farms, and their delicious home cooking. But the overwhelming reward, in my view, was the opportunity to experience a real spirit of community on these occasions.

Finally, there were also a number of geographical "firsts." Four of the states I had never visited before, and nineteen of the twenty parishes were located in towns or cities that were also new territory for me. The opportunity to observe in person these isolated and relatively poor parishes expanded my understanding of the context of the women pastors' work. These visits to parishes throughout the country also enriched my personal experience of racial and ethnic diversity. I heard accents and singing, watched dancing and experienced camaraderie that were new and refreshing.

I would like to thank the Lilly Endowment for a grant (#890087) that provided the time and the resources for my travel throughout the United States to collect the data, and allowed for the transcription of interviews and other related expenses. I am also grateful to the National Science Foundation for an award (#SES 89–12263) which provided for a graduate student assistant to help in the processing of the data.

There are others whose help at various stages of this study was invaluable to me. In particular, I want to thank Kay Sheskaitis, Kathryn Meadow-Orlans, Jenifer Oberg, James Coriden, Sheila Harvil, Sally Davis, Peter Gilmour, Phillip Murnion, Fred Hofheinz, Phyllis Moen, Helen Kelley, Helen Fuchs Ebaugh, Janet Saltzman Chafetz, Dorothy Smith, Arlie Russell Hochschild, Jacqueline Wiseman, Shirley F. Hartley, Carla Howery, Martin Mangan, and Maureen Healy.

•1•

Why Women Pastors?

"A woman in charge of a Catholic parish? You've got to be kidding."
"I can't imagine it in my wildest dreams! You must be talking about something happening on another planet, or at least in another country."
"Well, I can assure you that I've never experienced or heard of such a thing, and I've been a churchgoing Catholic all my life."

These reactions are typical of what I heard over and over again from people who listened as I described my research, a study of women administering priestless parishes in the United States. Many Catholics, particularly those living in the northeastern part of the United States, are unaware of the priest shortage, which is particularly acute in rural areas in the Midwest, the South, and western regions of this country.[1] Though these same Catholics may have heard of dioceses where the bishop has decided to close some parishes because of staffing problems, they were not cognizant of other alternatives like this one, now available to bishops.

Given the patriarchal structure of the Catholic church, and the conservative stance of the current members of the Roman Curia[2] regarding the role of women in the church, one would not expect to see women appointed to significant leadership positions. The women I interviewed have been entrusted by their bishops with the pastoral care of parishes where there are

1

no resident priests. In this capacity these women exercise overall responsibility in the parish for worship, education, pastoral services, and administration.

When, why, and how did it happen that Catholic bishops can appoint lay people, even women, as administrators of priestless parishes? This chapter provides a fourfold answer. First we look at the Second Vatican Council and subsequent changes in church law, and then we turn to the remaining facilitating factors, demographic changes and the contemporary women's movement, before describing my research.

THE IMPACT OF THE SECOND VATICAN COUNCIL

Shortly after Pope John XXIII was elected pope, he expressed his desire to bring about some changes in the church that would allow for better adaptation to modern society, changes which he referred to as *aggiornamento,* an updating or modernization, that would result in an opening of the "windows of the church" to the contemporary world.[3] To that end he convened all Catholic bishops throughout the world for the Second Vatican Council. These council sessions took place in Rome for approximately three months, from September through November, for four consecutive years, beginning in 1962 and ending with the fourth session in 1965.

The central participants in the Vatican Council deliberations from 1962 to 1965 were the 2,540 bishops and a few male heads of religious orders who had voting rights. In addition, there were approximately 450 priests invited as experts (*periti*), and some Protestant observers and representatives from non-Christian religions, all of whom were men.[4] These experts were allowed to be present at the Council deliberations but had no voting rights.

Beginning with the second session of the Council in 1963, a few lay auditors were also invited. By the end of Council deliberations in 1965, there were twelve laywomen, ten religious women, and twenty-seven laymen from different parts of the world present in Rome and participating as auditors.[5] These forty-nine lay auditors were present during the Council deliberations, but they had no vote and they could not speak, except at the various commission meetings held all over Rome. The list of auditors included one woman and two men from the United States: Sister Mary Luke Tobin, the mother general of the Sisters of Loretto, James Norris, and Martin H. Work. There were also a few well-known American Catholic laywomen, such as Dorothy Day, Patricia Crowley, Abigail McCarthy, and Mary Daly, present at peripheral activities, like the noontime Council summary and the daily press briefings on the Council debates. Some women were also present at public talks given occasionally by eminent theologians, and a few women could be seen at occasional weekend conferences and informal gatherings at Roman restaurants.

Some of my personal observations in Rome during the fourth session of the Council in 1965 may be helpful for an understanding of a woman's "place" during the Council.[6] There were many dramatic displays of patriarchal symbolism. An unforgettable sight, for instance, was the daily convergence of hundreds of bishops from all over the world dressed in their colorful regalia at the doors of St. Peter's Church. No layperson could be seen among them because the front entrance was reserved solely for the voting members of the Council. Women who were not auditors participated in the Council itself only by attending the Mass celebrated before each day's Council session. However, they were instructed to leave immediately after the liturgy, because only bishops, *periti,* auditors, and staff could be present for the Council deliberations. (There were some mornings when we felt we were literally being shoved out of St. Peter's, like uninvited guests at a party, because the church ushers pointed to the door while announcing in very loud and insistent voices, *"Exeunt omnes,"* indicating that we were to exit immediately.)

During Council deliberations, the authorized presence of twenty-two women auditors and a total of approximately three thousand men afforded women a very low profile at best. In addition, a woman's voice was *never* heard during the Council deliberations because of the limitations placed on the role of auditor. In general, women were virtually invisible and entirely silent when decisions were made regarding important structural changes affecting all members of the church.[7]

Vatican II Documents and Their Implementation

A perusal of the Vatican II documents reveals that there were only a few instances where any attention was given to the contribution of women to the church. Given the invisibility and silence of women during the Council, it is not surprising that women's issues are seldom addressed in the documents themselves, even in the document on the laity that was supposedly addressed to laywomen and laymen alike.

However, one statement in the document on the laity that was inserted only during the final drafting, reads: "Since in our times women have an ever active share in the whole life of society, it is very important that they participate more widely also in the various fields of the Church's apostolate."[8]

How was this Council statement regarding women's increasing participation implemented? There were some women in important positions before the Second Vatican Council convened in 1962. In fact, looking back historically to the medieval Christian church we can point to abbesses who wielded a considerable amount of power over priests and bishops. Many people will be surprised to learn that some or all of the following rights and duties belonged to abbesses:[9] licensing bishops to exercise pontifical rites in her district; licensing priests to say Mass in her churches; absolving in cases of excommunication; walking in front of the clergy and carrying the pastoral cross in processions; establishing new parishes; holding places in councils with a rank above the clergy; reading the gospel; suspending clergy subject to her; and even, at one time, hearing confessions and preaching in public. It is all the more amazing to realize that this quasi-episcopal status of abbesses did not come to an end until after the French Revolution in the late eighteenth century.[10]

In the period just prior to the convening of Vatican II women could be found in such important positions as administrators of Catholic hospitals, presidents of Catholic women's colleges, and principals of Catholic high schools and grammar schools. However, these were not viewed as strictly "clerical" roles, and the vast majority of women occupying these positions were members of religious communities.[11]

In those sections of the world where bishops and priests

encouraged the laity to participate more actively in the post-Vatican II era, some women gradually assumed more prominent roles. At the parish level they accepted new ministerial roles such as lectors, eucharistic ministers, acolytes (altar servers), and directors of religious education. A study of Catholic parishes in the United States twenty years after the Council found that fifty-two percent of the members of parish councils, sixty percent of eucharistic ministers, and half of the lectors were women.[12] The response of the laity has been largely supportive of this trend. When asked who were the "most influential parishioners," exclusive of the pastors, the respondents produced a list that was fifty-eight percent women.[13]

In our national study of the laity we found that a majority of Catholics think laymen and women should have the right to participate in the following areas which pertain to parish life: deciding how parish income should be spent (eighty percent agreed); giving occasional sermons at Mass (sixty-nine percent agreed); deciding whether to have altar girls (sixty-six percent agreed); being in charge of a parish when the priest is absent (sixty-five percent agreed); and selecting the priests for their parish (fifty-seven percent said they should have this right).[14]

Prior to Vatican II, women were excluded from such roles as students or faculty members in seminaries. It was only after the Vatican Council ended in 1965 that women were admitted to schools of theology for ministerial preparation. Before 1965, then, only those priests who went to college before entering the seminary had the experience of a college education that included women as students and/or teachers. Before the Council ended, most future priests studied for their college degrees in seminaries or schools of theology, where the only women visible were the "good Sisters" who did the cooking, laundering, and other housekeeping tasks. Thus many Catholic priests today, as well as most of the bishops, have had little experience beyond high school in working with women as intellectual equals.

The admission of women students to Roman Catholic schools of theology has resulted in an influx of women ministerial candidates. At the present time, approximately one-fourth of the students enrolled in Roman Catholic theological schools in the United States are women.[15]

Training in theology certainly enhanced a woman's chances of being appointed to positions that were formerly reserved to the clergy, such as superintendents of schools, chancellors of dioceses, canon lawyers, professors in seminaries, directors of Catholic charities, editors of diocesan newspapers, chaplains, spiritual guides and leaders in retreats and Bible studies, and even, as we shall see, as administrators of priestless parishes.[16] Since the percentage of women entering seminaries as students is on an upward trend, we may expect that the daily interaction among these women, their fellow students, and coworkers will have a positive influence on the attitudes and future behavior of these seminarians and priests as they become pastors of parishes and administrators in chancery offices.

Prior to Vatican II, many of the new activities currently assumed by lay people were restricted to the clergy by church law, thus conferring a legitimacy and seeming immutability to the existing structure. We turn now to a discussion of the ensuing revisions of the Code of Canon Law necessitated by the decisions emanating from this historic Council which ultimately sanctioned far-reaching changes, particularly for women's roles in the church.

The New Code of Canon Law

Realizing the importance of changes in church law for the implementation of Vatican Council decisions, Pope John XXIII called for the revision of Canon Law in 1959. The new Code of Canon Law, promulgated in 1983, made some provisions for the expansion of women's roles in the church. While still excluding women from the ordained ministry, the new code opened the following positions to women on the diocesan level: diocesan chancellors, auditors, assessors, defenders of the marriage bond, promoters of justice, judges on diocesan courts, and members of diocesan synods and financial and pastoral councils.

The legal change that opened the door for the recruitment of women as pastoral administrators in priestless parishes can be found in this revised code. In recognition of the priest shortage, the new code included a provision for people other than priests to exercise pastoral care, that is, to perform some of the duties of the pastor in a parish. The new canon (or ruling), 517.2, reads thus:

If the diocesan bishop should decide that due to a dearth of priests a participation in the exercise of the pastoral care of a parish is to be entrusted to a deacon or to some other person who is not a priest, or to a community of persons, he is to appoint some priest endowed with the power and faculties of a pastor, to supervise the pastoral care.[17]

For women, of course, the inclusionary clause in the wording of canon 517.2 is "some other person who is not a priest," because women cannot be ordained as priests or deacons. This could be viewed as a Pandora's box for the church, because the wording of this new law opened the door for female leadership on the parish level, and consequently created a new role for women in the Catholic church.

As in other complex organizations, the process of canon law revision involved a number of stages. Committees made up of bishops and canon lawyers (all males) spent many years analyzing the decrees of Vatican II, and then making the necessary changes in church law in order to bring the Code of Canon Law in line with the Vatican II documents. The earliest version of canon 517.2, published in 1977, was sent to the Catholic hierarchy and other consultative bodies of the church throughout the world in 1978. After observations of these groups were forwarded to the Vatican office, discussions on this proposed canon took place on April 19, 1980. As expected, some of the discussants in Rome "did not welcome the notion that a parish be entrusted, even in part," to a nonordained person.[18]

It was the intervention of Archbishop Rosalio Jose Castillo Lara from Venezuela that was the turning point in this deliberation.[19] He told the committee about the experience in his own diocese, where the priest shortage was particularly acute, and where the pastoral care of some communities was entrusted to nuns. Archbishop Castillo Lara expressed satisfaction with this arrangement, and he also argued that it was spiritually fruitful. This intervention by a Third World bishop was what finally convinced the committee, and the proposed canon was approved. If the earlier arguments of some of the committee members had prevailed, the inclusionary clause would have been deleted.

Thus, in 1983 when the new Code of Canon Law was promulgated, the door was opened for the appointment of women to a role that had previously been closed to them. Since canon 517.2 stipulates that a priest must be appointed to moderate the pastoral care provided by lay people, how radical a change is this, after all? Catholics who were parishioners before the decrees of Vatican II were promulgated can answer that, for they will remember that women were always seen but never heard in church, except as choir members. In fact, this author can recall being told by a priest in the early 1960s that it was a "mortal sin" for a woman to be present in the sanctuary (altar area) of the church during Mass. In the past twenty-five years, however, Catholic women had begun gradually to participate in parish roles which *required* their presence in the sanctuary during Mass, such as lectors (reading scripture), eucharist ministers (distributing communion), altar servers, and most recently, since the promulgation of canon 517.2, as administrators of priestless parishes.

The answer to the question, "Why Women Pastors?" is only partly answered by pointing to Vatican II changes and the revision of the Code of Canon Law. For a more complete answer to this question, we need to look at some external factors as well.

DEMOGRAPHIC CHANGES AND THE
CONTEMPORARY WOMEN'S MOVEMENT

Important demographic changes in the United States and the contemporary women's movement are the external factors that have expedited women's entrance into new roles in the church. Chief among the external demographic changes are women's greater participation in the labor force, their increased rate of college attendance, and their completion of postgraduate degrees.[20]

Concurrently, broad changes in external demographics are affecting the internal demographics of the Catholic church. The increasing shortage of priests is an example of these internal changes, and it is a key factor in the appointment of women to church positions that had previously been reserved solely for priests. Like the subject of the song, "Rosie the Riveter," written during the Second World War, women are being recruited to help out in a manpower shortage crisis. Appointing women as chancellors of dioceses, as canon lawyers in the diocesan tribunal, and as administrators of parishes can free priests for other diocesan needs, just as women working in factories freed male factory workers to fight in World War II.

The priest shortage is already in the crisis stage in some dioceses, as Schoenherr's national study indicates.[21] With regard to the situation in the United States, between 1966 and 1984 there was a twenty percent drop in the number of active diocesan priests, and it is predicted that between 1985 and the year 2005, there will be an additional twenty percent decline in the number of such priests available for active ministry. The most significant factor is recruitment: forty-six percent fewer priests were ordained between 1980 and 1984 than there were from 1966 to 1969. By the late 1990s the ordination rate will be sixty-nine percent lower than it was in the mid-sixties. Only six of every ten vacant positions are currently being filled by newly ordained priests.

The lower recruitment rate contributes to the rise in the average age of priests: forty-six percent of active diocesan clergy will be fifty-five years of age or over by the year 2005, and only twelve percent will be thirty-five or younger.[22] In contrast to the World War II manpower shortage, there is no anticipation of a future influx of male workers, because this shortage is due to retirements, resignations, and a steady decrease in recruitments over the past twenty-five years.

Were it not for the continued growth in Catholic membership in the United States, the situation would be less critical. The ratio of laity to priests over the past fifteen years has increased from 1,102 Catholics per priest in 1975 to a ratio of 1,418 in 1985, and Schoenherr predicts that there will be 2,193 laypersons per priest by 2005.[23] Since the priest shortage shows no sign of abating, and at the same time Catholic membership is steadily increasing, the recruitment of women to pastoring positions is not expected to be short-term.

The contemporary women's movement, which entered a phase of intense mobilization soon after the adjournment of the

Vatican Council, had important repercussions for Catholic women. It raised public consciousness regarding the second-class rank of women in the church. The gender caste system of the Catholic church, in which only men can attain the higher status of clergy while women—even those who join religious communities—are relegated to the ranks of the laity, was suddenly and starkly illuminated.

Have Catholics become more critical of the church's official position regarding the ordination of women? Greeley analyzed data from general social surveys at the National Opinion Research Center. Asked whether they thought "it would be a good thing if women were ordained as priests," American Catholics showed a fifteen percent increase in positive responses over an eight-year period. In 1974, twenty-nine percent agreed with the statement, but by 1982, forty-four percent agreed.[24] At present, slightly over half of Catholic adults no longer view the priesthood as a male prerogative, a twenty-three percent increase from 1974 to 1985.[25]

Some support for the ordination of women has come from professional groups within the church, such as the Catholic Biblical Association of America, which issued a report in 1979 concluding that the evidence in the New Testament, "while not decisive by itself, points toward the admission of women to priestly ministry."[26]

Individual members of the clergy have spoken out at various times in favor of women's ordination. For example, as early as 1970 sociologist Joseph Fichter, S.J. presented this challenge:

> What I am suggesting here is full equality of opportunity for women in the Catholic church. This means that women priests should be selected, appointed and promoted according to the same criteria employed for male priests. They should engage in both the parochial and special ministries of the church, receiving monsignorial honors if deserved, being appointed as chancery officials if competent, and reaching even the bishopric, cardinalate and papacy. Sex discrimination should go the way of ethnic and racial discrimination.[27]

In the early 1980s a few Catholic bishops in the United States wrote statements published in their dioceses addressing the problem of sexism in the church, and encouraged a rethinking of the role of women.[28] In 1990, the American bishops published the second draft of a pastoral letter[29] as a response to women's concerns. On the one hand the document condemned sexism as a sin, supported the theological preparation of women to preach the Gospel, recommended that "an incapacity to deal with women as equals should be considered a negative indication for fitness to ordination," and credited the women's movement for the part it played in helping nuns and laywomen to discover a new solidarity.

On the other hand, the document fell far short of the expectations of many Catholics. While admitting that there are "many women who can do what priests do," it sidestepped the issue of women's ordination by appealing to "unbroken tradition." It only went so far as to recommend that the question of women being ordained *as deacons* "be submitted to thorough investigation."[30]

The final vote on the proposed pastoral letter, which was to have been taken at the November 1990 national bishops' meeting, was postponed indefinitely on September 13, 1990. The explanatory statement by the committee making the decision cited as the principal reason "the need for more time and more consultation before the project reaches a conclusion." Another reason for the delay was that the Vatican had "suggested that consultation with bishops' conferences of other countries on this pastoral letter would be appropriate." Finally, it was argued that responses from the second draft of the proposed letter were still being received, and that the additional time would "allow a more reflective consideration of these responses."[31]

The women's movement was instrumental in other ways as well in regard to this movement of women into new roles in the church. Many American Catholic women experienced a heightening of their critical consciousness as they worked for the passage of the Equal Rights Amendment. These experiences helped some Catholic women to reflect on their countless hours of parish service and their exclusion from the most important functions in the ministry.

The use of gender-neutral language, an important agenda item of the contemporary women's movement, has gradually penetrated the Catholic church in the United States. For example, an excerpt from a consensus statement resulting from a symposium on Women and Church Law sponsored by the Canon Law Society of America in 1976 reads:

> We ask that the National Conference of Catholic Bishops, in conjunction with other Episcopal Conferences, work to replace sexist language in liturgical texts. We ask that such language be replaced in Conference statements, in existing Church legislation, and carefully avoided in any future statements and legislation.[32]

Some language revision in scripture readings, in hymns and prayers, and even in the revised Code of Canon Law has been accomplished, though much still remains to be done. The documents of Vatican II, some provisions in the new Code of Canon Law, demographic changes, and the contemporary women's movement have expedited the movement of women into new roles in the Catholic church. These facilitating factors help to explain why there are a few Catholic women serving as pastors of priestless parishes in the United States.

PREVIOUS AND CURRENT RESEARCH

One of the few previous studies of Catholic women pastors is Peter Gilmour's dissertation on priestless parishes, limited to nine rural parishes in the midwest: five in the west north central and four in the east north central regions of the United States. All of his parishes were predominantly white, and all were headed by nuns.[33] While he touches on some of the dilemmas experienced by the women administering these parishes, his book is predominantly descriptive of the context of the pastor's experience in each of these parishes. He focuses on this context in his interviews with the women pastors. Although there are a few statements from parishioners and priests in some of his chapters, it does not appear that he systematically interviewed parishioners and priests who were serving as sacramental ministers in each of the parishes.[34]

A national survey of administrators of priestless parishes in the United States that will be conducted under the auspices of the Institute for Pastoral Life is currently in the preparatory stage.[35] Located in Kansas City, Missouri, the Institute for Pastoral Life is a national center serving home mission dioceses characterized by vast geographic distances, sparse populations, and a poverty of resources. Established by a group of Catholic bishops in 1985, the institute focuses on the lay ministry needs of the parishes in these rural dioceses, and offers a direct training program of pastoral life coordinators (their title for laity heading priestless parishes) consisting of a three year cycle summer institute.

A perusal of the 1990 edition of the *Official Catholic Directory* revealed that there were 210 parishes in the United States administered by nonpriests. The largest portion of these parishes, sixty-one percent (129) were headed by nuns, twenty-two percent (47) were headed by deacons, nine percent (19) by laity, six percent (12) by religious brothers, and one percent (3) by pastoral teams.[36] Keeping in mind that the data for each edition of the *Directory* are gathered during the previous year, and the number of parishes headed by nonpriests increased from the previous edition (1989) by twenty-five, we can assume that at the present time there are approximately three hundred parishes or two percent of a total of 19,069 parishes in the United States being administered by nonpriests.[37] A recent edition of *Corpus Reports* cites a Vatican report that 157,000, or thirty-four percent of parishes worldwide, are without a priest; whereas in the United States ten percent of parishes are priestless.[38]

A research project on women appointed to administer parishes outside the United States was conducted by Katherine Gilfeather in Chile. Her study, entitled "The Changing Role of Women in the Catholic Church in Chile," was published in 1977. She reported that there were over eighty nuns acting as administrators of priestless parishes in many dioceses, doing tasks traditionally reserved for priests, and, as she said, "in general, taking the lion's share of responsibility for the spiritual welfare of the inhabitants."[39] As we know from the section in the earlier part of this chapter, these women were serving as pastors in spite of the fact that the new church law had not as yet been promulgated.

In 1987 I conducted an exploratory study of a small number of Catholic women who were in church positions that had been previously monopolized by men: chancellors of dioceses, canon lawyers, and administrators of priestless parishes.[40] The focus of that preliminary study, published in 1988, was on the creation of a new social reality for Catholic women; that is, on the causes rather than the consequences of recruitment to these new roles. Nonetheless, the data from those in-depth interviews shed some light on the consequences of women's movement into these new roles. For example, I found that there were considerable limitations to the power and control exercised by Catholic women administrators.

The results of a national survey of American Catholic laity also shed some light on the acceptance of women as pastors.[41] A majority (sixty-five percent) of the respondents said that Catholic laity (men *and* women) should have the right to be in charge of a parish when the priest is absent. A quarter (twenty-seven percent) said the laity should not have this right, and eight percent said they were not sure. There were no significant gender differences on this item. Thus, women who are placed in charge of priestless parishes can expect to find that about two-thirds of the parishioners approve of their appointment and about one-fourth disapprove.[42]

What the survey could not tell us was how parishioners translate these attitudes into behavior as they interact with a lay administrator appointed to head their parish, particularly when the layperson is a woman. Left unanswered were such questions as the following: Do her parishioners give a woman leader the same quality and quantity of support they gave the previous pastors? What are the types of behavior which show that parishioners affirm or reject her position as parish leader? What are her perceptions regarding the constraints and resources experienced in her everyday life in this new position?

MY RESEARCH

During the month of May 1989, I wrote letters to twenty women throughout the United States who had been appointed by their bishops to administer priestless parishes—and who had been doing so for at least a year—asking them to participate in my study. Most of the names and addresses of the women included in this study were obtained from the 1988 *Official Catholic Directory,* others came from women pastors whom I had interviewed in an exploratory study, and a few names came from other people knowledgeable about this phenomenon.[43]

In the letter I identified myself as a sociologist and a lifelong

Catholic who was embarking on a research project on women who had been appointed to pastoral leadership roles in parishes with no resident priest. I expressed the hope that the findings of my study would help to smooth the transition process for women who would be appointed to this role in the future.

My letter explained that I planned to visit twenty parishes throughout the country, where I would spend the weekend conducting interviews with the woman heading the parish, with the priest who provides sacramental ministry, and with two elected lay leaders of the parish (one male and one female).[44] I also said that I planned to participate in all of the liturgies and other parish activities taking place that weekend.[45]

When I phoned them a week later to schedule my proposed visit to their parishes, all twenty of the women said that they were willing to participate in the study. In spite of the fact that they were leading very busy lives, they were willing to contact the priest and parishioners and to arrange the time and place for my interviews prior to my arrival. When I asked them to recommend a hotel or motel nearby where I could make a reservation, most of them invited me to stay with them, either at the parish house or at their own homes. They also agreed to send me a copy of the history of the parish, where such a document existed, so that I could acquaint myself with the context of their situation before I arrived on the scene.

However, in making those initial phone calls, I discovered that two of the women had been recently terminated by their bishops, and a month later, I learned of a third termination. I substituted the next three names on my list for these three who were no longer living in their parishes; but I asked all three terminated women if they would agree to an interview, even though they would no longer be working in the same location. All three agreed, and I was able to conduct in-depth interviews with them as well.

One criterion for inclusion in the study was that these women appointed by the bishop as pastoral administrators had served in this capacity for at least one year. The total number of women who had been appointed to administer a parish before July 1, 1988, and whose names, addresses, and phone numbers were on my list, was eighty, so my sample represents one-fourth of the total population.

Initially I assumed that nuns would have an easier adjustment to the new role than laywomen, because parishioners
would perceive them as having a higher religious status as
exemplified by their vows, their title, and, in some cases, their
dress. Although nuns are not members of the clergy, and they
are, strictly speaking, laywomen, Catholics tend to place them in
a separate category, "a level above" the laity. Even though they
cannot be called "Father," religious women do have the title "Sister," which is not shared by their lay counterparts.

In order to compare the experiences of laywomen with that
of nuns, I chose nine parishes headed by laywomen and eleven
headed by nuns. To my knowledge, these nine laywomen were
the only women who had served as a pastor for a year or more,
and who were not members of religious communities. As mentioned earlier, sixty-one percent of nonpriest-headed parishes in
the United States are led by female members of religious communities. However, this proportion will change radically in the near
future because women's religious communities, like the priesthood, are experiencing a steady decrease in numbers of applicants.[46] Thus we can expect to see a continuing increase in the
numbers of laywomen appointed to head parishes. Therefore, I
overrepresented the number of laywomen in my sample, because
I considered their involvement to be the wave of the future, given
the increasing shortage of both priests and nuns.

Parishes headed by laywomen who were not nuns were
geographically dispersed in four of the nine census regions in
the United States. In order to include the eastern and southern
part of the United States, I included parishes headed by nuns in
two additional census regions. Although I traveled to twelve
states in all, I will not reveal the specific states in order to safe-
guard the anonymity of the people I interviewed.

The following are the six census regions represented in my
study and the number of parishes I visited in each: (1) Middle
Atlantic (New York, New Jersey, Pennsylvania), two parishes; (2)
East North Central (Wisconsin, Illinois, Indiana, Michigan, Ohio),
four parishes; (3) West North Central (Minnesota, Iowa, Missouri,
North Dakota, South Dakota, Nebraska, Kansas), three parishes;
(4) South Atlantic (Delaware, Maryland, West Virginia, Virginia,
North Carolina, South Carolina, Georgia, Florida, District of

Columbia), three parishes; (5) West South Central (Arkansas, Oklahoma, Louisiana, Texas), three parishes; and (6) Pacific (Washington, Oregon, California, Alaska, Hawaii), five parishes. In all, then, I traveled to twenty parishes representing fourteen dioceses and located in twelve states.

How "representative" was my sample? I combined the census regions into four categories and compared my sample to the total number of parishes headed by nonpriests in the United States (210) as reported in the 1990 *Official Catholic Directory*.[47] What I found was that in three of the regions my parishes were very similar: The largest cluster of nonpriest-headed parishes nationally is in the Midwest, forty percent (84), compared to thirty-five percent (7) of my parishes. The next largest cluster is in the South, thirty-two percent (68), compared to thirty percent (6) of my parishes. Another large cluster is in the West, twenty-six percent (55), compared to twenty-five percent (5) of my parishes. The region where I purposely oversampled, because I was aware that very few parishes were headed by nonpriests, was in the Northeast. Nationally only two percent (4) of the parishes in the Northeast are headed by nonpriests, compared to ten percent (2) of my parishes.

Another key assumption was that the climate of opinion created by supportive bishops would ease the transition into the new role for all women pastors. Thus I wanted to compare the experiences of women who were administering parishes located in dioceses headed by supportive bishops with those whose bishops were either neutral or nonsupportive. Bishops who engaged in activities such as the following were considered supportive: writing a public statement in support of women's greater participation in the church; visiting the parish prior to the appointment to explain to the parishioners the reasons for her appointment; making a public announcement of the appointment in the diocesan newspaper; participating in her formal installation ceremony in the parish; and including her in all the official mailings sent to other (male) pastors. Based on these criteria, half of the parishes in my sample are located in dioceses with supportive bishops.

I was also interested in rural-urban differences. My assumption was that Catholics living in large cities where there are many churches could simply attend Mass at another church if they did not approve of a woman as pastor. Likewise, Catholics living in smaller communities would have fewer alternatives for Sunday worship services, and would be more inclined to cooperate in order to keep their parish open. I wanted to compare the experiences of women whose parishes were located in large cities with those located in smaller communities. However, I soon found that the great majority of parishes headed by women were located in small rural communities, so only two large city parishes could be included.

When I visited these parishes between June and December 1989, I stayed for the weekend, usually three days and two nights, and in most cases I was their guest in the rectory or parish house. I conducted taped interviews not only with the woman in charge of the parish, but also with the priest who came to celebrate Mass and administer the sacraments (often called the sacramental minister), and two parishioners, one male and one female, who were members of the parish council.[48] I describe these interviews as in-depth because I spent approximately two hours interviewing each pastor, and one hour each with the priest and two parishioners. The interviews were also semistructured because, although there were specific open-ended questions asked, I also probed wherever feasible, and gave the interviewee many opportunities for input that was not included in the interview schedule.[49]

In addition to four interviews at each parish, I also conducted taped interviews with the three women who had been terminated as pastors shortly after they had agreed to participate in the study. The total number of in-depth interviews, therefore, was eighty-three.

While visiting at the parishes I would often hold informal interviews with parishioners, that I recorded in my field notes. I also gathered data by observing the interaction between the woman who was pastoring the parish and her central role partners (priest and parishioners) at the various parish functions occurring over the weekend, such as the worship services where she and/or the priest are the presiders, and other church activities, like baptisms, weddings, visits to the sick, coffee and donut gatherings after Mass, church dinners, and meetings of the parish council. Since in most cases I was a guest in their homes, and often traveled with the women pastors to church functions, I was able to observe them in their daily lives and to discuss a variety of topics with them.

With the cooperation of the woman pastor, I was also able to collect some documentary data such as parish histories, church bulletins, diocesan guidelines regarding lay pastors, contracts, letters of appointment, and relevant local newspaper articles. The data for this book, then, include the tape-recorded interviews, the informal conversations and observations that I recorded in a notebook during my visit to the parish, and documents.

The Lilly Endowment grant enabled me to hire a professional person for the next stage of the research project, the transcription of the interview tapes that were stored on disks as well as printed out. The database also included participant observation field notes and documentary material that were likewise stored on disks. After completing the coding of the data, I was aided in the data-retrieval stage by a graduate student research assistant, provided for by the National Science Foundation grant. Data were retrieved and analyzed by using a variant of Word Perfect's search and retrieve functions. When this was completed I was then able to begin the final write-up stage of the project.

The title of this book is *They Call Her Pastor.* Although the title "pastor" is, strictly speaking, reserved for priest-pastors,[50] I soon found that not only were these women doing the work of priest-pastors, but they were often referred to as the pastor. For instance, at least three of their bishops introduced them as pastor in public, and the mail they received from the diocesan administration offices often addressed them as pastor. Most of the parishioners I interviewed said they considered their woman administrator to be their pastor, and referred to her as pastor when speaking of her to people outside the parish.

Several of the priests who were serving as sacramental ministers for the parish also called them pastor. One of the priests put it this way,

> The sense that I got right away is that she is in many ways the pastor of the parish. I remember telling other people this. If there is a problem, they always go to a pastor. So I guess I knew right away that she really was the leader of the parish.

•2•

A Portrait of the Pastors and Their Parishes

This chapter is an attempt to present a picture of the women pastors in this study and their parishes. In filling out the portrait we look first at who the women are, in terms of some of their background characteristics. Then the question, "Where do they come from?" is answered by looking at how they were recruited to their present positions. Finally, we look at some of their personal characteristics as seen by them, by their parishioners, and by their sacramental ministers.

WHO ARE THEY?

What do these women pastors look like? Their ages range from thirty-three to sixty-seven, averaging fifty years of age. In general their ages help them to blend in quite well with their parishioners, even the women at the extremes of the age range. For example, the youngest was appointed to a rural parish of predominantly young families, and she and her young family fit right in. The oldest woman pastor told me that she thought her grey hair was an advantage in her dealings with the priests of the diocese. She is convinced that they would not have accepted her as readily, nor would she have been taken as seriously by them, had she been a younger woman. Seventeen of the woman pastors are white, and three are Mexican-American.[1]

Eleven of the parishes were headed by nuns, eight by married women, and one by a single laywoman.² All of the married women had children, from a low of three to a high of six, with an average of 3.5 children. However, only five of the married women had children who were still living at home with them. The husbands of the married women had full-time jobs with the exception of one who was retired. All of the husbands were living at home, though two of them had jobs requiring considerable out-of-town travel.

In general, all of the women pastors are college educated women. Although not all of them have college degrees, they had some college experience. Seven had one to three years of college, and thirteen have bachelor's degrees. Of the thirteen with bachelor's degrees, twelve have graduate degrees as well: three have two master's degrees, eight have one master's degree, and one was currently a master's candidate. In order to keep abreast in the field of parish ministry, several of the women were taking courses in theology at nearby colleges, attending workshops and seminars, and participating in in-service training conferences. When we discussed their preparation for church services, it was evident that they also made a serious attempt to keep up with their reading.

Some of these women have achieved a higher level of education than their sacramental ministers, although many of the women draw on the greater pastoral experience of the priests.

During an interview with a priest who had never received a bachelor's degree, he proudly described his role in the in-service training of the woman pastor with a master's degree:

> So I really was available to train her. I wish now, looking back, that she had enrolled in a couple of different kinds of programs that would have given her a little bit of experience with something like canon law. She had no idea what dispensations were for marriages, why you might need a dispensation for one thing and a permission for another, how you set up sponsors for baptisms, and what you require of people and what you do for marriage preparation.

He continued:

> I had to get books for her and I had to explain to her what our policies were here, though I did not impose those policies upon her. I tried to explain to her, one by one, when situa-

tions arose what to do. "What do I do with this bill that came in from the chancery?" It took a lot of time. I was on call for the first year, and then it still continues where now (she) prepares a yellow pad of questions and things she wants to talk about and then she'll say, "Can I get together with you?" And we'll just go through the whole number of things and she'll ask about them.

The education differential becomes more apparent when the preaching styles of priest and woman pastor are compared. I heard the women preach in eleven of the parishes I visited.[3] In five of the nine parishes where I was unable to hear the woman preach, it was the priest's "turn" that weekend. In the remaining four parishes, the woman pastor only preached rarely and/or on special occasions.

With respect to the preaching that I did observe, my impression was that these women not only prepared their sermons very carefully, but they also delivered them well, and tended to make a connection between the scripture reading and the daily lives of their parishioners. Some of the women pastors were very creative in the way they asked questions of the congregation while they were preaching. For example, when one of them asked, "Who would rather die than sin?" in the middle of her presentation, you could have heard a pin drop in the church.

Because they cared deeply about communicating effectively with their parishioners in their homilies, preparation time was a priority for these pastors. As one of them explained, "I don't think I would want to preach every week. I wouldn't mind every other week because I prepare, and I don't think I would have time."

One of the priests, well liked by the parishioners, delivered a weak and somewhat disconnected homily[4] during the Mass I attended. The woman pastor, who had a good sense of how to touch the parishioners, gave him an article as we were drinking coffee after Mass, about the scripture readings for a future Sunday, and he was most grateful for it. He explained that she often shared valuable preaching material with him.

One of the sacramental ministers, whose education was equal to or greater than the pastor's, praised her creativity in this way:

I think she is more creative and more personally attentive to things, whereas I might accept doing something just because that's the way it's always been done, or doing something because that's how the book explained it should be done right then or take the easy way out that way. I don't think she does that very often. I think she really sits down and thinks, "What is this?" and how it should be done and "What's the reason for it?" and "How should I go about it." At least I see some of that.

An example would be the commentary at Mass. I just take a commentary that's canned, and I will clean it up a little if it needs it. It is one that somebody else does and I take it. I think she does her own always. I am sure she may use some other sources on occasion, but I am sure she puts more energy into that than I do.

On the other hand, one of the woman pastors, with less education than her sacramental minister, only rarely preached, even though urged to do so by priests and parishioners. She described herself this way:

I am an introvert and he [the previous pastor] was a one hundred percent extrovert, very outgoing and expansive. For me, it isn't a natural thing to get up and do some of the things I am now doing, so in that way I have to work at it harder.

The real problem...for me is the preparation time. But both of them [sacramental ministers] give excellent homilies and so I am nervous about getting up and giving it, but I do it.

With regard to previous work experience, there is a range among the women pastors, varying from teaching to sales and clerical work. When asked about previous full-time occupations, fifteen women mentioned more than one; twelve listed two previous full-time jobs and three of them mentioned three occupations. Fourteen of the women mention teaching as an earlier full-time occupation; ten of the fourteen former teachers are members of religious communities. All of the former teachers viewed their previous experience as a good preparation for the job of pastor. One of them, who had been a primary school teacher, explained:

I think I have an intuition about people because I had to when I was in a classroom with little kids in the very beginning stages of learning. I don't mean that as a putdown at all, I just mean that I don't take some things for granted. It is something where you have to explain things clearly, and don't make assumptions that people know what you are talking about, using phrases and words that you assume they know. They don't always. Church jargon is a jargon, and sometimes it isn't understood. It's a whole different language sometimes. And because so much of what I do is teaching, I am grateful for the skills of group process and dynamics that I have developed.

Another former teacher told me that she writes her sermons almost a week ahead of schedule because the unexpected (like funerals) can always happen. She said she felt that her twenty-two years as a teacher making lesson plans for her classes were a good preparation.

Two of the women had previous experience as a pastor; this is their second parish. Seven of them list "pastoral associate" as a former full-time occupation; seven of them had experience in managerial or administrative positions; five are former directors of religious education; and three mentioned sales and clerical as previous occupations. All of them had worked primarily in the United States, but four of the eleven nuns had spent some time working in Third World countries as well. Table 1 summarizes the pastors' characteristics.

WHERE DO THEY COME FROM?

Half of the women could be described as "outsiders," meaning that when they were appointed to the parish, they were recruited from another city or town. Only four of the ten outsiders were recruited from outside the diocese, and those four were members of religious communities. One was asked by the diocesan personnel director to apply for the job; another belonged to a religious community that had asked the bishop to appoint a member to head the parish. In the third case, the sister was recruited from outside the diocese through a priest who had had a positive experience with a sister who had served under him as a pastoral associate in charge of religious education. As he described it,

> About twelve years ago, at another parish where I was, I approached the...Sisters and asked them if they had someone who would want to come and share a ministry in a parish. Then they contacted me and told me that someone was available and a few people came up for interviews, and we hired

Table 1
Characteristics of Women Pastors

	Age*	Education	Occupations**	Married
1.	Middle	Some College	Teacher/Sales	Yes
2.	Younger	Some College	Teacher/Mgr.	Yes
3.	Older	M.A.	Teacher/PA	No
4.	Middle	M.A.	PA	No
5.	Older	Some College	Mgr./PA	No
6.	Younger	B.A.	Mgr./PA	Yes
7.	Middle	M.A.	Teacher/DRE	No
8.	Younger	M.A.	Teacher/DRE/Mgr.	No
9.	Middle	Some College	Teacher/Mgr.	Yes
10.	Middle	M.A.	Teacher/DRE/PA	No
11.	Middle	M.A.	Teacher	No
12.	Younger	B.A.	Teacher/DRE	Yes
13.	Middle	M.A.	Teacher/Mgr.	No
14.	Middle	M.A.	Teacher/PA	No
15.	Middle	Some College	Sales/Clerical	Yes
16.	Middle	M.A.	Teacher/PA	No
17.	Older	Some College	Mgr.	Yes
18.	Younger	Some College	Clerical	Yes
19.	Older	M.A.	Teacher/DRE/PA	No
20.	Middle	M.A.	Teacher/PA	No

*Age categories: Younger (Under 46), Middle (46–55), Older (56+).
**Previous Full-Time Occupations: PA denotes either pastoral associate or pastoral administrator; DRE denotes director of religious education; Mgr. denotes managerial/administrative positions.

one as a pastoral associate. At that time I didn't bother to check through the diocese. We just hired [her] and then I informed the diocese that there was a sister working in the parish and there was no problem with that at all. And then it became a very acceptable situation when we found out just how well we were working together.

This strategy, hiring a woman as a pastoral associate to be in charge of a specific program—such as religious education or liturgy—and to work with the resident priest, has been used by some priest pastors as a "first step" toward the recruitment of women pastors. In a sense this is a form of in-service training for the women, and it is especially helpful in dioceses headed by bishops who are reluctant to appoint nonpriests as pastors, where there is no training program available.

This same priest quoted above became alarmed when he was appointed as pastor to a large parish where the neighboring pastor who administered two additional parishes was due to retire. Realizing that he might soon be asked to take over the duties at the neighboring parish, he contacted the sister in charge of religious women in his diocese and told her that he would like a sister to come up and administer these parishes. Because he succeeded in convincing the bishop of the need for alternate staffing, he was able to recruit a sister as pastoral administrator.

The fourth "outsider" sister who came from another diocese to be in charge of a parish took the initiative herself by asking the bishop to appoint her:

> I called [the bishop] up and said to him, "I am thinking of changing my job, and I wonder if there is anything in your diocese." And he said, as he always does, "Well, let's talk about it." So I had an appointment in January and I went up to [his diocese] and he said to me, "Well, what do you really want to do?" And when he said that, it freed me up to muse with him about it. But I never really said I wanted to be in charge of a parish until, as we talked, that is what it was leading to. And he listened. And then he began to talk about the shortage of priests.

She continued:

> It wasn't that long a visit, about forty-five minutes. After that, I said to him, "Would you ever consider me?" And he said, "Yes." He said, "I will be in touch with you within a couple of weeks." And within a couple of weeks I heard from him, and he said, "I am putting this in the hands of [the sister who was Personnel Director for the diocese]. I want her to negotiate how this will all work, and I have two places I have in mind, and I want to see how you feel, and we will work it out."

This bishop quoted above is very supportive of the idea of laity running parishes. In fact, his view is that ordination does not always produce good pastors, and he tries to place his priests in positions where they can utilize their strengths. So he appointed someone from outside the diocese with the gifts for pastoring, rather than closing the parish, or appointing an unsuitable priest.

ENTERING THE PARISH

Outsiders tended to experience more difficulty as they moved into the new role of pastor than did insiders. One of them described what she saw and did when she arrived at the parish house:

> The first week I moved into this house it was filthy dirty because no one took care of it. I came in and this house was overrun with mice, and dirty. I just started cleaning. And the people watched, and nobody came over and said, "Can I help?" They all knew what I was doing. This whole village knew what I was doing, but they were so nervous and so unsure of who I was or what I was doing here that they didn't approach me.

In fact it took most of the outsiders an entire year before they felt that they were accepted by the parishioners. The first few weeks were especially painful, as one of the outsiders attests:

> In the beginning I knew that if I didn't get out, I would just be sitting all by myself in here [the parish house] and I would never meet anybody because they certainly were not going to come to me. They were not going to come up and say, "Welcome!" I had to walk out or else I would die here. So I would just walk around town and meet people on the streets. Then, of course, they talked to each other. It's such a small town that everybody knows everything. And the same way at church, I would make sure I talked to every single person as much as I could. But it was real important; otherwise I would never get into their lives because they would not include me or invite me.

An outsider who described her parishioners as shy and low on self-esteem said,

> They are hard to get real close to because they don't communicate in terms of telling you how they feel. They have told me that unless you are born here, you will always be an outsider.

A parishioner described a confrontation that took place between an "outsider" woman pastor and another parishioner soon after the woman pastor's arrival at the parish. One of the parishioners who came to the parish house took it upon herself to inform the pastor that "the people do not want you here and (they) want you to leave." The woman pastor responded by explaining that she had been assigned to the parish by the bishop, that it was he who had invited her. Clearly this kind of confrontation could have been avoided or at least alleviated if the bishop had involved the parishioners in the recruitment of the pastor.

One of the four women recruited from outside the diocese—and had been serving as the pastor for four years by the time I visited her—made this observation about coming from a city in another diocese to her rural parish:

> The framework of social life revolved in circles here. I had never lived in a rural area. I didn't expect that I wouldn't be included in social things because in every parish I've been in I had always been part of the social fabric of people's lives—invited to parties. I always was. And here I'm not, even now.

She continued,

> I don't even get invited to all the weddings that I slave over. I don't get invited to the receptions. Some I do, but not all. I don't get invited to parties after baptisms. I think it isn't that they are rejecting me. I think they are just so used to their groupings being family that it doesn't occur to them to extend invitations to outsiders.

Perhaps the fact that these outsiders were also members of religious communities was a partial reason for the lack of invitations. Although I had predicted that nuns would have an easier adjustment to this new role because of their perceived higher religious status, this was not always true, especially for those who were outsiders in the sense that they had not previously worked or lived in the parish. One of the parishioners explained her community's reaction to the appointment of an outsider nun as their pastor:

> In the beginning it was like, "Oh my God, a nun is going to start ruling, and things are going to be so strict." It's been so lax with the priests, because they haven't been here to enforce or meet the needs. Even fifty percent of the time they're not here; they're doing a job somewhere else. So the idea that someone was going to come here with new ideas and new

rules who was from a city—that created a problem also—the fact that she was not a rural person. A city person tends to have different ideas and run a faster pace than we're used to. We're a laid-back, rural community.

One of the outsider nuns described the parishioners' resistance to her appointment this way:

It was like, "This is our place; you are the outsider. You aren't like Father So-and-so; we have always done it this way."

Another woman coming from outside the diocese described the way she attempted to move toward becoming more of an insider, and compared herself to the previous resident pastor.

They [the parishioners] just stared straight past me. They were shy. They didn't know what I was doing here. It was not clearly explained to everybody. They didn't know what I would be doing, and they didn't know how to reach out to me. They are very, very family-oriented people. They are not like a city or suburban parish where everybody is a stranger to each other, so you are forced to relate to each other. They are very groupy. So, as they stood outside on the steps after Mass, I had to go and insert myself into their groups. Otherwise, they just ignored me. Now that's different, of course, but in the beginning that's how it was.

She then compared herself to the previous pastor:

I am doing it differently. I think that the deacon ahead of me had good administrative skills, but he was not a pastoral person. He didn't have that charisma. I have a good combination of both, so I am doing it differently. I am more outgoing than he was. I open the [parish] house; he never opened the house, letting people come in and have meetings in the living room. Generally, there is a different atmosphere.

A male parishioner from this same parish corroborated her analysis when he praised her for the way she had reached out to all members of the community for the past four years. As a consequence, he said,

We have a community spirit here. She has her finger on the pulse of the parish much more so than the deacon or the former priests.

One of the "outsider" women pastors used the strategy of involving the parishioners in more of the parish decision making, and thus making them more like "insiders." She explained,

> It's important to bring people into the planning, and on a much bigger level, of course, it's critical. They will never feel that it's their own parish if an outsider like me comes in and does what I want. It has to be done with the people. So we have committees and commissions. We move any kind of project into those commissions.

An outsider who was a member of a pastoral team and had just completed her first year in the parish had this to say about the acceptance of sisters as opposed to priests on the part of older parishioners.

> Father is very taken care of and he won't go hungry and he will always be invited to dinner. We are not invited to dinner. Some of our close friends and the younger families are real good. "Sister, come on over," and they are real informal. But the older ones, the staid relationships in the parish that have been here for years, that have always had Father at their dinner table, they don't have Sister at their dinner tables.

RECRUITMENT ROUTES

Although I had assumed that most of the women I would be visiting were recruited initially by their bishops, this was not the case for the four mentioned above who came from outside the diocese. I soon discovered that there was a variation in recruitment. The variations could be a function of the lack of planning in some dioceses, where the shortage of priests either took the bishop by surprise, or he had hoped to find other solutions, like recruiting priests from foreign countries. Even today there are many dioceses where no guidelines regarding training or recruitment to these positions exist. These tend to be dioceses with an adequate supply of priests, where the bishop has not addressed future shortages.

On the other hand, some dioceses have recently turned to national advertising. For example:

The Archdiocese of Anchorage is recruiting for pastoral administrators in rural parishes. Qualifications: M.A. in divinity or
theology or equivalent and experience in parish ministry. Must
be willing to live in a rural setting that calls for flexibility. Send
resume to: Director of Pastoral Services and Ministries, Archdiocese of Anchorage, 225 Cordova St., Anchorage, AK 99501.[5]

As more and more dioceses turn to national advertising, we
can expect to find an increase in the number of lay pastors who
are recruited from outside the diocese. Advertising in the local
diocesan paper would probably be the first choice for most bishops, who would consider someone from the diocese as less an
"outsider." In fact, it was extremely successful in one parish I
visited, where there had been fifty applicants for the position
advertised in their diocesan newspaper.

There was a variety of "paths" to the door of the parish house
for the women pastors interviewed. Although all of the women
were appointed by the bishop, in seven of the cases a priest
(either a local pastor or the diocesan personnel director) recruited
her, as in one of the examples above. One of the priests, aware
that his term of appointment at the parish was in the final year,
recruited a sister as pastoral associate and after training her for
the job, convinced the bishop to appoint her to head the parish
after his departure. One of the sisters who was recruited as part of
a team by the diocesan personnel director said,

> We have begun to establish a trust level here. Father _____ is
> convinced that if people have a good experience of liturgy,
> and have good, solid homilies, and you are there for them in
> their grief, that they will come, no matter who you are. And
> that has certainly proved true. We have listened to them, we
> have identified their pain [regarding the loss of a resident
> priest pastor]; we have given them permission to be angry.
> And then we have buried them, married them, blessed them,
> prayed with them, cried with them. So, therefore, when we go
> to them and say, "Would you help us?" nobody turns us down.

In five cases the parishioners chose the woman to be the
pastoral administrator, and recommended her to the bishop. All
five of these were insiders, meaning that they had lived or
worked in the parish prior to their appointment. Three were laywomen who had been active members of the parish for many

years, and two were nuns who, at the time of the appointment, had been serving as pastoral associates in the parish for more than four years. The general scenario for the recruitment of these five insiders was similar. Typically, the bishop met with the parish council to explain that he had no priest to replace the one who was leaving or retiring. He explained that they could close the parish, recruit a foreign priest, advertise the position in the diocese or nationally, or appoint one of the members of the parish. After weighing the alternatives, the parishioners said, "We want her!" and the bishop complied with their choice.

In four cases it was the woman herself who was the initiator; two of them applied for the position that was advertised, and two asked the bishop to consider them for appointment to a parish which had recently lost its pastor, but where no decision about the successor had been made. One of the outsiders who took this latter path to the parish house described her experience earlier in this chapter. The other unique path to the door of the parish house was taken by a married woman who was aware that a neighboring parish had recently lost its resident pastor. Apparently no steps towards the recruitment of a replacement had been taken. She, however, could be considered an insider, because she had previously been a member of this parish, and knew many of the parishioners very well. Her strategy was to write a letter to the bishop, which she shared with me. The following are excerpts from her letter:

> Dear Bishop _____ :
> It is my understanding that the [parish] is still without a pastor at this time. I would like to ask that you consider appointing me as a [pastoral administrator]. I feel that my background in the church has given me the skills that would be valuable in this ministry.

After enumerating her training in pastoral ministry and her years of experience in working for the church in many capacities, she continued,

> Although we are registered at [her own parish], we live in the boundaries of [the parish without a pastor], and I am well acquainted with the needs of that parish. There are many challenges in serving that parish due to its essentially rural nature

and ethnic composition. The...area in the past has demonstrated its openness to fresh approaches to the presence of the church among its people, and I feel would be receptive to the appointment of a [pastoral administrator] to serve the...area.
Thank you for your consideration.

The bishop in question referred her application to the members of the diocesan personnel board, who recommended that she be appointed to the position. Before her appointment, however, the bishop asked her to consult with the parish council to see if they would support the appointment. She felt this was a good move on the part of the bishop because, as she explained, "If they don't support me, I would not be able to function effectively in the first six months anyway." However, she also realized that the bishop's condition of prior consultation with the parishioners might have some long range effects. She continued,

> However, he may not know that he is setting a precedent that may come back and haunt him when he gets ready to assign a priest somewhere and a strong parish council says, "We want to be consulted." I did not point that out to him, because I didn't think about it at the time.

In most of the parishes I visited, the process included consultation with the parishioners before the appointment was made. One of the women pastors who had been interviewed by the parishioners before her appointment, explained why she considered herself a good "fit" for her rural parish in a small town.

> I was really interested in getting involved in total parish activity. I felt this kind of parish would give me that possibility. It was very similar to my hometown situation, and I felt I could identify with that. I felt I could relate to the people in a town like this.

There were, however, three cases where prior consultation would have smoothed the process considerably for women who were outsiders. Because these women were "foisted on them" by the bishop without any parishioner input, the parishioners were understandably upset, and put themselves at a distance from their woman pastor. Needless to say, these three women pastors did not see any welcome signs when they arrived at the parish; in fact they felt that they were ignored by most parish-

ioners in the first weeks of their ministry. One of the parishioners said that there was only a small group who accepted her
as pastor at the very beginning. As she explained,

> I think she felt a cold shoulder from the majority of the people
> here, and that was very, very hard for her. And I know that
> she presented herself a little more gruffly to people because
> she didn't feel accepted. And her front was to buckle up and
> be very stern, and that came across like, "Oh boy, is she ever a
> strict nun." Their strict-nun image was really there anyway for
> a lot of people.

One of these three also had multiple stresses during her first
year as pastor, and she told me that she cried herself to sleep on
more than one occasion that first year. She was described by a
female parishioner in this way:

> She's a very tough lady. She puts up a very strong front and
> then when she accepts the situation for what it is, she kind of
> goes forward and attacks that situation and tries to break it
> down. And she's very good. I've seen her go up to people
> who are not accepting of her and give them a hug. And it's
> hard to resist somebody who's giving you a hug, somebody
> who's sharing themselves with you that way. And I've seen her
> break through on a lot of people. Sometimes it just takes time;
> sometimes they're just not ready to accept her and she just
> needs to leave it go. But if she sees that they are a receptive
> person at all, then she is very quick to go forward and try to
> break the ice herself. And it takes a lot of energy, a lot of emo-
> tion to do that.

What were the recruitment routes of the four remaining outsiders whom I visited? In three cases it was the bishop who initiated the recruitment of the woman pastor, and in one case it
was the head of the woman's religious community who asked
her to consider accepting the position, once the community convinced the bishop to appoint one of their members.

The other half of the women pastors were insiders. One of
them had lived in the parish all her life, and another had only
worked in the parish for a year before her appointment, but the
median amount of time spent in the parish prior to the appointment by these insiders was six years. The ten insiders had a distinct advantage as they moved into their new role as pastor, in

that they were already known, respected, and loved by many of the parishioners. In addition, their parishioners feared for the survival of the parish. As one of them told me,

> I think we were all leery because of the new situation. We had always had a priest being our administrator. Right from the time I started going to church here, we felt our church continuing was a precarious situation because we were small, and there were many larger parishes in need of priests. And we were really told that our doors may be closed if it came to the point where we couldn't afford to keep ourselves open to have a priest available to us. So when we heard that we were not going to be a parish that had a full-time priest anymore, we were all very shaken for fear that the church may cease to be.

THE CONTEXT OF THEIR PARISHES

As described earlier, the women pastors are located in twenty parishes dispersed in twelve states in six of the nine census regions in the United States. Thirty-five percent (7) of the parishes are in the Midwest (East and West North Central regions); thirty percent (6) in the South (South Atlantic, East and West South Central regions); twenty-five percent (5) in the West (Mountain and Pacific regions); and ten percent (2) are in the Northeast (Middle Atlantic region). All but two of the parishes are located in small towns or villages in rural areas that are not identified in order to protect the anonymity of interviewees.

The eastern part of the United States, and in particular New England, is not well represented in this study, although two of the women pastors are located in the Middle Atlantic region. Unfortunately, it was impossible to select any parishes in the New England region, which includes Maine, Vermont, New Hampshire, Massachusetts, Connecticut, and Rhode Island, because there were no women appointed in any of these states as pastoral administrators with the requisite experience when the research was planned.

Initially, I expected to find each woman in charge of one parish where a priest, appointed as the sacramental minister, appeared each weekend to celebrate Mass and preside at the sacraments. I soon discovered that there were many "atypical" situations.

First of all, there were only twelve parishes where the woman pastor was administering only one parish, and the appointed sacramental minister arrived every weekend to celebrate Mass. Secondly, there were three parishes where the interview with the pastor involved two people. In one case I held a joint interview with a married couple who were copastoring in a parish, and in two cases I held joint interviews with two nuns who were part of a diocesan team serving four parishes. The other members of the team were the priests, and in one case, a deacon also, all of whom took turns presiding at either Mass or communion services in the parishes they served.

However, even in some of these "typical" parishes, the responsibility for providing a sacramental minister was often placed in the hands of the woman pastor when the appointed sacramental minister was on vacation or had responsibilities elsewhere.

In four of the "atypical" parishes, there was a Mass every weekend, but the same priest did not appear each time. Two of the women pastors had two priests who rotated as sacramental ministers every weekend, one woman pastor had three rotating priests, and one had four different priests per month. In the latter case, both pastor and parishioners mentioned that they enjoyed having different preachers each week, even though much of the pastor's time had to be spent in contacting and scheduling the priests' visits. The fact that these priests had other full-time jobs made rotation necessary. For instance, one of the priests assigned as the sacramental minister for one of the parishes was also the vocation director for the diocese. He explained his limitations thus:

> I don't go out there [to her parish as sacramental minister] every weekend. As vocation director, I have to keep two weekends a month available when I go out to fill in for priests, or go to their parishes to speak on vocations during weekend Masses. And then the two or three weekends that I am here I fill in. When I am gone, [she] has to find another priest in the area who is available, or she has to hold a communion service.

In the remaining four "atypical" parishes the priest did not appear every weekend, usually because he was serving two or three other parishes in addition to his own, and/or because the driving distances were so immense. Three of the parishes had Mass every other weekend; in one of these it was the same priest who appeared, but in two others there were two different priests who appeared on alternate weeks. Finally, in the most atypical case, the parishioners in one parish sometimes saw a priest only once a month. The woman pastor explained,

> He [the bishop] promised to send a priest twice a month and that was not fulfilled. In the beginning, yes, but after awhile whoever was available would come and sometimes three Sundays in a row we wouldn't have anybody. In the beginning [of her term as administrator] I would call him and remind him, and there came a moment in which I thought that he is the bishop and he is the one who has the responsibility. If we have several Sundays without a priest, it is his responsibility. We are doing the best we can. Now, again, we are having this priest twice a month. For awhile we went three or four weeks without one.

In those eight parishes where the priest does not appear each weekend, the woman pastor presides at a word and communion service. This service consists of introductory prayers, readings from the scriptures, a reflection on the scripture readings (sermon), and the distribution of communion. The hosts used for this service were previously consecrated by a priest during Mass, and preserved for this purpose. I was able to observe four of the women pastors presiding at these services.

Most of the women (15) were in charge of only one parish, four administered in two parishes, and one was in charge of a parish and two missions. How many parishioners were these women responsible for? Most parishes count members by families or households, but "family" was the term that was used most often. The range in number of families in the twenty parishes was from 339 to 50. There were five "large" parishes (200–400 families), ten "medium-size" parishes (100–199 families), and five "small" parishes (under 100 families).[6] The median number of families for whom the women pastors were responsible was 147, which is roughly three hundred-fifty parishioners.

With respect to racial or ethnic characteristics, fifteen of the parishes could be described as predominantly white. The two that were predominantly Mexican-American were situated in the South and in the West. There was one black parish located in the South. In addition, there was one in the South that was almost equally black and white, and another in the West that had an equal portion of white and Mexican-American parishioners. Most of the white women pastors were heading predominantly white parishes, though one was pastoring a mixed black and white parish and another a predominantly Mexican-American parish. One of the Mexican-American women pastors headed a predominantly Mexican-American parish; one headed a black parish; and the third was a member of a pastoral team serving a parish that had an equal mix of Mexican-American and white parishioners.

Ten of the women live in a rectory, usually situated next to the church. Most of them refer to it as the parish house, because by definition a rectory is the residence of a parish priest. Half of the women living in the parish house live with someone else, either a member of their religious community, or in the case of one young married woman, with husband and children. The remaining five live in the parish house alone and are ambivalent about their living situations. One of them told me that she doesn't mind living alone because she is so busy throughout the day, and gone so much, that she appreciates the quiet and space when she returns home. Ideally, however, she would like to have someone to share with, to pray with, to "do things" with. However, she said she would prefer to live alone rather than have someone thrust on her, someone she hadn't chosen as a living companion. At least two of the others are "loners" and their attitudes about their present living situation is very positive.

Seven of the eight married women live in their own homes situated within the parish boundaries. Two of these married women have converted a room in their home to an office, because the church has not yet been built. The three remaining women pastors are living in rented homes near the church.

There was no church building in three of the twenty parishes I visited, although building plans are in progress in two of these parishes. In one case the land for the church had already been donated, and the building campaign was underway. When the woman pastor showed me the site for the church, she estimated that the building would be completed within a year or two. In the second parish, the building plans were limping along, and the parishioners were skeptical about the outcome.

Church services are held in nearby Protestant churches in two of the three parishes without their own building. In one case the Mass is celebrated on Saturday evening, a time when it is not needed by the host congregation. In the other case the Mass is celebrated early on Sunday morning, just before the Protestant service. In the third parish, Mass is held in the auditorium of a public school building on Sunday morning. These situations present constraints for all three of the women pastors. Problems include lack of adequate storage space, of classroom space for religious education, and of a meeting place for committees and social gatherings. Two of the women pastors have converted space in their own homes to be used as a temporary parish office, and one of them uses a rented office near the church. Needless to say, these women and their parishioners are looking forward to the day when their church buildings are completed. One of the male parishioners located in the parish where Mass was said in a public school building said,

> Speaking of funerals, one of the things that's been real difficult is that we don't have a church, so we have to make arrangements with other parishes in order to have a funeral service. [The woman pastor] has to do that.

The yearly salary of these women ranged from $3000 to $25,300. The two women with the lowest salaries did not work full-time, so if we subtract their wages in order to calculate the average full-time salaries, the average salary is $12,000. What we should keep in mind is that the salary is paid by the parish, which in this study was typically located in a poor and isolated area. Understandably, then, the women pastors cannot expect higher salaries, even though their education and experience dictates that they should.

Half of these women lived in the parish house rent-free, so their actual remuneration was higher. When I calculated the free housing as an additional salary of $500 monthly for those who lived in the parish house, then the average full-time salary comes to $15,500. Although the contracts varied, other monies were also usually allocated for medical and health insurance, gas for the car when used for parish business, and continuing education courses or workshops. Also typically provided were one day off per week, a week for spiritual retreat, and two or three weeks for summer vacation.

A laywoman who was not married explained how she was able to supplement her salary in order to meet expenses.

> I found it necessary to supplement the salary they could offer me here because of the fact of having left religious life at the age of thirty-nine, and not having any income accrued for retirement. So to do that, it was part of the agreement that I established with the parish from the outset and also with the bishop, that that would be the only way I could consider doing this, if I could supplement my income by doing additional ministry. Originally I wanted to put in the equivalent of about ten hours a week [in additional ministry], but I found that was impossible, so I cut back to approximately six hours a week.

Only ten percent (2) of the parishes I visited were situated in urban areas; the rest were located in small parishes in rural towns or villages. Thirty-five percent (7) of the parishes were in towns with populations of 1,000 to 9,999; and the largest percentage, fifty-five percent (11) were in towns or villages with populations under one thousand.

One of the priest interviewees was critical of the policy of placing women to head small parishes in small rural areas. He said,

> I was a little disappointed in the sense that if the diocese is going to make a commitment about women in ministry, I felt it was wrong that they started here [in a small parish]. Now they talked about it in two veins. One was the role of women. They wanted to encourage women in ministry. And then a second area was the shortage of priests. Well, if they're going to deal with the shortage of priest problem, they should have put (the woman pastor), or any other sister, at the Cathedral parish, a big parish. I mean, that would make a statement. This was not a statement parish, so I felt it was kind of a weak statement on their part that we're really concerned about putting women in the roles of ministry. If they really wanted to, they would have picked a larger parish, I think, with more visibility.

Table 2 summarizes the characteristics of the parishes. The average amount of experience as a pastoral administrator is four years, and the range is from one year to eight. Eighteen of the women are pastoring for the first time; two of them had served at another parish prior to this, their second appointment.

Table 2
Characteristics of Parishes

	Census Region*	Population**	Parish Size***	Race/Ethnicity
1.	West	Small Urban	Small	White
2.	West	Medium Rural	Medium	Mexican-Amer.
3.	South	Small Rural	Medium	White
4.	South	Medium Rural	Large	Black
5.	South	Large Urban	Large	White/Black
6.	Midwest	Small Rural	Medium	White
7.	Midwest	Small Rural	Medium	White
8.	Midwest	Small Rural	Medium	White
9.	Midwest	Small Rural	Small	White
10.	Midwest	Small Rural	Medium	White
11.	Midwest	Small Rural	Medium	White
12.	Midwest	Small Rural	Small	White
13.	Northeast	Small Rural	Medium	White
14.	Northeast	Medium Rural	Large	White
15.	West	Medium Rural	Small	White
16.	South	Medium Rural	Large	Mexican-Amer.
17.	South	Small Rural	Medium	White
18.	South	Small Rural	Small	White
19.	West	Medium Rural	Medium	White
10.	West	Medium Rural	Large	White/Mex.-Amer.

* Northeast (Middle Atlantic and New England); Midwest (East and West North Central); South (East and West South Central and South Atlantic); West (Mountain and Pacific).
**Large Urban (over 250,000); Small Urban (10,000 to 49,999); Medium Rural (1,000–9,999); Small Rural (Under 1,000).
***Large (200+ families); Medium (100–199 families); Small (Under 100 families).

Thus far we have explored some of the background characteristics of the women pastors, their recruitment processes, and the general context of the parishes they are heading. Now I want to complete the portrait of these women by looking at their personal characteristics as seen by them, by their parishioners, and by their sacramental ministers.

PERSONAL CHARACTERISTICS

One of the descriptive words used often by parishioners when they are referring to their woman pastor is "approachable." A female parishioner who had four years of experience with her pastor said,

> She is just so easy to work with and approach when you have something you don't like or want to talk to her about. She is so receptive and much easier to talk to.... I had never done that before with a priest. That's my point of view and I am sure that is shared by others.

A male parishioner in the same parish said,

> She is available every day and we can always call her. She is so close. The priest, either he was gone on business, or [at] a meeting.

The previous resident priests, in many cases, had been ill and therefore less approachable. As one of the women pastors explained,

> The last two [resident priests] were very old and very ill, and they were really not pastors. In fact, the last one was so ill that when he said Mass the last three years he was here, two men had to support him at the altar, stand on either side of him and hold him up. And he never gave a homily.

A female parishioner said she felt that her pastor's administrative skills and knowledge were less important in the adjustment to her new role than the fact that she was compassionate and patient when she interacted with parishioners. She argued that these personal qualities made the woman pastor more approachable, and thus more effective.

One of the sacramental ministers used the term "click" when he described the approachability of a woman pastor who had previously served in the parish as a pastoral associate.

They knew her before; that helped. But the key has been her personality. I believe that just as individuals click or don't click that the same thing happens for parishes and priests or administrators. Either they click or they don't, and I think with [the woman pastor] it clicked. She was secure enough as an individual not to take the nonacceptance as personal. She was secure enough; she was patient enough. She fits with the community because the community is very, very down-to-earth and she is down-to-earth. So it has worked for a whole bunch of reasons.

The woman parishioners were especially effusive about the approachability of their women pastors. Having a pastor who could understand from experience what it meant to be a mother, daughter, or sister was a new experience for them. One woman stopped me after Mass on Sunday, and with tears in her eyes told me that her pastor had helped her through some very difficult times, and had been like a sister to her. I observed the approachability of the woman pastor "in action" on several occasions during my parish visits when I saw the parishioners enthusiastically approach her before and after Mass at the entrance of the church, at wedding receptions, at local community gatherings, at restaurants while we were eating dinner, and on the streets of her town or village as she gave me a guided tour. On the other hand, one or two of the women pastors were not as approachable as the others, and parishioners were not afraid to voice their concern about it. One of the female parishioners said, "I would like to see (her pastor) handle people a little smoother. I feel bad for her because she does make enemies because of her abruptness."

In another parish one of the male parishioners said he felt that his woman pastor could still learn to be "a little more tactful in getting people to do what they ought to do." He said that when she first took over she had to go through the process of learning that "you don't treat volunteers the same way you do military people." He said she had to learn that these people "were willing to give their time, but they weren't willing to be pushed around." He quoted another male parishioner's reaction to her tactics who said, "The next time that bossy bitch tells me I have to do something, I am going to tell her to take a flying leap and take my kids to another church."

Learning to combine approachability with a measure of toughness did not come easy for some of these women. One of them described her confrontation with a male parishioner at a parish council meeting during her first year on the job.

> I said, "Let's stop right here. First of all, you do not speak to me in this tone of voice. I will not take that ever again." Well, he got up and said, "I'm going to get out of here and I'm leaving this parish, and I'm taking a whole bunch of families with me." And he stormed out. And I said, "God knows what I've done now."

Even though his family may have stayed away for a short time, they soon returned to the parish and became active again. The fact that she took a stand with him went down well with the parishioners, as a male parishioner attested:

> She handled it very well. I can remember times at a council meeting when she had to be very tactful in dealing with some of the people who had been on the council for years. In my opinion, she handled it very well. She was really patient. She was firm, and can be very firm, but I think just being intelligent and patient and understanding of what the situation was.

One of the women pastors reflected on the need to deemphasize the virtue of humility, especially in the beginning:

> If I could do it over I would exude more self-confidence, take a stronger role in the beginning, not be afraid of being called pastor. I think I had a hang-up about that, that that was prestigious, and I shouldn't be going around making myself important or something.

Another personality dimension often mentioned was introvert and extrovert. Because the "good pastor" is depicted as one who is outgoing, the introverts tend to have a more difficult time adjusting to the role. One of the sacramental ministers explained why the woman pastor was reluctant to visit the homes of parishioners.

> We've had a number of conversations about Myers-Briggs.[7] We've talked about that, and on the Myers-Briggs she certainly is an introvert. She shared with me that she's not overly comfortable in that kind of setting, going into the home and sitting

down and having a cup of coffee, and some people are. But she finds that very difficult. So I'm not sure if it's exactly because she's an introvert. It may be more her formal style, too, that you don't go to someone's house unless you're invited, and then it's okay to stop by.

One of the women who was having trouble adjusting to her role as pastor said,

Myers-Briggs checks me out as an introvert. I don't like talking in front of people. I'm not comfortable with it. If you are not comfortable, you don't do a good job. I am getting better. Obviously I can't get any worse, but it isn't my thing.

One of the women pastors described herself as an introvert with "a tendency to internalize a lot of the feelings that come from negative presence and vibrations." As I watched her preside at a word and communion service one Sunday, and observed how well she communicated with the congregation, it was difficult to view her as an introvert.

Another woman pastor who had been an aspiring actress earlier in her life, told me that she still teams up with a friend to put on a comedy routine for parties and special occasions that "has people falling over with laughter." Although I was unable to observe her in action, I was told that she often receives applause from the parishioners after she preaches.

Another example comes from an extroverted woman pastor:

I feel that through these other experiences I got to know how to approach people, how to be available to people, how to be more aware of needs. And especially I think this is very much a part of my temperament, but I like working with all this. I hate doing things by myself. In my religious life, it was kind of a difficult situation, because in the old times you were supposed to fulfill everything [yourself], and I always like to do things with other people, teamwork.

This view of some of the personal characteristics of the women pastors completes the portrait of the women and their parishes. We turn in the next chapter to a discussion of a quality unique to these women, the "pastoral heart."

•3•

The Pastoral Heart

The word "pastoral" comes from the Latin *pastoralis,* meaning "of or relating to herdsman or shepherd," and in a religious context the word "pastor" has come to mean a "spiritual overseer; especially a clergyman serving a local church or parish."[1] In the Christian tradition the gospel account of the good shepherd portrays the ideal characteristics for a pastor, whose "flock" consists of his parishioners. The pertinent scriptural passages from the Gospel of John (10:2–3, 14) are the following:

> The one who enters through the gate is the shepherd of the flock; the gatekeeper lets him in, the sheep hear his voice, one by one he calls his own sheep and leads them out.... I am the good shepherd; I know my own and my own know me...[2]

One of the key ingredients for a good shepherd is his intimate knowledge of his flock which enables him to call each of his sheep by name. As a result of this familiarity, the sheep recognize his voice and follow him. In this scriptural passage we are not told how the shepherd becomes familiar with his flock, but we can imagine that he had to spend a considerable amount of time and effort in distinguishing one from another.

Note how the masculine gender predominates in this English translation of the scriptural passage. Just as the word "shepherd" calls forth the image of a man with his sheep, so does the term "pastor" conjure up the image of a man with his parishioners. Interestingly enough, there is a feminine term, "shepherdess," that is well known, but the word "pastoress" is not commonly used. No wonder, then, that people have difficulty picturing a woman in charge of a parish!

The title for this chapter came from an incident in one of the parishes I visited, that captured a quality of these women pastors. This characteristic was something that the parishioners mentioned again and again. When they described how she interacted with them, parishioners usually began by stating that first of all, she knew their names, and they deeply appreciated her calling them by name.

Secondly, the parishioners mentioned the fact that she went out of her way to visit them in their homes and to spend time in their family settings. Thirdly, they treasured her visits to sick and dying parishioners both at home and in the hospital. Finally, the parishioners cherished their warm relationships with her.

All of the information from these parishioners' testimonies could be embodied in the term "pastoral heart," a term that I first heard in an interview with a woman pastor who was quoting a bishop when he was presiding at a meeting with the pastors of his diocese. The bishop had just returned from a confirmation ceremony held the previous day in her parish where he had accompanied her on a visit to a little girl who was dying of cancer. He had been deeply touched by this experience, and it was evident in his talk to the pastors. The following is the woman pastor's account of the meeting.

> The next day we were at a deanery[3] meeting and he started making his remarks and [said], "Yesterday I had the opportunity to visit a family and a little girl," and he described what the disease was doing to them. And he said, "But I could tell, as I was there, the interaction between Sister and the family, how much love and care there is between them and how much a support they are to each other. And that's what I mean when I talk about having a pastoral heart."

She continued,

> He used that as an example. I wasn't expecting him to say it. I didn't even know he was observing me. That kind of thing I don't think he sees that much among his priests. So I think it's a different dimension that women, in general, bring to it.

The "different dimension" was also attested to by one of her parishioners, who said,

Any family you talk to, in their bad moments you can feel the good that they feel when she walks in. We just had a little girl who died a month or so ago and she did everything she possibly could with that family. She even stayed with the children. She really went out of her way.

Seldom did any of the women pastors discuss their strategies for living out the ideals of the pastoral heart. But this dimension was a constant in every parish I visited. I saw it lived out as I followed them around during the weekend. I read about it in some of the parish evaluation sheets I perused. It fairly shouted at me when I read the weekly church bulletins composed by them, and I heard parishioners and priests alike attest to it. There was one woman who spoke of it as a strategy for women newly appointed as pastoral administrators. The following is her advice to women who are considering an acceptance of an appointment to a priestless parish:

Talk to people in the beginning. Live with them for a weekend. Just move around with them for awhile. And when you get to the place, the first thing is to be friendly with the people. Do that before you make any other moves. That's so important because you have to gain their trust. If you don't have their trust, you can turn the world upside down and they aren't going to like you. You have to win their hearts.

Why the need for such strategy? It could be their gender and/or their lay status that causes women pastors to look for ways to win the parishioners' hearts. It could also be that any new pastor would be inclined to utilize this strategy. Both are partial answers.

As we saw in the last chapter, most of the women pastors had previously performed the nurturant role of teacher. However, even the laywomen who had functioned in and competed successfully in a "man's world"—the military, business, etc.—and of necessity had taken on more "male" characteristics *also* perceived the need for the "pastoral heart," and strove to realize it.

Perhaps the newcomer status of these women combined with their position as laity and as women prompted them to develop the characteristics of the pastoral heart. What must be kept in mind is that all of the previous pastors in their parishes were clergy, so these women were not the kind of replacement that Catholic parishioners would expect or, indeed, want. Time and again I heard references to a "grieving process" that many parishioners experienced, and I saw references to it in articles on pastoral ministry. Evidently, losing the parish priest is like a death in the family for some parishioners, so the newly arrived woman pastor finds that she must work harder than any previous pastor to win the hearts of her parishioners.

These women initially had two strikes against them: their gender and the fact that they were replacing a priest in a nontraditional context. But the reason so many of them scored instead of striking out was that they went out of their way to learn the names of their parishioners and called them by name, they visited their homes and got to know the family situation, and they did all of this in a warm and caring way. In short, their words and actions embodied the pastoral heart. In the remainder of this chapter I will elaborate on these three characteristics of the pastoral heart: naming, visiting, and personal warmth.

NAMING PEOPLE

The ability to call people by name is an important one. Naming confers or at least implies validation of the person. To name someone suggests familiarity, but it also underlines the worth of the individual. In the context of this study, when the pastor calls her parishioners by name, it means not only that she is including them as esteemed members of the parish, but she is also acknowledging their gifts to the community.

When I visited these parishes, I made it a point to arrive early for the Sunday Masses, and to stand outside the church afterwards to observe the interaction between the woman pastor and her parishioners. Typically she would be standing outside both before and after the service, greeting each parishioner by name, and asking about other members of the family. Later on during Mass, when she helped to distribute communion, she also called each communicant by name.

In some parishes she would announce the names of those

with birthdays or anniversaries during the coming week, and the parishioners would sing to them. In one instance, each child was invited to come forward to receive a small birthday gift. One young teenager beamed when he was congratulated by the pastor during her announcements at the end of Sunday Mass for having been elected the president of his class.

One of the female parishioners described how her pastor made a public announcement every Sunday of the names of parish helpers:

> One of the things that [she] does is announce right before the Mass begins who they (the congregation) are going to be seeing visually—the eucharistic ministers, the altar boys, the choir, the celebrant, the lectors, the people bringing up the gifts—by name. It is important that everybody knows everybody in our parish, maybe not by name, but as a member of (our parish), and a conversation starts. And they realize how much they have in common once they start talking.

One could argue that the parish bulletin typically includes the names of the persons who are performing these tasks, so this oral announcement really is not necessary. And that is indeed true—for those few parishioners who already know everyone in the parish. But for the majority who do not, the added effort to point the person out by name can serve as a weekly "getting to know you" exercise.

Even more important, the oral announcement can also function as as an occasion when family members can point with pride to their relatives who are serving on the altar on that particular Sunday. I observed some of this family reaction when I saw parishioners smile and nudge one another at the announcement of a family member's name. They not only appreciated the public recognition, but it was a confirmation that they, the parishioners, were important to the working of the parish.

The oral announcement is also consistent with the conviction voiced again and again by the women pastors—that each person's gift should be acknowledged. One of them described a strategy she used to accomplish this:

> We are having an Appreciation Day, and I want to name every single person. So there would be parish council, all of the

commissions, the administration committee, the cemetery committee, the people that clean the church, the person that sends the bulletin to the shut-ins, the person who calls the family mid-week to remind them that they are bringing up the Offertory gifts. There are the eucharistic ministers, the lectors, the youth ministers, the religious education teachers. It goes on and on.

How does she learn all of their names? In one parish of five hundred the pastor showed me the calendar hanging in her kitchen where she had inserted the names of each parishioner's birthday, and said she tries to remember to wish them a happy birthday. Another had a picture of each parishioner with their names inserted on their birthdays on a large calendar on her desk.

The parishioners responded with gratitude to these efforts. A male parishioner said,

> I think she knows just about everybody and their kids on a first-name basis. She is always going out of her way to meet you. She worked hard to get to know everybody. Every Mass she stood outside, no matter how cold or hot it was, trying to get to know everybody on a first-name basis, so her efforts were apparent.

Another male parishioner described his pastor this way:

> She gets involved with everybody. She knows everybody's name. She knows who you are, where you live, what you do for a living, what your needs are, and so on. She is very, very much a part of the community.

Another parishioner said that he thought the people in his parish gave her more support than the previous pastor "because I think Father _____ had a tendency to forget names. He kind of drove some people away because he didn't remember names."

One of the women pastors said it took her awhile to figure out why it was that everybody was zipping in the back door each weekend, without even looking at her. She explained,

> I think I figured out Father _____ did not take time to learn people's names. He didn't know their names. I think people don't feel important enough to be spoken to. You know how when you don't know somebody's name, and you are too embarrassed to ask. So they zipped past.

Not all priest-pastors have a tendency to forget names, of course, but it is impossible for most priests who are serving as many as three parishes to learn the names of all the parishioners. In several of the parishes I visited the priests had to leave immediately after Mass in order to reach the next parish in time. One priest, in fact, went right into the sacristy after Mass, took off his vestments, and jumped into his car without a word. So they tend to adopt an attitude like the sacramental minister who gave me the following rationale for avoiding a "divided heart" situation:

I don't know these people's names. I know their faces and something about them, and there are a few over four years I've begun to recognize. But I have never given my heart to this community, on purpose. My heart belongs over there [in his parish]. I worked that out. I have gotten criticized by parishioners here because I end every Mass in [my parish] by saying, "I love you, have a good day." And I do that on purpose. I don't say that here. That's not my role here. That is Sister's position—to be the heart of the community.

To this priest, knowing the names of the people, calling them by name, and showing affection for them were necessary actions if the pastor was to take his or her position as the heart of the community. One of the priests I interviewed testified to the success of a woman pastor in this regard, and described a recent reaction of the local bishop to a woman pastor's winning way in the community.

I think [she] has won over the hearts of the people up there [at her parish]. I think they have a genuine affection for her. She has many important gifts. She can call almost everyone by their first name. At confirmation last Saturday she had thirty kids and she just called them all by name, one by one, and asked them to stand as she called their names to introduce them to the bishop. That's very impressive. The bishop was impressed. He leaned over to me and said, "She's not using a list." And I said, "She isn't, Bishop." And he said, "Not very often can the pastor do that."

Not every woman pastor was as effective with regard to naming, however. One parishioner whom I interviewed expressed her concern about this. She wanted her pastor to be more outgoing and caring, and to call the parishioners by name more often. In fact, she pinpointed the pastor's failure to be able to name her parishioners as a key problem in the parish at the present time.

Naming their parishioners will undoubtedly become more and more difficult for priest-pastors who, because of the clergy shortage, are increasingly being assigned to serve more than one parish. It is not only sheer numbers that stand in their way, but also the hours spent in travel leave less time for parishioners on a day-to-day basis. Eighteen of the twenty parishes had sacramental ministers (priests) who traveled to one, two, or even three other parishes to celebrate Mass on a weekend. In the remaining two cases, the sacramental ministers were elderly priests who had come out of retirement to help the woman pastor. They were physically unable to serve more than one parish.

By contrast, only five of the women pastors were administering more than one parish or mission, and three more were helping out part-time in another parish in only one program, for example in the liturgy or religious education programs. Like the circuit-riding priests, these women found that they had less time to learn names, and fewer opportunities to address parishioners by name. The divided commitment also cut into the time they would have preferred to spend in visiting parishioners' homes.

VISITING PARISHIONERS

In a certain sense, visiting parishioners at home or in the hospital can be seen as a way to achieve a deeper understanding of them, beyond the naming stage. These visits might also function as a way to write the names of the parishioners indelibly on one's memory. The sharing of parishioners' experiences in their own living environments could also serve to bring the parishioners' joys and sorrows into the weekly sermons. As one woman pastor said, in explaining why she spent time with parish teenagers, "I need to be in touch with what's going on and I need to hear their stories."

Other than pastors, what other professionals are expected to make home visits in today's society? For many Americans a home visit by the family doctor is a thing of the past. Even patients being treated in hospitals complain about not seeing their own doctors very often. Welfare workers could be listed, but their visits are limited to only one segment of society. In addition, the brief, formally bureaucratic, and therefore alienating visits of the welfare worker are a far cry from the visits expected of pastors.

Women pastors interviewed cited the visiting of parishioners as a top priority, and parishioner appreciation of this effort was a recurring theme. The following statements illustrate this:

> From talking to her and observing, I think she spends quite a bit of time one-on-one with people, visiting. She likes to do that, plus from what I have heard, people that are in need and need someone to talk to or need counseling like to talk to [her].

Many of the pastors visited every single home in the parish during the first year of their appointment. In one such parish a parishioner said,

> When they see her come up to their house, they enjoy seeing her coming, especially the older people. And the young kids— my daughter really likes to see her come to the house. We always invite her when we celebrate birthdays or anniversaries. And then the whole family gets to meet her.
>
> She works with the poor people and the sick people of the parish. She is always there. Anytime of the day you call her, if somebody is sick in the parish, like [when] I had surgery, she came to stay with the family. She does things that people don't expect, but she does them out of the goodness of her heart.
>
> Just to give you an example, my mother was in ICU just before she died. She thought the world of [the woman pastor]. [She] was just going through [town] during the week and decided to stop, and when Mama opened her eyes and recognized her, Mama said, "I hadn't realized it was Sunday." She would associate [the woman pastor] with communion. Mama was almost out of it but she still recognized her.

Many parishioners compared her visits with that of former pastors, as in the following:

> I think [she] is more available to the people. The priests we have had, they were there, but the attitude was the people come to them. They had office hours and would schedule them.

In the beginning she had big shoes to fill. We had had a parish priest who was here four or five years and he was like a member of all of our families, and when he left it was hard. She has become that same type of person who is irreplaceable in our hearts.

Priests likewise attested to the priority placed by these women on visiting parishioners. One of the priests described a woman pastor's reaction when she received the news that a twenty-year-old parishioner, working in another part of the country, had committed suicide.

As soon as she found out she called me and said, "I think they need a priest out there. Would you like to go along?" I said, "Pick me up and I'll be ready." We went out there and we didn't really do much except sit there and be with the people. They were just in shock. So we sat there for about an hour and a half and [the woman pastor] made coffee and we hugged and kissed everybody and sat around. Afterwards I found out that [she] had gone out there every day after that to be with the family. It was a whole week before they got the body here. We got the news on a Thursday night and the wake was the next Thursday. So she was very supportive. And they know that.

In a similar vein, another priest said,

She visits the sick very well. I am amazed of her knowledge of everybody, all the families, who is sick. She is just wonderful with being on top of what is going on in the people's lives here, and she seems to visit a whole lot.

Another priest, by contrast, was concerned that the woman pastor, who was experiencing a number of stresses in her life, was finding it difficult to make home visits. He said,

But pastorally, probably [she] struggles with being comfortable in the home situation. Now this could be a cultural thing with coming from [the city] or it could just be a personality thing. Some people are very comfortable walking into somebody's kitchen and sitting down and having a cup of coffee. And a lot of church happens in that context. There aren't many farmers left in the parish who are running active farms, but the farm mentality and rural mentality is here. People choose to live iso-lated, and I think their world is their home, more than people who live in a city where the neighborhood might be more significant and people may be more outgoing in city living. So a lot of church, I believe, happens here over a cup of coffee. So that aspect is lacking a bit.

One of the circuit-riding sacramental ministers expressed his own frustrations about "skimming through" people's lives.

As far as my own feelings about that go, I think it is more [a matter of] dealing with my own frustration at not being able to do some of the things that I really enjoy about the priesthood. The biggest problem that we face that colors everything we do is the amount of driving. It's an hour and forty-five minutes from one end of the parish to another. Yesterday and today I was out visiting people and did sixty miles round-trip. So I figure we spend an average [of] seven to ten forty-hour workweeks just driving. So that limits what you do. And when I do have free time I am so glad to have a night off I don't want to see anybody. So what I end up doing is skim through people's lives. It takes three times as long to get to know your parishioners when you have them in two or three communities.

Another priest who was, in general, very impressed and highly supportive of the woman pastor, felt that the parish was, in a certain sense, being shortchanged because, although she was living in the parish just a few blocks from the church, she chose not to live in the rectory. He stressed the importance of availability as well as visiting, and he described her predecessor this way:

He was quite popular, had been there [in the parish] for a long time, lived there, interacted with the people...was involved with families in a hundred different kinds of ways. Really involved in people's lives. He lived alone, had no community life to sustain him, and [was] available twenty-four hours.

The description above would fit only two of the immediate predecessors of the women interviewed. As one of the women pastors put it, "Most priests want the people to come to them. We go out to the people." This same woman described an exchange with her predecessor—a retired priest from another diocese—that occurred while she was serving in her present parish as a parish associate in charge of religious education.

I think it was a little too much for him to be here. He was very lonely, he didn't want to go around and visit families. I would tell him, "Father, go and visit people." And he would say, "No, because they don't invite me." I told him, "Father, people don't work this way. You go out to them and then they will start inviting you." But it didn't work out. He started getting very defensive because I was many times telling him, "Father, I don't think this is the right way to do it."

To understand these older priests, their seminary experiences before Vatican II must be appreciated. The other-worldly spirituality that prevailed in that era dictated a cautious attitude regarding the visiting of parishioners. They were warned about "playing favorites," and about adopting surrogate families, thus causing divisiveness in the parish. In particular they were warned not to visit only those parishioners who invited them to come for a meal, for that would exclude those who couldn't afford a meal that would be "fitting" for a priest.

One of the women who had been pastoring for four years was commenting on an article analyzing the impact of Vatican II on priests, where the author stressed the idea of a priest visiting every home in the parish at least once a year. She said,

In the hearts of the people, that's what they really want. My hunch is that most people don't care about what goes on at parish council, don't care about what goes on in finance council, but their stories are, "I remember when Father So-and-So came over and did such and such," or "He was at the hospital," or "He came to our reception."

Many of the women pastors began the home visits almost immediately upon their arrival at the parish, because it helped them to learn the parishioners' names. One of them who also used her camera as a strategy described her visits thus:

The thing that helped was that I went around and visited every household. I also took pictures when I went. I had a little routine when I went to the house. I said, "I brought my camera. I want to take your picture because on my desk I have a little flip photograph album, and every day I turn the page and that's the household, and those are the people I remember at Mass." So those kinds of little things were impressive to the people. I always gave them a copy of the photograph.

Several of them described incidents when parishioners called on them, rather than the priest [sacramental minister], in time of need:

About three months ago, it was late, about 10:30, and I was on the phone. The operator interrupted the call and asked if I could please hang up, that there was an emergency. So I did, and immediately one of our parishioners called and said, "Could you come out right away? Grandma is very, very sick. We don't know what is going to happen." And I said, "Yes, I'll be glad to. Do you want me to call Father?" "Oh yeah, maybe you could." They called me first. It wasn't even on their mind to call Father.

Another woman pastor also attested to being called instead of the priest:

As far as death, there is so much to being with a person or with the family when someone dies that the priest is not there for anyway. I am there at that time. Father comes in and puts a little oil on them, but he usually does that six months or more before they die. I am the one who brings them eucharist every week. I am the one who is with them or helps the family. I was the one that when [a young parishioner] died, they called me. She died real early in the morning. She was getting worse and had a little coughing spell. They had nurses around the clock in the home because they wanted to keep her in the home to make her as comfortable as they could. She was unconscious most of those last few days. I would stop in and I would talk to her when I would be there because I still felt like she could hear. They didn't call the priest to tell him. They called me.

This same woman explained why she felt that women pastors' attitudes about visiting parishioners were different from those of their predecessors when she said, "I think there is more of a going out to people, a caring for people."

Not everyone finds it easy to visit people in the hospital, especially when they are at the point of death.[4] During one parish visit, shortly after Sunday Mass, the woman pastor received a call from the daughter of a parishioner who was in the hospital with cancer. The family thought the ninety-four-year-old woman was near death, so the pastor decided to go. I accompanied her and the priest to the hospital. The priest recited the opening prayers, and then the woman pastor spoke to and blessed the dying woman, who showed signs of recognizing her. About halfway through the administration of the sacrament, the woman pastor left the room because, as she explained afterward, she was feeling ill. Nonetheless, she returned shortly thereafter. In the car on the way home, she told me that she finds it very difficult to be present at a death, and this is not one of her favorite duties. Who, after all, looks forward to such an occasion?

The final example regarding the practice of reaching out to parishioners comes from a woman pastor's reaction when she heard that some of the parishioners were disturbed because they heard that the parish council was considering a replacement for the old altar in the church. Although this was a seemingly insignificant issue, she went to the home of an elderly parishioner to speak to her personally because she sensed that the woman needed reassurance. In her words,

> When I heard that there was this one lady who was really kind of upset about it, I went to her house and I said I heard she was upset. And she said she was wondering why, so I told her why. I said, "Well, first of all, the other one is cracked and in need of repair. And, secondly, the tabernacle should not be on the altar; it should be separate." She said, "Well, that's good then. If that's the way it's supposed to be, I guess that's the way we ought to do it." It was kind of the sentimental value of the old one, but once you gave her a reasonable explanation, it was fine.

Although the reason for this visit was not the physical suffering of a parishioner, and thus could perhaps have been dismissed as not critical, nonetheless the woman pastor responded, and the visit had a healing effect. The visit itself was not sufficient for the healing; it was the way the pastor interacted with her once she arrived. In addition to naming people and visiting parishioners, the pastoral heart requires a third ingredient—personal warmth.

PERSONAL WARMTH

When parishioners described their pastors, invariably the word "warm" emerged in the conversation. I observed many examples of their personal warmth in the pastors' responses to parishioners in a variety of settings. On the two occasions when I accompanied them to visit dying parishioners, I was struck by the pastor's sensitivity to pain, and the loving way she conducted the ritual. The way they greeted people who rang the doorbell at the parish house, their readiness to embrace parishioners at social gatherings, and sometimes just the eagerness with which parishioners approached them—all were outward signs of the personal warmth of these women. Even inside the church itself they would often give members of the congregation warm hugs as they extended the kiss of peace prior to the distribution of Communion during a service. Their caring is evidenced in some of the following statements by parishioners:

> When [she] came, she actually knit the parish closer together. It did happen. People got to know her, respect her and love her. Now, if she leaves, I don't know what's going to happen. The older people got to love her so much. When she is not down there Saturday night at Mass, there is something missing.
>
> [She] is there for every Mass. She is the first one there and is always at the door saying, "Hi," hugging, greeting people.

In eighteen of the twenty parishes parishioners expressed their appreciation for the warm and outgoing manner of their pastors. They feel "very close" to her. Many said, "She's one of us."

Priests also testified to the personal warmth of these women. One of them said, "She is hugged and kissed before and after Mass by everybody every week." Another priest, reflecting on this aspect of her ministry, said,

> I think people are touched by her. And, in a way, I would guess, too, they would not be and probably could not be by a man, by a priest. What I sense is that she is able to plug in, to express or open up or invite a different part of people than what probably most priests would touch. I don't know if this will sound contrived, but to me it is the feminine level of life. She even talks different. The words she uses are different than the words I use. She is able to feel more what especially the women of the parish—what's happening to them and within them and their life, and the experiences they are having. I think she is able to identify better with that. And also with men, in some ways.

Another priest who was comparing the woman pastor with her immediate predecessor said that she had "much more warmth in her dealings with people. And I just think she has a better concept of being a pastor."

One evening at a parish "ice cream social" held in the church basement immediately after the Saturday evening Mass, there was a good example of the different stances of priest and woman pastor. The woman pastor joined right in with the parishioners, kidding them, and accepting their joking in a very friendly way. In contrast, the priest kept himself aloof. His clothing and bearing did not invite informal interaction from the parishioners. In fact, his behavior on that occasion contradicted what he had told me earlier regarding his eagerness to be with the parishioners, and how much he enjoyed the interaction with them. He was not very outgoing in this instance, and had he chosen to wear a sportshirt rather than a Roman collar, he might have mingled more easily. In contrast, the woman pastor's clothing, a summery dress with a white jacket, blended with the parishioners' dress.

During Mass on weekends when the sacramental minister was presiding and the woman pastor was present, I often wrote in my field notes how much warmer and more outgoing was she than he. Parishioners, too, made those comparisons. A male parishioner said,

> I think, rightly or wrongly, that [she] should be our priest. That's how I feel about it. I have no other feeling. My mother died last January, and [she] was a great comfort to us. I love Father _____; don't misunderstand me. But we are here, this is our locale, she is the person here; she should be taking care of us.

A female parishioner put it this way,

> I feel very comfortable with [her] as a woman being administrator and counselor and everything else, the whole ball of wax that she is. I feel a woman has more empathy and understanding of a lot of things that are happening in home life and parish life that a man can't understand and be sympathetic to. I think it's made a difference and would make a big difference in the whole country.

In fairness to the priests who are serving as sacramental ministers, it is important to remember that they are not the resident priest in the parishes I visited. Instead they are "visitors" in these situations, and resident pastors only in their own parishes, so their own parishioners are their first priority. Thus part of the explanation for the failure of some of the priests to be as outgoing as the women I visited was due to their extensive travel schedules. The role of circuit riding sacramental minister depleted the energy needed by these priests to extend themselves to parishioners.

Because parishioners value personal warmth in their woman pastor, they tend to be disappointed when they fail to see it displayed by them. One parishioner complained about the lack of warmth in her pastor. She was especially disappointed because her pastor did not make it a point to greet people individually before Mass.

> She greets them as a whole [in the church], like "Good evening." But she will be running back and forth to and from the sacristy, and passes people and doesn't acknowledge their presence. Again, I don't think it's deliberate. Maybe she thinks they won't respond back, I don't know. But that means a lot to those people.

On the other hand, women pastors were concerned about the response of the parishioners to their displays of warmth, especially during the first year of their appointment, when their acceptance is in question. One woman, who was appointed head of an Hispanic parish explained,

> In the Spanish tradition, especially with the male, you would know if you were accepted if you received the *abrazo,* which was a chestlike hug. I guess in American slang we call it a big bear hug. And you were pummeled on your back. When you got that, you knew you were in, because there was an intimacy to that. It was an acceptance. It was very public so it was sending a message to the community. I waited about eight months until I got that from the head usher. When I got that I floated on air. I knew I had arrived.

One of the pastors I visited was especially good at combining a personal warmth with a strong sense of justice. She had a wonderful open and loving way with her parishioners. For instance, she was a great "hugger," and also loved to tease and joke with her parishioners. But she was also a realistic and confronting pastor. For instance, she continued to counsel the young people in her parish who dropped out of school, repeating over and over again, "You can *do* it." She expressed the deep sadness she felt when "her kids" got pregnant or took drugs because she is so convinced that they can and must break out of the cycle of poverty. She took every opportunity to affirm the individual personhood of her parishioners.

Up to this point we have examined the characteristics of the pastoral heart from the vantage points of parishioner, priest, and woman pastor. In the final section of this chapter we look at some of the effects of this phenomenon for parishes.

CONSEQUENCES FOR THE PARISH

During the Mass or communion service, there is one moment called the "kiss of peace," when the consequence of the pastor's naming, visiting, and personal warmth was acted out in the ritual. At this point in the service, after the "Our Father" is recited, and just before the distribution of Communion, the person who presides says, "Let us offer each other the sign of peace." Parishioners then usually shake hands with those on either side of them, and the priest may come down from the altar and shake hands with a few parishioners. This whole "event" usually takes just a few minutes in most parishes.

In parishes with women pastors, however, this "moment" stretches out in many directions. First, there was hugging and kissing as well as shaking hands by both parishioners and presiders. Secondly, the woman invariably came down from the sanctuary and literally made the rounds of the entire congregation. If the sacramental minister was presiding, both he and the pastor might come down from the altar, and each would cover half the congregation, shaking hands or hugging each person on his or her side of the church. Thirdly, parishioners did not limit their greetings to those people standing on either side of them. Often, everyone around them, and even those located in other parts of the church, would receive their handshake, hug, and/or kiss.

Several of the women pastors would ask visitors from outside the parish to identify themselves before Mass began, or just before they announced the kiss of peace, so that parishioners could greet the visitors by name. Needless to say, the enactment of this joyous moment often took a good deal of time.

In one parish, for example, the choir and the congregation repeated many verses of the song "Reach Out and Touch Somebody's Hand," during the kiss of peace, because most of the parishioners moved out of their pews to greet people in other parts of the church, and the priest and pastor each greeted every single person, about eighty in all. At the very end of Mass the woman pastor thanked me publicly for visiting the parish, and invited me to come to the center of the church so that the members of the congregation could give me their blessing. All joined in singing their version of "Aaron's Blessing," with their right hands extended toward me. They were allowing me to share their spirit of community for a short time.[5]

One priest testified to the "great spirit of family" that had been built up in the parish in the two years since the arrival of the lay pastor:

> There are certain things that...you notice is giving you clues as to the spirit of the parish. One is how long and how many people hang around after Mass on Sunday at the door. If they all disappear right away, there is not much of a sense of community in the parish. Here I have noticed more and more people who are standing outside and talking.

How is the parish affected by a parish leader who lives out the characteristics of a pastoral heart? Probably the most important consequence of the willingness of the pastor to name people, to visit parishioners, and to interact in a warm personal manner is a growing sense of community throughout the parish. It is exemplified in moments like the extended sign of peace ritual, in the smiles of parishioners as they greet each other outside the church, the hours of voluntary service they contribute to the parish, and in the sacrifices they make in another parishioner's hour of need.

•4•

Collaborative Leadership

One of the striking differences between the women pastors and their predecessors is their collaborative leadership style. A collaborative relationship, where all of the persons in the group or organization work together jointly to achieve a common end, is based on equality rather than hierarchy. In a collaborative relationship, one individual works *with,* not *for* another.

Is the label "collaborative leadership," then, a contradiction in terms? It may be a contradiction if leadership means a relationship in which one person has the commanding authority or influence, and others are expected to obey her or his commands. In a parish situation this would mean that parishioners are basically passive rather than active participants, and the principal actor, or "leader," is the pastor.

On the other hand, if leadership means a relationship where the leader guides rather than commands, and in so doing, draws on the talents of others, then collaborative leadership is possible. This means that parishioners take part in activities that have an impact on the parish and are not confined merely to sitting in the pews on Sunday.[1] This is basically how women pastors define their leadership roles in their parishes, and it generally contrasts with their predecessors' definition. The women see themselves as copastors in the parish, and this is manifested in the way they work together with their parishioners on a daily basis. Evidence for this generalization was found in field notes and interviews.

AVAILABILITY

A key ingredient for collaborative leadership requires that the leader be available to his or her coworkers. In every parish visited, the previous pastor had been a priest, and in fifteen of the twenty parishes these priests were resident pastors (that is, they lived in the rectory or parish house) prior to the woman's appointment. Although the priests had lived in the parish house, and supposedly were available to practice collaborative leadership, this was seldom the actuality. In most cases availability to the parishioners was not possible because the priests had other duties outside the parish: some worked full-time in a diocesan office, others served another parish or two in addition to their own.

By contrast, none of the women pastors had other full-time jobs, yet five of them were in charge of a second church, and five were sharing parenting responsibilities because of children living at home. In general, however, their parishioners who typically had limited access to the previous pastors found that their pastor was more available to them. One parishioner expressed it this way:

> She is more visible than he [the former pastor] was. Again, he had two parishes, plus he was very active in AIDS education, and working with people with AIDS. And I think that was part of the reason he requested some help here because we hardly ever saw him. We would see him on Sunday and Saturday night for the services, and that was pretty much all we'd ever see him. Maybe that's part of the reason this transition went so well, too, because all of a sudden we have someone a lot more accessible than Father [the former pastor] was.

LINKAGES

Another key ingredient for collaborative leadership is that the leader have connections or linkages to the community. Creating and maintaining such linkages requires a certain amount of accessibility to the leader. Half of the women pastors I visited were living in the parish house. Five of the parishes had no parish house, and three of the rectories were too small for a family. In general, the married women remained in their own homes situated in the parish, and the nuns and the single lay-woman lived in the parish house. Exceptions to this were the married couple recruited from outside the parish who lived in the parish house, and three nuns who lived in rental units reasonably close to the church.

One of the women described her role with regard to the linkages with the community as a "hub." When someone asked her how she saw her role in the parish, she told me that she answered in this way:

> I see myself as the hub. I am connected to all these committees and I let everybody know what is going on. I am the one who is keeping everybody connected to each other.

Keeping everyone connected means that she must be accepted by all segments of the parish so that she can bridge them and thus begin to form the linkages between and among her parishioners. One of the male parishioners attested to this:

> In any community, the more people you have—we are still very small—but you have diversity. We have a conservative segment, and a very liberal segment, a charismatic segment, and [the woman pastor] is one of the few individuals in our parish group who is respected by all segments. So she has the ability to pull it all together.

Another parishioner described the segments in social class terms in the following way:

> In a rural area especially, if you spend too much time with—I want to use the word cliques—there are people who tend to find it very important socially to be active in the church, and I believe a lot of time spent with those people can narrow your social focus to that group of people and I think it's more damaging. Sister has tried to not have that occur. So she's focusing on all the social-economic aspects of the parish.

After I had attended a coffee and donut reception following Sunday Mass in the church basement, the married woman pastor who had been a parishioner there before her appointment explained to me that the occupants of each of the tables represented various cliques in the parish. She said that she systematically moved from table to table each week, so as not to be seen as favoring one clique over another.

However, some of the women I visited were more available to their parishioners than others, and thus better able to form linkages. As mentioned above, one-fourth of the women pastors interviewed were administering another parish or mission as well as their own, which lessened their accessibility. There was one case, in fact, where she was administering two mission churches in addition to her own parish.

Because I had made it a practice to follow each of the women pastors as they performed their various duties, I was exhausted after my visit to the last mentioned parish. On that occasion I traveled with her for many miles over winding roads to the three churches, attended three Masses, a baptism where she preached and assisted the priest, a baptismal party following the ceremony, and a parish potluck dinner.

Since women like her are "on the road" so much, their parishioners likewise have less access to her than they would if her sole responsibility was one parish. She is, of course, aware of that, and tries to "make up" for it by visiting the parishioners in their homes, because she values the linkages with them. As she explained it to me, she always accepted any invitations from parishioners to visit their homes if she could do so, because she got to know them better. As she put it, "People are open to visits; in fact they are thrilled to have someone visit their homes."

This outreach orientation, the practice of visiting parishioners' homes, was very prevalent in the parishes I visited. It was not only appreciated, but it was typically a "first" for most parishioners. In fact, many of them testified that her visit marked the first time a leader of the church had ever come to their homes.

Women pastors reciprocally valued their connections with the parishioners. One of them spoke very warmly about her linkages with the parishioners, and particularly about how her parishioners included her in their lives. For example, she said,

> A lot of the young women were having a housewarming across the street and they'll call and say, "We're having a housewarming. Come on over." I can't imagine they would have called a priest. Even the guys wouldn't have said, "Hey,

Father, come hunting with us." So you are included a lot in their life.

Another instrument they use to create linkages with the parishioners is the Sunday bulletin. In contrast to the formal style of most church bulletins, the ones I collected in my visits to these parishes are both more creative and more personal. Not only is the name of each parishioner with weekly liturgical duties listed and help solicited for projects in the future, but parishioners are also thanked by name for their work on previous church activities. The artistic talent of some of these women also makes reading their bulletins a more pleasant experience. Due to lack of secretarial help, about half of the women I interviewed told me that they typed the bulletins themselves.

Another means of communication and linkage to the parishioners was mentioned by a woman pastor:

> I inform them [parish committees] of every single thing that's going on so that they always know they are on the inside, and somehow just knowing what's going on helps them to believe they are making a decision about it, too. And they are. So I think communication is just very important that way.

LAY IDENTITY

Besides their greater accessibility, and the priority they place on making connections with their parishioners, there are other reasons why women tend to evidence collaborative leadership, rather than the hierarchical leadership style of their predecessors. They identify very strongly with the parishioners who, like themselves, are laity. This is in contrast to their predecessors, most of whom perceived themselves as occupying a special status, apart from and well above the laity.

We have to keep in mind that these women were not prepared for the the role of pastor in the same way as were their predecessors. In contrast to their predecessors, they were not exposed to the clerical socialization process where they learned the appropriate behavior expected of priest-pastors. Although over half of the women have master's degrees in theology, they did not earn their degrees in classrooms solely occupied by clergy or clerical aspirants, as did many of their predecessors.

The parishioners whom I interviewed not only recognized but tended to accept this hierarchical type of leadership of the priest when he was their pastor. As one female parishioner whose parish has had a lay pastor for two years explained,

> I didn't always feel like a lay person or a deacon could replace a priest because we always used to put priests up on a pedestal. And they were really special and nobody could fill their shoes. But my thinking has changed over the past few years.

Likewise, a male parishioner whose parish had a woman pastor for three years described how she truly labored together with the parishioners:

> [She] is not afraid to get out and minister, to get out and work at things and not sit back and give orders to somebody else to do the work. [She] is not afraid to pitch in, will go anywhere, anytime, for a meeting, to give a class, anything that needs to be done, to get a program going. [She] will devote her time and energy to it. She makes sure it's done; she doesn't just drop the ball. [She] does a good job of that, and that's something we didn't have before. Priests we have had don't take the initiative. They put themselves on a pedestal and let somebody else do the work. Right now we are getting more total community effort than we ever have because she is so active. We have had priests who would sit in this rectory while classes were going on next door and go for months without showing up.

In another parish, with four years of experience with a woman pastor, a parishioner stated:

> I think they [the parishioners] give her more than they did to the priests because previously, as I mentioned, the priests were more aloof, and there is a one-to-one thing going on here. We have a closer relationship [with the woman pastor], I think.

This does not mean, however, that all priests exercise leadership like the predecessors of the woman pastors in my study. Priests in various parts of the country, considered "good pastors" by their parishioners, tend to emphasize collaboration rather than authoritarianism. However, we should keep in mind that most of the parishes I visited were small isolated rural parishes, not the kind of parish that tends to get the "cream of the crop" for pastors. Some of these parishes, in fact, were viewed as the "last choice" by the priests of the diocese, and so were the first to lose a resident priest when the diocese felt the effects of the clergy shortage.

One of the parishioners, who was describing the problems the parish council had with the previous pastor, put it this way:

> It was just the priest who was here. He was very sick, became very sick mentally. He was here for [a number of] years, and the pressure was always there because we were always a small parish. We always had to respect the priest, and he had the run of the mill and we couldn't say anything. We had no say. We had a council in name only.

A male parishioner in another parish said,

> We had a priest who wanted to do everything and the parish, as a whole, became crippled, I think. And we are just learning that we can walk. The lay people are real good at fundraising and teaching for CCD, but I think we forget that we can minister to each other.

A female parishioner from the same parish said,

> [The lay pastor] is very good at delegating authority and letting people then do [the job]. That was a problem that Father [the previous pastor] had. He would ask for sharing of responsibility but didn't delegate to a point where a person would really feel they were fully sharing it, so they would sort of draw back and then the job wouldn't get done.

On one of my parish visits I observed a ceremony that exemplifies the delegating of authority to parishioners. At the end of Sunday Mass, the priest announced that the woman pastor would give some announcements and commission a eucharistic minister. The pastor then proceeded up the aisle, and went to the lectern. After making a few announcements, she called a parishioner by name to come up to the sanctuary, and explained that this woman, as a representative of the parish, would be taking Communion to parishioners in a convalescent home. The pastor then solemnly commissioned her to do so, and symbolically placed her hand on the woman's head as she made the invocation.

Another point to keep in mind is how these women were recruited to their present position, because it has a bearing on their leadership style. Although all of them were ultimately appointed by the bishop, in only a fourth of the cases was the recruitment initiated by the bishop or another diocesan official. Over half were recruited by the parishioners themselves or by a local priest. Three of the women applied for the job, and in one case it was the woman's religious community who asked the bishop to appoint one of their members. Because of the way they were recruited, many of these women have a strong sense of loyalty to the parishioners, and tend to see themselves as sharing their leadership with them.

The importance of their identity as laity is especially true for the seven women who were active in the parish as parishioners themselves before the appointment, and the three women who had worked in the parish as parish associates for a number of years prior to the appointment. As I mentioned in chapter 2, in these ten parishes the person chosen for the leadership role emerged from the parish itself. Although officially appointed by the bishop, in the last analysis she was chosen as head of the parish by the parishioners themselves, who knew her, trusted her, and recognized her leadership abilities.

Parishioners described some rather dramatic instances when the bishop or his representative came to meet with the parish council to explain why there would no longer be a resident priest assigned to the parish, and to discuss the situation. The alternatives he proposed included the following: closing the parish, advertising nationally for a priest to fill the position, recruiting a priest from a foreign country like India or the Phillipines, finding a male deacon, or recruiting a nonordained lay person. Invariably the parish council members, who recognized the quality of leadership that she had already exercised in the community, told the bishop, "We want _____," and pointed her out.

In one diocese the bishop sent a representative from the chancery office to meet with the parish council and to discuss the possibilities of a pastoral team made up of parishioners with one person as their leader. The council members pointed to one of the women on the council and said, "She will be that person for us, because she's our spokesperson."

One of the women chosen by her parishioners, who is deeply loved and respected by them, explained her perspective on leadership:

> Leadership is listening to parishioner's initiatives. A leader listens and then articulates the needs and direction of the community, and finds ways to name it and to facilitate it. The most valuable thing I think anybody could have who would find themselves in this position [as pastor] would be to maintain their sense of deep respect for all of the people that you work with and not think that you are in a position of authority over them; that's not what being a parish leader is about.

By contrast, another women pastor who likewise emerged from among the parishioners did not find it easy to exercise a collaborative leadership style. She explained that her previous experience as a business administrator for several years "got in her way" at times. As she explained it,

> I was a real tough Sarge; it was my way or no way. And it got done and it was right. But you can't work that way in the church. So I really had to turn around and really learn collaboration. I find it frustrating because I can get things done and get them done in a hurry, and when I give it to a committee, six months later they are still fighting about it. But my whole style of leadership has changed from the business world, very consciously.

The tendency to take over and do it herself when a project was limping along was simply not an option for most of the women I visited. These women were very talented, and could easily have taken over a myriad of additional jobs in the parish, like training teachers and teaching in the religious education programs; running the liturgy program, including directing the choir and playing the organ; running the youth programs, etc. Indeed, the list of their possible contributions, in addition to their pastoral duties, is almost endless. The temptation to take on some of this additional work is more acute during the first year of their pastoral experience, when they were "groping their way," and learning how to keep a parish running. But the reality is that, short of acquiring the miraculous power of bilocation, they simply don't have the time to take on these extra tasks. In fact, only about half of them consistently take a day off, which is provided in their contracts.

After at least one year's experience in the position, however, the women pastors learned not to give in to the temptation to take over, because of the long-run implications, certainly including a possible burnout for them. How did they accomplish this?

STRATEGIES: LETTING GO AND INCLUSION

Their chief strategy could be described as "letting go," or "forgetting." This simply means that they consciously "forgot" that they had talents like playing the organ, leading the choir, running youth programs, etc. Indeed, some said they had to keep reminding themselves that these talents were forgotten! But, as one put it, "It takes time and it takes letting go, and it takes letting people fumble around."

One of the rewards of letting go that was mentioned by many was "watching people grow." Here is an example:

> Sometimes I have a hard time letting go of things and I have to be real careful of that. I had done the liturgy and process for an Evening of Prayer for three years. I enjoy doing that. This last spring [one of the parishioners] asked me if she could do it, and I had an awful time letting go of that, but I said, "Yes." And I watched her put together something that was better than I would have done because she took more time at it, and it was a new experience for her and she wasn't relying on things that had worked in the past. She put together something that was better than I would have done. And I sat back and said, "Okay."

What they found was that parishioners were more willing to be active participants, and even to "fumble around" when the agenda was theirs, not the pastor's. One of the parishioners described a "listening session" conducted by the lay pastor soon after her arrival, where the parishioners were asked what they wanted to see done and how they wanted their parish to grow. One of the results of the listening session was the formation of a liturgy commission headed by and composed of parishioners, who then continued the listening process in this way:

> One of the first things we did as a commission was put a survey out to the people and try to get a feel of specifically what things in the liturgy they wanted to see changed, or how they feel about this or what made them feel good, or what they didn't like. So that's what our goal is, to try to make the Sunday Mass and special liturgies more meaningful.

We can expect a more collaborative style of leadership in parishes where the leadership of the women emerged from the parish itself because she is not an unknown entity, a stranger who was thrust upon them by the bishop. She has already earned the trust and esteem of the parishioners; in a real sense she was their candidate. In none of the parishes had the previous [priest] pastor ever been a member of the parish prior to his appointment. One of the predecessors had served as an associate pastor earlier in his priestly career, but his appointment came directly from the bishop; the parishioners had no say in the matter. In fact, most current diocesan norms [written and unwritten] in this country tend to prohibit or at least discourage the assignment of priests to their own family parishes.

One can only speculate about the ultimate advantages and disadvantages of appointing someone to this position who is already a member of the parish or who has worked in the parish previously. That it was an advantage for the women in my study may be a function of the parishioners' anxiety about the survival of their parish. All of these parishes suffer this anxiety. The very fact that they have been designated for alternate staffing and do not have a resident priest places the parish in a precarious state.

Therefore, the parishioners in these "priestless parishes" are ripe for a strategy of inclusion. Reaching out to the parishioners and attempting to include them in the business of keeping the parish operating has every chance of success in a situation like this one. It is a basic sociological tenet that a group threatened by an outside force tends to experience an increase of solidarity, and to stand together as they struggle for their survival.[2] The women who were parishioner-pastors are not newcomers to the threatened parish. It follows, then, that cooperation is not diffi-

cult to come by, as the following statement attests: "We worked
it out. We said, 'We are all in this boat together. We either go
down or stay afloat.'"

Another parishioner in a parish with an "insider" pastor said,

> It's hard to say no to [her] because people respect her and you
> want to help her. And she just has a way of asking you that
> puts you at ease. It's not in a demanding sort of way at all. She
> always *asks*, never says, "Do this."

The acceptance by the parishioners was not automatic, however. One of the women, who had grown up in a neighboring
parish, described an incident that happened on the occasion
when a representative from the bishop's office came to
announce her appointment as head of the parish.

> Then [the bishop's representative] came and celebrated all the
> Masses and told the people what was happening and intro-
> duced me at the Masses. That was an interesting experience
> because a lot of the people didn't know me. I was sitting behind
> a couple of women who were sitting there saying, "No way, no
> way in the world will I accept a woman in charge. No way." Out
> loud, during the homily. The reaction was that strong.

When the woman pastor was asked to stand, she said that
the women sitting in front of her "would have liked to have
crawled under their seats." However, both of them eventually
became strong supporters of the parish, because she always
greeted them by name and took Communion to them when they
were sick. As she explained, "After that I could do no wrong."
Again, the strong belief in making linkages by reaching out to
parishioners paid off.

In parishes where the woman pastor was not an "insider,"
there were similar sentiments voiced by parishioners regarding
the way they were enlisted to help in the running of the parish.
Here are three examples:

> She's got a certain way about doing it. It is the way she comes
> on. She is very, very pleasant and she is the type of person
> that you want to help because you know she is doing so much
> within the parish. So you feel, "I am part of this parish; I want
> to take some of the load off of her." And it is very hard to say
> no to [her]. That is the bottom line.

We have far more leadership and caring, nurturing, bringing out of talent than we have ever had here. [She] is always involved and always present, and I have worked with so many priests who don't care. [She] is involved in the planning and cares.

Personal contact, a lot of personal contact, and of course, the usual, the blurb in the bulletin and having other people to spread the word around and ask other parishioners if they would be involved. She has a way of knowing what an individual's talents are and calling them forth.

When I asked the women pastors how they went about getting the parishioners involved, most of them replied that they did it on an individual basis as well as on a group basis, asking people in general to help, but then contacting people directly and suggesting some specific project to them. Most of the time they received positive responses, as this pastor indicates:

I ask more of them. They weren't asked to do these things [by the priest]. They respond. Sometimes it scares me because some of them will say to me, "Sister, I can't say no to you. I don't want to do it but I can't say no to you." They said that with a little bit of fear, too, that "if I don't do it she might leave and then we won't have a parish." But I also think they do it out of affection.

One of the women pastors elaborated on the consequences of the inclusion strategy.

This is quite a breakthrough for people who formerly had little say in parish direction or planning. In this and other rural areas, the priest-pastor frequently acted as the parish council, the bus driver, the school superintendent, the choir director, and even the athletic coach. The one way that people knew to do something was "Father's way," or "the way we always did it." Now we are discovering better ways of meeting today's needs by drawing on all the personal insight and initiative available to us.

Women pastors tend to be very sensitive about the problem of usurping the parishioners' authority, even in seemingly small ways. For instance, the parishioners in one parish had experienced a period of nine months without a resident pastor before her arrival, and they had taken over a variety of duties to keep the church activities going. She explained one of her efforts to continue the empowerment of the parishioners.

> When I came, there was a group of women in the parish that met every morning for a Communion service and when the deacon left nine months before he said to them, "You can still continue to meet even though I am not going to be there." And he gave them a missalette[3] and he showed them which prayers to read and they simply carried on in a real simple way. They just simply read the prayers, found the reading, read the reading and had Communion. So when I arrived they assumed that I would just take over and that they would go back to their places. And I didn't. I said, "Oh, this is the future. We'll just take turns."

She then continued, revealing her commitment to training for lay leadership:

> But then I knew that I wanted to help them develop that presiding skill, because they weren't doing it well, and sometimes they weren't even finding the readings for the day. But now we have a beautiful, prayerful sharing of the Scriptures every morning. They never talked about the Scriptures before. They just read them and then they went on. Now they sit right down and we share and it's real different. So I am glad that I didn't just take over. I could have.

Another example of the careful attention to the problem of usurping parishioner's rights was presented by a parishioner who described the lengths his pastor went to in order to bring parishioners into a renovation process.

> She's currently involved in renovating the church. We've done an awful lot with the inside of the church, but she really tried very hard to meet the wants of the people. She had an idea of how she wanted the church to be laid out, but rather than just go ahead with that she talked to several people that were very active in the church, and asked for their suggestions. And we came up, in the end, with five possibilities.

He then continued to describe the process:

> So what we did is we rearranged the church in those five different ways. Each week we would come to Mass and the church would be laid out in a different fashion. The seats were

all unbolted from the floor so they were adjustable. But Sister did it over a period of time and she asked for input from the people. As each step went by, she kept saying, "Is this the way you like it? Keep in mind this because next week we're going to try something different." And then, in the end, after five weeks of having things rearranged and having people totally confused, she asked for the consensus of opinion as to which was the most effective way. So even for something as small as laying out the church, it wasn't her rule.

CONSEQUENCES OF COLLABORATIVE LEADERSHIP

Two of the most apparent consequences of the collaborative leadership exercised by these women were increased participation of the parishioners and a growing spirit of solidarity within the parish. The first, parishioner participation, could be quantified by increased numbers of committees and active committee members, an increase in church attendance, and in contributions to the Sunday collection. The contributions were usually reported in the Sunday bulletin, and a perusal of these revealed that there was, in general, an increase in contributions, particularly after her first year as pastor. One of the women pastors attributed the increase in contributions to the inclusion process. She said,

> When I came the contributions increased quite a bit, actually. Now it has continued to be on a pretty stable level. And the people have told me they are beginning to see where some of their money is going. They liked the fact that I was putting a little more into education. It came in when they saw where the money was going.

Many of the parishioners I interviewed attested to the fact that more families had joined the parish, and attendance at other parish activities had increased. My examination of parish attendance records corroborated the parishioners' perceptions. Summing it up, a parishioner said, "There are definitely more people at Mass now, more people at everything and more people doing things."

In a similar vein, parishioners told me that there were people in the parish who had not been involved for twenty years prior to the arrival of their woman pastor, but who were now actively working on parish committees. As one parishioner put it, "The same old people did everything until she came."

The second consequence of collaborative leadership—a growing spirit of community—is more elusive, and difficult to quantify. A careful reading of the parish bulletins prepared by the women pastors indicates how they foster a feeling of "we-ness" in the parish. Terms like "our church" and "our parish" are used over and over again. What I observed in the friendliness of the atmosphere at various parish functions, the warm greetings to each other on arriving and leaving the church, and the words used by parishioners to describe their solidarity all attested to this phenomenon. Time and time again, both in the interviews and in casual conversation, parishioners would refer to the parish in the first person plural.

An example of the feeling of we-ness comes from one of the poorest parishes I visited. One Saturday afternoon I observed a female parishioner who was helping to clean the interior of the church. She was not only dusting the furniture and vacuuming the floor, but she was also sweeping down the walls of the church, as far as she could reach. When I complimented her for her thoroughness, she said that she was pleased to participate in keeping "our church" clean, and proudly introduced me to to her son who was also a member of the cleaning crew.

In another parish on a Saturday morning, several male parishioners arrived at 8:30 to work with steel brushes on the exterior of the church, preparing it for a new stain job. About the same time a few of the women arrived to begin preparing strawberry shortcake as a treat for the workers. I observed the camaraderie that existed among the workers on the ladders and on the roof as well as in the kitchen. Later as I sat among them, enjoying the strawberry shortcake and listening to their conversations, I heard the words "we" and "our" whenever they referred to the church or to parish activities.

One of the parishioners described his sense of solidarity with his parish this way:

> I was baptized here, confirmed here. All my kids have been baptized and confirmed here. My Dad is also buried in that cemetery. All my grandparents and aunts and uncles are buried down there, also. My daughter is buried there. So I

have a real tie to that church, and my feelings for that church—I mean, if it closes it is going to be very hard, very troublesome for me to accept. I have been on the parish council now, my second term. I am treasurer of the cemetery committee, and I just love helping that church, my church.

Another manifestation of the spirit of parish solidarity that I observed occurred after Sunday Mass, when the parishioners congregated outside the church or in the basement drinking coffee together, a recent phenomenon at some of the parishes I visited. Parishioners reported that prior to the arrival of the woman pastor, people usually went directly home after church services, but that now they typically hang around and visit with each other before leaving. The "hanging around" could last anywhere from fifteen minutes to an hour, and it tended to be more prolonged when it included donuts and coffee. It may be, in part, a function of their location in isolated rural areas, and the distances some of them must drive in order to participate in parish activities, but these parishioners seemed genuinely glad to see each other, and enjoyed "catching up" on each other on these occasions.

One of the pastors talked about her bishop's reaction to the leadership style of women pastors:

> He [the bishop] said that what he sees in the parishes where there are pastoral administrators [lay pastors], is a real sense of community and a special something that he can't always identify that he sees there that he doesn't see in the other parishes. And I am not saying those parishes aren't good, but he can see something distinctive about the leadership of the women as pastoral administrators, and community was the thing.

A priest whom I interviewed also attested to the spirit of community in a parish headed by a woman. He said,

> I guess I feel, in a sense, there is a loss for the people here without a resident priest, just because I think the very nature of priesthood has something basic to do with Catholic life and they don't have that. But on a more personal level, in terms of what I see happening here, she's been the best thing that's happened to this parish in twenty years because she has been able to pull the community together and get them working. I feel an incredible sense of community here that she, in her

very humble kind of way, has been able to do. People have accepted her as a leader and I really don't feel the parish is missing anything.

A female parishioner from the same parish echoed his sentiments when she said,

> We were losing parishioners and losing the feel of community. It didn't have the closeness it had before.The priest coming in from St. _____ was doing a very good job, but it was just that he didn't have the time to dedicate to all of the extracurricular activities that we did have. This is a community where the church is the central location because there is nothing else. So we would come to church activities that would build this community. We don't have a store or central post office or town, not even a meeting place. Our meeting place is here at the church. And we were losing that.

My last example of increased solidarity as a consequence of collaborative leadership is one that emerged from what I observed when I accompanied a woman pastor on her visit to the home of a parishioner with a terminal case of cancer. Although very weak, and scarcely able to speak, the woman's face lighted up when her pastor asked her if she was remembering to take her medicine. The pastor explained that the woman who was ill had difficulty remembering to set her alarm clock, so a team of parishioners volunteered to take turns phoning her at various points of the day, including at two and four in the morning, to remind her that it was medicine time. Though her words were barely audible, it was obvious that this woman was expressing her appreciation for the efforts of the parishioners on her behalf, and was deeply touched by the expressions of their commitment to her.

In summing up the different leadership style of women pastors, it is clear that although the road to collaborative leadership is not always smooth and can be very circuitous and time consuming, it is the direction they are taking. Clearly some women pastors have moved further along in their collaborative efforts than others, but I found that all of them are clearly oriented to that type of leadership style. In fact, a female parishioner labeled collaborative leadership as a "movement" in the right direction. She said,

I don't see this whole movement as something negative. I see it as something that's really positive because I think the Church is going back to what it was very, very early when it was much more people-oriented, and much less run by a hierarchy. I like seeing control and responsibility being shifted to the laity. I don't think we would ever be getting this if we did not have a priest shortage.... That's a new idea for a lot of people, to have this much involvement in running your church, in deciding your liturgy, and still remaining Catholic, true to the faith, I think is healthy. I think our faith is becoming ours rather than belonging to a priest.

What this parishioner is alluding to is the movement toward a restructuring of authority in the parish, from a hierarchical to a circular relationship between parishioner and pastor. This type of parish restructuring, both a cause and a consequence of the collaborative direction these nonordained pastors are taking as leaders of the parish, is the topic I will discuss in the next chapter.

•5•

Parish Restructuring

When Pope John XXIII convened the Second Vatican Council in 1962, he made it clear that he wanted the Church to move in new directions. He stressed two changes in particular. First, he underlined the importance of *aggiornamento,* an updating or modernization process, which he often described as "opening the windows of the Church to the outside world," thus signaling an end to isolationism. For instance, when he publicly embraced a prominent rabbi, and referred to him as "Joseph, my brother," Pope John was acting out his belief in *aggiornamento.* This symbolic moment was an impetus for the ecumenical thrust of Vatican II. Although the ecumenical movement has experienced a series of reversals in the past twenty-five years, that new direction taken by the Catholic church received international press coverage, and one could argue that the President of the Soviet Union, Mikhail Gorbachev, was borrowing from Pope John's *aggiornamento* when he launched his *glasnost* program.

The second direction proposed by Pope John XXIII, and the one most relevant to the topic of this chapter, which he labeled coresponsibility, also bears some resemblance to Gorbachev's second key concept, *perestroika.* Both coresponsibility and *perestroika* represent proposals for a serious restructuring of institutions in order to bring about internal changes. In the case of the Catholic church, coresponsibility means that there will be significant changes in the relationships between clergy and laity. Without a change in ideology regarding the meaning of the church, that is, an ecclesiological redefinition, coresponsibility would not be possible.

A REDEFINITION OF CHURCH

The Vatican Council's definition of the church simply as the "people of God" required a radical change in thinking for both clergy and laity, from "we-they" to "us." It meant that the laity were no longer "quasicitizens" of the church, with the clergy alone retaining full citizenship. Inclusion of the laity gave them the right to participate in making decisions, in shaping policy, and in changing legislation, all of which had been seen as the prerogative of the clergy. One of the women who had been a parishioner in her parish for several years before her appointment as its pastor described how some changes in thinking came about as parishioners moved from quasi-citizenship to full citizenship in her parish:

> We had a group of parishioners that studied some of the documents on Vatican II that said the people are the Church. That was a whole new experience to think of yourselves as church because we always knew that the priests and nuns were the church and the rest of you were just there. So we went through a number of months of formation forming the parish council and identifying, and beginning to say "we are the Church."

We can expect that the process of moving from a hierarchical or pyramidal structure to a circular one will not be smooth, especially in a church that has a long history of hierarchy with clergy on the top and laity on the bottom. As one woman pastor put it, "The laity as laity have been peasants." The Soviet Union's experience has thus far illustrated that the restructuring process is fraught with difficulties, not the least of which is persuading the people of the value of *perestroika,* so that they will be willing to do their part toward moving their society in this new direction.

It may be that a lay pastor will be more effective in restructuring the parish than a priest, because a priest's presence may intimidate parishioners and inhibit their adoption of a new way of thinking about the church. A male parishioner who had four years of experience with a woman as the leader of his parish put it this way:

I feel part of the church now. I didn't feel part of the church before. It was the priest. He did everything; he did all the thinking. Now the responsibility has been sent down to us and in our parish it is working great. I think it's the best thing that ever happened here. I am encouraged. I love it. It's our church.

For the average Catholic, whether clergy or laity, thinking of the Church as the people of God requires a radical change in consciousness. It means changing the meaning of church from an institution owned and operated by the pope, bishops, and clergy to an awareness that we—that is, clergy and laity alike—are the church; in short, a belief personified in the quote above that it's "our church," not "theirs." The change in thinking then leads to relationships that are egalitarian, nonhierarchical, and mutually supportive.

We cannot expect a more active participation on the part of the laity without this change in thinking, because the pre-Vatican II definition of church placed the laity in a predominantly passive position, much like that of an audience during a theatrical performance. The priest-pastor was often depicted as a "one-man band," who did everything of significance in the parish, especially the thinking and decision making, and who shared no leadership with the laity, as the male parishioner attests in the above quote. The women pastors whom I observed, on the other hand, tended to be more like the conductor of an orchestra, who oversees all of the activity in the parish, but calls forth the talents of the parishioners who then willingly cooperate in taking on the responsibility for running the parish. In short, the laity "make the music," while the woman pastor orchestrates it.[1]

PARISHIONERS AS COPASTORS

This restructuring of the parish places the laity on stage as the principle actors in the performance, rather than in the audience or backstage. Because they are sharing in the leadership of the parish, the parishioners are more like copastors since they share in the decision making and in the activities that were formerly reserved to the priest. The dramaturgical concepts of frontstage and backstage regions in a performance are relevant here.[2] One could argue that the traditional stance of the priest-pastor was like an actor performing in the frontstage region, where he defined the situation for those observing his performance by the use of "expressive equipment," like his Roman collar, vestments worn during liturgical ceremonies, and his general demeanor including posture, facial expressions and body gestures, all of which enabled him to place himself on a level above his parishioners. In this hierarchical situation the majority of the parishioners are silent and passive members of the audience; a few are backstage assisting the main actor [priest] to succeed in his performance as the person solely in charge of the parish: the housekeeper, secretary, altar servers, janitor, etc.

By contrast, women pastors do not place themselves above the parishioners, and tend to find ways to eradicate, or at least to decrease, clerical privilege and status, and to reaffirm their positions as members of the laity. As one of them said,

> There are different ways of leading, and I would never want to see any one person taking over the role. Some people have called me "Pastor," and I always say, "No, I am not the pastor. We are all pastor together."

Some of the women pastors make the point of copastoring symbolically by sitting in the pews with the congregation during Mass, so that they are seen as an equal among equals. They also place laity with leadership responsibilities [like the lectors, eucharistic ministers, and song leaders] in the sanctuary with the priest, thus forcing the priest to "share the limelight," as it were, with other frontstage performers.

One woman pastor made this comparison:

> I don't think that the priest I am working with has the same vision of empowerment of lay people. He can say all the right words, but at the gut level he doesn't allow it to happen.

One could argue that the reason the vision cannot be shared is that the two principal "viewers" are standing in different positions. The priest is looking on from above, as it were, from his privileged position as clergy. He was once a layperson, but for most priests that was a long time ago, in the days of his youth. Understandably a priest would find it hard to remember how it felt to be a layman, and what the church looked like from that vantage point.

On the other hand, the women pastors, nuns and married women alike, have always been laypersons, even though they are temporarily in charge of a parish. They continue to be reminded of their limited empowerment as they struggle to perform a job without the proper credentials. Therefore, their vision of the empowerment of lay people tends to be crystal clear, as is evidenced in the following statement from a sister who had been pastoring for over five years:

> In my heart I consider myself laity, and the more enabled I can move this [parish], not only for women but for laity.... The other kind of hierarchical church is gradually going to become extinct, and then we will have the laity more enabled and ready.
>
> And another thing is because I am not in a class, in a sense, like a priest would be, I see where I can get in there and be part of that change without a class system attached to me. Even if there was ordination [for women], if that would ever come to be, I am sure I don't want it to be what it is. So I question ordination as such, because one of my firm beliefs is we could ordain women who would be doing the same things as men, but living in female bodies, and then we would still have the hierarchical [structure]. And that isn't the ordination that I'm looking toward. I am looking toward a more circular ordination that puts together the gifts of all people.

Parish restructuring has not been a smooth process. It requires power sharing, often a painful experience, because those in power are not in a hurry to give it up, and parishioners may require much persuasion to take on parish responsibilities. Thus the attitude of the "one in charge," the pastor, who proposes the restructuring in the first place, is the key to the success or failure of parish restructuring.

POWER SHARING

One of the first signs of parish restructuring is evident as one enters the door of the church. There, inside the entrance is a bulletin board filled with information about upcoming events and other announcements, but always in a prominent place are the names of parishioners who comprise the numerous parish committees. Over fifty percent of parishioners in most of these parishes are active members of a committee, and some estimates of parishioner participation were as high as eighty or ninety percent. As one parishioner described it, "There are some members in this parish who were inactive for over twenty years until she came along and recruited them." These committees are chaired and run by parishioners who are totally "in charge." The woman pastor oversees them, but rarely overrides their decisions.

Some dioceses provide guidelines for lay leadership. For example one such guideline states that all laity should be encouraged to participate in some sort of service to the church. It further instructs the pastor to join with the pastoral council and staff to discern the gifts of leadership among the laity and to facilitate this leadership by providing educational programs and training sessions. Thus, the promotion of lay leadership may not be initiated by the woman pastor in some cases, but she is typically very diligent in pursuing the movement towards lay participation.

This is accomplished in a variety of ways, but most of the women pastors talk to people individually about their participation. Their appeal to the parishioners tends to be very effective, because of the their common bond as members of the laity. One of the women pointed to her preaching as a source of recruitment:

> When I preach I always come back to how do we minister in the parish and what are some of the needs. It is so automatic that I don't realize I am doing it until I reread it and see what I am doing. Everything that I do encourages people to do something.

Another tool, which many of the women utilize, is a yearly sign-up sheet that is distributed to every parishioner. One woman describes her method in this way:

> Every year at our stewardship drive before we talk about money we talk about time and talent. And we ask people to fill out a Time and Talent sheet that has so many different things on it that there is something everybody can commit to, including praying for the needs of the parish. So we invite people to do something, even if it is something like doing nothing but saying an "Our Father" once a day at home. And we don't have very many who only accept that [responsibility].

Another way to encourage participation is to recognize the parishioners who are active. Most of the parish bulletins that are distributed each week listed all of the members of the parish committees and the names of those who had specific duties for the current week. But some women pastors found additional ways to acknowledge parishioner participation. For instance, as mentioned earlier, during the announcements made before the beginning of the Sunday Mass, one woman pastor read the name of each parishioner who was performing a duty during the ceremony. Although the names of these parishioners were listed on the bulletin board, this additional recognition in the form of a public act of gratitude was impressive, and was well received by the congregation.

A final example of parishioner encouragement comes from a parish that initiated an "Appreciation Day." As the pastor described it,

> Three years ago at the parish council meeting I said, "Now we are going to have the picnic again and I am wondering if it might be a good time to express our gratitude to each other because we've really developed over the past year and a half" [because that's how long I had been there]. "We need to recognize people." So the parish council really picked up on that and we decided that we would combine recognition and appreciation with the picnic. And at that time I made out certificates for every single person and [distributed] them, and we got balloons and had a big sign made and had the picnic outside.

The parish council, composed of elected parishioners, is the key group for parish decision making. Important decisions from other committees are usually filtered through the parish council before any action is taken. Although the woman pastor typically attends all meetings of the parish council, she is usually on an equal footing with them with regard to voting, and if she has an override vote she seldom uses it. The priest who serves as sacramental minister does not attend the parish council meetings in most of the parishes I visited. In one parish where he did attend, a parishioner explained his role:

> He is usually at our parish council meetings. He is a real quiet man. He'll sit and listen, and then he may say something, or if he is asked for a comment, he'll comment on it. He doesn't try

to take over. This is very much our parish and he assists us.
He does not take a leadership role. He doesn't want one.

Parishioners and pastors alike described the decision making
in parish council meetings as a consensus situation. As a woman
pastor, a nun with many years of experience in rural ministry
explained it,

> It's really their agenda that we have to deal with. And so it is a
> gradual kind of process of getting them to own the agenda.
> The agenda includes many things now that were never talked
> about before.

In addition, the meetings of the parish council are typically
open to all members of the parish, so that any member of the
parish can attend if he or she wishes.

This is not to say that the decisions of the parish council are
accepted by the parishioners without question. Changes made
inside the parish church, like taking away the Communion rail
or moving the statues from the front to the back of the church,
are sometimes strongly resisted. One woman pastor described
the reaction of some parishioners who protested the proposal of
the parish council to remove the Communion rail:

> They would come to meetings of parish council to protest.
> There was a group of four or five who would come to several
> of the meetings that we had right after that. I didn't ever feel
> like I was doing it nor did I ever really feel like I was being
> attacked in that whole situation because it was not my plan; it
> was our plan. I never took ownership of it all by myself. I was
> not the only one who wanted to get rid of the communion rail.
> In fact, I almost tried to remain neutral by telling them that this
> was what Vatican II was really encouraging and trying to
> almost remain a neutral person, but educating them as to why
> we were going to be doing this. I would have comments like,
> "I am not going to come into the church again if you take out
> the Communion rail," or I would hear that through someone
> else. Very often I was not the one who was hearing this, but it
> would be said in downtown cafes and people would come
> back to me saying that this was being said.

The parishioners opposed to the removal of the altar rail
threatened to obstruct its removal, but when the truck arrived at

the church on the appointed day and time, no parishioners showed up to hinder the operation. Had they not been allowed to voice their criticisms throughout the decision-making process, the outcome might have been very different, because the removal of any of the treasured objects from the church can be a sensitive and painful issue, especially for elderly parishioners. Some of the priests interviewed, in fact, said that they wouldn't dream of bringing up the question of such changes in their church until several years after they had taken over as pastor.

What are the specific responsibilities taken on by parishioners in these parishes? I asked pastors and parishioners this question at each parish I visited, and was amazed at the length of the list presented to me. First of all, parishioners are in charge of scheduling classes, training teachers, and teaching in the religious education programs of the parish, which usually include both elementary and high school-aged children. Most parishes also have adult religious programs as well. Though the woman pastor oversees these programs, she seldom has the time to participate in any of the work of this committee, though she may occasionally teach a class in a teacher's absence.

Three-fourths of the parishes I visited were small, with less than two hundred families; the largest had 339 families registered in the parish. Not one of them owned a school building, so most of their religious education classes were held in the church basement. I watched the miraculous transformation of one church basement, where partitions were pulled out to transform it into eight classrooms in about ten minutes. The parishioner in charge of the religious education programs was very visible, answering parishioners' questions and supervising every aspect of the program.

I also observed one session of a confirmation class that was held in a parishioner's home one Sunday afternoon. Three parishioners took turns at teaching the groups of teenagers, while the woman pastor, other parents, and I sat quietly on the sidelines. However, during the last half hour, when she led them in a brief prayer session, it was evident that this pastor was no stranger to the children, for she called each one of them by name.

Another important committee, usually called the liturgy committee, assists in the choice of hymns for each Mass, trains and assigns parishioners as lectors, altar servers, participants in the offertory procession, readers of the prayers for the faithful, eucharistic ministers, and ushers. They usually set up the altar before Mass, and see that all of the musical equipment is in its proper place. This committee also has jurisdiction regarding any changes to be made inside the church itself, like placement of statues and pews.

The finance committee is in charge of parish accounts, the counting of collections made at Mass, making decisions about expenditures, and all other aspects of the parish budget. Although the financial report to the diocesan office is usually done by the pastor each year, most of the ingredients of that report are the responsibility of this committee. In some parishes the chair of this committee cosigns the checks with the pastor.

A married pastor's description of her parish finance committee is a good example of parish restructuring. She explained that the finance committee, made up of four parishioners and herself, arrives at the yearly budget by consensus. She explained:

> When I meet with them I give them an update of where we stand. And they see everything. This is something that they have been absolutely flabbergasted with. They never saw the books before; they never saw anything. They get an accounting of every last penny. They see everything that comes in, and how it is spent, and where we stand.

The outreach committee, often called St. Vincent de Paul, is responsible for collecting and distributing clothing, money, and food to those in need. Membership in the parish is seldom a requisite for aid from this group. Other outreach groups visit the sick and the elderly, and *ad hoc* groups are often formed in crisis situations. An incident I described earlier regarding the parishioners who came to the aid of a woman dying of cancer is a good example of one of these groups.

The altar society, usually composed of women parishioners, is in charge of cleaning the church, decorating the altar with flowers, and often sponsors cake sales and other events in order to raise money for church needs. In the previous chapter I described one of my observations of the work of a parish altar society on a Saturday afternoon when I talked to a woman who was sweeping down the walls of the church while her son was vacuuming the floor. She admitted that she took as much pride in this as in her own housecleaning, because it was "her church."

The building and maintenance committee is in charge of the maintenance and upkeep of all parish buildings and grounds. Since many of these parishes have very old buildings, this is a key committee. Half of the women interviewed were living in the parish house or rectory, and since I was their guest for the weekend I had a chance to witness some of their many "calls for help" as they phoned members of the maintenance committee when pipes burst or refrigerators needed repair. Help usually arrived within the hour, and the worker's typical attitude was that he was repairing "his" parish house. The grounds of these parishes were all well kept, but in one parish, the grounds were so unusually beautiful that I inquired about its upkeep. I was told that the groundskeeper was a retired person who took great pride in the maintenance of the lawns and flowers on the church property, spending many hours each week on this endeavor. Again, the superb groundskeeping was another indicator of parishioner ownership.

The young adult or youth committee organizes programs for the teenagers of the parish. This committee was defunct in many of the parishes, and this was a matter of concern to the pastor and parishioners, who realize that the future of the parish is in the hands of the younger generation. The enlistment of the youth in the running of the parish does not seem to be high on the current agenda in most parishes, however.

The Knights of Columbus, open only to men of the parish, was also defunct in most of the parishes. This is primarily a fraternal organization that provides male fellowship for members who desire it, and it also hosts fund-raising events for the parish.

All of the work on these committees is voluntary and unpaid. In two or three cases a small stipend was paid to the choir director and the director of religious education, but this was not usual. Almost all of these parishes are struggling financially, and the parishioners not only are well aware of their economic situation, but they also take an active part in the financial decisions of the parish.

As has been evident from the foregoing discussion, the

women in charge of these parishes have limited empowerment in a formal sense because they are not priests, and they cannot have the title of pastor because they are laity. They have been recruited to their position in the parish because of the clergy shortage, not because of a movement toward the inclusion of women in leadership positions, and this aspect of power sharing will be treated in a later chapter. Women pastors have a different view of the role of the parishioner than did their predecessors, as the following statement illustrates:

> I very much did not want to be a leader like some pastors I have seen, that they did everything they wanted to do and the people had no say about it. There were some things I saw would be an improvement or I really wanted to do but [decided] to be patient and wait until I knew that they agreed with it rather than just doing it, and then letting them say or not say what they felt about it afterwards.

One of the women pastors, who had been a member of the parish for several years before she was appointed to head the parish, described the consequences of her predecessor's stance thus:

> He didn't work well with people, was very demanding and argumentative, didn't want to be bothered half the time, saw no point in having people involved in things. The idea of eucharistic ministers was ridiculous, and all the things we had built up over the years. The unfortunate thing was he still wanted to be in a church of thirty years ago and we were at a point, as a parish, having established our parish council and over the years [had] come to see that we had to be the church here, because we would either have priests with bad health or no priests. So if the people didn't see to the life of the church and the activity and all the other things—if we didn't see to it, it wasn't going to happen. So we have developed a strong sense of involvement and ownership.

For the married women pastors, their prior experience as parishioners in the parish they were heading enabled them to encourage the emergence of a strong sense of community among the parishioners. They were leaders who had a history of sharing in the sufferings and joys of their parishioners.

FACILITATING FACTORS FOR LAY OWNERSHIP

As I see it, the following are the factors that facilitate the restructuring of parishes: (1) close identity of a pastor with lay parishioners; (2) previous membership in the parish (an "insider" pastor); (3) pressure felt by parishioners to help in the survival of the parish; and (4) the base community model. The first three factors were dealt with earlier in the previous chapter, so I begin with a discussion of the fourth factor, base communities.

Some of the nun pastors whom I interviewed had Third World experience, which was an important preparation for parish restructuring. In particular, four of them had participated in the development of basic ecclesial communities, often called base communities, as part of their parish work in Latin America. Base communities are small groups led by laity that gather together for word and Communion services in the absence of a priest, for discussions of the connection of the Bible to people's everyday lives, and for social activism resulting from these discussions.[3]

The concepts of empowerment and active participation are at the heart of base communities. Drawing from the writings of liberation theologians and Paulo Freire,[4] literacy courses were taught, not as a matter of teaching a specific skill, but of liberating the whole person with a new consciousness of his or her dignity as an active subject in the world, rather than a passive object that is merely acted upon. Teaching literacy in base communities is designed to give voice to the voiceless and to help people to understand their capacity to transform their social realities.

One of the nuns who had experience in base communities in a Third World country explained that she did not have a leadership role in the base community. She said,

> Priests and religious do not have leadership roles in these communities. They are made up of the people of the community. It is a lay-centered church there. It is the laity that has the power.

The nun pastors translated their experiences in the base communities of Latin America to their present parishes, which are made up of predominantly poor, blue-collar parishioners, and with a high unemployment rate. For instance, one of the nun pastors, while serving as a pastoral associate prior to her appointment, had organized a literacy program for the parishioners, many of whom had only rudimentary skills in reading and writing, both in their native language and in English. As pastor, she was constantly conveying to her parishioners her belief in their capacity as change agents. Over and over again, almost like a refrain, I heard her say to individual parishioners, "You can *do* it."

Other women pastors, married women and nuns alike, who had no Third World experience, had at least read the works of liberation theologians, and were likewise engaged in making the parishioners conscious of their gifts and encouraging them to share these gifts with the parish.[5] On a smaller scale, it seems that these women pastors are using the same principles of base communities in their parishes, even though they might not recognize it themselves. They think of themselves as serving and guiding, rather than dictating to people how they should act. Like the workers in base communities, they seek to foster relationships that are horizontal or circular, rather than vertical or hierarchical. As a result, decisions tend to be made in a democratic and participatory mode, where bishops, priests, and laity are all perceived as equal because they are all part of the people of God.

One of the nun pastors, who had not had Third World experience, used the term "faith communities." She stressed the need to enable the parishioners to be leaders in the parish faith community. In her words,

> If their leadership continued to be enabled for a number of years, I think that this parish would continue on. I see such gifts in the small community that are sometimes lost in the mob or in the big mass, and that is why I am out here, because I believe in that, and I believe I have gifts to bring out that will help them to somewhat determine their own destiny and their own self-worth as faith communities.

As mentioned earlier, the collaborative leadership style of women pastors is in contrast to the hierarchical style of previous male pastors in these parishes. These women administrators provide training in lay leadership, encourage the parishioners to become involved in the business of running the parish, and empower them to do so. Because they view the parishioners as owners of the parish and themselves as enablers, the women work very hard to include as many parishioners as possible as active participators. As one explained,

> Our styles are different. He had a different vision of his role than I have of my role as a pastor. I suppose I am more people-oriented, and by that I mean that each person has something valuable to share with everyone else and that I try to recognize that, help them identify it, and draw it out because I think that the whole parish is enriched when everyone is sharing their ability in ways of ministering to the parish. And so that we do it together, so it isn't just that one person ministers to a community, but the community is ministering to each other, and my role is to help activate that and to encourage and nurture it.

This allusion to a "different vision" runs like a theme throughout the interviews with the women pastors. This is not surprising, given the very different vantage points of priest and laity.

There are several reasons why these women are successful in their efforts to encourage the parishioners to cooperate in the running of the parish. First of all, they can identify closely with the laity, and this includes the nuns who are not members of the clergy; therefore, they, too, are nonordained pastors. There are some advantages for women who had been active parishioners before they were appointed to head the parish, as one priest explained:

> There are some things that couldn't happen with a priest there [at her parish]. For example, one thing that is very highly stressed over there is lay leadership. I can talk about that all day here [at my parish] but it doesn't have the same impact because you might have a parishioner who doesn't want to talk with Father, but will talk with [the woman pastor] because she lives down the street. When [the woman pastor] says, "Well, I'm a mother, too, and I have kids at home," or whatever, "and being the lector is something I enjoy and you would enjoy it, too," they take it in a different way than if it came from me. So in many ways she is better [than I am] with the laity because she is a laywoman. She is excellent at getting people to participate.

Another priest voiced a similar opinion about the effectiveness of religious women who had not been members of the parish before being appointed as pastors:

> Because the sisters are doing a really good job and helping the people in [their parishes] to have more choice and ownership of what they are doing here, people see them as sort of one like themselves.

The ability of women pastors to restructure the parish is also enhanced by the fact that most of their parishioners are worried about parish survival. As I mentioned earlier, in many cases their grandparents and great-grandparents are buried in the parish cemetery. In a few of the parishes I visited, where the cemetery is placed adjacent to the church, I noted graves dating back to the mid-1800s.

In addition, some of the parishioners mentioned names of their ancestors who had helped to build the church. They have vivid memories of the stories told them about important contributions made by their relatives to the establishment of the parish. Because their families have been baptized, married, and buried in the parish, the parishioners want it to be there for the future generation as well. The appointment of a nonpriest as parish leader suggests to them the possibility that their parish could close in the future, unless they become involved in keeping the parish going. Thus, they cooperated willingly in keeping the parish open with their voluntary services.

Parishes differed in their efforts toward the development of lay leadership, however. One parishioner complained:

> With any nonpriest-pastor situation, I think what is important is the development of lay leadership, lay ministry. To do that you cannot just grab people off the street. You have to give them a spirituality; you have to give them basic skills. And you have to either plug them into programs that are available in the diocese or you have to have certain ideas in mind and be a mentor to these people who want to be involved in lay ministry. This is where our parish needs some real hard work. We need the structures for, not short-term development of lay ministry, but long-term. We have to engage people on a short-term basis to help them understand they can contribute. But given the realities of peoples' lives, a lot of them can't make

the two-year commitment for a leadership role. But what we need to do is to get them in and get them out and build up the idea within them that they are necessary to the community.

One of the women pastors described how she has trained eight of her parishioners as presiders at the Communion services held on weekdays in their parish. They take turns presiding at these services, and the pastor herself presides only once a week. As she said, "It's *our* parish, not mine." While I visited that parish I had a chance to observe this shared leadership in action when I watched one of her parishioners presiding at a weekly Communion service. I sat in a pew with the woman pastor and watched as the parishioner greeted the people, led the prayers, read the scripture, gave a reflection on the scriptural readings, and distributed Communion. Clearly this was not a "first" for her, and the congregation seemed quite comfortable with her as presider. The pastor proudly told me after the service that this same woman had taken care of all arrangements for the funeral of a parishioner who died while she was on vacation, arranging for the Mass, contacting a priest, arranging for the liturgy, music, and readings.

In another parish the parishioners also managed funeral arrangements during the pastor's vacation:

> They [the parishioners] tried to get one priest, but they couldn't get him. The other priest was busy. The third priest said he could come for the wake but could not come for the funeral, and they said, "No, Father, we don't need you for the wake. We can do that ourselves. But we need somebody for the funeral." So, as it turned out, they did the wake themselves. And then they did get a priest for the following day for the burial.

Because of the growing shortage of priests, it becomes more important for priest-pastors to develop lay leadership in their parishes also, and there are signs that this is happening. One of the women pastors described a clergy education workshop, where she had been invited to make a presentation to the priests of the diocese. She said, "Some [priests] wanted to know what they could do to prepare their parishes, not only for alternate staffing, but also to help the laity take ownership. I thought that was a sign of life."

These women are also preparing their parishioners to take over in their absence. One of the women pastors in a very poor parish with high unemployment, who in her own way was forming base communities in her parish, described it this way:

> I feel very optimistic because I know they are already a new people. They know how to stand on their own feet. They have had experience that they are someone, that they are capable, that they can speak out. I say to them that they have to question things, to me or to the bishop. They have that right to speak out and question things. It is not any more blind faith. I know they can handle it.

These women pastors tend to be very committed to preparing the laity to take over when they are no longer there. In particular, they train the parishioners with a talent for leadership to preside at the word and Communion service, so that the parishioner-presiders can take over when they are on vacation. This "in-service training" was also extended to week-day services in some priestless parishes, as mentioned earlier. Parishioner-presiders have substituted, on occasion, for a priest who failed to show up for Mass, as this parishioner testifies:

> We have had substitute priests not show up. A priest from the home office didn't show up because he went to the wrong place. Our schedules are such that he thought he was supposed to be someplace else. We came into church and there was nobody. Everybody sat around for a few minutes and one of our parishioners who has done some presiding overseas, came forth with no notice at all and did a service, and did a really respectable job, delivered a sermon off the top of his head. And we found out if we have to we can do it.

•6•

Support Systems and Resources

Anyone seeking to enter a new role within an existing institution can expect to encounter some resistance.[1] This is especially true when the process involves a complete redefinition of role attributes and activities. Then the innovator is by definition questioning certain widely held assumptions about the role. While women pastors experience constraints and tensions, there are resources available to them as they meet the obstacles to the successful performance of their new role. In particular, support systems exist in the form of aid and encouragement offered by bishops, priests, and parishioners, as well as other resources both inside and outside the diocese.

BISHOPS

Data regarding the support of the local bishop are based on the interviewees' perceptions of his support. Although I did not interview the local bishops, I asked how the woman pastor, the sacramental minister, and the parishioners assessed the bishop's support.[2] Thus all the interviewees were asked if they thought the bishop was supportive of the woman pastor's presence in the parish. Also, the women pastors, priests, and parishioners were asked to describe how the bishop showed support or non-support for her activities.

Some of the interviewees said that their bishop evidenced support at the earliest phase of the recruitment process, at the point when a parish was first designated for alternate staffing.

This designation meant that the parish would soon have a deacon or a nonordained person as its resident pastor. The initial support took different forms, but it usually involved the bishop himself making a visit to the parish, where he consulted with the parishioners before completing the recruitment process. As might be expected, the bishop's effort to involve the parishioners in this initial phase of the process paved the way for the arrival of the woman pastor.

The most dramatic example of this early support was related by a male parishioner. In his account, corroborated by others, he stated that the bishop asked the retiring pastor to announce to the parishioners that he would arrive on a specified day to meet with them to explain his plans for the parish. This event was described as a public forum open to all. Parishioners were encouraged to bring questions to the meeting.

The parishioner who described the bishop's visit attended the meeting, and he estimated that thirty parishioners (in a parish of 145 families) were there ("a good turnout"). During the meeting the bishop made it clear to the parishioners that it was *his* decision to appoint a layperson as head of the parish. He explained his reasons for this decision, and opened the meeting for questions from the floor. After answering questions posed by the parishioners, the bishop said, "Now, here's my telephone number." After repeating his number, he then reminded the parishioners that it was *his* decision to designate the parish for alternate staffing. He then instructed the parishioners to phone or come to him directly if they had problems with his decision, and not to whomever was appointed to head the parish.

The time and effort to travel to the parish and the long meeting with the parishioners were evidence of the bishop's support, but the fact that he took personal responsibility for the decision to designate the parish for alternate staffing added to the strength of his support of the lay pastor. Although the quality and quantity of initial support on the part of this particular bishop was a unique occurrence in the parishes I visited, the consequences were so dramatic for the lay pastor that the event merits emphasis.

In addition to meeting with the bishop, some of the parishioners in the same parish were involved in a later phase of the recruitment process, when they interviewed prospective candidates for the position. Because they had a chance to meet the candidates and the parishioners' input was solicited, one parishioner said, "They were very favorable" when the final choice was made. However, on reflecting on the recruitment process, my informant told me that he was convinced that by taking a "strong, no-nonsense position" at a very early stage in the process, the bishop made the adjustment to the new role much easier for the lay pastor.

Some bishops also sought the advice of the parish council in the prerecruiting phase. One priest said,

> [The bishop] has tried and is increasingly allowing for the advice of the parish councils. Through official letters to them with a questionnaire, he will get back from them what the needs of the parish are, and what they are looking for in terms of a pastoral leader. I know for a fact it has had [a] great impact on him about what kind of person should be selected.

One of the women pastors explained that the bishop sent a representative from the diocesan personnel office who met with the parishioners and "tried to develop a process to help them to deal with the fact that they weren't going to have a priest, and what did that mean." In another parish, a parishioner told me that the bishop came into a parish council meeting soon after the appointment of the woman pastor. On that occasion the bishop answered questions from council members, and then at the end of the meeting he legitimated her position in the parish by saying, "I have assigned her here, and she is here."

An additional resource for the lay pastor can be provided by the bishop after the candidate has been chosen, and the appointment had been made. This support, often initiated by the bishop, but sometimes by the parishioners or by the pastor herself with the bishop's approval, takes the form of an installation ceremony. The ceremony usually occurred during the first two or three months following the new pastor's arrival. It took place as a public ritual in the parish church with the bishop or his representative presiding. The principal function of the installation ceremony is the legitimation of the new pastor's leadership. I asked every interviewee if there had been an installation ceremony, and if so, to describe it.

About half of the pastors had been formally "installed" by the bishop. After speaking about the installation ceremony with pastors and parishioners, it became clear that the women pastors viewed it as a form of very positive support because they saw it as a conferring of public ecclesiastical approval on them in their new role.

The most dramatic example of the support afforded by an installation ceremony occurred in a parish where the nun pastor had previously served for four years as a pastoral associate in charge of religious education. In this case the bishop informed the new pastor when the installation was to take place, and asked her to involve the parishioners in designing the ceremony itself.

The parishioners not only chose the appropriate readings and hymns, but also wrote into the ceremony the symbolic moment when the power was to be passed on to the pastor. According to the program for the ceremony that was printed and distributed to the congregation, a parishioner was to give the processional cross to the bishop, who turned to the woman pastor and said, "I present you with the visible sign that unites this people. Take this cross as a symbol of the ministries of this community. It is the burden and glory of those who seek to love and serve Christ." Her response was, "On behalf of all who minister here at [the parish], I accept this cross as a sign of God's eternal and embracing love." The printed instructions stated that she was then to raise the cross before the people. As she was recounting that experience, tears welled up into her eyes. In her words,

> It was a very joyful affair, and the part that I think stands out the most for me was that after the homily [by the bishop] at the official installation time in the ceremony, one of the ushers was supposed to bring up the processional cross, and I was to simply raise it. Just as that happened, Bishop _____ whispered to me, "Sister, you can bless the whole community if you want to." So instead of simply raising it—I hardly knew what I was doing, to tell you the truth because I wasn't quite expecting that—I made the sign of the cross, and it was a very moving time. I could see lots of people with tears. It was a very joyful time. At that point it was very spontaneous, the applause afterwards. The whole community was caught up in it, and it was beautiful. I think it was a standing ovation. There was a lot of clapping.

When I asked her how the bishop responded to her blessing, she said that she was so shocked by the bishop's invitation
that she couldn't remember how she did it, but somehow she
managed not only to raise the cross, but to bless the congregation as well. She was able to describe the parishioners' response,
but she was so nervous about her first public blessing that she
did not observe what the bishop's response was. Luckily the ceremony had been videotaped, and I had time to view the tape
before I concluded my visit at her parish. The videotape showed
that the bishop himself received her blessing; that is, he made
the sign of the cross (blessed himself) as she blessed the congregation with the processional cross. This was a dramatic recognition of her legitimate authority on his part; in fact it could be
described very aptly as a ritual that "worked."

When I described to the woman pastor what I had seen on
the tape, her first reaction was shock and disbelief. However,
after she sorted it out, she rejoiced at his unexpected response.
She then interpreted the bishop's reception of her blessing as a
partial explanation of the parishioners' standing ovation.

Equally important, symbolically, was the fact that the processional cross, which had been carried in by a member of the
parish council, was passed from a parishioner to the bishop,
who in turn gave it to her. This procedure was written into the
ceremony by the parishioners, and it represented a direct
involvement of the parishioners in the conferring of that authority on her. In fact, it suggested that the conferring of authority
began with the parishioners, and passed then to the bishop,
who finally conferred it upon her.

Most of the other installation ceremonies were described as
more modest affairs. For instance, a woman pastor said,

> It was a very simple ceremony, the vicar general and sacra-
> mental minister and myself. We processed in. It was just a very
> simple ceremony. After the homily I was called up and
> received a candle as a symbol of leading the people, and then
> was asked some questions.

Another form of support can be found in the contracts
between the bishop and the women pastors. The terms of the
contract varied from diocese to diocese, but the supportive bish-

ops tended to specify three or six years as the appointment period, with the possibility of renewing the contract for an additional three or six years. In many cases the women were given the
same appointment period as the former priest-pastors.

Once the women were appointed and installed as the leaders of the parish, most of the bishops continued to support them
in a variety of ways. Sometimes it was in the form of a public
statement. One bishop, according to a lay pastor, "keeps telling
people that this [appointing laity to head parishes] is the way of
the future." Many parishioners reported that the bishop often
thanked the woman pastor publicly for her work in the parish.
In particular at the ceremony of confirmation in the parish, many
parishioners and priests stated that the bishop thanked her for
her work in the parish, and complimented her on the way she
prepared the children for the sacrament.

A parishioner described her bishop's support thus:

> When he was here I know he did make the remarks about Sis-
> ter _____ as far as the role in the parish and how good she
> was doing. I don't remember exactly what he said, but I know
> we had a service with the bishop for the anointing of the sick,
> and he came for that. I know he did make remarks then about
> things Sister _____ was doing in the parish. I know he is real-
> ly happy with what she is doing.

Another parishioner described a "town meeting" with the
bishop:

> The last time he [the bishop] was here we had a potluck meal.
> Everybody showed up and we had a town meeting and peo-
> ple asked questions. He said, "You know, you have a terrific
> person leading you, and I can see by this turnout how well
> she is supported." So he verbally on occasions has come here
> and said, "You have a terrific person, I am proud of her, she is
> doing an outstanding job."

One of the women pastors said that the bishop always
affirmed her in public. On one occasion when he came to the
parish while she was away on vacation, the parishioners told her
that the bishop really supported her. In her words,

> They [the parishioners] said something about the Catholic
> Church doesn't have women priests. And he [the bishop] said,

"You're right, and [she] is not a woman priest, but she might as well be."

One parishioner said that the bishop both privately and publicly "went out of his way to use the word 'Pastor.' He says, '[she] is your pastor.'" Another woman said that she was listed as pastor in the Diocesan Catholic Directory, something that would not have happened without the approval of the bishop.

One lay pastor showed me the tape of the bishop's formal dedication of her new church building and grounds. In the procession to and from the blessing of the cemetery she and the priest walked side by side directly in front of the bishop. Later, when the bishop was given the key to the church, he said, "I'd better give it to the pastor." And the bishop handed the key to the woman pastor, who unlocked the door.

This incident and the two mentioned in the paragraphs above may seem inconsequential, but such manifestations on the part of the bishop can be extremely important in establishing the woman pastor's legitimacy with her parishioners.

Some bishops also showed their support in a less public way. As a woman pastor explained,

> The other way he has shown support is about once a year he gives me a telephone call and he'll just kind of ask how things are going in the parish and how I'm doing. And that's been nice. He doesn't grill me with questions but just generally wants to know how things are going in the parish and what new things are going on. More of a concern than a questioning.

In the event that the sacramental minister cannot be present for the Sunday Mass and is unable to find a substitute priest, some bishops authorize the woman pastor to lead a service of God's Word and Holy Communion, often referred to as a "word and communion service." While this service is not, strictly speaking, a Mass, the bishop often helps the woman pastor by making it clear to the parishioners that the word and communion service led by their lay pastor serves as the parish community's Sunday celebration and fulfills their Sunday Mass obligation. In fact, one of the bishops instructed the woman pastor to post the following letter in the vestibule [foyer] of the church and missions which she was administering:

When the priests at _____ are unable to celebrate Sunday Masses at _____ and its missions, either because of illness or bad weather, and no other priest is available, Sister should conduct the Liturgy of the Word with a reflection talk[3] and appropriate prayers for the distribution of Holy Communion. In these instances, this Sunday service will enable the people to fulfill their Sunday obligation of worship.

Another way a bishop can support his woman pastor is by treating her as if she is the one in charge when he visits the parish. Many of the parishioners mentioned this type of affirming behavior on the part of their bishop.

Another support, and a very practical one at that, is the bishop's willingness to substitute for the priest [sacramental minister] when he is sick or on vacation. One of the women pastors said that her bishop came to her parish to say Mass five or six times a year; another said that her bishop came to the parish whenever she invited him, and would even give her feedback on her homilies when she sent them to him.

One of the priests spoke of the support given to women in general by his bishop. He described it this way:

When Bishop _____ gave his guidelines out for eucharistic ministers, he said that every woman has to wear an alb[4] if they want to be a eucharistic minister. I don't know his reasoning behind it, but I thought to myself, he is reaffirming the role of women in a liturgical setting.

Another priest described his bishop's stance as feminist when he explained that the bishop seeks out parishes where he can place a woman. He said that this is a deliberate move on the part of the bishop, because he wants more women as pastors. In at least two of the dioceses I visited, I discovered that there was a diocesan policy of not ordaining deacons, because to do so would rule out leadership roles for women.[5]

One of the women pastors who often had difficulty finding priests to administer the sacraments in her parish told about admitting to the bishop that she had, on occasion, administered the sacrament of baptism herself. She quoted her bishop's affirming response thus: "You've got to do what you've got to do, and if that's what needs to be done at the time, that's your pastoral duty."

These instances that indicate support on the part of bishops were described to me very enthusiastically by lay pastors, priests, and parishioners. They all seemed to sense that these words and actions of the bishop represented an important source of legitimation for the new pastors. However, some bishops are more supportive than others; in fact, the level of support varies from very supportive to supportive to neutral to nonsupportive. As I mentioned earlier, the bishops divide equally on this dimension, with half [seven] on the supportive side and the other half [seven] on the neutral or nonsupportive side. The next chapter will elaborate on the neutral and nonsupportive bishops. Now we turn to the supports provided by priests, and in particular, by the sacramental minister assigned to the parish.

PRIESTS

The relationship between the woman pastor and the priest who provides sacramental ministry is an extremely sensitive one, and it is fraught with potential tensions, constraints, and conflicts. Because of parishioners' high regard for the priest, he has the power, wittingly or unwittingly, to undermine the authority of the woman pastor in the parish. On the other hand, because of the parishioners' veneration of his priesthood, the sacramental minister also has the potential to support her position when he visits the parish by his words and actions.

When I interviewed the sacramental ministers, I asked each one how he supported her leadership in the parish. I also asked each of the women pastors how, in her view, the sacramental minister supported her parish leadership, and I asked the same question of the parishioners. Because I not only interviewed the sacramental ministers, but in many cases was able to observe them in action on the weekend, I thus have an additional source of data regarding the priest's support.

How did these priests lend support to the leadership of the women pastors? Many of them see to it that the woman pastor is physically placed in a position of equality during the church services, and I saw this in action at many of the parishes I visited. As one of the priests described it,

We walk up [to the altar] together in the opening procession. We preside together. In fact, lately I open the Mass with the sign of the cross, and she will do the penitential rite, and then the opening prayer. And then above and beyond that, of course, if she is preaching that weekend it would be the homily. I think she has a nice presence for the sake of the people, and she is the pastor here, for all intents and purposes.

When observing during Mass at these parishes, I often watched the priest and woman pastor walk in procession up the aisle side by side, and take their places in the sanctuary next to each other. Her voice was often the first heard by the congregation, because the service began when she greeted the congregation and gave a short commentary on the theme of the day's liturgy. The woman pastor often read the scriptures and/or preached the sermon, and sometimes she distributed Communion alongside the priest. Her voice would often be the last heard, when she made the announcements at the end of Mass. The supportive priests showed by their demeanor that they not only approved of her near-equal status, but that they recognized and affirmed her leadership role in the parish.

Another priest described their sharing of the baptismal rite:

At baptisms she has a prominent role to play in the rites. She will do the questioning of parents and godparents, all of those initial prayers, the blessing of the water. She will be present for the actual baptism of the child and the signing of the chrism.[6]

A woman pastor described her participation in a baptism:

Father _____ did let me participate in the baptism. I introduced them, called them by name, asked some of the questions.

In one parish the priest had a very egalitarian relationship with the pastor, but she was reluctant to preach during Mass. The priest explained how he interpreted the bishop's homily at her installation ceremony, and thus his rationale for urging her to preach.

In his [the bishop's] homily, he was really commissioning her to be leader of the parish, spiritually and in every other way, and to teach. As I heard it that day I said to myself, "Aha, if she's going to teach, she's going to have to preach, because if he's commissioning this woman to teach, that means she'll have to preach." Most of your folks are there on Sunday, and if you're not talking to them you're not communicating anything to your parish. So I thought, "Aha, good."

Like some of the bishops mentioned in the section above, there were also priests who referred to the woman as "pastor." In the words of a woman pastor, "Sometimes priests will call me and tell me I am the pastor. Lots of them do that." One of the sacramental ministers said, "When people ask me what her position is, I tell them she is the pastor of the church."

In some of the parishes, the parishioners would wait until the priest arrived on the weekend, and then bombard him with the kinds of questions and requests that should have more appropriately been addressed to the woman pastor. The priest's response to these questions and requests is critical, because it can help to make or break the acceptance of the woman's position in the parish. A supportive strategy used by many of the priests was to make it clear that she was, indeed, the pastor of the parish. One of the priests said:

> In regard to acceptance, when we [he and the woman pastor] were first here the first months, they [the parishioners] would often still stop and ask me questions instead of her. I would plead ignorance and I said, "That's not my role. Sister is it, so it would be most important to talk to her." So, certainly within the last eighteen months no one really asks me questions. I don't go to parish council meetings or anything like that.

A woman pastor explained the same strategy used by her sacramental ministers:

> If the parishioners go to them with something they should be going to me about, they [the priests] immediately refer them to me.... They [a family in the parish] tried to catch him [the priest] and ask him if they could have a baptism outside the Mass, and he said, "Go ask your pastor. If she says yes, I will do it."

One of the woman pastors said that the priests who served as sacramental ministers for her parish were very supportive. She said, "They [the priests] make it clear to the people by their comments that I am in charge. The priests will refer to me as 'your pastor.'"

This same priest's stance on the altar underlined his support of her position. While the woman pastor was preaching one Sunday, he focused his whole attention on her words, turning and facing her throughout the sermon. He was a good role model for the parishioners, for his body language proclaimed to the congregation that they should pay attention to their pastor's message to them.

One of the parishioners explained this same priest's strategy this way:

> Father was very quick to support everything that Sister was doing, and he tried to offer an explanation as to why. But when it came right down to it, it was, "Do it, folks, because she's not doing it because she wants to; she's doing it in your best interest." And he was very supportive of her.

In addition to the priests who are the sacramental ministers for the parish, the support of a previous pastor who was highly esteemed by the parishioners can also be an important resource for the woman pastor. One of the married women who had been a parishioner before her assignment as pastor, told me that the previous pastor encouraged her to attend classes on all aspects of pastoral ministry a few years before her appointment. In a few of the parishes I visited, the previous priest-pastors had met with the parish council to prepare them for the arrival of the woman pastor, and others used their homilies at Mass prior to the arrival of the woman pastor for the same purpose.

In one case the previous pastor helped to design the liturgy for her installation ceremony, and took an active part in it. As the woman pastor described it,

> He [the previous pastor] handed me the scripture, telling me I would be the spiritual leader of the community. He handed me a rosary which was a very prominent devotion here for the people. Those were the symbols. Also, he handed me the checkbook, saying I would have the responsibility of keeping the place going, and the bills paid. The last thing [the priest] handed over to me were the people.

Another priest who had previously been pastor at the parish, assessed the success of the current woman pastor in this way.

I ran that place for seven years. But I really think it is running better today. The church is full. Things are better than they ever were when I was pastor. That place has grown in wisdom, age, and grace. And the people are really participating. I didn't have that when I was pastor.

PARISHIONERS

While the bishop's and priest's support are important resources, they alone could not offer adequate support to a new pastor. After all, the parishioners interact with the pastor on a daily basis, and without their help and/or encouragement she would be ineffective.

Parishioner support of women pastors takes a variety of forms. One would assume that initial manifestations of parishioners' help and encouragement would spring from deeply held convictions and feelings about their responsibility to support their local pastor. We would also expect such support to be forthcoming from those who had strongly held convictions about gender equality. Later on, as parishioners learn to love and respect her as a person, we would also expect their help to be forthcoming. However, parishioners' support is also offered for a pragmatic reason—the fear that their church might close. In this section we will examine both parishioners's feelings and actions that serve as a support to the woman pastor.

A female parishioner described her feelings about the appointment of her woman pastor:

> I felt at that point when Father _____ was here, he had two parishes and it was a lot of work for him. And I know when he talked about Sister coming and helping out as our pastoral administrator I felt good about it because he really had an overload. I felt it was important that the women should play a role, have some role in the Church. I felt really good about it. I felt good that she was coming here.

Another parishioner said,

> I think this is the best thing that ever has happened here. I like to say when [she] moved in, the spirit moved in with her. We have seen more growth; we have seen people grow closer together; we have just that spirit that never was here before.

People are beginning to participate more, to volunteer more readily, to be friendlier. And I am speaking as an outsider. It is a closed community, I feel, and we've been here for twenty-five years, and I always felt [as an] outsider. And now we are beginning to feel like we belong here, and this all came about after [she] was here.

Parishioners sometimes showed their support even before her arrival at the parish by cleaning and renovating the parish house. In one such parish a female parishioner said,

> There were some repairs that had to be done on the house when [she] came, and there were people who helped with it. A lot of people came and helped before she came, to clean the house and get everything cleaned up and ready for her to live there.

One woman pastor mentioned that her parishioners welcomed her to the parish by organizing potluck dinners two or three weeks after she arrived. She saw it as their way of getting better acquainted with her.

Soon after the arrival of the woman pastor, parishioners tended to offer their help as they assessed her needs. For instance, in a parish where the pastor was a young married woman with small children, a parishioner told me that people were "volunteering like crazy to help with the kids." The pastor herself told me that she never had to worry about child care.

A male parishioner described a variety of supportive actions on the part of parishioners:

> We have a small parish here, and of course, financially we are not able to have a custodian. We have cleaning teams made up of people that alternate taking care of the church. We have ladies that come in and make the flower arrangements for the altar. Just about anything that needs to be done has to be done on a volunteer basis. We had people come and trim the shrubs recently. I had volunteer work to build that ramp [an access to the church for the handicapped]. That was all built since Sister _____ was here with volunteer labor. A lot of times they will have cleaning bees for special occasions like Christmas or Easter, and the ladies will turn out for that. Sometimes there will be a small cleaning bee in the church cemetery.

One of the male parishioners told me that even the non-Catholic husband of a parishioner often shoveled the walk to the parish house. He added,

> There's always somebody around [to help]. Sometimes I'll come around and take the blower out. Three or four ladies count the collection on Monday morning.

Contributions of food were a regular occurrence in rural parishes. One of the women pastors told me that the parishioners brought her a lot of produce from their gardens, and the very next day, while we were sitting in the kitchen drinking coffee, a parishioner stopped by with several bags of fresh vegetables. She said that she never refuses any of this food so as not to hurt the parishioner's feelings. Instead she either gives it away, cans it, or freezes what she cannot immediately use.

Another woman pastor stated:

> They continued to be so generous with their garden foods. I don't think I was here three days when I got a big bag of corn. It just made me feel like they would want me to stay.

Another lay pastor, in describing how food often appeared almost miraculously, said, "We find food on the porch—a peach pie, tomatoes. One time we found it in the back of the car."

One of the parishioners mentioned that his pastor received many gifts from various parishioners at Christmastime. In another parish a woman pastor who had unexpected surgery told me how thrilled she was at the outpouring of flowers, etc., from the parishioners. She said that she received over one hundred get well cards from the parishioners, and so many flowers that she was afraid she wouldn't have enough space in her hospital room. Another pastor said that she also viewed her parishioners' expressions of gratitude as a form of gift to her.

Another support comes in the form of invitations to share a meal with a family in the parish, especially on the occasion of a birthday, an anniversary, or other family celebrations. One of the married lay pastors, who was beginning to feel overwhelmed by the numbers of such invitations, said,

> Sometimes it's really hard. We had three Saturdays in a row where we had to go out after Mass for these family celebra-

tions. As time goes on, you can see it happening more and more. It's great; you really feel loved, but...

A sister who lived alone in the parish house had this to say about the invitations:

> And there is support in [the parishioners] just being friendly and inviting me out to different occasions. They want me to be part of their family gatherings. The fourth of July, for instance, a whole family reunion was happening. Memorial Day, Christmas. Many people check [me] out, "Are you going to be home?" They don't want me to be here by myself and would like me to be part of their family gathering. [They] really want me to be part of the parish family. I feel real well accepted and liked.

Some of the dioceses have guidelines for lay pastors which specify that they should wear an alb on any occasion when they are expected to take their place in the sanctuary, with or without a priest. This presents a dilemma for women, because albs for Catholic priests are made for men. In two of the parishes I visited the parishioners made the alb themselves and presented it to their pastor. In another parish the members of the Women's Guild, with the help of the local Methodist minister, purchased a female alb for their pastor from a Methodist catalogue. As the pastor herself described it, "The Women's Guild, without even asking me, offered to buy me an alb, because I was wearing all those men's things that looked just terrible on me."

Two very important indicators of parishioner support—the bottom line, as it were—are attendance at Mass and weekly financial contributions. Most of the parishioners whom I interviewed stated that their parish experienced an increase in numbers at Mass and in contributions to the Sunday collection soon after their pastor arrived. Several also mentioned that fund-raising events had been successful since her arrival. In most parishes the amount of the previous Sunday's collection are published in the church bulletin, so that the parishioners are able to chart the increased giving. They could also see the evidence regarding church attendance and participation in religious education classes in the enrollment figures and in the numbers of people kneeling in the pews on Sundays.

For instance, a female parishioner in a parish where the previous pastor had been semiretired and where a young woman pastor and her husband had recently been appointed as copastors described it this way:

> We had about eighty-four or eighty-five families before [they] came, and now I think our enrollment is 111 families. It shot right up. There are a lot of kids and a lot of very young families, and more since [they] came. Our CCD[7] enrollment, our Christian youth classes have really increased. There are definitely more people at Mass now, more people at everything, and more people doing things.

A male parishioner in another parish said,

> I would think there is a little bit more [money] given since Sister came and everything stabilized. She never asks for anything personally. Within the next few months we started a building fund. We knew where the monies were going, and they weren't being wasted.... She didn't have a microwave and we gave her one. She didn't ask for one. She didn't ask for anything.

One of the women pastors attested to her parishioners' support in this way:

> They give a good [amount of] time commitment. The contributions have risen a lot. Attendance has increased dramatically. And people are affirming.... I feel a satisfaction in seeing attendance go up and seeing the income go up.

A female parishioner summed up the support in her parish in this way:

> I personally see it as an affirmation when I see people stepping forward and doing things [in the parish]. A lot of people who have been there in the pews for twenty years [seemed] like bumps on a log, and now they are beginning to do things. I think that's affirming. More and more, after Mass people want to stop and talk to her. There will be a group of people waiting to see her after Mass. I think that's good and affirming because it used to be they were all gone immediately.

The final form of parishioner support that I will mention is a verbal one, which I heard at virtually every parish I visited. It is

simply this: THEY CALL HER PASTOR. Here are some examples:
   A female parishioner, in describing her to me, simply stated,
"She is our pastor." A·nun pastor said,

> When they [the parishioners] introduce me to people, they
> always say, "This is our pastor." And they do refer to me as
> their pastor, and I know this because I have heard it from
> other people.

A married pastor explained,

> Usually they'll say, "Oh, she's our pastor," or "She's our minis-
> ter." It's usually in those terms. Some of them have gotten into
> the hang of saying pastoral administrator, but they usually will
> just say, "She's our lay pastor, or our pastor."

Each time I heard a woman explain how her parishioners
usually referred to her as their pastor, I noted that it was said
with much pride and with a smile. They all know that the title
"pastor" is reserved solely for priests, but their experience in the
parish has convinced them that in spite of that institutional constraint they are, indeed, pastors in the true sense of the word.
And like true pastors, their reason for accepting the job and for
remaining in the position, in spite of the constraints, conflicts,
and tensions, resides in their parishioners. To my question,
"What is it that keeps you going in your ministry?" the answer,
unanimous and unequivocal, was "The parishioners." Here are
two examples of their responses. The first is from a sister who
said,

> I ask myself that a lot of times. I really am very energized. A
> lot of times it is on a person-to-person level. When I see new
> life happening, and that I could be part of that happening, or
> new levels of faith happening in them, excitement about them-
> selves, excitement about their parish, more belief in them-
> selves, more self-identity, a better image of themselves and
> also as a parish—this is a real plus for me. I guess I have
> always compared it to giving birth. That gives birth to me,
> when that happens. And open-mindedness: a futuristic look,
> open to new aspects, especially when I see new leadership
> happen among them, and they start to identify, and to own.

A married lay pastor put it this way:

If it wasn't for the people, I don't think I would stay, because I would say somebody else can go be on the cutting edge for awhile, and take care of the headaches and hassles. I think what would keep me from leaving this parish is some of the relationships we've already developed with the people. And I feel like I can't leave these people like that, despite any other difficulties that might come along.

OTHER RESOURCES

In addition to the supports provided by their bishops, priests, and parishioners, two types of networks also serve as resources for the women pastors. The first can be found in the Office of Ministry which has been established in many of the dioceses throughout the country. Often this office not only provides in-service training, but staff from the diocesan office will answer questions by telephone as they arise, and will sometimes visit the parish when called on by the woman pastor. The director of this office or, in some cases, the personnel director, will also schedule periodic group meetings of lay pastors, and this group can become an important resource. One woman pastor described such a meeting:

> The other thing we do is meet monthly with the pastoral administrators, and our agenda is, "What are some of the things we are having questions and problems with?" And then we get either the vicar general[8] to come in and talk about some of these things, or address a certain topic, or get somebody from the state to talk about some legal issues. So we do get some of those questions answered through some of the meetings and speakers that we have, or people that come in and share.

As the women reported, the more important function of such meetings was the opportunity to meet and know their counterparts from other parishes in the diocese. As a result of these meetings, several of them communicate regularly by telephone. About five of the women interviewed were the only lay pastors in their dioceses, and all of them expressed their disappointment that such a resource was unavailable to them.

The second resource mentioned by many of the women I interviewed is the Institute for Pastoral Life, based in Kansas

City, Missouri, which I briefly described in chapter 1.[9] This center, established by some Catholic bishops in 1985, offers a three-year training program for parish life coordinators [their term for lay pastors] from poor rural parishes. It lasts for two weeks, and is held during the summer in Kansas City.[10] In addition to the summer training program, the Institute for Pastoral Life also publishes a newsletter that often includes articles written by lay pastors throughout the country. It also occasionally sponsors teleconferences and symposia on various aspect of lay ministry, and makes available videotapes of these meetings.

Twelve of the women I interviewed had attended the two-week institute in Kansas City for three summers, and they were very enthusiastic about their participation in this program, primarily because it gave them the opportunity to share their experiences with other women pastors throughout the country. As some of them expressed it to me, if this program provided nothing more than the acquaintance of other women pastors, it was well worth their time and effort. After spending two full weeks for three summers together, some of them developed important friendships with other women pastors throughout the country, and they continue to communicate with each other by letter or by telephone.

This chapter has shown that in some instances bishops, priests, and parishioners can provide some support for women pastors, and that several of them have also benefited from diocesan and national support networks. However, we have been looking with rose-colored glasses at the woman pastor's relationships. In order to see the entire picture we need to look beyond the supports and resources, and examine the other side of the coin, the constraints, conflicts, and tensions experienced by women in this position.

•7•

Constraints, Conflicts, and Tensions

No matter how supportive the bishop, priest, and parishioners may be, no matter how many other resources she may have, there are built-in constraints for the woman pastor that persist in spite of all of the supports available to her.[1] These institutional constraints, in turn, often lead to conflicts and tensions in her everyday life. The role of lay pastor of a priestless parish is not only a new role, but it is one that has been redefined to exclude some of the key duties of previous pastors. Assuming that parishioners and priests share the desire to keep the parish operating, we would expect cooperation, rather than conflict, to predominate. However, conflict and tension can arise from a lack of any definition regarding what constitutes "appropriate behavior" for the woman pastor. In particular, the circumstances surrounding the liturgical and sacramental functions are especially sensitive.

In fact, the role of woman pastor is fraught with ambiguity that can be a constant source of strain in her daily relationships with parishioners and priests. In order to understand the role ambiguities involved in the relationships between women pastors and their role partners, it is necessary to shed some light on the institutional constraints placed on the activities of the women in this new leadership position.

The primary source of these conflicts and tensions is, of course, on the institutional level. It is the combination of teachings, laws, policies, and practices of the Catholic church that prohibit the woman appointed to head a parish from exercising all

125

the powers of a priest-pastor. In earlier chapters I have alluded to some of these institutional constraints in the lives of the women I interviewed, but I will elaborate on the nature of these constraints in the first section of this chapter. The rest of the chapter will examine the consequences of these constraints in the daily encounters of women pastors with priests, bishops, and their parishioners; and how these women, their parishioners, and sacramental ministers think and feel about these constraints.

INSTITUTIONAL CONSTRAINTS: CHURCH TEACHINGS, LAWS, AND PRACTICES

The chief institutional constraint for the woman pastor results from a law of the church which restricts priestly ordination to males, so that even though they are doing the work of a priest-pastor in these parishes, they are not, and cannot be members of the clergy. In the final analysis, then, a woman pastor is not a priest, and her nonordained status is the bottom line that places her in a position which, in institutional church terms, carries a liability from the outset. Her position is "in the red," as it were. Continuing the financial analogy, we can say that her liabilities may be perceived as exceeding her assets, because she does not and cannot have the "proper" credentials.

If women could be ordained deacons, which present church law does not allow, then they would have the right to give homilies, to baptize, and to preside at marriages outside of Mass.[2] In one of the parishes I visited I found that this constraint was particularly painful for a woman pastor whose husband, with whom she was copastoring, was to be ordained a deacon in a few months. She was well aware that, as an ordained deacon, he would then have a higher status in the parish, and this would mark an end to their equal sharing of the position.

Because women pastors, including nuns, are officially laypersons, some of the central pastoral duties, such as the celebration of Mass, hearing confessions, baptizing, and presiding at marriages and funeral Masses are reserved for the sacramental minister, the "real" priest. On these occasions, when the woman must take a "back seat," the limitations in her new role are quite evident to her and to the parishioners.

A major bone of contention in many of the parishes I visited, is the role of the woman pastor in the Sunday liturgy. The built-in constraint results from the way her role has been circumscribed by the church. As one priest explained it:

> Obviously it's an auxiliary role simply because of the way the Catholic setup is. We've tried to create a style so that she has some appropriate prominent [role]. She greets the people, I don't. The first words that go through the mike to the folks are from her. She welcomes them and welcomes visitors, and talks about the theme for the day. Then I walk to the microphone and say the prayer of the day, and then the liturgy goes on.

These limitations follow her, even when a woman pastor travels outside her parish. One of the pastors reported the following incident. A priest who taught at the diocesan seminary invited her to give a talk there, but attempted to circumvent the issue of her preaching. As she explained it to me,

> He didn't say, "Preach." He said, "Talk about what you are doing." And I said, "When am I doing this, at the lunch?" And he said, "No, at Mass." I said, "What time in the Mass?" And he said, "Well, at the homily time." I said, "You say I'm preaching, then." "Well, no," he said, "I can't." I said, "I can't speak after the gospel without preaching, whether you want to call it preaching or addressing. I can't just get up and talk about something that is divorced from the gospel, because I have enough of a liturgical background to know that I don't believe that ought to be done." So he said, okay, he would stand up and say something. So he did. And then nobody could stand up and say Sister _____ preached at [the seminary]. Father _____ said three or four sentences first.

What "game," you might ask, was the priest in the above incident playing? Strictly speaking, laypersons are not permitted to preach at Mass immediately after the gospel has been read, which is "homily time." In order to avoid this prohibition, the presiding priest sometimes says a few words immediately after the gospel, and then invites a layperson to preach. The priest in the example above was circumventing the prohibition.

According to church law, the right to preach during Mass is conferred at the time a man is ordained a deacon, so it is an exclusive privilege of ordained deacons and priests. As we have seen, however, this law is open to interpretation, as is evident from the following argument from a sacramental minister:

> We can't have church without priests because then we aren't sacramental, and the Catholic church is a sacramental church. We would just simply be congregational without the priests. Obviously I am biased, but I think priests have a very important role in the church, and [the woman pastor] does not want to take my job away from me. She is quite happy to let me do my part and that is why we don't have a competition or a clash because she is happy to let me do my sacramental role, I am quite happy to let her fulfill her role and I don't see a problem with that. In fact, my allowing her to preach once a month, I think, says very clearly that [it] is not something I see as a threat to my priesthood.

A sacramental minister in another parish, however, felt differently about the situation. His more traditional stance dictated that he should ask permission before allowing the woman pastor to "cross the line," as it were. He said,

> My impression in all the years I have been involved in the church and parish work has been that when people see people doing things, then the question doesn't become, "Should we or shouldn't we?" It is more or less, "They are doing all this stuff, why can't they be ordained?" And a lot of women I have worked with have elicited that response from people. To me that is really important because I think there is a lot of anger tied up for a lot of women with the institutional church which gets transferred to priests, and then we sort of take it in the shorts for being part of the institution because we are priests. And yet there [are] a lot of limitations on us. As much as I would love to ask for permission for sisters to do things like baptisms or witness weddings and so forth, we don't have that permission here yet.

Phrases like "allowing her to preach" and "asking permission for" underline the institutional constraints placed on the role of woman pastor. In addition to the limitations placed on them in their liturgical and sacramental roles, two additional constraints concern title and dress.

About half of the women I visited have the title "pastoral administrators," some are called "pastoral coordinators," a few are "parish ministers," and one each has the title of "pastoral director," "parish lay administrator," and "parish life coordinator." Why is there such a variety in titles for these women who are pastoring parishes? Although they bear the responsibility of pastoring a parish community in their exercise of overall responsibility for worship, education, pastoral services, and administration of the parish, the title of pastor is restricted, by church law, to ordained priests, and at the present time no nationwide title has officially been bestowed on them; thus the title differs from diocese to diocese.

One could argue that there are very few examples of a role that has been so thoroughly monopolized by men as that of a Roman Catholic priest, who is typically called "Father," a title that explicitly excludes women. As we saw in the preceding chapter, however, parishioners, priests, and even bishops sometimes refer to these women as "pastor," and many of them receive mail from the diocesan office addressed to "pastor" or "reverend."

The significance of "naming" of their parishioners by women pastors as an important and positive attribute was discussed in chapter 3. Similarly, "naming" by title is significant for those so named with regard to role definition. Thus, the role ambiguity experienced by these women is both reflected and partly determined by the confusion in "naming" them.

The various titles for lay pastors were bothersome to many of the people I interviewed. For instance, one lay pastor, expressing dissatisfaction with the title, said,

> This is the typical institutional church [saying], "We can't call these people 'pastor'." Well, what are we? If a banana's a banana, you call it a banana. Why do they have to come up with pastoral administrator, parish director, pastoral agent? What are we doing? We're doing the ministry of pastor, right? Then call us that and simplify it.

In regard to the question of dress, the clerical collar can be worn by women clergy in Protestant denominations, but it cannot be worn by the women pastors in this study because it symbolizes the clerical state. Unlike their Protestant counterparts, Catholic women pastors are also prohibited from wearing a chasuble or a stole. The chasuble is a sleeveless outer vestment worn by the officiating priest during Mass, and the stole is a vestment consisting of a long cloth band worn traditionally around the neck, like a scarf hanging down in front, by bishops and priests, and over the left shoulder by deacons.

However, there were two or three dioceses I visited where the guidelines require that pastoral administrators wear an alb at all ceremonial functions. The alb, a full-length white linen vestment with long sleeves gathered at the waist with a cincture, and worn during Mass by priests under the chasuble, was described in the previous chapter. As one of the lay pastors explained to me, the diocese views the alb as the dress of the layperson, and the stole, described above, designates ordination. In fact, I was told that there are some parishes where the eucharistic ministers [the parishioners who help to distribute Communion] also wear some sort of vestment. Therefore, if the altar servers, the priest, and the eucharistic ministers are all wearing vestments, then the woman pastor would look "out of place" on the altar without an alb.

In four of the twenty parishes I visited, the women pastors regularly wore an alb while on the altar during liturgical ceremonies. Many of those who wore lay clothes on these occasions, married women and nuns alike, argued vehemently against ever accepting any of the "clerical trappings," like a collar, chasuble, stole, or even an alb, because they identify very strongly with the laity, as the following statement from a married woman pastor illustrates:

> I dress in liturgical colors. In other words, if I am preaching during Advent, I wear a purple dress. My whole message to everyone in this parish is that I am a layperson and they are lay people. We had a group of people here who wanted me to wear an alb, and I said that just separates me from the people. I am just not into clerical dress.

Some of the nun pastors were equally vehement, for example, one of them explained:

> Even in the first pamphlet they gave us on what a pastoral administrator is supposed to be, they said that for the Communion services or the Sunday liturgies we were supposed to

wear an alb. But the albs that were here were extremely long. I thought I wasn't going to spend that much money for that. My whole thinking was: "I am part of the people; we are the church." So there was no need to be dressing any special way because I am one of them. I don't want to be different. I don't want to pull myself away from them; I want to be with them.

Another woman pastor who wore only lay clothes in her parish said that perhaps if she went to another parish, she might wear something symbolic. However, she was undecided about wearing liturgical garb, and she explained,

I go back and forth because, on the one hand, there is something about having them say, as they do to me, "You're one of us," in looking like that. There is something about that that is very precious and I don't want that to be erased because I am wearing liturgical garb. On the other hand, I have done some reading and heard some people talk about the importance of the presider's role and the liturgical vestment, and I do key into that, too. So I don't know. I'm back and forth on that.

Do women who are members of religious communities, who have the title "Sister," and who may wear clothing symbolic of their religious state, experience an easier acceptance by the parishioners than married women or single women who are not nuns?

This question, of course, is difficult to answer for a number of reasons. First of all, I found that the title "Sister" does not lessen the resistance of some parishioners who are distrustful of outsiders in general. For instance, in a rural parish where the nun pastor was from a large city, the sacramental minister said,

I believe when a priest walks into a parish, they are immediately accepted. It's just a strong tradition and no questions are asked. And there's kind of a sense of, "We know who he is because he's wearing a Roman collar." But I would say when [the nun pastor] arrived here, because she was a woman, and because she was [from a large city], there was a lot of skepticism, and people were going to kind of step back and wait and see who this newfangled minister was in town. So she didn't get the immediate reception that I think a priest would.

On the other hand, a woman parishioner who described herself to me as a conservative Catholic had this to say:

The shock was very hard for people to handle, that it was just done so fast. And certainly from my point of view, I was happy we were getting a sister rather than a "layperson." I know nuns are officially "lay," but nonetheless it's a committed, dedicated religious life. That distinction is very important to me personally, so I've always felt we were very lucky to have a nun heading the parish.

Since Vatican II most nuns have adopted the clothing of the laity, so they no longer "stand out in a crowd" as do priests wearing clerical collars. In fact, in only one of the eleven parishes run by nuns did I see a woman pastor wear anything that resembles a religious habit. In this case she wore lay clothes most of the time, but she donned a "modified habit," consisting of a blue street-length dress with a small blue veil on her head for Sunday services. Several of the woman pastors, nuns and married women alike, wore a small cross during the Sunday liturgies. In fact, the cross worn by the woman pastor in two of the parishes I visited was given to her by the parishioners.

CONFLICTS AND TENSIONS IN DAILY ENCOUNTERS

As might be expected, bishops, priests, parishioners, and women pastors did not always agree about the constraints of the institutional church. Some held more traditional positions, and some less so. These differences, in turn, often caused conflicts in daily encounters, and increased the tension as they attempted to work together in the parish.

These kinds of encounters, critical to the woman's success as a pastor, could never be adequately understood by analyzing responses to a written survey. They can, however, be examined by interviews with the principal informants and by observations in natural settings. Because an understanding of both the supports and constraints involved in the everyday activities of women pastors was my chief goal in undertaking this project, my research design included both depth interviewing and participant observation.[3] Another source of knowledge about these everyday encounters, of course, would be autobiographical accounts of the principal informants. To this end I have been and continue to encourage women pastors to keep a journal and eventually write of their experiences in order to expand our understanding of this phenomenon.

Woman Pastor and Priest

In looking at the consequences of institutional constraints on the role of a woman pastor in everyday encounters, I will focus first on the relationship between her and the priest assigned as the sacramental minister. This is a sensitive relationship, because the pastor must depend on him to perform ritual activities central to the pastoral role. The moments of his interventions are, therefore, illustrative of the restrictions on her power in the parish.

Typically, the sacramental minister travels from his own parish on the weekend to preside at the Mass, and often he would leave immediately afterward. The role of the pastor during the Sunday Mass was more restricted in some parishes than others. As a male parishioner described it:

> There are several priests that come here who will not allow her on the altar with them, and that's a bone of contention with the parishioners, because she is our pastoral director. She is our spiritual leader at this point, the person we go to when we need advice and help and leadership. I feel uncomfortable with the fact that she cannot be part of the service.

A female parishioner in the same parish said,

> Everybody mentions that we would like to see her be more a part of the Mass. That seems to be a constant topic of conversation, I would say especially from the women. But also some of the men feel like [her] role in this whole thing is very spiritual, and sometimes she gets lost in the administrative end.

In general, much of the conflict between pastor and sacramental minister was related to different expectations about how this new role was to be acted out in the parish. One of the women pastors said:

> For me, the constraints continue to be around the expectations of the ordained ministers. Their expectations and my expectations are really different, and their perception of what we are working toward does not always jibe. Sometimes it does intellectually, but I don't find the practices always working in the

same direction. I think the various expectations, and not being able to come to some "clicking" on those, continues to cause tension that is hard periodically, especially with certain things in the ministry that make it obvious. That is a constraint for me.

Several of the women I interviewed expressed their disappointment at not being encouraged to preach by the sacramental minister. One of the priests explained why he did not encourage the woman pastor to preach during the Sunday Mass. He said,

> For me the presider is to be the homilist. So I do not invite her to homilize as frequently, for example, as my predecessor did. I am more of a stickler on some liturgical things. One of the things I believe is that if I am presiding at the eucharist, then normally I should be the one who gives the homily. Now I am not a stickler in the sense that I would be hung up on it, and if she ever came and said, "I would really like to give some words on this at this Mass," I would say, "Great, go ahead."

Even the practice of a woman pastor presenting a summary of a priest's homily can be resisted by priests who object to a woman's presence in the sanctuary. The woman pastor in a Mexican-American parish said that among the priests who served her parish, there was only one who could speak Spanish, and he came only occasionally during the summer. She said,

> The others don't know Spanish, so after they finish the homily in English, I give the summary in Spanish. One [priest] told me it wasn't necessary, and I said it is necessary because there are some people who don't understand English.

Because he often serves two or more parishes, the role of the sacramental minister has its limitations as well. One of the women pastors said,

> I think we want to be very sensitive to the priests so they don't feel like they are somebody who just comes in here because we have to have this warm body, that they are valued, too, that they have something to give to our community. So that takes some balancing to work that out.

The "balancing" can be difficult. This is especially true in the typical situation where only one sacramental minister has been assigned to the parish. In these cases, the two must work out any conflicts between them, since there are no alternatives.

By contrast, a woman pastor in a diocese critically short of priests had no single priest assigned to her parish. Instead, the bishop gave her the task of locating the priests for the sacramental liturgies in her parish. She had this to say:

I do have the choice of who comes for Mass. I make the arrangements; nobody else makes them for me. If I have somebody who is undercutting me, he doesn't come back. I had that happen my first three months here and he didn't come back. If somebody told me that this person was going to be my sacramental minister, I would fight that tooth and nail. I want to choose that. I will take the hassle of having to find priests any day over having somebody imposed on me.

Sometimes the priests who are substituting for the sacramental minister during his vacation have difficulties accepting the woman pastor as leader of the parish. A nun pastor described just such a situation.

He didn't want me sitting next to him [on the altar] to begin with. I said, "This is what we do here." And I sat next to him. But he never looked at me. I was a nonperson. And those are the kinds of things where my frustration hits.

Some of the women resolve the conflict about their role with regard to the sacraments by taking a more active stance. Several of them reported having heard confessions informally, although they cannot validly give absolution. A married woman pastor explained:

I have found when people are sick that they are really confessing a lot of the time. I had one person say to me, "I have told you, and God is listening, and that's enough." I agreed.

A nun pastor described her response when parishioners came to her for confessions. She said,

We were having a penitential service[4] and this person came to me and said, "Sister, could I talk with you?" I told him, "Yes, you can." So right there he started to talk, pouring out the whole thing. When he finished I told him, "Why don't you go now to Father and he will bless you." He said, "Do you think I am going to repeat what I told you to that man?" I said, "He is representing Jesus. He is only going to confirm the blessing." He said, "No, I am not going to. Do you think my sins are forgiven?" I said, "Of course your sins are forgiven. If you want to go, go, and if not, don't go." When they ask me if they need the priest for confession I tell them no, they don't.

Only two women pastors reported that they presided alone at baptisms. One of them explained,

One time when we had baptisms, the priest didn't come, so we had a Communion service and I baptized the baby. Later on the young mother told me, "Sister, I'm so glad you did it."

Although nonordained persons are not permitted to perform the sacrament of the anointing of the sick [often referred to as one of the "last sacraments"], it is often difficult to find a priest to officiate at the critical moment, and if they are not able to find a priest, some of the women pastors perform the rite themselves. In one parish the woman pastor told how she solved a dilemma for a dying woman who was in dreadful pain, but who, as her husband described it, was "holding on" for the sacrament of the anointing of the sick. After trying unsuccessfully to locate a priest, the woman pastor arrived at the hospital room, leaned down to speak into the ear of the dying woman, and, as she reported it:

I made sure she knew who I was and what I was doing, and I said we would go through the whole rite just as if she had a priest. Her husband said that was what she wanted, and I wasn't gone ten minutes when she let go. And she was in terrible pain.

Although the woman pastor is also responsible for the preparations for the sacrament of confirmation, she does not expect to preside because this is typically the bishop's responsibility. However, even on these occasions there are tensions with the priest who is also present on the altar. A woman pastor described such a scene thus:

So the bishop comes and they do their little thing. In the end Father is thanking everybody who helped, the musicians and everybody who helped. He didn't say my name. This was to the whole congregation. I could have just throttled him.

Another aspect of the conflicts between the woman pastor and the sacramental minister is that he is often late, or fails to show up for the Sunday Mass at her parish. When the priest knows that he will consistently be late because of his schedule in other parishes, and it is impossible to change Mass schedules in the parishes, he may even work out a compromise with the woman pastor where she would "start" the Mass by presiding at the first part of the service consisting of the opening prayers and the liturgy of the word [scripture readings and homily]. As as soon as he arrived, he would "take over," because only a priest can preside for the second part, the liturgy of the eucharist [offertory, consecration, and Communion]. One sacramental minister described such a situation:

> Many times because of the schedule, they [the woman pastor and her congregation] would start and I would come in after the start. Many times I would leave before Communion would start because I would have another Mass to go to.

A similar incident was reported by a woman pastor who said,

> He was a prison chaplain and he got locked up...during a breakout, and he couldn't make Mass. We knew this was going to happen someday. It was on a Saturday and I had two hundred children in church. It was the kickoff Mass for the religious education program. I waited twenty minutes and the children became restless, so we started Mass without him. I figured he would get there sometime and if not, I would do a dry Mass,[5] that's all. And I explained this to the children. I was in the middle of the homily when he came racing down the aisle, and then afterwards he said, "I bet she was going to put on the vestments." And all the kids giggled.

Celebrating Mass as a "team" can be an awkward situation, involving logistics that are both liturgically questionable and perhaps incomprehensible to the congregation. I should hasten to say that the above situations were reported to occur only rarely.

What was reported more frequently to me, however, was a real "no show" on the part of the priest, either because he misinterpreted the schedule, or because he was sick or was called out of town unexpectedly. In these cases, the woman pastor would announce the priest's absence to the congregation and explain that she would be presiding at a word and Communion service.

I was an observer in such a situation, and I noted that prior to the beginning of the service, the woman pastor asked if there were any visitors from out of town in the congregation. After a few people identified themselves as such, she then very carefully described a word and Communion service. After that she explained to those gathered in the church that the service to be performed, although strictly speaking would fulfill their Sunday obligation, it would not be a Mass, and she invited those who wanted to leave in order to attend Mass elsewhere to do so. No one left the church on that occasion, and from what I heard in the parishes I visited, only rarely did people ever leave; in most instances the entire congregation remained to participate in the word and Communion service.

When the priest's absence was unexpected, there is always the danger that there may not be an ample supply of consecrated hosts available. Such was the case in a situation described by a woman pastor:

> We had four hosts for 136 people. I turned and there were all these people and I had four hosts. They saw my face and they all looked and I said, "Let's pray for the multiplication of the loaves here." So we broke and broke and broke, and I told the people, "This is where I feel my poverty of the nonordained because there is a bowl of [unconsecrated] hosts in the sacristy." So I held up Jesus between my fingers and said, "Trust me, this is the Lamb of God." And everybody got a little piece.

As I explained in an earlier chapter, there are some parishes where the priest comes for Mass only twice a month, and in one or two parishes he appears only once a month. In these parishes the woman pastors regularly preside at word and Communion services on the weekend. A male parishioner reported that one of their former priests expressed his reservations about the word and Communion services at a parish meeting. As the parishioner described it,

> He was very threatened by the fact that we had women doing these services. Someone [a parishioner] said, "Well, Father, after people start seeing what's going on at the Communion services you may not have as many at your Mass." And it was almost as if somebody dropped a bomb.

The same parishioner continued with a reflection on the collaborative stance of the women who were presiding at these services:

It's ministry not by a person on a pedestal. It is out there at the level of the people, and the sisters are doing it and are not putting themselves on a pedestal. Sometimes priests tend to do that. So that was a power situation.

As we saw in chapter 4, where the collaborative leadership style of woman pastors was discussed, there is often a stark contrast between the extent of parishioner participation in parish activities before and after her arrival. However, there are some situations where the sacramental minister is not in agreement with this new direction. One of the women pastors complained about this when she said,

I really don't think I am free to pursue what I believe needs to be done in order to prepare the people. And I don't think that the priest I am working with has the same vision of empowerment of lay people. He can say all the right words, but at the gut level he doesn't allow it to happen.

At the heart of the tensions involved in the encounters between woman pastor and sacramental minister is the question of power. As a priest-pastor in his own parish he traditionally had [and may still have] virtually unlimited power. And his travels to her parish are for the specific purpose of fulfilling functions that are beyond the limits of her authority. He has a "piece of the pie," so to speak, in her parish. What does this look like from the priest's vantage point? One of the sacramental ministers explained,

I find among the priests, as a whole, just a general acceptance of them [woman pastors] and the situation. Everyone knows it is going to happen. Now there is a lot of comparison [of woman pastors] that happens, and a lot of it has to do with—and this is priest talk—"She'd really want to be a priest." And so if there is some sense that they are intruding in our space, then I think that causes tension. There was a situation in this deanery that was difficult because the priest felt his space was being [intruded]; he was being told what to do [by the woman pastor] in an inappropriate manner.

On the other hand, every time the sacramental minister arrives at her parish to fulfill his sacramental functions, in a sense he is invading the woman pastor's "turf," because she has overall responsibility for the parish. And since he is accustomed to being the authority figure, it may be very difficult for him not to revert back to "putting himself on a pedestal," expecting the people to come to him, and "taking over."

Some of the priests did take over in the sense of limiting the woman pastor's opportunities for preaching, for example. But not one of the sacramental ministers was seen as trying to move her out of her position and take it over himself. Most of the priests were overburdened, in fact some were already suffering from burnout, and had neither the time nor the energy to take on another parish.

Pastor and Parishioners

One of the first obstacles the woman pastor meets on her arrival is a reluctance on the part of the parishioners to accept her as their leader. One of the female parishioners attributed this reluctance to the the parishioners' attitudes regarding the traditional authority of the priest. She said,

> Her predecessor had Divine Rule because he was a priest, and what he said was readily accepted as God's law. I think what Sister says isn't quite accepted, but she's willing to discuss it with the parishioners, to make the parishioners part of as many decisions as she possibly can.

Parishioners' views regarding priestly power was also mentioned by a married woman pastor when she recounted her confrontation with the parish finance council. She said,

> We were doing the budget. I said I really needed a secretary. I said I have a typewriter and phone at home, but I don't have the time when I'm home, and I really felt a need for a secretary, probably eight hours a week. I approached the finance council about it, and they said they would talk to the parish council. So they talked to the parish council, and the parish council bounced it back to the finance council. I went to the finance council meeting and said, "Hey, guys, if somebody with a Roman collar said, 'I want a secretary,' you would say, 'Yes, Father.' I am telling you we are having a secretary." And that was the end of it.

Another married woman pastor, who said that some of her parishioners were constantly asking the sacramental minister to perform various functions for them, decried the fact that she needed to clarify publicly again and again precisely what the duties of the sacramental minister were. She said, "That's one of the things I don't think we will ever get over as long as we don't wear the Roman collar."

Some of the conflict between a woman pastor and her parishioners revolves around her role as presider at word and Communion services. Older and more conservative Catholics are especially bothered by the sight of a woman leading the services at the altar. A male parishioner explained,

> The first three months were very hard on [her], and were hard on a lot of us, too, because we were not well prepared. There was a fair amount of resistance, and quite a bit of initial change, especially going from Mass to Communion service, and some of these kinds of things. The parish suffered maybe a little bit in those few months, and I know [she] suffered a lot.

One of the female parishioners compared her change of attitude with that of others in the parish when she said,

> It really doesn't bother me as much as I thought it was going to. The sisters have done such a good job with the eucharistic service, I am not missing the consecration part of the Mass, and we have everything else. So it really hasn't bothered me. Some people it has; it depends on who you are going to talk to. There are going to be a few who don't accept the fact that sisters can do it. But I think they are effective, and it doesn't bother me that I don't go to Mass, because they do such a good job with their services. And we've had better sermons from them than we have had from some of the priests we've had.

The church's position regarding the right of a layperson to preach the homily during Mass, for instance, inspires many different interpretations, and thus creates some controversies. A woman pastor described such a conflict situation in her parish.

> Last year there was an uprising because I was doing the homily, and there was an article in the [diocesan newspaper] that stated that women shouldn't be doing the homilies. And before you knew it, there was this whole ferment going on in

the parish. I knew who the people were, and they had given me a problem ever since I came here. They don't like the changes and would like to see me out. So I said to [the sacramental minister], "I think the only way to handle this is to confront it face on."

She explained how the priest took the occasion to raise the issue while she was on vacation:

He did it during the homily. He kind of used the scriptures of the day and then went into [explaining] we're all family and how we support one another. Then he went into the fact that there had been some rumblings about my doing the homily, and he said how he suggested it right from the very beginning, and how the bishop knew about it, and how I had given homilies that are much better than some of the priests that he knows. I mean he just laid it on the line. That was very important.

In this instance, the priest took the responsibility for authorizing her to preach during Mass, and added further legitimacy to her actions by arguing that the bishop was aware of the situation.

PERSONAL CONCERNS AND TENSIONS

In the previous chapter we concentrated on the bright side of the coin, the supports and resources available to women pastors, but, as we have seen, this chapter looks at the flip side. In order to have a more complete understanding of that "dark side" of the role of a woman pastor we will now look at those personal concerns and tensions that are in part a consequence of the institutional constraints and the conflicts she experiences in her relationships between herself and the other key individuals, that is, the parishioners, priests, and bishop. The question we are raising here is, "What do these key individuals think about the limitations of this new role, and what are their feelings about it?"

One of the priests whom I interviewed spoke about the "whole liturgical tension of what their [the women pastors'] role really is." For example, he cited baptisms that are done during Mass, and asked what is appropriate for women pastors to do. As he said,

We are really trying to give them everything that they can do that is appropriate, or maybe even stretching the appropriateness canonically. So they [women] lead the community in the renewal of baptismal promises and do the giving of the candle and the garment, and basically we [priests] do the anointing and the pouring of water.

A nun pastor expressed very strong feelings about her lack of credentials when she said,

This is the first time in any ministry I have been in where I have not had the credentials to do what I am asked to do. When I taught, I was certified to teach, and when I worked in the retreat apostolate I was certified as a spiritual director. But now we are asked by [the bishop] to pastor these parishes and to be the spiritual person to lead them, and we can only do so much, and then we have to put the skids on. We can't give absolution, though we hear confessions all the time down in the parlor. We can't anoint when we go to the hospital, though we bless them. They ask, "Is this going to be okay now, Sister?" I say, "Yes, it is. I am sure God has forgiven you. Father will be in to give you the blessing of the church."

Another nun pastor used the analogy of trying to dig a hole without tools. She said,

The most difficult moments were helping persons get ready for the sacraments and not being able to celebrate the sacraments with them. The image that comes to my mind is: you give someone a job...for instance, "You need to dig this hole here, but I tie your hands, so do it." Or, "The tools are there, but you cannot touch them." I really think that deep down I am called to minister. That is why sometimes it makes me feel so bad that they give me a job and then they tie my hands up.

On the other hand, how do sacramental ministers feel about their role, particularly those who minister in two or more parishes? A young priest who was reflecting on his role as sacramental minister to three parishes said that he felt he was becoming a sort of "sacramental parachuting priest," and this discouraged him. Another sacramental minister said that the woman pastor did all of the preparations for the sacraments in the parish, and his role, as he described it, was to "come swooping in from heaven and lay on the appropriate magic." A third sacramental minister who had a full-time job teaching at the local seminary, and who did not have his own parish, expressed his reservations in this way:

> I have on occasion found it very difficult to come and do the sacramental thing, and then leave. We were joking in the diocese once that I was the sacramental stud. I'd just go and do my thing, and that's it. I don't think that that can work, and so that's a real concern I have about this whole direction.

In this instance the priest was expressing a lack of connectedness, or anomie, as sociologists call it. Although in most cases the sacramental minister scarcely knew the parishioners, he had to be called in to perform their baptisms, marriages, and the final anointings at their deaths. The women pastors who are responsible for preparing their parishioners for these occasions reported that the greatest point of tension is here, at the moment when they must place themselves "in the back of the church," as it were, and let the "real priest" take over. A nun pastor said:

> I would like to get more involved in the sacraments because I do the preparations for baptism and I'm not able to do anything in the actual baptism. The sick—we have a little boy here who is nine years old who is dying of leukemia, and I spent literally my first two years here in and out with the family, hours and hours. And then when it comes to the funeral, well I did the homily for that, so I did feel that I was part of it. But very often I almost feel as though I am on the outskirts of it, and I mind that.

She continued,

> I don't even like to think about it too much because I get feeling a little like, "This is really dumb." I try not to think about it too much. Like the sacrament of reconciliation [confession], for instance, I prepare those kids for the sacrament. One of the kids came up to me one day and said, "Why can't I go to you for confession? I'd rather go to you." And I know some of the couples, too, they really want me to be there and want to make sure I am going to be at the wedding or reception. I guess they know very well that I can't do much more. Deep down I wish it would change.

She summed it up by saying that she felt "kind of on the fringe" when it comes to the sacraments. Terms like "on the outskirts," "on the fringe," and "feeling like a nonperson," kept emerging when the woman pastors discussed their role in the sacraments.

A married woman pastor who had talked about it with her priest, reported,

> He tells me that part of my frustrations is that I am doing all this work and I can't actually do the sacrament. And I told him, "No, it's there. I realize it and know I can't do it, but it's a loneliness or an emptiness I can live with because I know right now I can't do anything about it."

The same woman talked about feeling like a nonperson because she was "not in the picture":

> You know, afterwards they take pictures of the baptism group with Father. And I'm not in the picture.

One of the women pastors explained how she felt when the priest she located for the anointing of the sick was someone who did not know the family.

> If it's a priest who knows them, I feel a little bit more comfortable. If it is [a situation where I] call the chancery and just a hot body with a Roman collar shows up, it really hurts. And I think it hurts more so because of the family who may be standing around the bed, knowing that this stranger is going to say some prayers for somebody they love very dearly. And, if it is somebody who is that kind of person, they normally do not ask me to participate, and I think it hurts the families more than it hurts me.

The parishioners, who observed the subservient role of the woman pastors on these occasions, also expressed their disappointment. A female parishioner, for example, said,

> I don't think that it's fair to [the lay pastor]. I can't think of a comparison, but it just doesn't seem like [lay pastors] should have all the work and not reap the final benefit. To me it's the most gratifying to actually perform the marriage and to actually do the baptism. That's where the real gratification comes in, so it is like they are doing all the work and they don't get to sit down and reap the rewards.

The parishioner quoted above stopped me the day after our interview to tell me that she had finally thought of a comparison

regarding the sacramental limitations of lay pastors. She presented the situation where someone performs all of the preparations
for a dinner, and then must leave the room when the guests
arrive and let someone else take over, thus forgoing the gratifica-
tions of eating the food and enjoying the company of the guests.

A parishioner in another parish who served as the organist
and choir director said,

> I resent it more and more because [the woman pastor] does
> such a beautiful job. She has done all the footwork. She's done
> everything. I just feel so frustrated for her because I just know
> how I would feel if I prepared all the music, did all the plan-
> ning, practiced [with] the folks, and somebody else came in
> and played the organ and directed, and I sat on the side and
> watched the whole thing happen.

Some of the priests were sensitive to the pain experienced
by woman pastors over the inequity of the sacramental situation.
A woman pastor described how a priest explained it to the congregation from the pulpit:

> At a wedding [the sacramental minister] said, "I think you all
> need to know that Sister _____ is the one who has walked
> with this couple all these months, and in some way it hurts—
> when the big day comes, she steps aside."

There is no doubt that the central concern and the point of
greatest tension for women pastors is that they cannot totally minister to their parishioners. Using the analogy of the shepherd, they
can watch over their flock, but they must call on someone else to
feed them. And it is this incompleteness—or emptiness, as one of
the women pastors put it—that is at the heart of their tensions.

But their limited empowerment is not the only issue that
causes strain. Finances are also a concern for all of the women
pastors. As we saw earlier, the compensation they receive is
minimal, at best. One might argue that nuns are accustomed to
receiving low wages, and they have a vow of poverty, so the
salary should be sufficient for them. On the contrary, most of the
sisters I spoke with were very concerned about their compensation because such a large percentage of the members of their
religious communities were elderly, and needed their financial
support. One of the nun pastors said,

It would be hard for me to ask for a better compensation, and yet I do support that, and I do get my word in because every one of us who is a working religious in our community supports two sisters who are retired. That's the state of every congregation.

What the nuns told me was that their salaries as pastoral administrators were much lower than what they could earn as teachers in a public school system, for instance. Nonetheless, their religious communities were willing to allow them to work for the lower compensation in a parish for a time, because their work in the parish was defined by the sisters as dedicated service to the church. However, the burden of supporting the retired sisters would force the community eventually to ask the women pastors to leave their present positions, unless their compensation could be increased.

The lay pastors, married and single, likewise suffer from the financial constraints of a low salary. Although all of the husbands are working full-time or are drawing retirement pensions, the married pastors have families to support, as do the nuns, who have the responsibility of supporting their religious community. An additional concern of some of the women pastors whom I interviewed was that they were working with overdue contracts; in fact, one of them was still operating without a written contract.

In general, finances are a major problem in poor parishes, and this is the case for the vast majority of the parishes I visited. The Sunday collection, for instance, is usually insufficient to cover any renovation expenses for the parish buildings. Fundraising events like annual bazaars and quilting sales are a necessity in most of these parishes. In a parish with a high rate of unemployment a nun pastor told me that she obtained some much needed funds by speaking about the pressing needs of her parish at all of the Masses one weekend at a wealthy parish in her diocese. Although she did not enjoy her "begging expedition," she felt she had no other alternative, and it enabled the parish to pay its bills.

Another cost for some of them is travel time. Women pastors who live in isolated areas, and who are in charge of more than one parish, share a deep concern about the time and energy they must expend traveling from parish to parish. As I accompanied them on their travels, I realized that an inordinate amount of their time was spent in the car. One of the nuns who was copastoring with a member of her religious community calculated that they put in about two thousand miles a month traveling from parish to parish. She said,

> We get very drained because we have a hard time getting the time we need for ourselves, with that kind of mileage. When we talk about a day off, we are talking about not a day off, but about doing all of the house-oriented kinds of things that have to get done, as any working person has to experience.

As I mentioned earlier, another concern for some of the women pastors is their living situation. The five women who live alone in their parish houses said that they did not mind living alone because they were so busy throughout the day, and gone so much, that they appreciated the quiet and space when they came home. Ideally, though, they would like to have someone living with them to share their meals, their prayers, and their daily joys and sorrows. In addition, two of the married women living at their own homes with their families had to create an office in the home because the parish, which had only been in existence for a short time, owned neither a church building nor a pastor's office. These were parishes mentioned earlier that rented space from a local Protestant church for Sunday services. Both of the women pastors were very anxious to move the parish office out of their homes, because it occupied space needed by the family.

This completes our glimpse of the personal concerns and tensions surrounding the role of the woman pastor. This chapter examined the conflicts and tensions engendered by church teachings, laws, and practices that serve to cloud the role of the woman pastor in varying degrees of ambiguity and uncertainty. These conflicts and personal tensions are present in their interactions with priests and parishioners because women pastors are reminded on a daily basis that as laity—and especially as women—they are not fully pastors.

That these women pastors are on the "frontline," so to speak, in a movement toward an altering of the limited image of the "good woman," may be of little solace to them in their day-to-day experiences. But the significance of what they are doing in these parishes must not be underestimated. It is these issues that I will address in the next chapter on the "Woman Question."

•8•

Gender and the Pastoral Role

The idea of a woman pastor is so incongruous for many Catholics that they can hardly imagine it. It is incompatible with their only image of a Catholic pastor: a priest, an ordained male, the dominant figure in the parish, whose parishioners traditionally both revere and obey him. A woman in charge of a parish does not look like a pastor, she does not sound like a pastor, and she does not act like most previous pastors.

How, then, do people react to a person in a new position like this, who is not of the "appropriate" gender? And how do women in this new position meet the challenges to an effective performance of their responsibilities?

These two major parts of the "woman question" are not unique to women pastors. They can be applied, in fact, to all women who are moving into occupations that were formerly reserved solely for males. How can this be so? It could be argued that most women in male-dominated jobs have challenges, but at least they have the law on their side. That is, there are no laws on the books that exclude women from jobs that were formerly male-dominated positions such as senators, Supreme Court justices, governors, mayors, military officers, corporate executive officers, construction supervisors, and university presidents. Women in these positions may not have an easy time of it, but they have no *de jure* constraints, as do the women pastors.

The *de jure* constraint, which prohibits women from ordination, still exists and is well known to all, clergy and laity alike.

Therefore, women in charge of parishes are aware of the constraints placed on them because of their gender. In fact, they were cognizant of their limited empowerment well before they arrived at the parish. Because they share their status as laity with their parishioners, they bring a different perspective to their ministry. As we saw in chapters 3 through 5, her experience as a layperson enables her to exercise collaborative, rather than hierarchical, leadership. Her experience as a laywoman is also the impetus for her attempts at restructuring her parish and for her efforts to forge a bond with her parishioners.

A nun pastor remarked that laity have been treated "as peasants" in the church, and she shares that aspect of her history as a Catholic with them. On the other hand, women as mothers have an exalted position in the Catholic church, as is evident in the devotion to the Blessed Virgin Mary over many centuries. But women in that honored position do not exercise any power beyond the confines of their homes; in fact, relegating women to the private sphere of the home reinforces their low status in the public sphere of the "real world." Thus laywomen belong on the lowest rung of the "peasantry" in the church, and, as in a caste system, their low status in the church was determined at birth and is presumably lifelong.

It is no wonder then, that the first few women appointed to head parishes became celebrities almost overnight. A few of them have been on television talk shows, and one of them who was featured in a special report on national television told me that the television crew spent a week doing the filming and interviewing in her parish. One of the women pastors showed me a large album filled with newspaper articles, pictures, and letters, and she described her reactions in this way:

> It was in the diocesan paper, the local paper, and the [metropolitan area] paper. All of a sudden I was a celebrity. It was unnerving in some ways because I began getting all of these cards and letters of congratulations. Of course, what I loved was that many of them were from women.

Women who are the "firsts" to move into positions previously held by men in secular institutions and organizations also experience the "instant celebrity" syndrome. However, unlike their counterparts heading Catholic parishes, they have no *de jure* obstacles. Nonetheless, they often find that there are a number of *de facto* constraints once they appear on the scene at their new job locations. And, in fact, these constraints may be more difficult to deal with, because they are often unwritten, almost always unexpected, and seldom acknowledged by the people with whom they are working.[1]

In the last analysis, what all women in formerly male-only occupations have in common is that some of the people with whom they must interact on their jobs may not welcome them. Such persons may, in fact, deter them in their daily encounters, primarily because of ingrained and long-held biases regarding a "woman's place" and limited capabilities, which lead to an uncomfortable clash of expectations with realities in these situations.[2]

In this chapter, as we focus on the woman question, we examine three of its components in the daily lives of woman pastors: patriarchy, gender discrimination, and progress toward nonsexist attitudes and actions.

PATRIARCHY AND GENDER INEQUALITY

The Catholic church as an institution is the personification of a hierarchical system based on patriarchy, where men who are considered superior hold all the positions of power. A belief in patriarchy guarantees a dominant position for males because the primacy of their authority is unquestioned. The use of terms like "your eminence" and "your excellency" reserved for cardinals and bishops, all of whom are men, is a case in point.

I found that the belief that men should rule was played out in numerous ways in the everyday lives of women pastors. It was particularly evident in the way some of the sacramental ministers related to them. As a nun pastor described it,

> At the beginning I was told I couldn't preach. He [the sacramental minister] talked about it and told me what I could do and what I couldn't do. He is a very dominating person. He's a good person and he would like to think that he is very supportive of me in leadership roles. But on the other hand, if I were to say something about "my parish," which I have, but I don't do it anymore; I never meant it as mine. But when I

would say, "out at my parish," he would say, "It's 'our.'" So I got used to that.

The same woman explained that this priest made it clear to her that he wanted to do things "his way," so she had to be tactful about making any suggestions or recommendations to him. As she described it:

> To put it most simply, I feel tired if I have to work at being diplomatic with [him], and make a suggestion and make it sound like he made it in order to make it work out right. And sometimes that wearies me.

A similar situation can emerge in the relationships between women pastors and male parishioners. A young married woman told of the conflict she had with a very domineering male parishioner, a leader of the parish, who was a member of the parish council. She said,

> I think the guy has a real problem with women in authority, no matter what. And as long as I would kiss up to him and let him have the upper hand, it was okay. One day I didn't do that, and he just blew up.

A middle-aged woman pastor encountered the same difficulty. She stated,

> There were people who had a very difficult time accepting a woman. It is an Hispanic parish, and we do have the macho Mexican there. I still am fighting with a couple of people where I have had to come down very authoritarian a couple of times, and I don't like to do that. That's not my style, but the only way I can get my point across sometimes is to say, "I'm the boss; you do it my way."

A similar statement came from a woman pastor in a predominantly white parish:

> Probably the main problem I had was being a female in a leadership role in a mining town that's very macho. I was very cautious in the demands that were made in the parish for the first year.

Likewise, a nun pastor described what ensued immediately after she stood up to a male parishioner at a parish council meeting.

Four of them [parish council members] stayed with me an hour after that, supporting me basically, because they said, "He had done this before; he's always ruled the roost." He had done it with the priests as well. So I didn't know what was going to happen. I certainly didn't want to cause a major eruption, but I wasn't going to let this man rule me for the whole time I was here. And the whole first year had been a real struggle with him. I tried to be gentle with him, but firm, listen to him, but he was totally disrespectful. He had no respect for me. It was really a woman issue. He is really a male chauvinist to the teeth.

A female parishioner said that there was a lot of "hell raising" when the parishioners heard that "a woman was going to be boss." She quoted one of the women of the parish who told her,

I know these men. They don't want a woman in charge. They think all we are good for is cooking in the kitchen, and making love, and having babies. We're going to show them.

Often I would hear my interviewees allude to the root of patriarchal attitudes and actions among Catholics, the stance of the institutional church. A male parishioner who was critical of the gender inequality in the church said,

I would like to see more liberal views towards women as far as active roles in the church because they are a valuable resource. I think we have done a disservice, especially to some of the sisters who have devoted their lives the same as a priest has. Why should they be treated different? Just because they are female doesn't mean they are not capable of the same feelings, the same actions, everything. They are no different. The hierarchy is totally male, so it is hard for them to accept that.

A married woman pastor stated:

It's just not right for the hierarchy to say to this group of people [women pastors], "No, you can't have complete and full action and movement in the sacraments, but only as we can dole it out to you according to some man, and [depending on] when he can come in here [to the parish]."

A nun pastor reported her perception of her bishop's reactions to the way she relates to him:

Probably he didn't expect my behavior to be what he has found. Probably he expected I was going to be like a little girl following orders, or something like that. And when he realized it was a woman who could confront him, I don't think he liked that too well because even his own priests don't speak to him like I do. There are some who disagree strongly with him, but I don't think he finds too much of that. Most of the priests who don't agree with him keep quiet.

This woman has no aspirations to membership in the hierarchy of the church, and indeed has no realistic grounds for such aspirations because as a woman she is destined to lifelong membership in the laity. In contrast to the priests who "keep quiet," she cannot identify with the hierarchy or aspire to any role within it. Thus she is free to confront the bishop since, in the last analysis, she has nothing to lose because she is not as closely connected to the diocese as priests are.

In a very straightforward statement about the consequences of working for a patriarchal church, a married woman pastor said,

I think it's the frustration of working on trying to break into the political system of the Catholic male church. I live in a relationship with the other half of mankind, my husband. We are equal. Somewhere around the tenth year [of our marriage] it was either we had this equality or we couldn't have a marriage, and we are happier. Our family's happier because of it, and it's very frustrating to go from that kind of a setting into the direct opposite. It frustrates me, and it doesn't make working there [in the parish] very joyful.

Prejudicial attitudes regarding gender based on centuries of patriarchal church tradition and practice clearly reveal themselves in many ways, as the above examples indicate.

GENDER DISCRIMINATION AND RESPONSES

In the case of a woman pastor, a belief in patriarchy on the part of bishops, priests, and parishioners often results in active discrimination against her. Reflecting on the source of gender discrimination, a married woman pastor said,

In all of the years of [my] gradually doing different things here, sitting on the council, being president of the council, leading prayer services, and all the other things, there was never any time where somebody said, "Wait a minute, [she] can't do that because she's a woman." It's only when you get into the areas of the Sunday Assembly, and then the actual, heavy-duty sacramental things, that the issue begins to surface. And it always comes from the top down, from the hierarchy. It's a problem for the hierarchy; it isn't a problem for the average people. And those people that do suffer from it and say, "Wait a minute, she's a woman," they didn't learn that themselves. It was taught to them, and they can learn to get past that, just as they can learn to get past judging a person because they are black or Mexican or Oriental, or any of the other things that they feel that puts constraints on them.

Some of the women pastors reported that they were often treated as if they were invisible when they attended meetings of the clergy. One of them spoke of feeling intimidated when she was the only woman among many priests wearing Roman collars, and another described a priest who kept his eyes down and would not look at her during a meeting. On the occasion of a Mass at the cathedral attended by all pastors, a woman pastor described how she and the only other woman pastor were treated:

Before the ceremony began, all the priests and the altar servers, and [the other woman pastor] and I were in the sacristy getting ready. We didn't wear albs. I'm sure I had a suit on. We processed in with them [the priests], and we bowed and went to our places in the sanctuary. But before we did that, in the sacristy when Father _____ and [she] and I were in conversation, the bishop came over and greeted Father and totally ignored [her] and myself. It was as if we weren't there. It was deliberate. And I knew it was deliberate because then five minutes later he crossed right in front of us again to greet the altar boys. As he crossed over, I was watching him just to see if he was going to say hello to us, and he caught my eye and put his eyes down, so I knew. And then at the end of Mass the bishop thanked everybody in the cathedral, from the choir through the people who set up the sacristy, for all their help, but he never acknowledged our presence. We went to the luncheon after, and he was there and he never talked to us there.

This woman expressed great anger at the way she had been treated by the bishop. She was equally critical of the first draft of the pastoral letter of the American bishops on women's concerns, which she analyzed as a statement of principles with no follow-up, that is, where they "say one thing and do another."

In an earlier chapter I described a decision of a bishop to ordain the husband of a woman pastor as a deacon. Not only was this an application of a law that directly discriminates against women because it states that only men may be ordained to the diaconate, but the bishop's decision was bound to cause tension in their copastoring situation. The woman in question explained her feelings about it when she said,

> I am happy for him [her husband], but I am sad for me. I don't think it's fair. It's really hard, that we have been doing this equally together for so long, and now he is going to be ordained and I am not. But that's reality, and you don't right a wrong by another wrong, like saying to somebody who has a vocation that they can't have it just because it's unfair to me. That's not how you right a wrong. So I have mixed feelings.

Several of the women pastors described how difficult it was for them to interact with priests when they were the only nonpriest in attendance at meetings held specifically for pastors of the diocese. One of them had the following experience:

> The very first time I went to a meeting [for pastors] was at one of the staid parishes down in the center of town. I had received a letter about it, and they told me over the phone that the lunch would be at 12:30, followed by the meeting. Somehow or other it was at 12:00, but I didn't know that. So I arrived at the door, and when I told [the housekeeper] who I was, she said, "You're a nun?" I said, "Yes." She said, "Why aren't you wearing a habit?" Well, she was an older woman, and I came so close to saying, "None of your business, sweetie." I just let it go.
>
> She took me to the dining room and they [the priests] were a good way through the meal. I picked up a plate, and when I walked into the room—I always think of when a conductor gives a signal to an orchestra to stop—*everything stopped.* I didn't say anything. I was a little surprised because I wasn't expecting that, and I think they were surprised, too.

They knew who I was, but they didn't quite know what to do with me.[3] I thought to myself, "I'm going to wait until one of them says something." So I looked around for a chair, and there was no place at the table. But somebody got up right away and he said, "Sister, why don't you take my place because I am finished." I thanked him and took his place. Some people just said, "Nice to have you with us, Sister," and they broke the ice. And then it was all right.

Her words, "everything stopped," and "they didn't quite know what to do with me" point up the awkwardness for both the "only woman" and for the men in such a situation. Priest-pastors are obviously not accustomed to dealing with women as colleagues; their training leaves them ill-equipped for this type of an encounter. A woman pastor who had reflected on this lacuna in priest's lives made it a priority to attend each meeting or "study day" for pastors to which she was invited. She explained,

I will go to the study days because the priests need to see women there. It is important for the priests to talk to me in a nonthreatening atmosphere because some of them are going to be dealing with people like me in the next few years more and more. And they need to begin to realize that we don't bite.

On the other hand, one of the women pastors pointed out to me that meetings with priests can also silence the women attending. She was initially enthusiastic about attending meetings to which both women pastors and their sacramental ministers were invited. She soon lost her enthusiasm, because, as she put it,

We noticed that the men were dominating. So last September we all got together and at that meeting we told the sacramental ministers that as much as we [the women pastors] appreciated them, we thought we needed just to be with us, that they tended to dominate, and we needed things that were just appropriate for us. And that worked.

Another aspect of overt gender discrimination is exclusion. This usually takes the form of not receiving invitations to meetings for pastors of the diocese. Several of the women mentioned their disappointment at being excluded from some of these meetings. In one instance I was told that there was a diocesan meeting devoted solely to a discussion of alternate staffing of parishes to which no women pastors were invited. It would seem logical to include those with the most expertise on the topic among those invited, but such was not the case.

Parishioners as well as priests overtly expressed their bias in regard to the presence of women pastors. A male parishioner explained,

> There is still a little bit of bias in people. It is not going to go away. It is unfortunate, but there is. And when people are seeing women taking the place of where they have been seeing a man in that position for, well, some of them for seventy or eighty years, it was difficult for some to accept. But generally everything worked out pretty well. There is still a small percentage, I would say less than ten percent, that are quite upset with the whole thing.

A woman pastor described her experience with parishioners who initially questioned the appropriateness of her preaching.

> The Sunday after I came, I preached to the people and told them what I was doing. They didn't all click on that. After I preached, several of them came and told me that I had no business preaching up there. But they've come a long way [since then].

A sacramental minister reported,

> There were some people who, I understand, left the parish and said they just had a difficult time with a woman. A lot of it, I think, centered around her preaching more than her presence here. People have adjusted to that over the years, but I used to watch the people [while she was preaching], and the men would look up at the ceiling, and the women would look sideways. So there was a struggle in that way.

A female parishioner who described herself as a conservative Catholic had this to say:

> I have heard adults tell me that kids say that a woman does not belong on the altar. I think there are a lot of people in this area that are threatened by changing female roles, and I think the threat goes very deep with them. By the way, I am not sure this is bad at all. There still is a certain security in raising boys and raising girls, and keeping sexes distinct. Homosexu-

ality really scares the [local] macho. They want their sons to hunt, and they want sex roles absolutely clear. They find the blurring of sex roles a threat to keeping their boys straight.

This same parishioner told me that it turns her off when her woman pastor mentions anything about the woman's movement, or quotes from people involved in the woman's movement. On the other hand, she thinks her woman pastor is wonderful, and she supports her one hundred percent.

The issue of "appropriate" behavior for the different sex roles came up in several of the interviews. For example, the question of whether or not to fire the housecleaner for the parish house was raised. A woman pastor described her response.

> I remember that [the woman who cleaned the house] came in tears after Father left and said to me, "I suppose now that Father's gone that they won't hire me anymore." She thought I was going to do the cleaning. I said, "That shouldn't make any difference. I am doing everything Father did. You can be sure as long as I'm here you are going to stay on." Then I heard comments from the people, "Now that Sister is hired she will have more time so she can do her own cleaning." That was all the more reason why I didn't. I said, "I really wasn't trained to do the work of a housecleaner. I know how to do it, but my work is not that. My work is ministry here, and if Father could have somebody, I don't see why there should be a difference and I can't have somebody." She [the housecleaner] stayed on then.

In a similar incident in another parish, the sacramental minister reported some of the initial negative responses on the part of the parishioners to the nun pastor. He said that one of the interesting things was the decision of the altar and rosary society that "they really didn't have to wash the linens any more because a nun would do it."

The attitude of the parishioners in the accounts above are classic examples of gender discrimination, and they also exemplify entrenched beliefs about "a woman's place." In spite of the fact that the woman pastor had a full-time job, and that all of the previous pastors had housecleaners, because she happened to be a woman, she was expected to work the "second shift."[4] In fact, eight of the ten women pastors I interviewed who lived at the parish house did their own housecleaning, some because of the impoverished state of the parish, and others because they said they preferred to do their own cleaning. But in each case it was their own decision or preference to do so.

Another example of the response to gender discrimination emerged when a woman pastor described her encounter with the diocesan school board representatives. The issue was the amount that the parish had been assessed for the support of the Catholic schools in the diocese. She was unsuccessful in her attempt to persuade the school board to decrease her parish assessment, and she reported,

> I knew there were other pastors who were upset about this, and I said, "I'm getting no place because I'm a woman, number one, and they aren't paying any attention to me." So what I did was I invited some of the pastors in the area to meet, and I got a very generous response from them.

She then gathered the priests for a meeting, and they submitted a recommendation to the priest's council to have regional meetings to study the issue of Catholic education. She was also given a reprieve on her parish assessment by the diocese in the form of a "donation" to help her parish to meet the assessment. This woman pastor was aware that her assertiveness might not be appreciated by diocesan administrators. She said,

> So what I've done is I've gathered the priests. That's why I said I might not be here next year. I don't know what they'll do, but I've gotten very good responses from the priests.

Aside from the abilities of some of the women pastors to transform negative situations based on gender inequality into positive outcomes for themselves and for their parishes, there are also some indications that the patriarchial basis of gender bias is moving toward identifiable changes in the direction of gender equality. These indications are reflected in the issues we take up next, nonsexist attitudes and actions.

PROGRESS TOWARD NONSEXIST ATTITUDES AND ACTIONS

What were some of the indications that patriarchal beliefs and gender discrimination were being replaced by positive feminist beliefs and gender equality in the parishes I visited? There were a number of occasions during my travels to these parishes when the question of inclusive language emerged, sometimes during our conversations, and other times when I observed it in action, usually during the liturgy. For example, I noticed in one parish that hymns on xeroxed sheets showed words like "his" and other exclusive language had been deleted, and more inclusive language was inserted. In another parish I noticed that when the priest gave the last blessing at Mass, instead of "Father, Son, and Holy Spirit," he said, "Creator, Redeemer, and Holy Spirit." On neither of these occasions did I witness an uprising or even a mild protest from the congregation.

As we might expect, the efforts of women pastors to promote the use of inclusive language were not always met with enthusiasm, and in particular by priests. A nun pastor talked about one particular Sunday when the gospel was "one of the worst in terms of lack of inclusive language." She then said,

So I went over to the church and took a pencil, feeling very secure in doing this, and changed the language in the lectionary.[5] [The priest who was the sacramental minister] came about an hour early, and he said to me, "Now is there anything we want to go over about the liturgy?" I said, "Oh, by the way, we're into some very sexist language in this translation, so I penciled in some changes." And he looked at me. I said, "You don't mind, do you? I've done just a little bit of changes to make it more inclusive, nothing drastic. I didn't change the sentence structure or anything, but I put in 'everyone' rather than 'men.'" And I tried to do it tastefully because I hate it when it's overdone. I said to him, "Are you comfortable with that?" And he said, "No, I am sad to say I am not comfortable with that. Now, if you had changed a psalm or one of the epistles or an Old Testament reading, I wouldn't have had any problem with that. But somehow I am not ready to change the wording of the gospel reading."

Without telling him, she then went back and erased the changes, and he thanked her for it, explaining, "I'm just not ready for that yet." She said that since that episode she has noticed that priests would change the language in the prayers, and would never say "mankind" or other exclusive words when they recited prayers, but they tended not to change the language of the gospel.

As I explained in a previous chapter, there is a difference of opinion among women pastors about their role during Sunday Mass. One of the women who usually wore an alb and was seated in the sanctuary next to the priest during Mass argued that it was important for her to take a public position in that setting. She described a meeting with other women pastors who differed with her.

> They [other women pastors] said, "That's okay for you, because you can get up there. You are good at being in the front and all that." And I looked at them and I said, "But I think that's a qualification to be a pastoral administrator, that you can be public. Otherwise I don't think we are doing anything that we haven't done as parish workers. It's just the whole concept of moving women into equal positions. And I don't see that as a power play, but rather as justice.

She continued,

> One of my strong convictions is that I am not up there for [myself]. I feel a real call to leadership for women, and so when I am up there I am representing women moving with more recognition into leadership as far as we can stretch that. And unless we do that, we are always going to just stay kind of the helpers for the priests, and I don't believe in that. I think that is a scary thing to deal with.

Another woman pastor spoke about the way she was treated when she attended local deanery meetings, where she was the only woman among five pastors. She said,

> But none of them greet me like I am second class. They respect my opinion and they listen. It's not a "me" and "them" situation.

Perhaps the change in attitudes and actions that have resulted from a woman pastor's activities in a parish can best be summed up by a woman parishioner, the parish organist and choir director, who said,

> I have really come to believe that women can do the job, not as well, but *better*. And believe it or not, when [the woman pastor] first came here, I didn't even change the words in the

hymns. That was not an issue at all. So I've grown a lot in the last four years, and realize what women can do for this church, and the position that women are in presently. And I don't think it's right.

At the beginning of this chapter I posed the "woman question" in two parts: how people react to the woman pastor and how she creatively meets the challenges of her new role. As is evident in the previous statement, it is the parishioners who witness the whole gamut of challenges stemming from patriarchal beliefs and practices that the woman pastor meets in her daily encounters. And it is the parishioners who, as laity, can identify with her treatment as a "second-class" citizen and who can also rejoice when they witness occasions when justice replaces sexism in her life as pastor. Even those parishioners who described themselves as traditional Catholics told me that they had changed their attitudes and actions regarding women in the church as a result of their experiences with their woman pastor. In short, the overwhelming majority of the parishioners I interviewed no longer support patriarchy and gender discrimination, and they attribute their change of attitude to their woman pastor.

•9•

Final Observations

This book has examined the woman-as-Catholic-pastor phenomenon from various perspectives as it exists now, in its early stages. The women pastors I interviewed can be described as pioneers or trailblazers because they were among the first to take on this new role in the United States. Therefore, their experiences may help to pave the way for others who will follow in their footsteps.

Any attempt to characterize this chapter as a conventional "conclusion" is tempered by an undeniable acknowledgement that the central subject matter of this book is still very much in process. I am well aware from current media accounts and information gleaned from several sources within the church, that more and more people are "calling her pastor" because her numbers are increasing, even as I write this. This is a phenomenon that will not go away, no matter how much resistance there is to women pastors. In fact, the actual instances in this book are merely the tip of the iceberg.

My solution is not to write a conclusion. Instead I will make some final observations about the following: (1) the creativity of women pastors in transforming constraints into opportunities; (2) recommendations for policy and for future research; and (3) the future of this new role for women, as seen by parishioners, priests, the women themselves, and this researcher.

TRANSFORMATION OF CONSTRAINTS

Constraints and opportunities are two threads that together form a theme running throughout this book. What is unique about the women pastors is the way they manage to transform constraints into opportunities in the daily enactment of their new role.[1]

As I listened to my interviewees, and when I examined the transcripts, the word "challenge" emerged again and again. Phrases like, "taking on other challenges and more visionary things," "helping the church move into the future," "needing new challenges," "being a link between an older model of church and a brand new vision of what church can and should be," and "being challenged and stretched beyond what I thought I was capable of doing" kept recurring. One of the women pastors, for instance, said that she saw herself as taking part in a "pilot project" in her diocese, and she labeled the appointment of women as heads of parishes a "creative solution" to the priest shortage. In a real sense it was the very challenge of the constraints, conflicts, and tensions that attracted some of the women pastors to this new role.

What are some examples of the ways that these women managed to transform constraints into opportunities? A constraint that caused considerable tension, and that was mentioned repeatedly in the interviews with the women pastors, was their experience of rejection by parishioners, especially during the first few months following their arrival at the parish. Obviously the women pastors had somehow survived this initial rejection, because they were still in charge of the parish when I interviewed them, and had served in this capacity for an average of four years. In chapter 6 I discussed some of the support systems that helped them to overcome the "rejection period," but moral support and advice from others was not the only solution.

One of the priests described how a woman pastor transformed the parishioners' rejection of her into an opportunity. He said,

> One way she coped with it is she went to a workshop. I can't even tell you the title of it, but it was in that area of how to understand parishioners that reject you, not just because you are a woman but just reject what you do, and how you reach them. That's the way she is. This is another mountain she's got to climb and she'll climb it. She is a strong woman.

One of the initial experiences of these women, sometimes occurring the very first day they take over as pastor, is encountering parishioners who are anxious, fearful, or angry about losing their priest. Such people tend to bombard them with numerous questions that demand immediate answers. As I explained in chapter 6, bishops who traveled to the parish before the arrival of the new pastor fielded these questions themselves, thus saving the women pastors a considerable amount of time and energy. One of the lay pastors, who had previous pastoring experience in another parish, described her strategy:

> We had xeroxed and stapled together a cover letter to the parish along with ten or twelve commonly asked questions and answers about pastoral coordinators, and we had those mailed out to the whole parish mailing list that first week. And then we were up in the pulpit the first Sunday.

This tactic was successful because it enabled the copastors at this parish to lessen the time spent in explaining over and over again who they were and what they would be doing, and instead to get on with the work of the parish more easily.

One of the very sensitive issues which sometimes caused conflict within the parish and was a source of tension for many of the women pastors was their "right" to preach. The ambiguity surrounding this aspect of their role as pastor allowed some of them a certain degree of freedom. Several of the women pastors preached regularly, and because they knew the names of their parishioners and had visited their homes, they found new ways of reaching them in their sermons.

I observed this creativity when a woman pastor preached during a word and Communion service on a Sunday morning. She was interpreting the gospel for the day, the story of Zacchaeus, who, because he was short of stature, climbed a tree in order to see Jesus. In her introduction she explained that she, who was also short of stature, had walked around examining the trees on the parish grounds to see if she might be able to climb any of them, and had decided that she could not. She then immediately caught the attention of her audience by directly asking three very small boys who were sitting with their parents in the bench next to me, if they could climb a tree. She called on each one in turn by name, and asked, "Could you climb a tree?" And each one, with his eyes riveted on her face, replied, "No." She literally had these children and the entire congregation eating out of her hand.

She continued with an analogy, describing the actions of a young boy and girl who had to stand at a circus and because of their height couldn't see the performance. They cried, whined, and threw temper tantrums, yet refused help from their parents, and so missed seeing the show. She mentioned as a parallel, the actions of people who are failing in school or who are alcoholics and refuse help from others, thus compounding their problem. She then compared all of these examples to the actions of Zacchaeus who not only went out of his way to see Jesus, but also accepted the Lord's help and thus changed his life for the better. She kept saying to them throughout, "You can *do* it, but you need to accept help from others."

During this sermon, while making her point regarding the individual's need for community, she kept eye contact throughout, was very expressive, and did not use notes. And all of this was done within the confines of a religious service which is defined as "second class" because it was presided over by a nonordained minister who cannot celebrate Mass.[2]

Later, when this same woman pastor discussed what it is that keeps her going in her ministry, she included her opportunities to preach:

> I think the people [are what keeps me going in my ministry]. And an inner call. I really think the Spirit is the one that speaks through me, that is doing things on Sundays. I prepare because I really love preparing my Sunday liturgies as best as I can. Once I have it all written and all prepared, I say, "Lord, it is your job." And He/She takes over. I think it is that inner calling, the experienciang of the Lord in my life, and the people. I think they deserve more than what they have experienced in the past.

From what I observed and heard from my interviewees, the preaching done by these women was a key element in changing peoples' attitudes about women's role in the church. One of the priests, commenting on her homily, told a woman pastor that she had "sure rattled some cages." As she reiterated the conversation,

> I said, "Is that good or bad? What does that mean?" And he said, "Well, if you don't rattle cages, you don't open doors, do you?" So I said, "Thanks."

The doors begin to open when the parishioners perceive their woman pastor as someone who has assumed a seemingly incongruous position in their parish since her appearance and actions differ quite obviously from those of their previous pastors. It is difficult for people who had never previously seen a woman in such roles as pastor, Supreme Court justice, construction worker, soldier, or astronaut, to imagine such an eventuality. Such an image runs counter to individuals' experiences in everyday life.

However, most of the parishioners, who encounter their woman pastor on an almost daily basis, gradually come to the conclusion that she performs her pastoral duties as well as or better than the previous priest-pastor. As a result of these observations the "doors" of their imaginations have been opened to the possibility that SHE can do it, and do it effectively.

As we have seen in the previous chapters, these women are able to identify with their parishioners to a much greater extent than any previous pastor because they are not members of the clergy. Thus the constraints and limitations of their nonordained state are transformed into opportunities by their creation of a new leadership style that incorporates their parishioners as peers, and eventually leads to a greater spirit of community in these parishes.

Because Catholic parishioners share membership in the laity with their woman pastor, they are also keenly aware of the limitations placed on her authority, and they are beginning to question this inequity. An increase in parishioner questioning of the limited empowerment of women pastors is a signal that the doors are opening still wider. Thus institutional constraints actually are providing the opportunity for changes in attitude at the grass roots level.

RECOMMENDATIONS

Having traveled across the country to collect the data for this book, and having analyzed it in the previous pages, I am now prepared to present some recommendations that could make the transition into this new role a smoother one. The Catholic church is in the throes of an evolutionary change process which is experienced more profoundly in the poor and more isolated areas of the country at the present time. Any organization anticipating change should·plan and prepare for it so as to be able to shape desirable outcomes.

One strategy that worked well in the parishes I visited was the active involvement of parishioners in the recruitment process. Some dioceses, in fact, have guidelines that require candidates to be interviewed by a committee of parishioners prior to the appointment by the bishop. As was shown in this study, it was not the status of nun or married woman, nor that of insider or outsider that necessarily made a "better pastor." It was rather the level of trust, which was enhanced by parishioner participation in the recruitment of the new lay pastor.

Other recommendations concern the role of the clergy in the legitimation of the newly appointed leader. The bishop should personally visit the parish prior to the arrival of the lay pastor to explain his reasons for alternate staffing, and he should also preside at the installation ceremony. He should appoint a priest-pastor as mentor for the lay pastor, at least for the first year. In addition, the bishop himself should visit the parish after the new pastor has been installed, so that he can periodically renew his support. Likewise, the priest acting as sacramental visitor should use every occasion to legitimize the authority of the lay pastor.

All of the strategies mentioned thus far also have obvious implications for secular organizations that are recruiting women into positions previously occupied by men.

It would certainly lighten the financial burdens in priestless parishes if the diocese would take on the responsibility of paying the stipend for the priest who performs the sacramental ministry. It does not seem fair that such a parish not only loses a resident priest, but also must incur a greater financial strain. In the interest of long-range planning, dioceses should fund scholarships to encourage laity to pursue master's programs in theology or pastoral studies. Perhaps seminaries and schools of theology could be persuaded to create scholarships for laity who are training for pastoral ministry.

Some recommendations regarding future research also come to mind. One of the central issues emerging from this study is the extent to which the patterns of behavior and attitude observed are due to the gender or to the lay status of the pastor. This issue can only be addressed with comparable data on male lay pastors.

However, at the present time, as I explained in chapter 1, there are only about twelve parishes in the United States headed by religious brothers, who, like sisters, are not ordained.[3] At the time that I drew my sample, there was only one married layman heading a priestless parish, and he is copastoring with his wife.[4] This points to the need for a study of male lay pastors of priestless parishes in the United States, so that we can make the basic gender comparisons.

As preceding chapters show, some evidence of bishops' support and nonsupport was gleaned from the interviews with women pastors, parishioners, and priests. What is needed now, however, is a research project focusing on the issue of alternate staffing of parishes that directly involves Catholic bishops. This proposed research would give us a better understanding of bishops' attitudes and behavior towards lay pastors.

Until the Catholic church allows ordination for women, there can be no direct comparisons with Protestant clergywomen. The women in my study lack the clerical privileges and rights that Protestant clergywomen possess; therefore their status is not comparable. Although many of the Catholic women pastors attested to the support of Protestant clergywomen in their local area, they were keenly aware of the difference in status.

Unlike Catholicism, which is experiencing continued growth in membership while the priesthood is shrinking, the mainline Protestant churches, with a surplus of clergy, are characterized by a declining membership.[5] Thus we cannot expect to see a similar phenomenon of increasing use of lay pastors in Protestant churches, at least in the foreseeable future.

My ethnographic research has given us a view of the behavior, perceptions, attitudes, and feelings of parishioners, women pastors, and priests in twenty parishes scattered throughout the United States that have no resident priest. This qualitative research should be complemented by a quantitative study with a national overview, which is already in progress. As I mentioned in chapter 1, a survey of parishes throughout the United States where there is no resident priest is now in preparation. It goes without saying that all of the research projects recommended above should also be extended to other countries throughout the world, so that cross-national comparisons could be made.

LOOKING TO THE FUTURE

What does the future look like to those who have experienced the pastoring of a woman in these parishes? Several of the priests who served with them as sacramental ministers offered serious reflections. One of them said,

> I really feel that these kinds of creative solutions are absolutely essential, not just because of the priest shortage. I think the grace part of the priest shortage is that it's allowing other ministries in the church to emerge. I think that's the gift from God...the shortage of priests. That other people, people who are not ordained, are in these kinds of roles is wonderful. And getting used to seeing a woman in that role is going to help visually for the day when finally God can break through in those places where it hasn't happened.

Parishioners also offered their views of the future. A woman parishioner who was in a diocese where the former bishop, who had appointed a woman pastor to head the parish, was recently retired, expressed some apprehension. She stated:

> From what I understand [the new bishop] is a little more strict about women's involvement and role in the church. For awhile there it gave us all a little bit of an uncomfortable, uneasy feeling about what the future was to hold. The possibility always is there that they could remove [her] or make a concerted effort to find a parish priest or bring in a deacon. So I think right now things are a little bit iffy, and I wonder if she is going to have the support of [the new bishop].

In several of the parishes I visited, women pastors, parishioners, and priests discussed the possibility of a rotation of priestless parishes, or "spreading it around." One of the parishioners put it this way:

> I had heard at a workshop that they were going to try working with these administrators [women pastors], to put as many as they can in the diocese to help the priests. They were talking

about moving priests around and putting administrators in the larger parishes, and giving everyone in the diocese a feel of having an administrator sometime or another. I would favor that kind of thing [rotation of priestless parishes]. I think people would feel more comfortable in the church, knowing that just because they are a small community, they would not always have a [lay] administrator.

The growing awareness by parishioners of the constraints and inequities faced by their woman pastors in carrying out their ministry led to another topic frequently mentioned by parishioners. This was the possibility of ordaining women. A male parishioner who was deeply concerned about the survival of the church phrased it this way:

> I think that whoever came up with this pastoral administrator job for the religious [women] and lay people should get into a position in our church that they would enlighten the view of our upper-echelon people. We have to do something. We are committing suicide. We just have to change. I feel we are wasting an awful lot of our resources. We should have ordination of women. It is just puzzling to me that we don't. People have to be protecting their own turf.

He continued with this same theme a little later in the interview:

> I just said a few minutes ago that we are committing suicide, and we are. We are losing members right and left, and we have no vision. In the Bible it says that Jesus founded this church and the gates of hell will not prevail against it. But I am afraid that we are prevailing against it, the members are.

What did the women pastors have to say about the future? Several of them had very practical recommendations, for example:

> I wish the church would wake up and start planning, not day to day. They keep putting Band-aids on situations, and now they have run out of Band-aids. I would love for them to look creatively at the diocese, places where they have mission churches and no community life—the people just use it as a place to go to church—[and] close them. To really study and see where community is, and to foster those communities of people.

Some of them offered carefully nuanced statements with regard to the ordination of women. One of the nun pastors stated that she "wouldn't want ordination to continue as it's been," adding that to ordain women in the current structure would mean having "a masculine structure with feminine bodies in it." She suggested a new, less hierarchical model of ordination that would reflect the more participatory style of leadership modeled by women pastors.

Similarly, a married pastor who always sat with the parishioners during Mass, and made it clear that she did not want to be placed on a clerical pedestal, said,

> If I were to sit in the presider's chair and do all those things, they [parishioners] would eventually do to me what they did to the priests. But I am always conscious that I want not only the sex to change, but the style of leadership to change. Even some people do this to me now, [saying] "Well, if you are not going to heaven, who is?" [I answer], "Just because I work in this position does not make me holier. You are just as holy as me. I could be a crook for all you know."

A nun pastor spoke of her dreams of the future church:

> I hope and pray, and keep wishing and dreaming that our church, especially our hierarchy, can open their eyes to the reality, and not continue burying their heads in the sand, [and] to face the reality with joy and optimism, and allow the lay people to really take over. If we are all baptized, and are all empowered, why can't we go ahead and minister completely? We would be more alive, more enriched. In one of the meetings I said, "I wish the Lord would come right now and tell us what He feels about our church, because we are massacring the whole thing." I wish we would open our eyes and our minds, and really allow the Spirit to do Her job.

As this study has shown, a change of parishioners' and priests' attitudes is already happening in parishes headed by women. I heard both laity and priests who were formerly opposed to women clergy describe their conversion. In the nine parishes headed by married women, this change of heart encompassed the issue of married clergy as well.

It is safe to say that the proportion of Catholics who have undergone this attitude change does not yet constitute a critical mass. At the present time there are only about two percent of the Catholic parishes in this country that have nonpriest pastors.

However, that percentage will increase as the priest shortage continues to become more critical. In increasing numbers the laity will be asking, "Why *not* women pastors?" and "Why *not* married pastors?"[6]

Whether this dramatic change in thinking will filter up to the hierarchy is not the question; it already has in some dioceses, and indications are that more and more bishops are appointing women to head parishes. Some dioceses that have enough priests at the present time will probably hold out for awhile, but by the year 2005, they will also experience the priest shortage, and will then have to decide whether to close parishes, import priests from other countries, or provide alternate staffing of them. It is my position that this slow but steady change in attitudes regarding women clergy and married clergy will, in the last analysis, portend well for the future of lay leadership in the church.

My prediction is, however, tempered by the awareness of the tendency to resist change, particularly on the part of those in positions of power. A striking example of the resistance to change came to my attention as this book was going to press. One of my interviewees, a woman who had been pastoring a parish for four years, wrote me a letter to inform me that she had been moved out of her parish by the bishop. Her replacement was a priest from a foreign country who, she wrote, "is destroying the beautiful community you witnessed there." She continued,

> And the bishop does *nothing* about it. For him the important thing is "having a priest in every parish," no matter what kind of a priest he is.

This is a clear reminder that institutional constraints cannot easily be transformed. It is also safe to predict that some bishops will opt for this type of alternate staffing, recruiting priests from other countries, instead of entrusting parishes to lay people. The notion of empowering the laity, even though supported by Vatican II decrees, runs counter to the Catholic tradition of hierarchical authority.[7] Those bishops who cling to that tradition will be more likely to go to great lengths to place a priest in every parish, no matter where he comes from. Such bishops will undoubtedly try to blind themselves to the problems caused in parishes led by pastors who are unfamiliar with the parishioners' language, values, and culture.

In this regard, the key issue is whether parishioners will continue to be submissive, and to accept the bishop's appointments unquestioningly. Some of them undoubtedly will continue to go along with all of the bishop's decisions, but there is evidence that the majority of American laity favor more democratic decision making at all three levels: parish, diocese, and Vatican.[8] Thus I predict that those bishops who appoint lay pastors to head parishes will continue to grow in number, until their decisions about alternate staffing of parishes will predominate in the early years of the third millenium.

Whether the movement toward greater lay participation will permeate the various offices at the Vatican is an open question. Unless the leader at the top accepts new roles for the laity, especially the inclusion of women in making decisions and shaping policy at the parish, diocesan, and Vatican levels, there is little hope for a restructuring that includes all levels of the Catholic church in the foreseeable future.

A significant obstacle to the appointment of lay pastors, which I discussed in chapter 7, is the financial one. How can poor parishes afford to pay them a living wage? This, of course, can only be answered on a parish-to-parish basis. However, most parishes that at one time had a resident priest own a parish house, and I would expect that many young laypersons interested in church ministry would find free housing a major asset. For example, the young couple who were copastors told me they were delighted to have a large parish house for themselves and their three children, and were well aware that most young couples their age could not afford such a home. Likewise, the laywoman and the nuns who were living in parish houses could not afford to accept the position without the rent-free housing.

Another financial solution is the "sharing" of a lay pastor by two parishes that together pay the salary. Still another solution, already experienced in almost all of the parishes I visited, is increased giving by the parishioners. As many parishioners told me, once they realized the benefits of having a woman pastor, they became actively engaged in the running of the parish. Thus the parishioners became part of the solution themselves, not only by their volunteer services, but also by contributing more to the Sunday collection.

There are some very poor parishes, however, with high unemployment rates, where contributing more money to the Sunday collection is not a possibility for the parishioners. There were a few parishes I visited that were able to raise money through annual bazaars and quilt sales, but this is less successful in a geographical area where the entire region is depressed. In such a case, wealthier parishes in the diocese could "adopt" the parish, and share their resources with them. Two of the parishes I visited were "adopted" parishes.

Poverty is not an insurmountable problem for pioneers, as we know from our own history as a nation. Needless to say, the image of the women and men who crossed this country in covered wagons includes few of the material comforts of life. These were poor but determined people who were risk-takers because they were in pursuit of a cherished dream. They were aware that they were participating in building the new nation that they had adopted.

The same can be said for these talented women pastors who are also encountering all of the obstacles that stand in the way of those who seek and accept the challenge of breaking new ground. Inspired by the Vatican II teaching that the church is the people of God, they are participating in the transformation of an institution of which they are an integral part. In parishes like those I visited throughout the country, the presence of women pastors is already beginning to change the face of Catholicism.

NOTES

CHAPTER 1

1. Although at the present time few dioceses in the Northeast have appointed nonordained persons to head parishes, Richard Schoenherr's recent research indicates that by the year 2005 dioceses in the New England region will decline most in the number of active diocesan priests, suffering an average loss of fifty-two percent between 1966 and 2005. See Richard A. Schoenherr and Lawrence A. Young, *The Catholic Priest in the United States: Demographic Investigations* (Madison, Wis.: University of Wisconsin-Madison Comparative Religious Organization Studies Publications, 1990), p. 23. Dolan et al. (1989:220) document an earlier period of leadership for women, prior to the establishment of parish programs. For instance, Mrs. John O'Brien was quite literally serving as pastor for twenty-five Catholics in Tallassee, Alabama in 1915. See also Weaver (1986:37–70).

2. The Roman Curia is the central administrative government of the Catholic church in Rome.

3. See Rosemary Ruether, *Contemporary Roman Catholicism: Crises and Challenges* (Kansas City, Mo.: Sheed and Ward, 1987), p. ix for a discussion of the meaning of *aggiornamento*.

4. See *Concilio Ecumenico Vaticano II: Commissioni Conciliari* for a list of the council participants.

5. See Walter M. Abbott, *The Documents of Vatican II* (New York: America Press, 1966), p. 500.

6. At that time I was one of the four American nuns invited to Rome by Cardinal Leon Joseph Suenens to organize discussions on topics that were on the current agenda of the Council.

7. No wonder, then, that Sister Teresa Kane's address to Pope John Paul II, on his visit to the United States in October, 1979 created such a sensation. She requested him to provide for women to be fully participating members of the church, and that they be included in all church ministries. See Dolan et al. (1989:189).

8. See Abbot (1966), p. 500. The term "apostolate" refers to the mission or activities of the church.

9. An abbess is a woman who is the superior of a convent of nuns.

10. See Joan Morris, *The Lady Was a Bishop* (New York: Macmillan, 1973), pp. 57, 75–77, and 85–86.

11. Some of this discussion is adapted from my earlier work on women in the church, in particular "Bringing Women In: Marginality in the Churches" (1975), "Catholic Women and the Creation of a new Social Reality" (1988), and "Women in the Church: Limited Empowerment" in D'Antonio, Davidson, Hoge, and Wallace (1989).

12. A eucharistic minister is a person who assists in the distribution of Communion. A lector is one who reads the scripture lessons during Mass or other liturgical celebrations.

13. David C. Leege and Thomas A. Trozzolo, "Who Participates in Local Church Communities?" *Origins* 15 (1985): 56–57.

14. William V. D'Antonio, James D. Davidson, Dean R. Hoge, and Ruth A. Wallace, *American Catholic Laity in a Changing Church* (Kansas City, Mo.: Sheed and Ward, 1989).

15. See William L. Baumgaertner, ed., *Fact Book on Theological Education: 1987–88* (Vandalia, Ohio:Association of Theological Schools in the United States and Canada, 1988), pp. 90–92.

16. In fact, some dioceses currently require that candidates for the position of pastoral administrator have already earned a master's degree in theology or its equivalent. Because only priests can have the title "pastor," these women are usually given the title "pastoral administrator" by their bishops.

17. See *Code of Canon Law* (Washington, D.C.: Canon Law Society of America, 1983).

18. See John A. Renken, "Canonical Issues in the Pastoral Care of Parishes without Priests," *The Jurist* 47 (1987): 506–19.

19. Ibid.

20. See Elaine Kroe, *National Higher Education Statistics: Fall 1989* (Washington, D.C.: U.S. Department of Education, 1989), pp. 11–13.

21. See Richard A. Schoenherr and Lawrence A. Young, *The Catholic Priest in the United States: Demographic Investigations* (Madison, Wis.: University of Wisconsin-Madison Comparative Religious

Organization Studies Publications, 1990). This exhaustive study was sponsored by the United States Catholic Conference.

22. Although Schoenherr's report did not include recommendations, Dean R. Hoge has suggested that the priesthood shortage would be alleviated if the laws regarding celibacy and male ordination were changed. See Dean R. Hoge, *The Future of Catholic Leadership: Responses to the Priest Shortage*, (Kansas City, Mo.: Sheed and Ward, 1987).

23. See Schoenherr and Young (1990), pp. 99–110.

24. Andrew M. Greeley, *American Catholics Since the Council: An Unauthorized Report* (Chicago: Thomas More Press, 1985), p. 182.

25. Hoge (1987). See also Kenneth L. Woodward, T. Stranger, S. Sullivan, M. Margolis and R. Vokey, "Church in Crisis," *Newsweek* (December 9, 1985): 66–75.

26. See *Origins* (December 17, 1979).

27. See Joseph H. Fichter, "Holy Father Church," *Commonweal* (May 15, 1970): 216–18.

28. The following are some examples: Matthew Clark, "American Catholic Women: Persistent Questions," *Origins* (1982) 12:273–86; Victor Balke and Raymond Lucker, "Male and Female God Created Them," *Origins* (1981) 11:333–38); and Peter Gerety, "Women in the Church," *Origins* (1980) 10:582–88.

29. A pastoral letter is the bishops' official guidance to American Catholics on how they should think about problems facing their church and their country. Previous pastorals have looked at such issues as the U.S. economy and nuclear arms.

30. See U.S. Bishops, "One in Christ Jesus: A Pastoral Response to the Concerns of Women for Church and Society," *Origins* 19 (1990): 717–40. See also Pat Windsor, "Weakland Advises U.S. Bishops to Drop Women's Pastoral," *National Catholic Reporter* (May 18, 1990:3), where it is reported that Milwaukee Archbishop Rembert Weakland advised the bishops not to issue this pastoral letter because it fails to mention the issue of power and decision making in the church, and how they are related to ordination. He predicted that until that relationship between ordination and jurisdiction is laid out clearly, "there will be no credible treatment of the role of women in the church. The gifts of women cannot be fully recognized if leadership roles have to be tied into ordination." A deacon is an ordained cleric ranking below a priest

who has the right to deliver homilies during Mass, and to preside at funerals and marriages outside of Mass.

31. See Daniel Pilarczyk, "Vote on Women's Pastoral Delayed," *Origins* 20 (September 27, 1990): 250–51.

32. See James A. Coriden, ed., *Sexism and Church Law: Equal Rights and Affirmative Action* (New York: Paulist Press, 1977), p. 159.

33. The term "nuns" historically refers to members of contemplative orders, and "sisters" denotes members of religious communities engaged in active ministries. However, modern usage tends to equate the two terms. In order to avoid any confusion with family relationships, I use the term nuns in most cases when I am referring to female members of religious communities.

34. See Peter Gilmour, *The Emerging Pastor: Non-ordained Catholic Pastors* (Kansas City, Mo.: Sheed and Ward, 1986). A sacramental minister is a priest, usually from a nearby parish, appointed to celebrate Mass and administer the other sacraments in parishes where there is no resident priest.

35. Professor Gary Burkart, chair of the Sociology Department at Benedictine College in Atchison, Kansas, is the principal investigator of this research project.

36. Totals ninety-nine percent because of rounding off percentages.

37. The data reported in the *Official Catholic Directory* are typically underreported, since they are compiled by the bishop's office in each diocese, and then sent to the publisher. Some bishops may be reluctant to admit that laity are administering their parishes, and instead list the priest who is the sacramental minister. For instance, I found five women whom I had interviewed in their parishes who were not listed as the administrator of the parish in the *Directory*. See *Origins* (April 19, 1990, Volume 19, No. 46: 758–65) for the full text of an address given on March 10, 1990 by H. Richard McCord, Jr., associate director of the National Conference of Catholic Bishops' Secretariat for Laity and Family Life, where he stated that already there are *at least* 201 pastoral administrators directing 193 parishes or missions in seventy dioceses in the United States.

38. See "Celibacy First, Eucharist Second," *Corpus Reports*, Vol. 16, No. 2 (March–April 1990): 3.

39. See Katherine Gilfeather, "The Changing Role of Women in the

Catholic Church in Chile," *Journal for the Scientific Study of Religion* 16 (1977): 53.

40. See Ruth A. Wallace, "Catholic Women and the Creation of a New Social Reality," *Gender and Society* 2 (1988): 24–38.

41. William V. D'Antonio et al., 1989.

42. For recent sociological studies of Protestant clergywomen, see Jackson W. Carroll, Barbara Hargrove, and Adair T. Lummis, *Women of the Cloth: A New Opportunity for the Churches* (San Francisco, Ca.: Harper and Row Publishers, 1983) and Edward C. Lehman, Jr., *Women Clergy: Breaking Through Gender Barriers* (New Brunswick, N.J.: Transaction Books, 1985).

43. I am especially indebted to Kay Seshkaitis, an expert on this topic, who was then working at the Office of Ministry for the Archdiocese of Portland, Oregon.

44. Here I draw on Robert Merton's work on role-sets. See Robert K. Merton, "The Role-Set: Problems in Sociological Theory," *British Journal of Sociology* 8 (1957: 106–20) and Robert K. Merton, *Social Theory and Social Structure* (New York: Free Press, 1968). The members of the woman pastor's role-set know that the individual who previously occupied her position was a member of the clergy, and his role performance was facilitated by a long tradition of clear-cut role expectations. Therefore I assumed that the members of her role-set would have different, and to some extent, indefinite or unclear role expectations. This is the reason why I wanted to concentrate on the role relationships between the woman pastor and the significant members of her role-set, the male and female parish leaders and the priest who was the sacramental minister for her parish.

45. My letter included two additional pieces of information: first, that the costs of my transportation, meals, and housing were covered by a grant from the Lilly Endowment; and second, in case they wished to check my references, I provided them with the names and addresses of three people in different parts of the country, all of whom are nationally known experts on aspects of pastoral ministry, who know me both professionally and personally.

46. A decrease in the numbers of Catholic women entering religious orders, and an increase in the numbers leaving, resulted in a total decrease of forty percent of the members of religious women's communities between 1966 and 1981. See Marie Augusta Neal, *Catholic Sisters in Transition: From the 1960s to the 1980s* (Wilmington, Del.: Michael Glazier, 1984), p. 19.

47. I combined New England and the Middle Atlantic to form the Northeast. The East North Central and West North Central were combined to form the Midwest. The South Atlantic, East South Central, and West South Central were combined to form the South. Finally, the West was a combination of the Mountain and Pacific regions.

48. Within the first hour of my arrival at each parish, before I began the first interview, I made it a point to describe some of my background to the women pastors, in particular the fact that I had spent eighteen years as a member of a religious community, and the rest (1970–present) as a laywoman. Thus I could identify with nuns and laywomen alike, and this commonality in backgrounds tended to "break the ice."

49. My research emphasizes the importance of the individual's interpretation of his or her situation, and the active employment of various strategies in order to manage one's behavior, thought, and feelings. Sociologists will recognize that symbolic interactionism is one of the key theoretical perspectives that informs this research. See Herbert Blumer, *Symbolic Interactionism: Perspective and Method* (Englewood Cliffs, N.J.: Prentice-Hall, 1969); Erving Goffman, *Presentation of Self in Everyday Life* (New York: Doubleday, 1959); George J. McCall and J. L. Simmons, *Identities and Interactions* (New York: Free Press, 1966); and Arlie Russell Hochschild, *The Managed Heart* (Berkeley: University of California, 1983) and *The Second Shift* (New York: Viking, 1989). Because I also emphasize the importance of institutional constraints and supports and demographic factors in an explanation of this phenomenon, this study is a combination of both micro and macro sociological analysis. See Anthony Giddens, *Central Problems in Social Theory* (Berkeley: University of California, 1983) and *The Constitution of Society* (Cambridge: Polity, 1984); and C. Wright Mills, *The Sociological Imagination* (New York: Oxford, 1959).

50. This restriction is contained in church law. Canons 150 and 521 state that the office of pastor requires the order of priesthood, and that it cannot be conferred on one who is not ordained to that order.

CHAPTER 2

1. Although there were no black women heading priestless parishes when I was collecting my data, a black nun was appointed to head a parish in Richmond, Virginia, and she assumed duties there on June 4, 1990. See Myra L. Dandridge, "Black Nun to Lead Parish in Virginia," *Washington Post* (May 26, 1990): D1.

2. Although both women and married persons are excluded from ordination to the priesthood, these restrictions do not apply in the case of pastoral administrators. As we saw in chapter 1, canon 517.2 did not exclude laity.

3. According to canon 766, laypersons can be permitted to preach in church in cases of necessity or usefulness.

4. A homily is a sermon presented to a congregation during Mass by a priest or deacon, usually after the scripture readings.

5. This appeared in the classified advertising section of the April 20, 1990 issue of the *National Catholic Reporter*, p. 21.

6. In a recent national study, Hoge et al. found the average size of Catholic parishes with no full-time clergy was 234 households (or families). See Dean R. Hoge, Jackson W. Carroll, and Francis K. Scheets, *Patterns of Parish Leadership: Cost and Effectiveness in Four Denominations* (Kansas City, Mo.: Sheed and Ward, 1988), p. 146. Therefore, my five "large" parishes would be interpreted as medium-size, and the rest would be labeled "small" on a national scale.

7. Myers-Briggs is the name of a personality inventory that is designed to characterize people on a number of psychological factors, one of which is introvert/extrovert.

CHAPTER 3

1. See *Webster's Ninth New Collegiate Dictionary* (Springfield, Ma.: Merriam-Webster, Inc., 1984), p. 861.

2. See *The Jerusalem Bible* (Garden City, N.Y.: Doubleday and Company, Inc., 1966), pp. 168–69.

3. A deanery is a geographical subdivision of a diocese comprising several parishes in a particular region, for example, a county.

4. In their study of the dying situation, Glaser and Strauss found that some nurses used strategies to avoid being near the patient during the later stages of dying because they found the death scene upsetting. See Barney G. Glaser and Anselm L. Strauss, *Awareness of Dying* (Chicago: Aldine Press, 1965), p. 202.

5. Robert Bellah defines community thus: "A group of people who are socially interdependent, who participate together in discussion and decision making, and who share certain practices that both define the

community and are nurtured by it. Such a community is not quickly formed. It almost always has a history and so is also a community of memory, defined in part by its past and its memory of its past." See Robert N. Bellah, Richard Madsen, William M. Sullivan, Ann Swidler, and Steven M. Tipton, *Habits of the Heart: Individualism and Commitment in American Life* (Berkeley: University of California Press, 1985), p. 333.

CHAPTER 4

1. See Doohan (1986:33–101) for a discussion of collaboration in parish ministry.

2. See, for instance, Emile Durkheim, *Suicide* (Glencoe, Ill.:Free Press, 1951), p. 156.

3. A missalette is a small book containing all that is said or sung at Mass.

CHAPTER 5

1. See Jay P. Dolan, R. Scott Appleby, Patricia Byrne, and Debra Campbell, *Transforming Parish Ministry: The Changing Roles of Catholic Clergy, Laity, and Women Religious* (New York: Crossroad, 1989), pp. 89–107, for a discussion of the emergence of the orchestra leader in contemporary parish life.

2. See Erving Goffman's *Presentation of Self in Everyday Life* (New York: Doubleday, 1959), pp. 106–40.

3. See Madeleine Adriance, *Opting for the Poor: Brazilian Catholicism in Transition* (Kansas City, Mo.: Sheed and Ward, 1986), p. 107.

4. Paulo Freire, *Pedagogy of the Oppressed* (New York: Seabury, 1970).

5. Neal recounts how the experience in base communities was the basis for transforming the forms of governance in women's religious communities. See Marie Augusta Neal, *From Nuns to Sisters: An Expanding Vocation* (Mystic, Conn.: Twenty-Third Publications, 1990), pp. 99–100.

CHAPTER 6

1. This chapter draws on role transition theory. See Vernon L. Allen and Evert van de Vliert, *Role Transitions: Explorations and Expla-*

nations (New York: Plenum, 1984), p. 3, who define role transition as "the process of changing from one set of expected positional behaviors in a social system to another."

2. I purposely wrote to the woman pastors for the invitation to visit the parish. Since they were in charge of the parish, I felt that this was the appropriate avenue. There were two reasons why I chose not to ask the bishop for either his permission or for the invitation. First, I feared that some bishops might refuse my request, thus eliminating those parishes from my sample. Second, if the bishop was the one who invited me to visit the parish, the woman pastor might be less than enthusiastic about having a researcher imposed on her by her bishop, with little or no say in the matter. Only on one occasion did I see the local bishop, who quite by accident happened to be a passenger on the same flight I was taking to his diocese. However, the woman pastor who met me at the airport quickly sized up the situation. After greeting the bishop, she very discreetly introduced me as "Dr. Ruth Wallace from George Washington University." Needless to say, a study of bishops' attitudes and behavior toward woman pastors is certainly in order, but this is beyond the purview of my research project.

3. The term "reflection talk" is sometimes used in order to avoid the word "homily," because church law denies laity the right to give homilies during Mass.

4. An alb is a full-length white linen vestment with long sleeves that is gathered at the waist with a cincture. This is worn by the priest officiating during Mass under the chasuble, a sleeveless outer vestment.

5. A newspaper article in the *Seattle Post-Intelligence* (May 19, 1990, p. A8) described a protest on the part of conservative Catholics against their bishop's stance on certain issues, including the following: "Using an alleged priest shortage to threaten practicing Catholics with priestless services and a denial of sacraments" to further the bishop's attempts to sanction women deacons and priests. In response the public affairs director for the diocese said that the bishop "believes women's rights is one of the most pressing issues confronting the church." Consequently the bishop canceled a training program for new deacons because he said "the church first should review the possibility of including women."

6. Chrism is consecrated oil used in the conferring of sacraments like baptism, confirmation, ordination, and the anointing of the sick.

7. CCD is the Confraternity of Christian Doctrine, the religious education program in the parish.

8. The vicar general is an administrative deputy of a bishop with authority second only to that of the diocesan bishop.

9. Shortly after I completed the data collection phase of this study, I traveled to Kansas City to meet with the director of the Institute for Pastoral Life, Jean Marie Hiesberger. I spent one morning with her and the members of her staff, conferring with them about topics for future programs sponsored by the Institute, and about the plans for their national survey of lay pastors.

10. The chief drawback of this program is that the funding is earmarked for poor rural parishes; therefore, women who are heading urban parishes would have to depend on their parish or diocese to cover the travel and housing costs. The material presented also would have to be expanded or adapted to cover issues peculiar to urban parishes.

CHAPTER 7

1. This chapter draws on the structuration theory of Anthony Giddens, who argues that structure is both enabling and constraining. In his book, *Central Problems in Social Theory* (Berkeley: University of California, 1983), p. 71, Giddens states: "According to the notion of the duality of structure, rules (or constraints) and resources are drawn upon by actors in the production of interaction, but are thereby also reconstituted through such interaction."

2. On the recommendation of the National Council of Catholic Bishops, a local bishop may request permission from the Vatican to delegate a layperson to witness a wedding. Archbishop Francis Hurley received the authorization in January 1990, and appointed six parish administrators—five nuns and one laywoman—as witnesses of Catholic weddings in the Archdiocese of Anchorage, Alaska. See *Origins* (February 15, 1990): 598.

3. Richard A. Schoenherr, "Power and Authority in Organized Religion," *Sociological Analysis* 47 (1987:68) argues that a variety of approaches is needed in order to have a better understanding of changing beliefs and shifting power in organized religion.

4. A penitential service is a preparatory ritual for the sacrament of confession.

5. A "dry Mass" literally means a "practice Mass" where a deacon who is about to be ordained a priest "goes through the motions," as it

were. What this woman meant was that she would simply distribute Communion after the homily if the priest did not appear.

CHAPTER 8

1. See Nijole V. Benokraitis and Joe R. Feagin, *Modern Sexism* (Englewood Cliffs, N.J.: Prentice-Hall, 1986) for numerous examples of both overt and covert sex discrimination in male-dominated occupations.

2. See for instance, Christine L. Williams, *Gender Differences at Work: Women and Men in Nontraditional Occupations* (Berkeley, Calif.: University at California Press, 1989).

3. Rosabeth Moss Kanter, *Men and Women of the Corporation* (New York: Basic Books, 1977) discusses the phenomenon of "solo hires," women who have the experience of being "tokens" in work settings in large corporations.

4. See Arlie Russell Hochschild, *The Second Shift: Working Parents and the Revolution at Home* (New York: Viking, 1989).

5. A lectionary is a book of biblical readings used in the liturgy.

CHAPTER 9

1. Giddens (1983:91–93) argues that individuals possess a transformative capacity because they can intervene in events in the world, and by their utilization of resources, produce definite outcomes.

2. In Giddens's (1983:88) view, this exemplifies the way that social transformations take place through innovative practices or "strategic conduct," to use his term.

3. One of the reasons why there are so few male lay pastors is that the majority of Catholic men who desire pastoral ministry are practicing it as priests. According to the 1990 *Official Catholic Directory*, there are 6,743 brothers in the United States, a three percent decrease from the previous year. This is a higher decrease than that of sisters, who now number 103,269, a one percent decrease from 1989.

4. Technically, deacons should not be classified as male lay pastors, because they are members of the clergy. Whether their perceived identity is lay or clerical, however, is not clear.

5. Schoenherr and Young call the Catholic situation the "dilemma of full pews and vacant altars." See Richard A. Schoenherr and Lawrence A. Young, "Quitting the Clergy: Resignations in the Roman Catholic Priesthood," *Journal for the Scientific Study of Religion* 29 (1990): 464.

6. Most Catholics are unaware that there are already married priests ministering with ecclesiastical approval in the United States. On May 20, 1989 the forty-second married Episcopal priest was ordained to the Catholic priesthood by Cardinal O'Connor in New York. See Joseph Fichter's study of this phenomenon in his book, *The Pastoral Provisions: Married Catholic Priests* (Kansas City, Mo.: Sheed and Ward, 1989), p. 1.

7. See, for instance, John Seidler and Katherine Meyer, *Conflict and Change in the Catholic Church* (New Brunswick,N.J.: Rutgers University Press, 1989), pp.158–68.

8. See D'Antonio et al. (1989:108–14).

BIBLIOGRAPHY

Abbott, Walter M. *The Documents of Vatican II*. New York: America Press, 1966.

Adriance, Madeleine. *Opting for the Poor: Brazilian Catholicism in Transition*. Kansas City, Mo.: Sheed and Ward, 1986.

Allen, Vernon L., and Evert van de Vliert, eds. *Role Transitions: Explorations and Explanations*. New York: Plenum Press, 1984.

Baumgaertner, William L., ed. *Fact Book on Theological Education: 1987–88*. Vandalia, Ohio: Association of Theological Schools in the United States and Canada, 1988.

Bellah, Robert N., Richard Madsen, William M. Sullivan, Ann Swidler, and Steven M. Tipton. *Habits of the Heart: Individualism and Commitment in American Life*. Berkeley: University of California Press, 1985.

Benokraitis, Nijole V., and Joe R. Feagin. *Modern Sexism: Blatant, Subtle, and Covert Discrimination*. Englewood Cliffs, N.J.: Prentice-Hall, 1986.

Biddle, B. J. "Recent Developments in Role Theory." *Annual Review of Sociology* 12 (1986): 67–92.

Blumer, Herbert. *Symbolic Interactionism: Perspective and Method*. Englewood Cliffs, N.J.: Prentice-Hall, 1969.

Bock, E. Wilber. "The Female Clergy: A Case of Professional Marginality." *American Journal of Sociology* 27 (1967): 531–39.

Burr, W. R. "Role Transitions: A Reformulation of Theory." *Journal of Marriage and the Family* 34 (1972): 406–16.

Carroll, Jackson W., Barbara Hargrove, and Adair T. Lummis. *Women of the Cloth: A New Opportunity for the Churches*. San Francisco, Calif.: Harper and Row, 1983.

Concilio Ecumenico Vaticano II: Commissioni Conciliari. Vatican City: Polyglot Press, 1965.

Coriden, James A., ed. *Sexism and Church Law: Equal Rights and Affirmative Action*. New York: Paulist Press, 1977.

Dandridge, Myra L. "Black Nun to Lead Parish in Virginia." *Washington Post* (May 26, 1990): D1.

D'Antonio, William V., James D. Davidson, Dean R. Hoge, and Ruth A. Wallace. *American Catholic Laity in a Changing Church*. Kansas City, Mo.: Sheed and Ward, 1989.

Dolan, Jay P., R. Scott Appleby, Patricia Byrne, and Debra Campbell. *Transforming Parish Ministry: The Changing Roles of Catholic Clergy, Laity, and Women Religious*. New York: Crossroad, 1989.

Doohan, Leonard. *Grass Roots Pastors: A Handbook for Career Lay Ministers*. San Francisco: Harper and Row, 1986.

Durkheim, Emile. *Suicide*. Glencoe, Ill.: Free Press, 1951.

Fichter, Joseph H. *The Pastoral Provisions: Married Catholic Priests*. Kansas City, Mo.: Sheed and Ward, 1989.

―――. "Holy Father Church." *Commonweal* (May 15, 1970): 216–18.

Freire, Paulo. *Pedagogy of the Oppressed*. New York: Seabury Press, 1970.

Giddens, Anthony. *Central Problems in Social Theory*. Berkeley: University of California Press, 1983.

―――. *The Constitution of Society*. Cambridge: Polity Press, 1984.

Gilfeather, Katherine. "The Changing Role of Women in the Catholic Church in Chile." *Journal for the Scientific Study of Religion* 16 (1977): 39–54.

Gilmour, Peter. *The Emerging Pastor: Non-ordained Catholic Pastors*. Kansas City, Mo.: Sheed and Ward, 1986.

Glaser, Barney G., and Anselm L. Strauss. *Awareness of Dying*. Chicago: Aldine Press, 1965.

Goffman, Erving. *Presentation of Self in Everyday Life*. New York: Doubleday, 1959.

Greeley, Andrew M. *American Catholics Since the Council: An Unauthorized Report*. Chicago: Thomas More Press, 1985.

Hochschild, Arlie Russell. *The Managed Heart: Commercialization of Human Feeling*. Berkeley: University of California Press, 1983.

―――. *The Second Shift: Working Parents and the Revolution at Home*. New York: Viking, 1989.

Hoge, Dean R. *The Future of Catholic Leadership: Responses to the Priest Shortage.* Kansas City, Mo.: Sheed and Ward, 1987.

Hoge, Dean R., Jackson W. Carroll, and Francis K. Scheets. *Patterns of Parish Leadership: Cost and Effectiveness in Four Denominations.* Kansas City, Mo.: Sheed and Ward, 1988.

Hurley, Francis. "Authorization Received for Lay Witnesses of Weddings." *Origins* 19.37 (February 15, 1990):597–99.

John Paul II. *Code of Canon Law.* Washington, D.C.: Canon Law Society of America, 1983.

Kanter, Rosabeth Moss. *Men and Women of the Corporation.* New York: Basic Books, 1977.

Kennedy, Eugene. *Tomorrow's Catholics Yesterday's Church: The Two Cultures of American Catholicism.* San Francisco: Harper and Row, 1990.

Kroe, Elaine. *National Higher Education Statistics: Fall 1989.* Washington, D.C.: U.S. Department of Education, 1989.

Leege, David C., and Thomas A. Trozzolo. "Who Participates in Local Church Communities?" *Origins* 15 (1985): 56–57.

Lehman, Edward C. *Women Clergy: Breaking through Gender Barriers.* New Brunswick, N.J.: Transaction Books, 1985.

McCall, George J., and J. L. Simmons. *Identities and Interactions.* New York: The Free Press, 1966.

Merton, Robert K. "The Role-Set: Problems in Sociological Theory." *British Journal of Sociology* 8 (1957) 106–20.

———. *Social Theory and Social Structure.* New York: The Free Press, 1968.

Mills, C. Wright. *The Sociological Imagination.* New York: Oxford University Press, 1959.

Morris, Joan. *The Lady Was a Bishop.* New York:Macmillan, 1973.

Neal, Marie Augusta. *Catholic Sisters in Transition: From the 1960s to the 1980s.* Wilmington, Del.: Michael Glazier, 1984.

———. *From Nuns to Sisters: An Expanding Vocation.* Mystic, Conn.: Twenty-Third Publications, 1990.

Pilarczyk, Daniel. "Vote on Women's Pastoral Delayed." *Origins* 20 (September 27, 1990) 250–51.

Renken, John A. "Canonical Issues in the Pastoral Care of Parishes without Priests." *The Jurist* 47 (1987) 506–19.

Report of Catholic Biblical Association. *Origins* (December 17, 1979).

Rosenberg, Florence, and Edward M. Sullivan. *Women and Ministry: A Survey of the Experience of Roman Catholic Women in the United States.* Washington, D.C.: Center for Applied Research in the Apostolate, 1980.

Ruether, Rosemary Radford. *Contemporary Roman Catholicism: Crises and Challenges.* Kansas City, Mo.: Sheed and Ward, 1987.

Schoenherr, Richard A. "Power and Authority in Organized Religion: Disaggregating the Phenomenological Core." *Sociological Analysis* 47 (March 1987): 52–71.

Schoenherr, Richard A., and Lawrence A. Young. *The Catholic Priest in the United States: Demographic Investigations.* Madison, Wis.: University of Wisconsin-Madison Comparative Religious Organization Studies Publications, 1990.

————. "Quitting the Clergy: Resignations in the Roman Catholic Priesthood." *Journal for the Scientific Study of Religion* 29 (1990): 463–481.

Seidler, John, and Katherine Meyer. *Conflict and Change in the Catholic Church.* New Brunswick, N.J.: Rutgers University Press, 1989.

The Jerusalem Bible. Garden City, N.Y.: Doubleday, 1966.

The Official Catholic Directory. New York: Kenedy, 1990.

U.S. Bishops. "One in Christ Jesus: A Pastoral Response to the Concerns of Women for Church and Society." *Origins* 19 (1990): 717–40.

Wallace, Ruth A. "Bringing Women In: Marginality in the Churches." *Sociological Analysis* 34 (1975): 3–11.

————. "Catholic Women and the Creation of a New Social Reality." *Gender and Society* 2 (1988): 24–38.

Weaver, Mary Jo. *New Catholic Women: A Contemporary Challenge to Traditional Religious Authority.* San Francisco: Harper and Row, 1986.

Webster's Ninth New Collegiate Dictionary. Springfield, Mass.: Merriam-Webster, Inc., 1984.

Windsor, Pat. "Weakland Advises U.S. Bishops to Drop Women's Pastoral." *National Catholic Reporter* (May 18, 1990): 3.

Wittberg, Patricia. "Non-Ordained Workers in the Catholic Church: Power and Mobility Among American Nuns." *Journal for the Scientific Study of Religion* 28.2 (1989): 148–61.

Woodward, Kenneth L., T. Stranger, S. Sullivan, M. Margolis, and R. Vokey. "Church in Crisis." *Newsweek* (December 9, 1985): 66–75.

INDEX

Skill, 80, 99
Social activism, 99
Solidarity, 11, 77, 81-84
South, 16, 17, 36, 39, 186n.47
Stewardship drive, 92
Suenens, Cardinal Leon Joseph, 3,
181n.6
Support, 5, 10, 14, 17, 27, 34, 43, 48,
52, 56, 89, 96, 105-121, 124, 125,
142, 146, 147, 153, 162, 165, 168,
172-4
Survival, 36, 77, 99, 102, 175; ances-
tors, 102; parishioners leery of
woman pastor, 36
Symbolic interactionism, 186n.49
Symposium on Women and Church
Law, 12

Tensions; dealing with priests not
showing up, 38
Term, 9, 32, 38, 43, 47, 48, 83, 100,
102, 124
Terminated, 15, 18
Third World, 7, 25, 99, 100
Title, 13, 16, 19, 48, 98, 122, 128, 129,
131, 168
Tobin, Sister Mary Luke, 3
Training, 6, 13, 22, 27, 31-33, 75, 80,
92, 95, 100, 104, 123, 124, 159, 172
Travel, 22, 54, 63, 106, 147; driving,
83, 92; travelling to meet multiple
responsibilities, 70
Turf, 140, 175

Urban, 17, 41, 190n.10; going from
urban to rural, 29-30, 56-57, 131;
urban parish with women pastoral
administrators, 18; outsiders, 26

Vatican II, 1, 2, 4-8, 12, 58, 87-89, 94,
132, 177, 179; second session, 2;
fourth session, 2, 3; women present at Council summary, 3; parish

committee to analyze Vatican II, 7
Venezuela, 7
Vestment, 130, 131
Vicar General, 109, 123, def. 190n.8
Virgin Mary, *See* Blessed Virgin Mary
Visiting, 70; by bishop, 27, 106, 123;
characteristic of pastoral heart, 50,
54-60; community as consequence
of, 64; reluctance, 45; to sick and
dying, 61, 84, 96
Volunteers, 118, 179

Warmth, 48, 50, 60, 61, 65, 82, 134
Wedding, *See* Sacrament of Marriage
West, 12, 16, 17, 36, 39, 186n.47
Women pastors; legitimacy of, 111,
142; limits of power, 14; married
pastor, 122; parishioners' confusion over her title, 19, 122, 129;
understanding women's experiences, 44, 101; parenting, 68;
parish life coordinator, 129; pastoral administrator; administrator;
pastoral associate, 25, 26, 32, 44,
99, 108; in larger parishes, 174-75
Women's movement, 8, 9, 11, 12, 13
Women's ordination, 10, 11
Women in the Church; as little girls,
156; caste system, 10; contributions
of, 4; exclusion from ordained
ministry, 6; in authority, 62, 117,
154; in leadership, 98; lay, 16, 41,
33, 49, 152; movement toward
expanded image of, 148; role of,
11, 13, 41, 112, 184n.39; taking a
public role, 164; woman question,
149, 151, 153, 165; women's place
during Vatican council, 3; *See also*
Altar and Rosary Society
Word and Communion Service, *See*
Communion
Work, Martin H., 3

Youth, 52, 75, 76, 90, 97, 121